VICTORIAN WOMEN POETS

Victorian Literature and Culture Series

Karen Chase, Jerome J. McGann, *and* Herbert Tucker

General Editors

Daniel Albright
Tennyson: The Muses' Tug-of-War
David G. Riede
Matthew Arnold and the Betrayal of Language
Anthony Winner
Culture and Irony: Studies in Joseph Conrad's Major Novels
James Richardson
Vanishing Lives: Style and Self in Tennyson, D.G. Rossetti, Swinburne, and Yeats
Jerome J. McGann, Editor
Victorian Connections
Anthony Harrison
Victorian Poets and Romantic Poems: Intertextuality and Ideology
E. Warwick Slinn
The Discourse of Self in Victorian Poetry
Linda K. Hughes and Michael Lund
The Victorian Serial
Anna Leonowens
The Romance of the Harem
Edited with an Introduction by Susan Morgan
Alan Fischler
"Modified Rapture": Comedy in W. S. Gilbert's Savoy Operas
Barbara Timm Gates, Editor
Journal of Emily Shore, with a new Introduction by the Editor
Richard Maxwell
The Mysteries of Paris and London
Felicia Bonaparte
The Gypsy-Bachelor of Manchester: The Life of Mrs. Gaskell's Demon
Peter L. Shillingsburg
Pegasus in Harness: Victorian Publishing and W. M. Thackeray
Allan C. Dooley
Author and Printer in Victorian England
Angela Leighton
Victorian Women Poets: Writing Against the Heart

VICTORIAN WOMEN POETS,

Writing Against the Heart

Angela Leighton

University Press of Virginia
Charlottesville and London

First published 1992 by Harvester Wheatsheaf

First published 1992 in the United States of
America by the University Press of Virginia
Box 3608 University Station
Charlottesville, VA 22903

© Angela Leighton, 1992

Library of Congress CIP Data No: 92–60971

ISBN 0–8139–1426–4
0–8139–1427–2 (pbk)

Printed and bound in Great Britain

For Kenneth
'the reed which grows nevermore again'

Contents

Acknowledgements

In the course of writing and revising this book, I have been indebted to many people who have been generous with their time and criticisms. My thanks, especially, to James Booth, for standing by with unfailingly perceptive criticisms, disagreements and enthusiasm from the first to the final drafts; to Harriet Marland for all her generous intellectual as well as practical support in reading and checking this book, and to Marion Shaw for many pleasurable discussions, as well as detailed, specific advice on the Victorian background.

My thanks, too, to those who read individual chapters, and who offered me their special literary expertise: Norma Clarke on Felicia Hemans, Sara Dodd on the Pre-Raphaelites, Margaret Reynolds on Barrett Browning, Patsy Stoneman on the Victorian context and Christine White on Michael Field, as well as to those who lent me their eyes and ears in reading sometimes unfamiliar and often unfinished material: Tom McAlindon, Neil Sinyard, Simon Wilson and Rowland Wymer. Thanks to Kelsey Thornton who generously passed on old notes on Michael Field.

In addition, my gratitude to Isobel Armstrong and Joseph Bristow, who offered their invaluable, expert advice at a crucial stage of revision – with, I hope, visible results – and to Jerome McGann for helpful corrections and comments on the final typescript.

To all those who responded to urgent questions, both niggling and overwhelming, and who supplied information, corrections and suggestions, my thanks: especially Judith Bryce, Marilyn Butler, John Chapple, Marysa Demoor, Antony Harrison, Owen Knowles, Margaret Reynolds, Jane Thomas, Rowland Wymer, William Zunder and members of the Hull University Classics Department.

I am grateful to Hull University for granting me Study Leave, and to my colleagues and students in the English Department for providing an intellectually stimulating and supportive environment for thinking, teaching and writing.

A Leverhulme research grant awarded in 1988 enabled me to make necessary journeys to various libraries to consult manuscripts and first editions.

Extracts from the manuscript letters of Alice Meynell to Katharine Tynan are reproduced by courtesy of the Director and Librarian of the John Rylands Library, University of Manchester. Extracts from the unpublished journals of Michael Field are reproduced by courtesy of the Manuscripts Librarian at the British Library. For permission to quote from the manuscript diary of Katherine Bradley and the notebooks of Christina Rossetti, I am grateful to the Librarian of Western Manuscripts at the Bodleian Library, Oxford. To Norma Clarke, for permission to use her unpublished paper on Felicia Hemans, my thanks.

Some parts of the chapters on Elizabeth Barrett Browning, Christina Rossetti and Augusta Webster first appeared in ' "Because men made the laws": the fallen woman and the woman poet', *Victorian Poetry*, 27(1989), 109–27, © 1989 by West Virginia University, and in ' "When I am dead, my dearest": the secret of Christina Rossetti', *Modern Philology*, 87(1990), 373–88, © 1990 by University of Chicago Press. I am grateful to the editors for permission to reprint.

Finally, to all those whose work on Victorian poetry has, at some unacknowledged level, affected and influenced my own, I remain gratefully indebted.

Abbreviations

(Primary works are given in parenthesis in the text)

Felicia Hemans
Works   The Works of Mrs. Hemans: with a memoir of her
                 life by her sister, 7 vols., Edinburgh, 1839.

L.E.L.
PW   The Poetical Works of Letitia Elizabeth Landon, ed.
                 William B. Scott, London, 1873.

Elizabeth Barrett Browning
Letters   The Letters of Elizabeth Barrett Browning, 2 vols.,
                 ed. Frederic G. Kenyon, London, 1897.
CW   The Complete Works of Elizabeth Barrett Browning,
                 6 vols., ed. Charlotte Porter and Helen A. Clarke,
                 New York: Crowell, 1900.
Sister   Elizabeth Barrett Browning: Letters to her sister,
                 1846–1859, ed. Leonard Huxley, London: John
                 Murray, 1929.
Boyd   Elizabeth Barrett Browning: Unpublished letters of
                 Elizabeth Barrett Browning to Hugh Stuart Boyd,
                 ed. Barbara P. McCarthy, London: John Murray,
                 1955.
Diary   The Unpublished Diary of Elizabeth Barrett Browning
                 1831–1832, ed. Philip Kelley and Ronald Hudson,
                 Athens, Ohio: Ohio University Press, 1969.
RB   The Letters of Robert Browning and Elizabeth

	Barrett Browning 1845–1846, 2 vols., ed. Elvan Kintner, Cambridge, Mass.: Harvard University Press, 1969.
AL	*Aurora Leigh and Other Poems*, intro. Cora Kaplan, London: The Women's Press, 1978.
MRM	*The Letters of Elizabeth Barrett Browning to Mary Russell Mitford: 1836–1854*, 3 vols., ed. Meredith B. Raymond and Mary Rose Sullivan, Winfield, Kans.: Wedgestone Press, 1983.
Corr	*The Brownings' Correspondence*, 4 vols., to date, ed. Philip Kelley and Ronald Hudson, Winfield, Kans.: Wedgestone Press, 1984–.

Christina Rossetti

Commonplace	*Commonplace, and Other Short Stories*, London, 1870.
PW	*The Poetical Works of Christina Georgina Rossetti*, with Memoir and Notes by William Michael Rossetti, London: Macmillan, 1904.
Letters	*The Family Letters of Christina Georgina Rossetti*, ed. William Michael Rossetti, London: Brown, Langham & Co., 1908.
Maude	*Maude: Prose and verse*, ed. R. W. Crump, Hamden, Conn.: Archon Books, 1976.
CP	*The Complete Poems of Christina Rossetti: A variorum edition*, 3 vols., ed. R. W. Crump, Baton Rouge and London: Louisiana State University Press, 1979–90.

Augusta Webster

BL	*Blanche Lisle and other Poems*, Cambridge, 1860.
LG	*Lilian Gray*, Cambridge, 1864.
DS	*Dramatic Studies*, London and Cambridge, 1866.
HO	*A Housewife's Opinions*, London, 1879.
Portraits	*Portraits*, London, 1893.
Sel	*Selections from the Verse of Augusta Webster*, London, 1893.
MD	*Mother & Daughter: An uncompleted sonnet-sequence*, intro. William Michael Rossetti, London, 1895.

Michael Field

NM	*The New Minnesinger* (Arran Leigh), London, 1875.
LA	*Long Ago*, London, 1889.

SS	*Sight and Song*, London, 1892.
UB	*Underneath the Bough*, London, 1893.
WH	*Wild Honey from Various Thyme*, London: T. Fisher Unwin, 1908.
PA	*Poems of Adoration*, London and Edinburgh: Sands, 1912.
MT	*Mystic Trees*, London: Eveleigh Nash, 1913.
WC	*Whym Chow: Flame of Love*, London: privately printed at the Eragny Press, 1914.
Ded	*Dedicated: An early work of Michael Field*, London: Bell, 1914.
SP	*A Selection from the Poems of Michael Field*, London: The Poetry Bookshop, 1923.
WD	*Works and Days: From the journal of Michael Field*, ed. T. and D. C. Sturge Moore, London: John Murray, 1933.

Alice Meynell

Poems	*The Poems of Alice Meynell*, London: Oxford University Press, 1940.
PP	*Alice Meynell: Prose and poetry*, intro. V. Sackville-West, London: Jonathan Cape, 1947.

Charlotte Mew

FB	*The Farmer's Bride*, London: The Poetry Bookshop, 1929.
RS	*The Rambling Sailor*, London: The Poetry Bookshop, 1929.
CPP	*Charlotte Mew: Collected poems and prose*, ed. Val Warner, Manchester: Carcanet Press, 1981.

Introduction

Nineteenth-century women's literature has attracted considerable critical attention in recent years, but women's poetry, as a distinct genre, has not. Individual poets like Elizabeth Barrett Browning and Christina Rossetti have always been, and continue to be, favourite subjects for biography, and, in the last decade or so, have also undergone something of a revival in critical status. None the less, nineteenth-century women's poetry as a whole has generally been neglected. Kathleen Hickok's ground-breaking book, *Representations of Women* (1984), makes a rare exception to this rule of silence.

The reasons for this neglect are hard to pinpoint. It may be that the hidden consequence of such pioneer studies as Ellen Moers' *Literary Women* (1963), Elaine Showalter's *A Literature of Their Own* (1977) and Gilbert and Gubar's *The Madwoman in the Attic* (1979) was to establish a canon of women's writing which is predominantly, though not intentionally, that of the novel. Neither Moers nor Gilbert and Gubar, for instance, consider the work of Augusta Webster, Michael Field or Charlotte Mew, though they are generous in their attention to Barrett Browning, Rossetti and Dickinson. This precedent of exclusion has tended to persist into the 1990s, exacerbated, perhaps, by a vague reluctance on the part of feminist critics to tackle the problem of poetry's ideological obliqueness and aesthetic self-sufficiency. In general, therefore, gender has tended to eclipse genre, 'a literature of their own' has tended to overshadow 'a poetry of their own'. Yet women's poetry of the nineteenth century, much more than the novel, was written and read as part of a self-consciously female tradition. Although there were women writing good poetry before the nineteenth century, as Greer's (1988) and

1

Lonsdale's (1989) anthologies amply show, and although many of these women, like Charlotte Smith, Jane Taylor and Mary Robinson, for instance, were professionals in the sense that they wrote for financial reward (see Curran, 1988), the woman poet as a self-professed, rather than just self-supporting, writer, appears, almost for the first time in history, in the post-Romantic decades of the 1820s and 30s. The mystique of the woman poet which develops at this time, partly as a response to the economic expansion of the literary market, offers to subsequent generations of women both an enthusiastic incentive to write and a subtly determining myth of what being a woman poet means. It is this emerging tradition of British women's poetry, falling under my intentionally capacious title of 'Victorian', and focusing primarily on those writers who considered themselves professional poets rather than novelists who wrote poetry, which forms the subject of my book.

Within this framework, I aim to do several things. On a simple level, this book offers an introduction to the lives and works of eight major women poets (counting Michael Field as one), who for some reason have been lost to the traditional canons of nineteenth-century verse. These are all writers whose work is of considerable literary as well as historical interest, while at least two of them, Christina Rossetti and Charlotte Mew, deserve to be placed foremost in any poetic evaluation of the period. Barrett Browning, Augusta Webster, Michael Field and Alice Meynell are more uneven in their output, but, at their best, emerge as intriguing, original voices, whose work has more than justified the simply recuperative purpose of this book. Their poetry, in my opinion, deserves at least as much recognition as that given to the minor male poets: Swinburne, Meredith, Clough, Dowson and Johnson, for instance, whose literary survival has been much luckier. My method of selection, then, has been unashamedly aesthetic. These are not historical or feminist curiosities, but poets who, I believe, merit a hearing in their own right. Perhaps such a hearing will help to shift the 'long border' (Jehlen, in Keohane, 1982: 199) between Victorian women's poetry and Victorian men's poetry, to make more room for these voices who for too long have remained unheard on the other side.

At the head of this tradition stand two poets who are not historically Victorians at all. Yet Felicia Hemans and Letitia Elizabeth Landon (L.E.L.), for all their limitations, are the true originators of a line of poetry which can be distinguished from the Romantics, on the one hand, and the modernists, on the other. To use the term 'Victorian' in this more elastic literary, rather than strictly historical sense, is, admittedly, to play on some of its more clichéd attributes; but it is also to acknowledge the obvious fact that literary movements do not start or end at certain fixed dates. Victorianism begins before 1837 and continues after 1901. My reasons for including Hemans and L.E.L., at one end, and Meynell and Mew, at the other, have more to do with a particular development of sensibility and style during the greater part of the nineteenth and early twentieth centuries, than with the presence or absence of a particular monarch. Although such a development is not cut off from others – Hemans is strongly indebted to an eighteenth-century cult of sensibility while Mew is distinctly modernist in some of her technical innovations – I would argue that its spirit is essentially different from either of those, in that it constantly sets women's imaginative experience at cross purposes with social and sexual morality. Such a cross is, in a sense, of the essence of the Victorian imagination, as well as being the especially burdensome anxiety of the Victorian *woman* writer.

Thus, while on one level this book simply offers an introduction to a select number of women poets, with separate chapters for each, recognising their differences and originality, it also, on another level, opens up into a continuous and connecting discussion of the nature of the nineteenth-century female imagination. Victorian women's poetry, I argue, grows out of a struggle with and against a highly moralised celebration of women's sensibility. Through Hemans and L.E.L. sensibility becomes, not only fashionable and profitable again in the 1820s and 30s, but it also accrues certain strongly prescriptive, gender-specific values of sincerity and purity. The exclusion of money, sex, power and, as it were, imaginative *in*sensibility from the poetic consciousness of women then becomes part of a more general, moral protection campaign of Victorian womanhood. This dissociation of sensibility from the affairs of the world – a dissociation already decried in the later works of Mary Wollstonecraft – is one of the woman poet's most disabling inheritances. The attempt to overcome that dissociation by writing not from, but against the heart, is an ambition which, although taking different forms, connects all these poets who follow in the wake of Hemans and L.E.L. Without the heart to guarantee femininity, feeling and truth, the imagination enters a world of sceptically disordered moral and linguistic reference. While the aesthetic possibilities of such disorder are seductive, the moral cost, especially for women, is high. The tension between these two recurs, in various patterns, in the work of most of these poets, and becomes the hallmark of their common creativity.

The argument about sensibility which weaves through my separate chapters centres on two models, whose influence can be felt in women's poetry almost to the end of the century: those of Sappho and Corinne. Epitomising, in some ways, the ideal of creative but suffering femininity which is of the essence of sensibility, these two models also, however, focus certain contradictions in the very ideal they seem to impress. On the one hand, lovelorn and suicidal, they seem to stand for a woman's

3

writing which is always on the brink of self-denial in the face of male rejection. On the other hand, triumphalist and obsessively self-expressive, they represent a flow of poetic inspiration which thrives on a covert, transmittable enthusiasm between women. The two strains can be detected from the start. As women's poetry develops in the course of the century, the myth of Sappho–Corinne unfolds in some surprising directions.

Although interest in nineteenth-century women's poetry is growing, as the fine work of Kathleen Hickok, Dorothy Mermin, Dolores Rosenblum, Marlon Ross and Stuart Curran bears witness, the names of Webster, Meynell, Field and Mew still remain largely unknown. For this reason, I have begun each chapter with a biographical introduction. The problems of biography are especially acute for critics of women's writing. Since Wimsatt's formalist rejection of 'the intentional fallacy', the sentence of death on the author (Barthes, 1977: 142–8) has been widely and wittily pronounced. Yet feminist criticism, by its very nature, needs to ask 'Who is this author?' who, far from having to die, has not yet been brought to life in the reader's consciousness. For these critics, the signature of the woman writer is not a dispensable addendum, because, as Nancy Miller points out, only those with a sense of the importance of their own signature 'can play with not having it' (in Hirsch and Keller, 1990: 118). Rosi Braidotti, similarly, challenges modern theory's failure to perceive that, in the case of women, 'one cannot deconstruct a subjectivity one has never been fully granted' (in Jardine and Smith, 1987: 237). The problem of the author, of the 'signature', remains central to any feminist criticism, but especially to one concerned with unknown or unfamiliar writers. To ignore the authorial name, and all the historical and biographical information that goes with it, would be to lose, not only an already lost history of women's writing, but also the rationale for writing about women poets at all.

Yet to offer biographical information is not therefore to subscribe to some form of authorial intentionalism. To emphasise this, I give the facts of the authors' lives in a section at the beginning of each chapter, and thus at a distance from my subsequent interpretation of their works. Obviously my selection of facts has some bearing on that interpretation, but not in any intentionalist sense. The split between the first and later sections of my chapters (paralleled by my use of the author's Christian name in the first and surname in the second) is intended to represent a split, not only between woman and poet, life and works, but also, in some ways, between one aspect of the author's psyche and another. The two parts are not necessarily either causally related or obviously compatible, but neither are they, therefore, totally unrelated and different. The self who lives is not the same as the self who writes, but

4

that is not to say that the first is simply irrelevant and 'dead'. As Barrett Browning's heroine asserts, at the beginning of *Aurora Leigh*:

> . . . I . . .
> Will write my story for my better self,
> As when you paint your portrait for a friend,
> Who keeps it in a drawer and looks at it
> Long after he has ceased to love you, just
> To hold together what he was and is.
>
> (*AL*: I, 4–8)

From the start, writing creates another self, 'better' perhaps, or less lovable than the first, but always requiring a little effort to 'hold together' with it. As Proust proclaimed, against the nosy biographism of the critic Sainte-Beuve: 'a book is the product of a self other than that which we display in our habits, in company, in our vices' (1988: 12). In Rossetti and Mew, the split between the self displayed in public and the self who wrote poems almost makes nonsense of any biographical explanation of the works. The extent to which art invents life, the writing self shapes the living self, is one of the themes which runs through this book. Much more than for the woman novelist, life, for the woman poet, is a text to be written according to certain contours of myth and desire. Renunciation, rejection and despair are thus gestures loaded with inherited, mythic meaning for the woman poet who, in the wake of high Romanticism, was still very conscious that being a poet was not simply a professional occupation, but an idea to be invented and lived out. The biographical sections of my chapters are an attempt to set the poetry, not squarely in the context of the life, but side by side with it, in a suggestively interacting tension, rather than a determining sequence.

There are a number of threads which run through this book and surface in the course of its argument, but at its heart there is one central idea. The relationship between aesthetics and politics has remained one of the most contentious areas of feminist criticism, as well as, in a sense, its very *raison d'être*. The opposition between them continues to irk and inspire critics. Elaine Showalter, for instance, has distinguished between the 'gynocritical' and the 'ideological' (in Abel, 1982: 12, 14) mode of interpretation, Myra Jehlen between 'appreciation and political analysis' (in Keohane, 1982: 194), Teresa de Lauretis between *'an erotic, narcissistic drive'* and *'an ethical drive'* (in Hirsch and Keller, 1990: 266). This inherent divergence of interests has been exacerbated by the awkward but sometimes fruitful 'bedfellowing' (Gallop, in Brennan, 1989: 27) of feminism with, for instance, Marxism, post-structuralism, psychoanalysis or postmodernism. None the less, it could be argued, the very energy of feminist criticism derives from this inner tension, which closely approximates the tensions of imaginative literature itself. Both outwardly referential and documentational and also inwardly self-referring and self-enjoying, the literary text is poised between opposite commitments of sense. On the one hand, it faces the world of literal politics and history, of identifiable events and intentions, but on the other, it asserts the alternative reality and pleasure of language for its own sake. In the case of poetry, that double view becomes extreme. To interpret the text only in terms of its politics or ideology is to risk becoming doggedly literal-minded. But to interpret the text only as a 'free play of signifiers', as a matter of endlessly intertextual style, is to lose the specific, evaluative reasons for selecting some texts rather than others.

Feminist theory, in all its diversity, seems to return to this resourceful contradiction. As Myra Jehlen argued, as early as 1981: 'contradictions just such as that between ethical and aesthetic that we have tried to resolve away lest they belie our argument frequently are our firmest and most fruitful grounds' (in Keohane, 1982: 200–1). Andreas Huyssen comes to a similar conclusion: 'The point is not to eliminate the productive tension between the political and the aesthetic, between history and the text, between engagement and the mission of art. The point is to heighten that tension' (in Nicholson, 1990: 271). The proposal that a new feminist theory would be 'more pragmatic, ad hoc, contextual, and local' (Fraser and Nicholson, in Nicholson, 1990: 21), that it would be essentially 'nonuniversalist' (34), seems to offer a return to certain pluralisms which were always at work in feminist criticism. Something of de Beauvoir's original defence of 'the dispersed, contingent, and multiple existences of actual women' against the essentialised 'Woman' (1972: 283) of philosophy and myth returns in contemporary theory, as a reassertion of a reality on which, even if only on one foot, feminist criticism must stand. Some women writers, in all their 'contextual, and local' reality, are the subject of this book.

None the less, although the biographical and historical context of my interpretations remains visible, it gives way, in the later sections of each chapter, to a more purely textual and aesthetic method. In these, the life story gives way to the story of imaginative creation, which is, very often for Victorian women, a death story, as well as the story of fantasy, invention, imitation, dream. In the best poets, it gives way to something which the idea of 'free play' defines quite suggestively. Evidently, this atmosphere of words for words' sake is what ultimately distinguishes imaginative literature from others. Post-structuralism, as a later phase of formalism, has at least kept attention focused on the figurative–linguistic pleasures of the text, though the fact that it has done so at the expense of historicism, contextualisation or even reference itself has left it in danger of becoming stranded, without oxygen, at the top of a formalist mountain.

To take the anti-representational impulse of the text, not as an absolute end in itself, but as part of a relation, between figure and referent, play and representation, fiction and ideological commitment, is a way of staying true to the relations of literature itself. Furthermore, to historicise that tension, as I will do in some of my analyses of particular poems, is to find that it takes on a specific significance for these Victorian women. The occasions when figurative 'play', with its connotations of laughter, freedom and heartlessness, seems in excess of the poem's 'extralinguistic referent or meaning' (de Man, 1979: 106) are often occasions for guilt (that crucially missing ingredient of post-structuralist theory). The counter-gravity of moral seriousness is at work in the playful inventions of these poets' imaginations, making those inventions, not absolutely 'free', but related to, for instance, suffering, sex and sin. The socio-political reality of women's lives remains embedded in the figures even of the most fantastical of their dream poems – embedded, not as a resolving explanation, but as a reminder, a catch, a grain of literal memory. Certain images, of laughter, music, entombment, heartlessness and whiteness, figure, in the work of many of these poets, as signs of a condition of suspended reference, of playful nonsense, achieved against the moral cost of what it means to be a woman. Such an aestheticism cannot be separated from the reality of the woman poet's life and history, her 'signature'; but such aestheticism also cannot be reduced to those facts. Between the biographical–historical matter of my chapters and the formalist–aesthetic interpretations of the poems there is a tension which is itself, implicitly, the literary argument of this book.

—1—

Felicia Hemans (1793–1835)

Mourn rather for that holy Spirit,
Sweet as the spring, as ocean deep;
For Her who, ere her summer faded,
Has sunk into a breathless sleep.
(Wordsworth, 1940–9: IV, 277–8)

Mourning the deaths of his eminent contemporaries in the 'Extempore Effusion upon the Death of James Hogg' (1835), Wordsworth added Felicia Hemans to the list of writers: Hogg, Scott, Coleridge, Lamb and Crabbe, who had preceded him to the grave. Hemans had died that same year, at the age of 41 and at the height of her fame. Wordsworth's commemoration is couched in the bland and churchy epithets which her name continued to inspire throughout the century. She is 'holy' and 'Sweet', less a woman than a spirit, less a poet than a saint. The ring of merely official sentiment which mars the whole poem becomes, in the case of Hemans, vague to the point of blank obviousness: she is 'Sweet as the spring, as ocean deep'. None the less, in 1835 Wordsworth could rely on his readers recognising the unnamed object of his praise. Only one woman poet had gained sufficient renown to be worthy of inclusion in his pantheon of great contemporaries and, furthermore, to be instantly identifiable by the religiose familiarity of phrases like 'that holy Spirit'.

The myth of Hemans as 'holy' and 'Sweet', which she herself had promulgated in her life and works, was thus already well established by the time of her death. On the one hand, a calculated self-projection on the part of the poet and, on the other, an invention of the age which needed it, such a myth profoundly influenced the history of women's poetry in the nineteenth century. Not only did it help to rescue the profession of writing from the scandals still associated with the names of Aphra Behn and Mary Wollstonecraft, but it also helped to promote, however apologetically, a seductively self-realising and self-admiring figure of the woman poet. Hemans' own writings project, in effigy if not always in conviction, the very thing long held inappropriate or contaminating to women: the idea of public artistic success. The ideological contortions which underlie that effigy are, however, a sign of the moral and social difficulties she encountered. To set the story of Felicia's life against the myth of Mrs Hemans, and then against some of Hemans' own poems, is to begin to perceive how the very idea of the woman poet, as she exemplifies it, emerges from a set of implicitly incompatible premises.

*　　*　　*

Felicia Hemans was born in 1793.[1] Soon after her birth, and as a consequence of financial reverses in her father's business, the family moved from Liverpool to North Wales, where she spent a largely happy childhood in a landscape which she loved and to which she returned throughout her life. She was, by all accounts, a precocious, literary child, capable, it was said, of memorising at a single reading 'whole pages of poetry by heart' (Williams, 1861: 406) – a feat readily attributed to a number of nineteenth-century women poets. This childhood contentment was broken, however, by an event which had a profound affect on her imagination. Her father, at some point, left home for Quebec from where he never returned, leaving his wife and six children in considerable financial straits. This first male defection in Felicia's life had a direct bearing on her early poetic ambition. At the instigation of her mother, and to help pay for the army uniform of one of her brothers (Clarke, 1989: 7), she published her first volume of poems at the age of 14. She thus, from the start, set her poetic talents to remedy her father's emotional and financial defaulting. The connection between male desertion and female creativity remains traumatically deep-rooted in her imagination.

It was this youthful volume of 1808 which fell into the hands of the 16-year-old Shelley, who eagerly wrote to its author 'soliciting a correspondence' (Dowden, 1886: I, 49), only to be brusquely rebuffed by her mother. Felicia's was not to be the life of a Romantic runaway, but rather the opposite. She clung tenaciously to the respectability which her provincial, non-intellectual background made both precious and yet precarious. In 1812 she published a second volume, characteristically entitled *The Domestic Affections, and Other Poems*, and that same year married Captain Alfred Hemans, an officer in the army. The first year of marriage was spent in Northampton, but Felicia and her husband then returned to her mother's home in Wales. It seems that Captain Hemans had been discharged from the army without pay (Clarke, 1989: 9), so the reasons for returning to the maternal roof may have been financial as well as emotional. However, for Felicia they were almost certainly emotional. Her poetry enacts a return to the mother with compulsive repetitiveness, and it may well be that financial exigency only gave her the excuse she needed to go back to the beloved home of her childhood.

During the first six years of marriage she gave birth, in quick succession, to five sons. ' "I have none but boys; a circumstance I often am inclined to regret" ' (in Chorley, 1836: I, 143), she wrote, years later. Sons, she feared, were bound to leave home, whereas daughters might remain. Then in 1818, before the birth of the fifth child, Captain Hemans took a trip to Rome, ostensibly for reasons of health. From there, he never returned. Early biographies of Hemans are anxious to gloss the event as discreetly as possible. Felicia's sister, Harriett Hughes, asserts in her 'Memoir' that it was 'a tacit conventional arrangement, which offered no obstacle to the frequent interchange of correspondence' (in *Works*: I, 30). The fact remains, however, that Felicia lived for the rest of her life as a separated woman – an unconventional, if not scandalous situation which, perhaps more than anything else, accounts for the sweet and holy attitude she cultivated so assiduously. Certainly in her poetry it was easier to turn the defection of men into a romantic drama of desertion than acknowledge it as a mutually convenient 'arrangement'. Yet in real life, the fact that two men had deserted the family home, leaving mother and daughter to rear and educate the children from their own resources, hints at something more than a cruel and unforeseen coincidence. It is possible that the arranged separation with her husband, however difficult to explain according to the mores of the day, was not entirely unwelcome to Felicia. The absence of men leaves women some real, if unusual, compensations. For Felicia one such compensation, though she emphatically refused to admit it, was her poetry.

She had published little during her six years of marriage, but in 1818 she was thrown once again on the resources of her pen. She wrote fast and apparently effortlessly, with a good eye to the market of annuals and pocket books which increasingly, during the 1820s and 30s, answered to the demand of a new, distinctly female readership. Between 1817, when *The Literary Gazette* was founded, and 1857, which saw the last issue of *The Keepsake*, these expensively bound and lavishly illustrated volumes flourished. They supplied the need for a purely literary and popular magazine, free from the political rancours of the main journals, and containing a light, readable mixture of poems, stories, letters and fashionable chit-chat. To a great extent, the annuals dictated the kind of writing expected of their predominantly female contributors, and although Hemans was not as dependent on them as L.E.L., her writing clearly betrays their influence. Some of her early, uncollected poems show a sense of humour and wit which suggests that the public register of mournful plangency, made fashionable by the annuals, was not necessarily her natural one. The 'Epitaph on Mr W——, a Celebrated Mineralogist', for instance, not only sounds uncharacteristically idiomatic and jocular, but also touches on a potentially anti-religious subject which would have been anathema to the older poet:

> His fossils, flints, and spars, of every hue,
> With him, good reader, here lie buried too –
> Sweet specimens! which, toiling to obtain,
> He split huge cliffs, like so much wood, in twain.
> We knew, so great the fuss he made about them,
> Alive or dead, he ne'er would rest without them,
> So, to secure soft slumber to his bones,
> We paved his grave with all his favourite stones.
> His much-loved hammer's resting by his side;
> Each hand contains a shell-fish petrified:
> His mouth a piece of pudding-stone incloses,
> And at his feet a lump of coal reposes:
> Sure he was born beneath some lucky planet –
> His very coffin-plate is made of granite.
>
> (*Works*: I, 20–1)

By comparison, the poem which was probably Hemans' best known in the nineteenth century, and which she first published in the *Forget Me Not* annual of 1826, is in her favourite public style of sanctimonious melancholy. 'Evening Prayer at a Girls' School' advises its readers, all girls themselves, to accept the 'lot' of womanhood with willing, if gloomy, zeal:

> Her lot is on you – silent tears to weep,
>   And patient smiles to wear through suffering's hour,
> And sumless riches, from affection's deep,
>   To pour on broken reeds – a wasted shower!
> And to make idols, and to find them clay,
> And to bewail that worship – therefore pray!
>
> Her lot is on you – to be found untired,
>   Watching the stars out by the bed of pain,
> With a pale cheek, and yet a brow inspired,
>   And a true heart of hope, though hope be vain;

11

> Meekly to bear with wrong, to cheer decay,
> And, oh! to love through all things – therefore pray!
>
> (*Works*: IV, 176)

All the light-hearted nonsense of the earlier poem has gone, and in its place is a declamatory mournfulness, a kind of high-handed emotionalism, which Hemans works, with unswerving commitment, through almost twenty volumes of verse. Yet it is precisely this style which contains the key to her immense popularity in the nineteenth century, particularly among women readers. The tone of exhortatory melancholy captures a potent combination of resilience and weariness, heroism and victimisation, importance and hopelessness in its female audience. The contradiction of having 'a true heart of hope, though hope be vain' points to a redundancy of purpose in this life which only heaven may reward: 'therefore pray!' None the less, through these awful warnings about womanhood comes something akin to a battle-cry. Hemans' undoubted technical facility is put to the service of a poetry which, while advocating languidly high-minded virtues in women, also rallies quite forcefully and insistently to their side. These girls are at least given the stature of martyrs to their fates, as well as of respected readers (however martyred) of the poem.

Thus the ethic of weary endurance is contradicted by the curiously ostentatious mechanics of Hemans' writing. The martial assertiveness of her rhythms and rhymes creates an energy in the verse which is often out of proportion to its softer, homely sentiments. In the much anthologised and parodied 'Casabianca', for instance, the pounding fist of her metre turns the boy's bathetic fate into a miniature military feat:

> The boy stood on the burning deck
> Whence all but he had fled;
> The flame that lit the battle's wreck,
> Shone round him o'er the dead.
>
> Yet beautiful and bright he stood,
> As born to rule the storm;
> A creature of heroic blood,
> A proud, though child-like form.
>
> The flames roll'd on – he would not go
> Without his Father's word;
> That Father, faint in death below,
> His voice no longer heard.
>
> (*Works*: IV, 157)

Yet, for all its faults, its mnemonic alliterations and hectoring rhymes, 'Casabianca' captures something of the child's stubbornly stupid heroism in the face of male, and specifically of course, paternal absence. Although a true story, the poem is also a fictional variation on an obsessively personal theme. Like the boy, women too must stand at the post of moral duty and hopeless devotion, whatever the cost or the absurdity of it. This, which is one of the most infamously unforgettable poems of all time, though most readers have forgotten its author, has lost none of its broadside effect on the ear. In the twentieth century, Elizabeth Bishop has paid her own, not entirely mocking tribute to its rhetoric:

> Love's the boy stood on the burning deck
> trying to recite 'The boy stood on
> the burning deck.' Love's the son
> stood stammering elocution
> while the poor ship in flames went down.
>
> (1970: 6)

John Stuart Mill may have had Hemans in mind when, in 1833, he made his famous distinction between poetry which is '*overheard*', and 'eloquence' which is '*heard*' and 'supposes an audience' (1981: 348). Yet her undoubted capacity for writing to be heard, and moreover to be heard by a new audience of women, is the key to Hemans' power. She, almost alone at the beginning of the century, asserts a woman's voice in poetry which, far from being closed in private introspection, is rousingly theatrical and catching. Her proper sphere as a poet is not the solitary bower of Romantic musing, but a 'burning deck' of public declamation.

Thus, while one of Hemans' obvious faults is an overbalance either of moral meaning or of emotional effect in relation to the situation, her strength lies in a technical confidence which, much more successfully than Wordsworth's, reached the ear of the ordinary (woman) reader, and continued to do so for much of the century. Behind the mild irony of William Michael Rossetti's comment, in 1873, that her poetry appealed 'to many gentle, sweet, pious, and refined souls, in virtue of its thorough possession of the same excellent gifts' (1873: xxvii), lies the fact that she was still being widely read by 'many'. Nor is the reference to 'refined souls' a class limitation. As late as the 1890s, the prefatory essay on Hemans in Alfred Miles's ten-volume anthology, *The Poets and the Poetry of the Century* (1891–7), reminds its readers that, although no longer 'a poet for poets', she continues to be a poet 'read by the people' (VII, 55). Writing for financial reward and therefore, unashamedly, for the sheer quantitative popularity the cheaper book market and increasingly literate population were able to supply, Hemans succeeded where almost no poet had succeeded before her. As Amy Cruse notes: 'Every young lady had a copy of her poems, and in every schoolroom they were read and learnt by heart' (1935: 178). Harriett Hughes set many of them to music, and they became a staple fare of the Victorian drawing-room. Evidently the poetry's simplicity and memorability made it publicly accessible, and crucially at a time when girls' education was not only a subject of controversy – Mary Wollstonecraft and Hannah More had both written about it in the 1780s and 90s – but also increasingly available to daughters of the growing trade and manufacturing classes. The very title, 'Evening Prayer at a Girls' School', carried, in 1826, a social pointedness which has been lost. Thus, out of the absence of fathers and husbands, whose voices in her own life she 'no longer heard', Hemans found a battling, affective and surprisingly public voice of her own. Her message to women may seem to be to stay at home and pray, but her rhetoric, in its tenacious eloquence, 'carries' well beyond the home.

Hemans' own views about poetry are simple and few. In a sense, her hard life left her little time for theories, and most of the statements which appear in her carefully edited correspondence are expressions of regret about its moral and domestic cost to women. However, one comment hints at a self-knowledge which is conscious of artistic failing. ' "It has ever been one of my regrets" ', she wrote, ' "that the constant necessity of providing sums of money to meet the exigencies of the boys' education has obliged me to waste my mind in what I consider mere desultory effusions" ' (in Williams, 1861: 473–4). The story of women writing to support sons, husbands or brothers recurs throughout the century. Wordsworth voiced the same regret when he commented that

> Mrs. Hemans was unfortunate as a Poetess in being obliged by circumstances to write for money, and that so frequently and so much, that she was compelled to look out for subjects wherever she could find them, and to write as expeditiously as possible. (1940–9: IV, 461)

The pressing reality of 'providing sums of money' is a subject which Hemans studiedly avoids in her poetry, in an effort to keep up a front of respectability unsullied by financial need. Her reiterated cry that ' "I have been all my life a creature of hearth and home" ' (in Chorley, 1836: I, 212) must be understood in the context of this public anxiety, as well as of a personal plight which, at least in the imagination, made the ideals of ' "hearth and home" ' all the more furtively desirable. Struggling to make up for the practical and emotional deficiency of her husband, she fills her verses with sweet ideals of domestic bliss, although it soon becomes apparent that the values of ' "hearth and home" ' have more to do with the resilient faithfulness of women than with the actual presence of men.

14

Wordsworth's comments about Hemans sprang from some personal knowledge, for, in June 1830, she spent two weeks at Rydal Mount. While there, she seems to have created certain divisions in the household. Sara and Mary found the time insufferably '"*long*"' and their visitor full of '"affectation"'. William, on the other hand, seems to have liked his guest, or at least to have defended her against their criticisms. Sara wrote grudgingly that '"Mr. W. pretends to like her very much – but I believe it is only because we do not; for she is the very opposite, her good-nature excepted, of anything he ever admired before"' (in Moorman, 1957–65: II, 484, note). It seems to have been Felicia's '"good-nature"', her spirit of sweetly suffering womanhood, which especially endeared her to William. He later recalled his 'true affection for her amiable qualities, and, above all, for her delicate and irreproachable conduct during her long separation from an unfeeling husband' (1940–9: IV, 461). Whatever buried guilts she stirred from the depths of William's own past, it is clear that Felicia's apparent loyalty to her irresponsible husband touched a chord of deep approval in the male head of the Wordsworth household.

Unfortunately, however, this model wifeliness was not matched by model housewifeliness. Wordsworth was shocked by his guest being 'totally ignorant of housewifery' and took it upon himself to direct 'her attention to household economy' (1940–9: IV, 461). He did so by pointedly mentioning a pair of scales which he was giving a young lady as a wedding present. Felicia failed or refused to take the paternalistic hint. '"Imagine, my dear,"' she reported to a friend, '"a bridal present made by Mr. Wordsworth, to a young lady in whom he is much interested – a poet's daughter, too! You will be thinking of a broach in the shape of a lyre, or a butterfly-shaped aigrette, or a forget-me-not ring . . ."' This poetical trinketry from the annuals would hardly have reassured her interlocutor. However, Felicia's response is not without its own rebellious sense of mischief: '"indeed I told him that I looked upon scales as particularly graceful things, and had great thoughts of having my picture taken with a pair in my hand"' (in Chorley, 1836: II, 125–6). The comment briskly turns Wordsworth's literal-minded culinary values into metaphorical ones. This woman will be, not the unpoetic skivvy of the kitchen, but an emblematic 'picture' of Justice with the balances in her hand. By turning the 'scales' against him, she shows something of that early provocative wit which, unfortunately, much of her verse damps down. In contradiction of the poems, with their recall of women to the duties of the hearth, Felicia herself seems to have felt little vocation for being a housewife.

For his part, Wordsworth might more usefully have directed his criticisms towards Hemans the poet, rather than towards the woman who had, after all, whatever her economic competence, reared five sons almost alone. Paradoxically, his reactions to her verse consist almost entirely of household praise. Of 'Flowers and Music in a Room of Sickness', for instance, he wrote: 'This was especially touching to me, on my poor sister's account, who has long been an invalid, confined almost to her chamber' (1967–88: V, 736). The young Mary Ann Evans quoted the same poem enthusiastically to a friend, as an example of 'our sweet Mrs. Hemans' language' (G. Eliot, 1954–78: I, 109). Such homely responses are characteristic of how her verse was read for much of the century. Intimate and utilitarian, it seemed to offer a comfortable domestic palliative to the troubles of life. Hers is a poetry which consoles, assuages, almost 'mothers' its reader; nothing is left over from its beneficently fortifying purpose.

No doubt this was why young women especially, like Mary Ann Evans, claimed her as 'ours'. They found in *Mrs* Hemans a mothering voice and a sweetness of phrase and message which seemed to speak of the very nature of woman. Charlotte Brontë in her mid-twenties made a present of Hemans' poems to the sister of her close friend, Ellen Nussey (1932: I, 284). Emily Eden found in Hemans a poet who '"just said the things I was thinking"' (in Cruse, 1935: 178). As Mrs Gaskell reminded her readers of the later 1860s: 'To be nearly as good as Mrs Hemans' was saying as much to the young ladies of that day, as saying that poetry is nearly as good as Tennyson's would be in this' (1986: 97). Hemans was a mother poet in both senses of the word. She was, to 'the young ladies' of the 1820s and 30s, the poet who seemed to speak most stirringly of woman's lot. But she was also, to many aspiring women writers, the poet who also stood as an example of what was professionally and publicly possible. Both a mother of the sickroom and a mother of the pen, the enthusiasm with which women greeted her work suggests, among other things, how disabling was the poetic silence which she seemed to fill.

Evidently Felicia's own most intense human relationship was with her own mother who had stayed faithful to the home, and who, from the first, had encouraged her daughter's writing. As William Michael Rossetti points out, perhaps with the insight of his own sister poet, 'the family affections of daughter and mother were more dominant and vivid in Mrs. Hemans than conjugal love' (1873: xv). As the poet who also makes motherhood, for the first time, a worthy subject for poetry, it is interesting that Hemans most often describes it, perhaps in recollection of her own mother's Italian–German background, as a remembered, exotic other country of the imagination, nourishing and southern. She mined innumerable books of history and travel, including Sismondi's influential *Rise of the Italian Republics*, for subjects for the many narrative, historical poems, like *The Abencerrage* and *The Widow of*

Crescentius, which she sets in other lands and times past. By the 1820s –
that most nostalgically Byronic decade in poetry – the south was already
a fashionable and rather formulaic geography. Hemans brings to it,
however, her own quite distinctive affiliation. Although not interested in
'character' as such, she is obsessed by gender. It is gender which gives
her poetry a dynamism which, in other Byronic narratives of this time, is
largely supplied by plot (see Butler, 1981: 125). Her southern tales and
lyrics not only look at history from the angle of forgotten mothers,
daughters, widows and wives, but also build up a powerful mythology of
motherhood as a socially self-sufficient state and a metaphorically longed-
for ideal. In 'Italian Girl's Hymn to the Virgin', for instance, she sets up
an emblematic little scene for female confidences which reproduces the
very woman-to-woman atmosphere of her poems:

> For thou, that once did'st move,
> In thy still beauty, through an early home,
> Thou know'st the grief, the love,
> The fear of woman's soul; – to thee I come!
> (*Works*: VI, 21)

The home, in many of these southern tales, is noticeably not the
bourgeois, peculiarly English norm which it will become for many
Victorians, writing in the wake of Burke's anti-Revolutionary rhetoric,
but an exotic, foreign, matriarchal place, remembered from the past and
in another landscape: most often Spain, Italy or Greece. A Romantic,
cosmopolitan streak runs through Hemans' verse, although it is a
pastoral cosmopolitanism, specifically recuperated for women.

Felicia's mother died in 1827. The loss to her 34-year-old daughter
was profound. Some years later she wrote that ' "the death-bed scene of
my beloved and excellent mother is still as mournfully distinct as the
week when that bereavement occurred, which threw me to struggle upon
a harsh and bitter world" ' (in *Works*: I, 294). The loss of her mother was
like a loss of Eden and a first encounter with the 'world'. The poems
written soon after her mother's death possess a new, toughened sadness
which, though it still seeks relief in lyrical platitudes and otherworldly
consolations, occasionally, also, betrays an edge of scepticism. 'No
More', for instance, pivots between the specific loss of a beloved
'mother's voice' (*Works*: VI, 150) and a more generalised grief for life's
betrayals. In two stanzas, Hemans rises to a declaration of hidden
passion worthy, at least in its sentiments, of Christina Rossetti:

> To watch, in dying hope, affection's wane,
> To see the beautiful from life depart,
> To wear impatiently a secret chain,

To waste the untold riches of the heart –
No more!
Through long, long years to seek, to strive, to yearn
For human love – and never quench that thirst,
To pour the soul out, winning no return,
O'er fragile idols, by delusion nursed –
No more!
(*Works*: VI, 151–2)

By comparison with 'Evening Prayer in a Girls' School', the note of weary faithfulness, here, sounds a little sour. The glimpse of a personal resentment in those references to impatience, 'waste' and 'delusion' hint at dissatisfied or squandered energies pressing against the poem's high-toned consolations. Hemans characteristically ends by disguising her autobiographical motives in public advice. But breaking through the 'chain' of her impeccable maxims and metre is an implicit 'I' which, though never voiced, can be felt like an unregulated, 'thirsty' presence in the poem.

This excision of the 'I' signals one of Hemans' most obvious differences from her Romantic contemporaries. By generalising unsatisfied desire into a human or female condition in 'No More', she censors both its personal and its sexual application. The difference emerges most suggestively in a comparison with Rossetti. Hemans' line 'To pour the soul out, winning no return' is almost identical, in imagery, to Rossetti's 'To give, to give, not to receive, / I long to pour myself, my soul' (*CP*: III, 265–6, ll. 25–6). Yet, while Hemans sounds religious, Rossetti sounds sexual; where Hemans sounds impersonally resigned, Rossetti is personal and passionate. The thematic substance of both poems is largely the same: women's desires are unsatisfied. But where Rossetti's 'I' energises such desire into an audible, verbal appetite: 'To give, to give', Hemans smooths it into an inaudible idea. None the less, many of the forms and images of later women's poetry are already, formulaically, present in her work. Such figures as that of the woman's wasted heart, her poured-out soul and idolising passions are adopted and repeated by other poets, but without her constraining sense of edification.

At times, Hemans seems to have recognised the disadvantages of this selflessness. ' "I fear that a woman's mind *never* can . . . attain that power of sufficiency to itself, which seems to lie somewhere or other amongst the *rocks* of a man's" ' (in Chorley, 1836: I, 294), she writes. Yet her own self-reliance in life, especially after the death of her mother, is notably at odds with such statements. In her poetry, too, the contradiction becomes apparent. In general, she keeps to an impersonal tone of consolatory orthodoxy, offering women a poetry of their own which sweetens their lot and eases their burdens – a domestic cordial

18

which turns loneliness, dissatisfaction, boredom and faithfulness into self-rewarding virtues. Yet these smooth, didactic comforts break, here and there, to suggest a deeper protest or trouble in the soul. In 'No More', the tiny metrical catch of the refrain and the hint of bitterness in 'To wear impatiently a secret chain', point to a more strenuous, even resentful self behind the sweet and holy spirit Hemans presented to the world. Paradoxically, her verse's very moral elevation of womanhood also exposes, here and there, the depth of its grievances: 'To waste the untold riches of the heart'.

In 1828, the year after her mother's death, Felicia published her best collection of poems, *Records of Woman*. That same summer Maria Jane Jewsbury, who had long been an admirer of her verses, took a cottage near by, and the two families, consisting of Felicia, her sister Harriett and the boys, Maria Jane and her two brothers, joined forces, and spent a summer walking, reading and talking together. This was Felicia's last summer in Wales, and one of the rare occasions, after the death of her mother, of literary companionship and domestic security. Maria Jane, for her part, recorded her memory of her friend in 'The History of a Nonchalant' (1830) – a story which, as Norma Clarke (1990: 83) has suggested, offers an intriguing confirmation of certain facts behind Felicia's broken marriage. The nonchalant protagonist of the title is in love with Egeria (a portrait of Felicia), who is described, in a subsequently much quoted passage, as 'a muse, a grace, a variable child, a dependent woman – the Italy of human beings' (Jewsbury, 1830: 189). But having been disinherited by his father, the nonchalant refuses to contemplate marriage on any but the conventional terms: 'live upon the money earned by a woman – that woman my wife – and that wife Egeria! – I could far sooner have died than permitted such a reversal of the order of nature' (193). If, as Jewsbury hints, Captain Hemans felt humiliated by his wife's capacity to earn, while she, for her part, agreed to the 'tacit conventional arrangement' of their separation because she preferred to be the wage-earner, then the story of domestic desertion is certainly not as heroically simple as the poetry, and the long-lasting popular myth of Hemans, would suggest. Her own need to elaborate that myth in her poetry, as a generalised story of woman's enduring domestic loyalties, was the means by which she both fended off the feared stigma of professional ambition and, at the same time, surreptitiously passed on to her women readers and successors a sign, almost a hidden code, for the power of that ambition. The contradictions of her life and work are in a sense the matrix from which the Victorian woman poet will emerge.

After 1828, Felicia's life became increasingly difficult and unhappy. Harriett married, and the family home in Wales was sold. Soon after, she herself moved to Wavertree, near Liverpool, and with the exception of her visit to the Wordsworths and another to Scott at Abbotsford, became ever more reclusive and despondent. Exiled, as it were, from the maternal hearth and home she had so devotedly tended, and feeling constantly hard-pressed by a literary fame which was as greedy as it was rewarding, she became weak and ill. Towards the end, she moved to Dublin to be near her brother. Evidently exhausted by a lifetime's continuous writing as well as by the domestic anxieties of her last years, during which she moved house several times, she died in 1835. She outlived her beloved mother by only eight years.

ROMANTIC EXILE

Chronologically, Hemans is a Romantic poet. Nevertheless, whether because much of her writing belongs to the post-Romantic twilight of the 1820s and 30s or because, as a woman poet, her perspectives were inherently different from those of her male contemporaries, her place is hard to fix. Certainly her poetry lacks the political and metaphysical speculation of those contemporaries, and seems, indeed, in its domestic and female concerns, to represent an early 'transition into the characteristic preoccupations of Victorian verse' (Curran, 1988: 188). On the other hand, if, as Marlon Ross has argued, 'romanticism is historically a masculine phenomenon' (1989: 3), which defines the poet as an imperial quester and ruler of high-altitude, visionary empires (25–6), then the women writers of the time are declassed simply because they do not fit this historically promulgated model. Their writings are not Romantic, because not driven by an apparently supra-social urge for 'self-identity, possession, and conquest' (49). While Jane Austen, Dorothy Wordsworth, Mary Shelley and Mary Lamb, for instance, might be found in another category as prose writers (although their status as Romantics has been the subject of recent reappraisal[2]), Hemans inevitably raises the problem of the woman poet's relation to the literary movement called Romanticism. As a woman, Ross suggests, she cannot be judged according to the 'problematic standard' (235) of originality, which is still strongly associated with a masculine–Romantic drive for 'individuality' and 'self-ownership' (161). For her, he claims, 'originality itself may be more or less a nonissue' (235). The problem with this argument, however, is that it both relies on a hidden intentionalism of 'desire' (Romantic originality is gained by wanting it) and that it also turns historical differences of gender (Hemans is a woman and therefore dutiful, self-denying and wary of poetic vocations) into rules of aesthetic value. Such separatism does a disservice to the indubitably greater and more original women poets who succeed Hemans and who struggle, not only to overcome her artistic limitations, but also to be heard on the same terms as men. To read her as a Romantic, as Ross has done, is certainly to prise open some intriguing ideological differences between male and female poets of the time, but it is as a 'Victorian' – one of the first – that her influence and significance in literary history is most profound.

Far from being original but different, Hemans' poetry is often highly derivative. Full of echoes of Wordsworth, Byron, Scott and to some extent Shelley, she ventriloquises the work of her most admired contemporaries and reproduces it with technical efficiency. However, although her language is always curiously familiar to the ear, her verse does achieve another kind of originality in the persistent and ostentatious gendering of its voice. The imaginative landscapes of Romanticism are thus constantly subjected to the critical and social bias of the woman. Such a bias, rather than any intrinsic distinction, becomes Hemans' true note. She writes with an unmistakably partisan devotion to the cause of women, and puts what seems a timidity of the imagination to the service of all the mothers, daughters and wives who have been deserted by the Romantic male's intrepid idealism. As a poet, she looks to the visionary quester's wife and children. Thus, her many poems about journeys and exile, while seeming to espouse the cause of political liberty, of spiritual adventure in distant lands, do so against the strong, underlying tug of home and social responsibility. Romanticism's wanderlust is acknowledged but distrusted by her; Promethean gestures become half-hearted and the wanderers, particularly the female wanderers, nostalgic for what has been left behind.

In *The Forest Sanctuary* (1826), for instance, an ambitiously long, narrative poem much admired by the young Mary Ann Evans (G. Eliot, 1954–78: I, 72), Hemans tells the tale of a family fleeing from the Spanish Inquisition to find a life in the New World. Having described, in some dramatic detail, the execution of the protagonist's best friend and his two sisters, she then describes the long sea journey which takes father and son to their land of liberty. The wife, however, dies of grief and weakness on the passage out. This difference in the fates of the men and the woman is not just a detail of the plot, but provides the main thematic interest of the work. The woman's perspective drags against the forward, political optimism of the men:

> For ever would she cling,
> A brooding dove, to that sole spot of earth
> Where she hath loved, and given her children birth,
> And heard their first sweet voices.
>
> (*Works*: IV, 50)

The Romantic impulse is thus obviously counteracted by the feminine impulse. The one travels outward in the spirit of freedom and adventure; the other looks back, homesick and regretful. Hemans' underlying signature, and the charged tremolo of her descriptions of home, would seem to be supporting the political conservatism implicit in the latter. As Marilyn Butler suggests, 'to become domestic, withdrawn, quietist, meditative and very consciously English' in the early nineteenth century 'was to make a choice which carried a specifically political connotation' (1981: 67). Hemans, more than any other, would seem to express that post-Romantic spirit of the age which, well before the accession of Victoria, was beating a retreat indoors, whether into the well-upholstered security of the English home, guarded by good wives, or into those more troubled towers and moated granges of the mind, haunted by restless, imprisoned Marianas.

However, the emotional direction of *The Forest Sanctuary* is not quite so easy to decode. Evidently the husband's drive for freedom costs the woman her life. She is a victim of that pioneering spirit which is not her own. None the less it is interesting that, just after her burial at sea, which seems to represent the last tragic gesture of female refusal and reluctance, the rhythm of the verse lifts audibly, to suggest a heart-free movement forward:

> The wind rose free and singing: – when for ever,
> O'er that sole spot of all the watery plain,
> I could have bent my sight with fond endeavour
> Down, where its treasure was, its glance to strain;
> The white foam flash'd – ay, joyously, and thou
> Wert left with all the solitary main . . .
>
> (IV, 62)

The idea of that feminised 'sole spot', which recurs throughout the poem like a motif of woman's earth-bound faithfulness to 'birth' as well as death, is almost brusquely abandoned as, 'joyously', father and son continue the journey. The emotional direction of the poem does not quite match its affecting declarations of loss. Male energy triumphs, almost brutally, over female nostalgia.[3]

This formula of sexual division is repeated in innumerable other poems. 'Song of Emigration', for instance, sets male against female voices, in a counterpoint of ideas as well as of metre:

> 'Away, away o'er the foaming main!'
> This was the free and the joyous strain,
> 'There are clearer skies than ours, afar,

We will shape our course by a brighter star;
There are plains whose verdure no foot hath press'd,
And whose wealth is all for the first brave guest.'

'But, alas! that we should go,'
Sang the farewell voices then,
'From the homesteads, warm and low,
By the brook and in the glen!'
(*Works*: VI, 29–30)

Romantic 'quest', here, is clearly defined as male 'conquest' (Ross, 1989: 15–55), as the voices of the women drag against the metrical energy of the men, in dismay at having 'to dwell / In a soil that is not ours' (*Works*: VI, 31). Hemans' literal-mindedness in the face of certain Romantic tropes makes her ideologically interesting in spite of the obsessive and somewhat overacted emotions of her verse. Her story-telling mode ensures that the social context of the Romantic quest becomes explicit: the men's freedom and joy is not a sign of transformed inner consciousness, but of pioneering greed; journeys are not ends in themselves, but routes to a territorially acquired destination. Meanwhile, her sense of gender also sets up a tension between what might be gained, in the way of freedom and 'wealth', and what might be lost: 'the homesteads'. The high cost of experience to women, which will become one of the main motifs of Victorian women's poetry, is already being movingly measured by her. Hemans' many displaced wives and daughters, by being exiled from their allotted 'sole spot', offer a socially critical commentary on the metaphysics of place which underpins Romantic idealism. Their nostalgia or their deaths conflict with 'the free and joyous strain' of the men's imperialist energy.

However, although Hemans repeatedly sets a myth of home against the gusto of adventure, a female pastoralism against male sublimity, she herself often seems uncertain of her position, being caught, somewhere at sea, between nostalgia and risk, security and liberty. Her imagination, far from remaining safe within its own 'spot' of home, constantly travels abroad (where she herself never travelled), in search of other lands for poetry. Furthermore, like many women writers after her, she envisages home, not as that 'very consciously English' place, which it became for the revolution-fatigued Wordsworth and Coleridge (Butler, 1981: 67), but as a foreign, matriarchal enclave, a lost primal scene which may, nevertheless, be recovered. Such a recovery is not acted out in terms of metaphors of nature, which ensure and also compensate for the orphaned imagination of the male poet. It is not mother nature that Hemans seeks, but real mothers, and her poems are full of them. Romanticism's mythologising of landscape as the original nurse, guardian or mother therefore does not affect her, as it does Emily Brontë and Emily Dickinson for instance (see Homans, 1980: 12–40). Instead, she writes about landscape with a highly domesticated, reductive literalism.

'The Chamois Hunter's Love', for instance, is a good example of the way Hemans sets herself in a Romantic landscape, but reads it from another perspective. In this poem, she takes the fashionable stage-set of Romantic angst – Alps and solitary male hunter – and turns on it the different view of the woman lover (and poet):

> I know thou lov'st me well, dear friend! but better, better far,
> Thou lov'st that high and haughty life, with rocks and storms at war;
> In the green sunny vales with me, thy spirit would but pine,
> And yet I will be thine, my love! and yet I will be thine!
>
> (*Works*: VI, 25)

The figure of the chamois hunter comes straight out of Romantic literature, most notably Byron's *Manfred*, suggesting that, at some level, Hemans is writing, like many women poets after her, not as the chamois hunter's love, but rather as the 'love' of Byron himself. Her role, as a poet, is determined in relation to his powerfully tempestuous psycho-dramas, 'with rocks and storms at war'. None the less, such a relation is swiftly resolved into gender polarities: the man aspires, but the woman mourns; he scales the heights, but she longs for home. Sexual difference, so apparently divisive and unbridgeable, is the constant nagging theme of Hemans' verses. Her Romanticism, however enticing, is challenged by the ordinary problem of what the abandoned, unloved women must do.

But in fact the woman, here, does not keep to her proper sphere of 'sunny vales'. She goes, as it were, halfway. 'And I will leave my blessed home, my father's joyous hearth . . .', she declares, 'To sit forsaken in thy hut' (25). This is not the old chant of the deceived maiden, for this maiden, interestingly, chooses deception on the heights rather than safety in the home. Ross's discussion of the poem's 'politics of possession' (1989: 313) misses this element of self-determining choice. There is a certain ambiguous exhilaration about the woman's own small gesture of risk:

> It is my youth, it is my bloom, it is my glad free heart,
> That I cast away for thee – for thee, all reckless as thou art!
> With tremblings and with vigils lone, I bind myself to dwell,
> Yet, yet I would not change that lot, oh no! I love too well!
>
> (25–6)

Whatever autobiographical conflicts lie behind this poem, it is also, clearly, a woman poet's commentary on the 'high' and 'reckless' ambitions of her poetic contemporaries. Male poets may scale the heights, like Manfred, but this woman poet chooses the middle slopes – somewhere between the peaks of the sublime and the vales of the beautiful. The poem betrays a certain imaginative envy of the exalted lovelessness of the male hunter; but it also expresses the dilemma of the woman. For to be the hunter's love is to miss being either the hunter or even much loved. Yet, at some level, Hemans chooses to miss both of them (as perhaps she did in real life). The place of Romantic ambition for the woman is a halfway 'hut', perched on the slopes of the sublime landscape of the imagination, but lonely and forsaken. In the end, Hemans' outsider's relation to Romanticism leaves her, however much protesting '"hearth and home"', only more homeless: somehow exiled both ways. She belongs neither to the family home nor to the wild homelessness of 'rocks and storms'.

These poems of exile and emigration thus bring to the extremist landscapes of the Romantic quest a certain resisting literalism. The woman's point of view counters the territorial ambitions of the male adventurer, as well as, more troublingly, the 'self-possession' (Ross, in Mellor 1988b: 49) or, as Hemans herself put it, the '"sufficiency to itself"' (in Chorley, 1836: I, 294) of the male ego. 'Are not the mountains, waves, and skies, a part / Of me and of my soul, as I of them?' (Byron, 1970: 220), asks Childe Harold as he approaches the Alps. Such metaphysics of the mind's mountains are not for Hemans. The chamois hunter's love speaks, not really of her self but, generically, of woman; hers is not a solitary, individual drama to be 'overheard', but a socialised public speech to be 'heard' by other women, and to be understood as their own. This ideological purpose cannot excuse the poetic weaknesses of her verse, but it does throw light on some of the contradictions in it between the woman's voice, as Hemans emphatically defines it, and the questing, self-tormented voice of high Romanticism, which she both admires and distances as other and male.

However, in her own small way, she too is inherently a poet of exile and displacement. Although literalised in stories of actual travel rather than internalised as a quest romance (Bloom, 1971: 13–35), she too, at her best, can convey a feeling of permanent discrepancy within. One short poem which sums up this sense of estrangement in much of her work is 'The Stranger's Heart'. The inspiration for the poem evidently came from Joanna Baillie's 'Introductory discourse' to her *Plays on the Passions* (1798), where she writes of the universal dramatic interest of 'the fall of the feeble stranger, who simply expresses the anguish of his soul, at the thoughts of that far distant home' (1851: 6). Hemans' poem is not just about a stranger, but also about the strangeness at the very 'heart' of the familiar:

> The stranger's heart! Oh! wound it not!
> A yearning anguish is its lot;
> In the green shadow of thy tree,
> The stranger finds no rest with thee.
>
> (*Works*: VI, 72–3)

Such restlessness marks many of the male characters in her verse. They are all, like her own father and husband, anxious to depart. But in her best poems she turns that restlessness, not into an object of emotional reproach, but into an alternative point of view, at odds with the rooting sanctities of the hearth. The stranger, here, is no particular stranger, but simply the 'other', the unbelonging, the one who 'finds no rest'. The poem avoids any more intimate relation between the speaker, the stranger and 'thee', the female reader.

Thus, the evidence of a great deal of Hemans' poetry is that the estranged heart belongs as much to women as to men. Exiled, restless and full of regrets, they too seem to suffer from that Romantic sense of alienation which opens up an impassable breach between subjectivity and the world. Without metaphorising such alienation, she gives it a local, literal, contingent meaning: the meaning of being, however much bound in love to men, to their voyages of exploration or visionary mountaineering, simply not 'at home' with them. The hint of scepticism, which occasionally ruffles the smooth public-speaking of her verse is, at heart, a scepticism about the very thing she was long held to epitomise: the conservative values of the marital home. In fact her position could be described as lying edgily between the amoral, cost-careless aspirations of the male Romantics, and the sweet and holy myth of the woman poet she herself so energetically, and disingenuously, upheld.

TOWARDS A DREAM OF PASSION

For all her Romantic themes of displacement and exile, Hemans' poetry also looks back to an earlier tradition of literature: the cult of sensibility. In some ways, she makes a bridge between the theatrical, extrovert pathos of eighteenth-century sentimentalism and the sincere, socially responsible pathos of Victorian sentimentality; between femininity as an aesthetic pose and femininity as a saving religious morality. Other poets before her, like Hannah More, Anna Barbauld and also Mary Tighe whom she much admired, had already in the late eighteenth century shifted their emphasis away from the emotionalism of sensibility, with all its increasingly Jacobinical connotations, towards the sober voice of public duty and domestic virtue. As More asserts in *Sensibility: An Epistle to the Honourable Mrs. Boscawen*, a poem written, consciously after the manner of Pope, to one of the first bluestockings:

On these small cares of daughter, wife, or friend,
The almost sacred joys of *home* depend:
There Sensibility, thou best may'st reign,
Home is thy true legitimate domain.
(1835: I, 35)

According to Marlon Ross, More and Barbauld represent the beginning of that widespread nineteenth-century myth of the woman poet as 'the conscience of culture' (1989: 202). Such a conscience may only speak from within the woman's 'legitimate domain' of home. However, Hemans' own position is, once again, not so simple. Both her 'Romantic' poems about exile and her 'Victorian' poems about female passion, set sensibility and home at odds. In spite of all her homely advice, she frequently projects herself in the image of the woman outcast, who sings, self-consciously and helplessly, of her feelings to the world at large. Between sensibility and the duties of home there is, for Hemans, a troubling gulf. The myth of her own domestic sweetness and holiness, coupled with a ready inclination in her reviewers to celebrate such a myth, became a useful cover for certain less obviously legitimate passions.

At a time when England was beginning to consolidate a sense of its own special moral and industrial worth, Hemans seemed to offer an exemplary model of the new literature of female conscience. Harriett Hughes' 'Memoir', published in 1839 at the beginning of Hemans' complete works, played an important part in this national recuperation. Near the start, to allay suspicions about Felicia's marriage, she quotes a review which emphatically endorses the myth of the saintly woman: '"the author before us is not only free from every stain, but breathes all moral beauty and loveliness".' The review then urges that women writers as a class assume responsibility for the morality of culture: '"it will be a memorable coincidence if the era of a woman's sway in literature shall become co-eval with the return of its moral purity and elevation"' (in *Works*: I, 33). Hemans' own saintliness of character, now fully disclosed to the world, is quickly transposed into a literary value for all women. The '"woman's sway in literature"' promises to effect a much-needed moral clean-up after Romanticism. Another quoted review makes the point even more strongly: '"wherever the power of true religion has been felt, there woman, more disinterested, more pure, and more moral than man, has exerted a constant influence to raise the character of society"' (in *Works*: VII, 312). Such confusions between goodness and literary success continue throughout the century. In 1861, Jane Williams fulsomely applauded the 'sublimely blended purity and piety' (490) of Hemans' work, while, in 1873, William Michael Rossetti reminded readers of her poems that 'beauty' is 'inherent as much in the personality of the authoress as in her writings' (xi). Sweetness and holiness, purity and piety would be heavy responsibilities for later poets to bear.

The emphasis on a new morality was often accompanied by a new critical sentimentalism. In 1840, for instance, the *Quarterly Review* carried an important article by Lockhart, which was one of the first to recognise a burgeoning tradition of women's poetry. Reviewing Caroline Norton, Barrett Browning, Caroline Southey and Sara Coleridge among others, Lockhart for the most part gives his authors serious critical attention. However, the defensively gallant antics of his opening paragraph betray his unease, whether real or pretended, at having to write about women:

> It is easy to be critical on men, but when we venture to lift a pen against women, straightway . . . the weapon drops pointless on the marked passage; and whilst the mind is bent on praise or censure of the poem, the eye swims too deep in tears and mist over the poetess herself in the frontispiece, to let it see its way to either . . . (*Quarterly Review*, 60(1840), 374–5)

This misting over of the critical eye, which renders the reviewer impotent to carry out his task, is caused by the softly pictured woman of the 'frontispiece'. Between the poetry and the life, the work and the woman, there is a fatally unmanning congruity. Thus, in a Sternian spasm of effeminate sympathy, the male intellect dissolves 'in tears' at the sight of the beautiful 'poetess'. Such sentimentalism became a favourite tactic among Victorian reviewers. In 1873, E. C. Stedman described Barrett Browning as 'surrounded with aureolas', and then declared: 'We do not see clearly, for often our eyes are blinded with tears' (1887: 114). Such spontaneous affectiveness quickly becomes a highly gender-conscious affectation. It mimics the idea that women's poetry is itself no more than a spontaneous flow of feminine instinct, a tearfulness raining onto the page.

The darker implications of this affective praise, however, are brought out in a review of Hemans by George Gilfillan, which appeared in *Tait's* in 1847:

> Mrs. Hemans's poems are strictly effusions. And not a little of their charm springs from their unstudied and extempore character. This, too, is in fine keeping with the sex of the writer. You are saved the ludicrous image of a double-dyed Blue, in papers and morning wrapper, sweating at some stupendous treatise or tragedy from morn to noon, and from noon to dewy eve – you see a graceful and gifted woman, passing from the cares of her family, and the enjoyments of society, to inscribe on her tablets some fine thought or feeling, which had throughout the day existed as a still sunshine

upon her countenance, or perhaps as a quiet unshed tear in her eye. In this case, the transition is so natural and graceful, from the duties or delights of the day to the employments of the desk, that there is as little pedantry in writing a poem as in writing a letter . . . (*Tait's Edinburgh Magazine*, 14(1847), 361)

Interestingly, while Hemans herself regretted the hasty hackwork which had resulted in too many '"desultory effusions"' (in Williams, 1861: 474), Gilfillan acclaims the effusion as the natural expression of the woman poet. The 'unstudied and extempore character' of her writing is a sign of its quintessential femininity – that is, its appearance of having been written with no intellectual effort, but as a 'natural and graceful' continuation of her equally effortless duties within the home. The extempore mode clearly protects the ideal of woman as unselfish, unthinking and sexually appealing, and thus, in spite of all that housework, aristocratically redundant in relation to the intellectual work-force. Her verse is, like a smile on her face or a tear in her eye, unconsciously and spontaneously physiological, but never sweaty or ungraceful. The nature of this physiology of creativity reflects the tastes of the reviewer, whose comments about 'papers and morning wrapper' then betray, behind all his readiness to worship, an inquisitional voyeurism. Like Pope's attack on Mary Wortley Montagu, which similarly linked female ambition with dirty underclothes: 'Sappho's diamonds with her dirty smock, / Or Sappho at her toilet's greasy task' (1963: 559–69, ll. 24–5), Gilfillan slyly resuscitates, in the guise of flattery, the old conventions of satirical chauvinism. The woman poet, in order not to offend, must be an object of conspicuous sentimentality, tearful herself and provoking tears in her reader. Only thus will she be able to reassure him that she is not a poet at all, but a clean and contented angel of the hearth.

Gilfillan's emphasis on the 'extempore' recuperates certain stock notions of the cult of sensibility. As Janet Todd summarises: 'Women were thought to express emotions with their bodies more sincerely and spontaneously than men; hence their propensity to crying, blushing and fainting' (1986: 19). Such an assumption does not disappear in the eighteenth century, but continues throughout the nineteenth, as a form of approval of women's naturally unselfconscious poetic artistry. Nevertheless, the connection which Gilfillan emphasises, between 'the unstudied and extempore' mode of Hemans' poetry and the attitude of femininity shown by the poet, is charged with contradiction. For as his very iconography tells, to be 'unstudied' as a poet is to be self-consciously and studiedly visible as a woman. True naturalness of attitude in fact belongs, not to the domestic angel, dressed to be looked at, but to the engrossed bluestocking in her unalluring *déshabillé*. Gilfillan's imagery works against him. Being 'extempore', as much of Hemans' stiffly metrical and mannered poetry shows, is a highly artificial and sexually strategic pose. Moreover, what Gilfillan has perhaps forgotten is that the great majority of the readers of Hemans' graceful, clean and effortless effusions were not men, but women. The 'unstudied and extempore' mode is performed specifically for them.

This gendered context gives to the cultivated sentimentalism of Hemans' work a double purpose. Addressed primarily to women, it is not only an apology for creativity, but also an ostentatious exhibition of it. The Romantic Hemans, whose women shrink from adventurous self-assertion and who, in the place of exile, remember their homeland, is crossed, particularly in the later volumes, with a more 'Victorian' Hemans, who is spelling out certain formulas for female passion which will become her most important legacy to later poets. It is not entirely true that she wishes 'to suppress', as Ross argues, the 'relation between poetic activity and vocation' (1989: 229). Rather, she moves from the didactic self-abnegation of her earlier work, 'therefore pray!' to emotional self-assertion in the later; from the heart's exile to passionate display. She does in fact develop a description of poetry as a woman's vocation and, specifically, a vocation outside the home. The impulse for this change of direction came from one particular work which, in a sense, recovered the cult of sensibility expressly for the woman writer.

Madame de Staël's *Corinne: or Italy* appeared in France in 1807, and subsequently went into many English translations, most notably that of 1833, with ode translations by L.E.L. This, as Ellen Moers has shown, was '*the* book of the woman of genius' (1978: 173). In particular, it was the book for women poets. At a time when the reality barely existed, de Staël created the myth of the woman poet and thus, in some ways, made the reality imaginatively possible. In *Corinne*, women read the story of their own ambitions, or, maybe, discovered ambitions to match its story. As Hemans herself commented: ' "some passages seem to give me back my own thoughts and feelings, my whole inner being, with a mirror, more true than ever friend could hold up" ' (in Chorley, 1836: I, 304). Yet the story of *Corinne* is that of an independent, family-less, free-spirited heroine, a poet and improviser, whose English origins are crossed with Italian blood, who is beautiful and powerful, and who has achieved the very public fame Hemans so frequently disclaimed. The plot consists of a lengthy walking tour round Italy, as the heroine journeys from one historical site to another, reciting her verses to the adoring crowds and meanwhile catching the eye of her English lover, Lord Nelvil. Yet in spite of all her gifts and success, Corinne is fated to be a tragic heroine of love. Lord Nelvil, torn between desire and duty, passion and propriety, eventually leaves her for the more domesticated English heroine, Lucile, and she dies, grief-stricken, though not before she has given her last, most inspired poetic performance.

It is hard to see how this pedantically high-pitched plot spoke to Felicia, the apparently devoted wife and mother, who clung to her domestic privacy, travelled little and constantly regretted her public fame. Yet evidently *Corinne's* glamorously staged expression of woman's creativity appealed to the English poet for reasons which were not part of the Hemans myth. The artistic triumphalism of Corinne's progress, although paid for in loneliness and desertion in the end, offers to the reader a distinctly new kind of female sentimentalism: non-domestic, energetic and public. While eighteenth-century sentimentalism, on the whole, insisted on 'the gentle feeling lady, entirely familial and entirely subordinate' (Todd, 1986: 20), de Staël brings the feeling woman out of the home and puts her on a public platform to perform. As a result, feeling becomes, as in English Romanticism, an end in itself, rather than a reaction to domestic catastrophe. It is this new, intransitive mode of sensibility – a sensibility put to the service of art rather than of the home – which marks the innovativeness of de Staël's novel. What today seem like *longeurs* of description, of Italy and of Corinne's own improvised compositions, were undoubtedly read as one continuous metonym for a female passion which had been liberated from its domestic history. If Hemans found, in its pages, the story of her own marital desertion, she also found in it the unprecedentedly long-drawn-out story of woman's creative vocation. *Corinne* recovered poetry for women, not as a moral campaign or 'market enterprise', but precisely as a 'calling' (see Ross, 1989: 268).

Hemans, more than any other, was responsible for transmitting de Staël's message to England as, increasingly, her own poetry came to focus on the woman artist, however misunderstood and tragic, however much pining to be a wife and mother instead. As a result, the thematic tension in her work shifts from external gender difference to internalised self-division. '"I wish I could give you the least idea of what *kindness* is to me – how much more, how far dearer than *fame*"' (in Chorley, 1836: I, 212–13), was one of Felicia's frequent complaints. Yet '"*fame*"', particularly woman's fame, is one of the central preoccupations of her work. 'Woman and Fame', for instance, sets out the contradiction which *Corinne* first dramatised. The speaker, addressing Fame, cries:

> Thou hast a voice, whose thrilling tone
>   Can bid each life-pulse beat
> As when a trumpet's note hath blown,
>   Calling the brave to meet:

But mine, let mine – a woman's breast,
By words of home-born love be bless'd.
(*Works*: VI, 182)

The trumpet of fame, with all its 'thrilling' clamour, enlivens the pulses and calls to adventure. By comparison, the last two lines fall with a dreary and dogmatic flatness. Certainly in Felicia's own life there is no evidence to suggest that she was willing to relinquish her poetry to save her marriage. Yet poem after poem concludes in the routine moral of 'home-born love'. ' "Of all things, never may I become that despicable thing, a woman living upon admiration! The village matron, *tidying up* for her husband and children at evening, is far, far more enviable and respectable" ' (in *Works*: I, 175), she insisted. Respectability haunts her poems about women artists, yet 'admiration', which is precisely the inspiration and the addiction of the Corinne story, is often the main response elicited from her readers.

'Corinne at the Capitol', for instance, reproduces the famous early scene in the novel, where Corinne is crowned, like Petrarch, at the Capitol in Rome. This incident, which Barrett Browning, Christina Rossetti and George Eliot all rework, is riddled with the contradictions which it deliberately landmarks. As de Staël writes: 'it might, indeed, be perceived that [Corinne] was content to be admired; yet a timid air blended with her joy, and seemed to ask pardon for her triumph' (1833: 20). Exposed on a stage of combined creative success and sexual allure, the poet heroine is demurely apologetic. But where de Staël insists on having it both ways – Corinne is both 'content to be *admired*' and yet 'timid' – Hemans turns the contradiction into a stark moral choice:

Radiant daughter of the sun!
Now thy living wreath is won.
Crown'd of Rome! – Oh! art thou not
Happy in that glorious lot? –
Happier, happier far than thou,
With the laurel on thy brow,
She that makes the humblest hearth
Lovely but to one on earth!
(*Works*: VI, 89)

This is, loud and clear, the moral of the tidy matron. With improbable conviction, Hemans turns the scene into a lesson in domestic humility, as the idea of that unnamed 'one' brings the 'Radiant daughter' of inspired creativity firmly down to earth as a cleaner of the hearth. In *Corinne*, the presence of Lord Nelvil, who sees the poet for the first time in this scene, similarly introduces the problem of domestic life: 'in the midst of all this success, it seemed as if the looks of Corinne implored the protection of a friend, with which no woman, however superior, can dispense' (de Staël, 1833: 21). Hemans, like de Staël, insists on the pathos of lovelessness at the height of triumph, while the ending of her poem seems to assert, unequivocally, that Corinne would have been happier '"*tidying up*"'.

Meanwhile, however, 'Corinne at the Capitol' has gorged itself on the spectacle of the admired, successful woman. Before she issues her punishing moral at the end, Hemans writes five stanzas of pure appreciation of Corinne's creative power. The anatomisation of this power is fully in the tradition of the cult of sensibility, but the context and meaning of such power are new:

> All the spirit of thy sky
> Now hath lit thy large dark eye,
> And thy cheek a flush hath caught
> From the joy of kindled thought;
> And the burning words of song
> From thy lip flow fast and strong,
> With a rushing stream's delight
> In the freedom of its might.
> (VI, 88–9)

Throughout the nineteenth century, the idea of the woman poet as a spontaneous improviser remained popular. In 1826, Mrs Jameson noted in her *Diary of an Ennuyée* that, far from 'living only in the pages of Corinne', the art of poetic improvisation was still widespread in Italy (1836: 132). The feminisation of this role in women's poems of the 1820s and 30s offered a model of creativity which, in its insistence on spontaneity, not only re-affirmed a Romantic view of 'poetry' as synonymous with the 'poet' (Coleridge, 1971: 173), but also exploited the artistic potential of femininity itself. Hemans is the first woman poet to embrace, so wholeheartedly, the woman artist as a subject for poetry.

Her tactics in 'Corinne at the Capitol' also point forward, rather intriguingly, to that late development of the whole tradition of sensibility in twentieth-century French feminism. As Catherine Clément puts it, recuperating for feminism the physiological emphasis of sensibility:

> This language which has not yet reached verbal expression, but is held within the confines of the body, which signifies the body on all sides but does not transmit it in the form of a thought-content, remains convulsive. Men watch, but do not understand. (in Marks and de Courtivron, 1980: 133–4)

In Hemans' poem, Corinne's creativity is indeed a body writing, an *écriture féminine*, which flows, unimpeded by thought or reflection, from her convulsed, highly visible body: 'And the burning words of song / From thy lip flow fast and strong . . .' Burning, flowing and flushing are signs of an inner passion which is written and read physiologically on the surface. Such a 'flush' of 'thought' or, to adapt a phrase from Meynell, such published blood (*PP*: 221), suggest a perfect confluence between inner and outer, impression and expression, poet and poem. The woman's body, her 'eye', 'cheek' and 'lip', thus turn naturally into parts of speech. The profound significance of *Corinne* was that it offered to women's poetry of the nineteenth century a model of female sensibility which was not only assertively public, self-possessing and self-admiring, but which could also be imaginatively inhabited, by women, from within.

Admittedly, Corinne's 'performing heroinism' (Moers, 1978: 173) remains tied, in terms of plot, to the male gaze. Lord Nelvil's eyes fill 'with tears', like those of innumerable subsequent reviewers of women's verse, not at the power of her poetry, but at the sight of her vulnerable femininity: 'in the midst of all this success, it seemed as if the looks of Corinne implored the protection of a friend' (21). The whole of the crowning scene at the Capitol is mediated by and staged for the male onlooker in de Staël's story. Thus, the free flow of poetry into physical beauty, art into anatomy, remains part of a strategic, heterosexual appeal: 'Her arms were transcendently beautiful; her figure tall' (20). By contrast, Hemans' version of the same scene is observed, not by a male lover, but by other women: 'Well may woman's heart beat high / Unto that proud harmony!' (*Works*: VI, 88), she declares. Characteristically, she has slipped into an implicitly matrilineal interpretation of the scene. Corinne's performance, here, is not for the male lover, but for these women who, like Hemans herself, find in her a symbol of their own hearts' pride and power. The excision of Lord Nelvil from the poem, at least until the punitive last lines about 'the humblest hearth', suggests the extent to which this Corinne is already part of another romance: with the women readers and writers who are her real admiring audience. The story of *Corinne*, Hemans' small revisionary swerve seems to hint, is not one of rejection in love, or even of the conflict between fame and domesticity; instead, it is the story of an 'enthusiasm of authorship' which she herself, like many other writers, caught from reading the novel. Corinne is already, not a character, but an intertextually invented myth of woman's power.

However, there is yet another text behind the novel. Corinne is no more than an updated and somewhat cleansed version of an older model of female creativity. De Staël herself comments on the fact that Corinne's crowning must have been identical to the tributes given to the first woman poet of all: 'Sappho' (22). In her posthumously published play, *Sapho* there is a scene in which the poet is crowned with laurel and improvises to an accompaniment on her lyre (1836: 701–2). The play tells the legendary story of Sappho's unrequited love for the boatman Phaon, and of her subsequent suicide by leaping into the sea from the Leucadian cliff. This, which was almost certainly a later invention of writings from the fourth century BC (Hallett, 1979: 448), is none the less the myth about Sappho which prevailed in the nineteenth century, and which profoundly influenced theories of female art. Evidently the suicide story was a convenient heterosexual cover for less acceptable stories about the poet, which also appear, in the course of the century, in the works of Baudelaire, Swinburne and then in the Sapphic lyrics of Michael Field. Tennyson, on the other hand, who created in 'Mariana' and 'The Lady of Shalott' two powerful emblems of the woman poet as reclusive and dying, exploited the suicide legend of Sappho as a figure for an art 'embodied' in the sensibility of women. Sappho's leap connects female creativity with death, in a pact which the Victorian imagination finds endlessly seductively appealing.

Nevertheless, this legend cannot altogether obscure the other fact about Sappho: she is the first woman love poet and, furthermore, the one who described, in elaborate detail, the physical effects of female passion. Of the two longer fragments of her poetry which were known in the early nineteenth century, the second, addressed to a beloved girl (but translated, before 1885, as a boy), is an enumeration of the bodily symptoms of love in phrases which pre-empt the formulas of sensibility:

> When I look on you, Drochea [Drochea], my speech comes short or fails me quite, I am tongue-tied; in a moment a delicate fire has overrun my flesh, my eyes grow dim and my ears sing, the sweat runs down me and a trembling takes me altogether. (Sappho, 1922: 187)

A number of Tennyson's poems about women, in particular 'Eleänore' and 'Fatima', are either direct translations or elaborations of this fragment (see Robinson, 1924: 55, 205). The objectification of the woman's body as a convulsively impassioned art form, as a self-improvising poetry as well as a sexual spectacle, finds its originating myth in the figure of that first female poet and lover in one. However, it is a long time before such a figure can be freed from the legend of sexual despair and death which accompanies it, and women's poetry be defined as something other than a lovelorn, suicidal enterprise. Sappho's leap gives to Victorian poetry a figure for women's creativity as penultimate and doomed – as on a cliff-edge of desire and death which is imminently self-silencing and punishing. *Corinne*, which ends with the heroine's 'Last Song' before she dies in despair, patently presents a Sappho *rediviva*, fated, in spite of all, to die for love.

Hemans' own poem, 'The Last Song of Sappho', begins a tradition of 'last songs' which are also, paradoxically, some of the first that women poets sing. Betrayed in love, this singer throws herself, lyre in hand, into the sea:

> I, with this winged nature fraught,
> These visions wildly free,
> This boundless love, this fiery thought –
> – *Alone* I come – oh! give me peace, dark sea!
> (*Works*: VII, 11)

Such a model of creative abandon tends to reinforce the notion of women's poetry as heartfelt, lovelorn and reluctant. As Susan Gubar points out, the 'hegemonic position of Sappho' emphasises the values of 'personal sincerity and passionate ecstasy' in women's verse (1984: 59) – values readily reinforced by Victorian critics. Yet it also emphasises desire and power. Wrung out of sexual betrayal and impending death, Sappho's last songs are also, as it were, a last fling of passion, a waving and drowning together, in which the woman's body is alluringly and unattainably displayed in a spasm of hopeless desire.

Thus death is at once a drastic apology for women's passion and a suggestively eroticised celebration of it. Hemans' innumerable wandering female singers tend to be, like 'The Sicilian Captive', literally fainting to death as they pluck the (heart) strings of their antique lyres: 'She had pour'd out her soul with her song's last tone; / The lyre was broken, the minstrel gone!' (*Works*: V, 234). This conventional yet catastrophic permission for passion (another pouring of the soul) is riddled with the contradiction of the Sapphic myth itself. Sappho's leap, on the one hand, is a gesture entrammelled with the heterosexual story which motivates it; self-pitying and reproachful, it takes place very much in the imagined eye of some treacherous Phaon who is to blame. On the other hand, Sappho's leap is also a bid for self-expression, physical passion and poetic power, as the woman's body takes centre-stage in an exhibition of self-confirming sensibility put on specifically for women readers. Such a double audience creates a deep emotional split at the centre of many of Hemans' poems about the woman artist.

Her best volume, which she published the year after her real mother's death and dedicated to her poetic mother, Joanna Baillie, ' "of whose name my whole sex may be proud" ' (in Chorley, 1836: I, 146), is *Records of Woman*. In some ways, the poems in this collection repeat old themes. Men are faithless – as Clarke notes, 'there are no satisfactory husbands' (1990: 80) in these works – and women, as a result, have a statuesque, if much lamented, independence. Arabella Stuart, Joan of Arc, Edith, the Indian Woman, Madeline, all suffer heroically and eloquently on their own. None the less, the emotional energy of these sufferers begins to show a certain dramatic, rather than merely elocutionary, power. Hemans' usual form of moral monologue is here clearly developing some features of the dramatic monologue:

> Now never more, oh! never, in the worth
> Of its pure cause, let sorrowing love on earth
> Trust fondly – never more! – the hope is crush'd
> That lit my life, the voice within me hush'd
> That spoke sweet oracles; and I return
> To lay my youth, as in a burial urn,
> Where sunshine may not find it. All is lost!
> (*Works*: V, 141)

Thus Arabella Stuart bewails the fate which has imprisoned her for life for a political misalliance. The intimacy of the suffering voice here, of an 'I' unmediated by moral dogma, begins to hint at that historical relativity which will mark the dramatic monologue proper. Certainly Hemans' poems contain neither the psychological 'morbidities' (Faas, 1988: 185) nor the de-stabilising ironies of 'moral and emotional Truth' (Langbaum, 1974: 132) which Tennyson and Browning will exploit. In fact such ironies are absent from most dramatic monologues by nineteenth-century women poets, perhaps because 'Truth' is still believed to reside, if nowhere else, in women. Even in Webster and Mew, irony is a social rather than moral or metaphysical strategy. In Hemans, the notion that 'the victim speaks in a pure voice' (Elshtain, in Keohane, 1982: 136) remains an essential ingredient of her poetic creed. None of her heroines are self-deceived, sophistical or criminal; most are victims of deception, sophistry or crime. But then, neither Tennyson nor Browning probe the immorality of women very much. Irony, it seems, is an essentially masculine device, suited to the sturdier inner 'build' of the Victorian male self. Hemans, with her clinging belief in women's victimised purity, cannot risk ironising that purity.

None the less, in *Records of Woman* she does forge a sense of the woman's voice as historically significant, and, in its own sphere, self-determining and self-asserting. The idea of that self as a product of history and temporal change emerges in the new flexibility of the speaking voice, which presses its own rhythms against those of the metre: 'Now never more, oh! never . . .' Such contrary pressure also carries a hidden moral meaning. The idea that metrical correctness is equivalent to moral propriety continued into the nineteenth century, at least as far as women's poetry was concerned. Anna Barbauld had laid down the rules, in the previous century, in 'On a Lady's Writing': 'Her even lines her steady temper show, / Neat as her dress, and polished as her brow' (1825: 1, 59). Hemans' *Records of Woman* at least shows her struggling free of that 'steady temper' which aims, not at poetic power but a respectable tidiness of dress. '"I have put my heart and individual feelings into it more than any thing else I have written"' (in Chorley, 1836: I, 160–1), she declared of her new volume. Something of woman's restless 'heart' and 'feelings' can be heard in these still heroic, but more intimately dramatised poetic declamations.

The best monologue in the collection represents Hemans' most ambitious version of the Sappho–Corinne myth: 'Properzia Rossi'. If eighteenth-century women poets 'rarely assumed the stance of the suffering artist' (Todd, 1986: 61), Hemans, however formulaic her representations, is increasingly obsessed by it. 'Properzia Rossi', as she explains, was 'a celebrated female sculptor of Bologna' who 'died in consequence of an unrequited attachment' (*Works*: V, 160). The sixteenth-century orphan and possibly courtesan, who was on several occasions in conflict with the law (Greer, 1979: 210), is thus politely transformed into a pure woman and passive victim of 'unrequited' love.

None the less, Properzia is also an artist, and this theme of creativity carries the conviction of a passion which has otherwise been blanked out of her character. The poem opens with an almost full-blooded cry for feeling and creative power:

> One dream of passion and of beauty more!
> And in its bright fulfilment let me pour
> My soul away! Let earth retain a trace
> Of that which lit my being, though its race
> Might have been loftier far. Yet one more dream!
> From my deep spirit one victorious gleam
> Ere I depart!
>
> (V, 160–1)

This is not womanly devotion, but a quite Wordsworthian demand for the inspirational 'gleam'. The note of didactic mournfulness has gone and, instead, the speaking voice, full of egotistical energy and desire, breaks the monotony of the rhymed pentameter. Hemans' technical proficiency here hints, through a lightening of the rhyme and the occasional enjambment, at the unsteady waywardness of desire: 'One dream of passion and of beauty more!' The act of pouring the soul is no longer a wasteful generosity, unrequited by men, but, as in Rossetti, a declaration of emotional purpose which is its own reward. The 'bright fulfilment' comes, not from any onlooker, but from the 'deep spirit' within.

Unfortunately, this purely artistic commitment does not last. Properzia has made a statue of Ariadne, the woman whom Theseus deserted and left to die on an island, and has cast her in a pose of grief which duplicates her own. Inevitably, Sapphic self-sufficiency gives way to Sapphic suicidalism, art to despair:

> Speak to him of me,
> Thou, the deserted by the lonely sea,
> With the soft sadness of thine earnest eye –
> Speak to him, lorn one! deeply, mournfully,
> Of all my love and grief!
>
> (V, 162)

For all its initial aspiration this is art, not self-sufficiently for art's sake, but as a plea for attention. The temptation to be a statue in a *tableau vivant* of self-conscious 'heroinism' is one which, to the end of the century, lures women into an easy association between the self and the work. This false Pygmalionism disguises the differences between subject and object, poet and lover, so that woman, as a creative subject, becomes her own mournfully static sexual object. The artist becomes an actress, the creator a victim, and the 'dream of passion', invoked at the beginning, freezes into a pose.

Barrett Browning, in the voice of her own poet-heroine, Aurora Leigh, acutely sums up the weakness of such a model:

> There it is,
> We women are too apt to look to one,
> Which proves a certain impotence in art.
> We strain our natures at doing something great,
> Far less because it's something great to do,
> Than haply that we, so, commend ourselves
> As being not small, and more appreciable
> To some one friend.
>
> (*AL*: V, 42–9)

The temptation to be 'more appreciable' is one to which Hemans too often succumbs. Whether it is a strategy to pacify the onlooking critic or a reaction to the facts of her own life, such special pleading risks turning her verse into a self-pitying and mercenary appeal. Properzia uses her statue, not to embody her 'dream of passion and of beauty', but only to propitiate or reproach the 'one friend'. She is, in fact, a courtesan in her art, displaying her emotional wares to the imagined eye of her lover. Such an eye will continue to dominate the whole tradition of sensibility in the nineteenth century, provoking later women writers to take a symbolic and melodramatic revenge on it.

As in much of her poetry, Hemans' tactics in 'Properzia Rossi' suggest a split purpose: on the one hand appealing, on the other self-possessed; on the one hand sexual, on the other artistic; on the one hand addressed to men, on the other to women. At one point Properzia, forgetting her cruel lover, exclaims:

> Oh! I might have given
> Birth to creations of far nobler thought;
> I might have kindled, with the fire of heaven,
> Things not of such as die! But I have been
> Too much alone . . .
>
> (V, 163)

Although this rounds on friendlessness once again, it also hints at some better knowledge, which lies deep in Hemans' consciousness: a sense of squandered gifts and unfulfilled potential. The thrill of a passion which is objectless and inborn comes through the poem's melancholy romance, though it comes, as it does in *Corinne*, more as an idea than as a reality. It will be for later poets to realise this formula of power which Hemans so obsessively and passionately reworks:

> It comes – the power
> Within me born flows back – my fruitless dower
> That could not win me love. Yet once again
> I greet it proudly, with its rushing train
> Of glorious images: – they throng – they press –
> A sudden joy lights up my loneliness –
> I shall not perish all!
>
> (V, 161)

Meanwhile, one solution to the contradictions of love and art, home and fame, heterosexual reproach and homoerotic enthusiasm, is, as always, to die. At least death offers woman an apologetic sort of grandeur – a momentarily prolonged cliff-edge of power from which to sing another Sapphic last song. The real 'dream of passion', unlike its heroically mimed replica, may never be achieved, but at least Properzia, like her author, knows it would be worth having.

Hemans, then, is to be credited with having helped to shift the tradition of sensibility away from its private domestic context of tearful but tidy femininity towards a public, socially purposeful platform of female inspiration and creative power. By putting her heroines on a stage, however unreal and mythical like the stage of the Capitol, she does at least liberate the *idea* of the woman poet from the (in some ways equally mythical) denials of history. Her Sapphos and Corinnes give later women poets a place, as it were, from which to start, even if it is to start to walk away. They also leave to them that large area of common reality which Hemans' own life and the tradition of sensibility denied. It will be for later, better poets to find ways of writing about power as well as goodness, money as well as love, sexuality as well as romance. It will also be for them to turn the lyre of spontaneous, heartfelt feeling into a colder, more secretive figure for what might lie at the poet's heart.

In the end, for all her brave statements, Hemans largely produced what was required, at a time when those requirements – sweetness, holiness and propriety – were being enthusiastically put on women. The Victorian rule for women writers would continue to be, to the end of the century, not to perfect the work but, in the words of Hemans' true descendant, Ella Wheeler Wilcox, to: 'Make thy life better than thy work' (1909a: 116). Hemans turned such rules into a quite profitable popular idealism about women. She was widely read and, in her way, influenced the whole course of poetry to come. Tennyson's mother 'read aloud from Mrs. Hemans' on country walks with her sons (C. Tennyson, 1968: 14) and Browning showed Michael Field the first book he bought as a boy: 'Mrs. Hemans' *Commonplace Book*' (*WD*: 15). That she did so by insisting, anxiously and self-protectively, on non-artistic values was perhaps as much a necessary disguise as an imaginative limitation. Those values, however, become daunting obstacles to the women poets who follow and who, for all their admiration and gratitude, must learn to throw open the narrow prison of theme and feeling which Hemans so competently and devoutly shut round her.

SATIN RIBANDS

In 1842, Elizabeth Barrett Browning wrote to Miss Mitford to express some of her reservations about Hemans' verses:

> I admire her genius – love her memory – respect her piety & high moral tone. But she always does seem to me a lady rather than a woman, & so, much rather than a poetess – her refinement, like the prisoner's iron .. enters into her soul. She is polished all over to one smoothness & one level, & is monotonous in her best qualities. We say 'How sweet & noble' & then we are silent & can say no more – perhaps, presently, we go to sleep, with angels in our dreams. (*MRM*: II, 88)

She had recently read both Chorley's and Hughes' memoirs of the poet, describing the latter as similar to Hemans' own work in having 'the taste of holy water' (II, 88) about it. Her admiration for Hemans' 'genius', as she briskly names it, quickly degenerates into a 'respect' for her 'piety', and it is clear that such formulas are repeated largely as a perfunctory obligation. Unlike Wordsworth, she then mocks the adjectives ' "sweet & noble" ' as descriptions of poetry. Characteristically quick to hear the class values of such descriptions, she repudiates them with the assertion that Hemans is a lesser poet for being 'a lady rather than a woman'. The cliché of angels at the end beautifully parodies the kinds of attributes commonly brought to women's verse. Angels are all very well in dreams; in poetry they are soporific.

Barrett Browning was always alert to the oppressive conventions of sexual praise. When Poe sent her his volume of poems and prose, containing a lavish dedication to herself, she was wryly nonplussed: 'What is to be said, I wonder, when a man calls you the "noblest of your sex"?' An appropriate reply, she thought, ironically, might be ' "Sir, you are the most discerning of yours" ' (*Letters*: I, 249). The fact that Hemans had been so fulsomely worshipped as noble, sweet and pious was calculated to offend the poet who, at the age of twelve, had read Mary Wollstonecraft and was determined to reject compliments based on gender or class. Some years later, she finely summed up the flaw in Hemans' work: 'she was bound fast in satin riband' (*MRM*: II, 425). The image perfectly suggests a form of constraint which is, in fact, luxurious and frivolous. Barrett Browning's own early verse has its faults of sentimentality and melodrama, but its verbal exuberance, even where inept or grotesque, at least breaks the 'satin riband' of moral delicacy and metrical correctness with which Hemans binds the ladylike body of her work.

The extent to which Barrett Browning realises and reacts against the vitiating features of the older poet's style is shown by the poem she wrote on Hemans' death in 1835. 'Felicia Hemans' was published in the *New Monthly Magazine* and was written as a revision of a poem by the other popular woman poet of the time, L.E.L. It thus, as Dorothy Mermin points out (1989: 74), unequivocally declares its line of descent on the female side. But it also takes issue with its two predecessors. L.E.L.'s 'Stanzas on the Death of Mrs. Hemans' insists on a sentimentalist transparency of life and art, which brings the character of the poet comfortingly within reach:

> With what still hours of calm delight
> Thy songs and image blend;
> I cannot choose but think thou wert
> An old familiar friend.
>
> (*PW*: 410)

L.E.L. is keen to insist, as she does in an article on Hemans published that same year, that 'nothing is so strongly impressed on composition as the character of the writer' (*New Monthly Magazine*, 44(1835), 425). The authenticity of the woman's poems comes from the moral values of her life, and L.E.L. repeats those values with fluent enthusiasm:

> So pure, so sweet thy life has been,
>   So filling earth and air
> With odours and with loveliness,
>   Till common scenes grew fair.
> (*PW*: 409)

The dead poet's 'songs and image blend' to produce the effect of a single, perfect identity, which is then canonised, through all the familiar adjectives, into a vapid saintliness.

By comparison Barrett Browning's poem, which takes L.E.L.'s to task for unnecessary mournfulness, edges on the grotesque in its rough heptameters and over-ambitious abstractions:

> But bring not near the solemn corse a type of human seeming,
> Lay only dust's stern verity upon the dust undreaming . . .
> (*CW*: II, 81–3, ll. 13–14)

Above all, Barrett Browning is at pains to separate the woman and the artist, and she implicitly rebukes L.E.L.'s suggestion that Hemans' art was not worth the sorrow:

> Nor mourn, O living One, because her part in life was mourning:
> Would she have lost the poet's fire for anguish of the burning?
> The minstrel harp, for the strained string? the tripod, for the afflated
> Woe? or the vision, for those tears in which it shone dilated?
> (ll. 17–20)

The baroque oddity of these double rhymes and the 'strained string' of the metre are very different faults from the sickly fluency of L.E.L.'s 'Stanzas'. The immature Barrett Browning is already struggling against the smooth correctness of her two predecessors, while repudiating the trick of self-pity which frequently mars their verse. 'Would she have lost the poet's fire for anguish of the burning?' directly challenges Hemans' own innumerable complaints about the emotional and domestic cost of fame. The poet, if she is a true oracle or prophet, will know that 'tears' are not a poetic end in themselves, but only an instrument for larger 'vision'. Barrett Browning's poem presses, albeit awkwardly, beyond the narcissistic consciousness of 'woe', which both Hemans and L.E.L.

ostentatiously parade, to the idea of the poem as a separate, impersonal object. Refusing to engage in an aesthetics of tearfulness, she roughly asserts that, if Hemans were worthy of the name of poet, she would not relinquish inspiration for happiness. The whole martyred ethic of her work – her constant assertion that security in the home is more to women than fame – is thus reversed. By separating writing and suffering,[4] Barrett Browning deliberately breaks the connection between art and femininity, between the 'songs' and the 'image', between the poems and the frontispiece, which the legend of Mrs Hemans was so influential in cementing. The very title of her poem has a touch of impolite unfamiliarity about it.

For all its tortuous immaturity, then, 'Felicia Hemans' expresses something of the struggle and the anguish of the younger poet's creativity. Its rejection of real-life compensations for fame, its substitution of the wild Delphic visionary for the betrayed heroine and its insistence on the harsher, impersonal meanings of art: 'Beauty, if not the beautiful, and love, if not the loving' (24), all mark out the divergent path that Barrett Browning's own poetry will take. Already she is refusing to say ' "How sweet & noble" ' with the general chorus. Instead, she forges her own description of imaginative truth as something less rarefied and less monotonous than Hemans' self-regarding, tightly ribanded melancholy.

None the less, it is from Hemans, rather than from any other Romantic poet, that Barrett Browning takes her bearings, and it is Hemans who, for good and for ill, will largely determine the course of women's poetry in the decades to come. Hers is a troubling and limiting legacy, but it is also the legacy of a woman who proved herself, against the seeming odds of history, and in spite of all her own versified disclaimers, the poet who wrote about and for women, and who, moreover, made a spectacular professional success of it.

2

L.E.L. (1802–38)

(Letitia Elizabeth Landon)

> 'What is my life? One day of drudgery after another; difficulties incurred for others which have ever pressed upon me beyond health, which every year, by one severe illness after another, is taxed beyond its strength; envy, malice, and all uncharitableness, – these are the fruits of a successful literary career for a woman.' (L.E.L. in Hall, 1871: 264)

The 'literary career' of Letitia Elizabeth Landon or, as she was known to her readers, L.E.L., makes a striking contrast to Hemans'. The two poets were near-contemporaries and often wrote for the same publications, but they never met, and it may be that Hemans, ever anxious about her reputation, intentionally kept her distance. For the career of L.E.L. provided a stark reminder of the risks of professional success for women. Living, not in de Staël's imaginary Italy, but in an England where moral values were already stiffening into a class-conscious, sexual puritanism, L.E.L. suffered the penalties of putting a myth into practice. She was a real-life, and therefore more tawdry, Corinne. Without Hemans' protective double standards of life and art, she fell victim to the altogether banal ' "envy, malice, and all uncharitableness" ' of a London literary world which was a far cry from the Capitol. Her scandalous death, only forty years after the death of Mary Wollstonecraft and at a time when, Flora Tristan noted, the *Vindication of the Rights of Woman* seemed unavailable in England and its mention filled even ' "progressive" women' with 'horror' (1982: 253), only confirmed the public's worst suspicions. The violent reaction of the reputedly 'gentle-hearted' Charles Lamb, for instance, suggests how readily disapproval and outrage could surface in the general consciousness. '"If she belonged to me"', he declared of L.E.L., '"I would lock her up and feed her on bread and water till she left off writing poetry. A female poet, or female author of any kind, ranks below an actress, I think"' (in P. G. Patmore, 1854: I, 84).

Yet if L.E.L.'s fate was to play out the story of Corinne to the life, her interest as a poet lies in the way that she develops and comes to distrust the public 'dream of passion' which de Staël and Hemans bequeath to women. In her early work she adopts their model of sensibility with fervour, taking its artistic exhibitionism to compulsive extremes. However, as she matures, a streak of scepticism begins to unsettle her grand poses and, though realised too late in her own career, it points forward to the devices of self-distance and doubt employed by later poets. Meanwhile, the story of L.E.L.'s life added its own cautionary significance to the contradictory myth of the woman poet which the nineteenth century enthusiastically created and embraced. This 'snub-nosed Brompton Sappho', as Disraeli called her, was fated to show that, in real life, Sapphic ambition was the material not of high and sublime but of rather low tragedy.

*   *   *

Letitia Elizabeth Landon was born in 1802. Her father was an army agent who, as a result of financial speculation, fell from relative prosperity to near poverty. Like Hemans, Letitia showed a surprising facility at an early age for both memorising and writing poetry (Blanchard, 1841: I, 13). In particular, her father's stories about his travels in Africa before marriage fed his daughter's avid fascination with the foreign as romantic and exotic. Highly imaginative and with a fluent ear for verse, Letitia was one of those 'gifted girls' (Moers, 1978: 197) whom the nineteenth century was all too ready to turn into lucratively performing prodigies. As it happened, next door to the Landons lived a certain William Jerdan who, in 1817, pioneered one of the first, new-style, popular magazines, *The Literary Gazette*, and who was prepared to publish in it the surprisingly accomplished verses of his 16-year-old neighbour. Thus L.E.L.'s poetic career began early and effortlessly. Like Hemans, she was cultivated from the start as a 'natural' poet, whose improvisatorial methods needed no training or harnessing, and whose facility for writing long, perfectly metrical poems was of itself a sufficient cause for wonder. In a few years she became one of the most sought-after names in the annuals. Bulwer Lytton recorded how, when he was a student at Cambridge, 'there was always, in the Reading Room of the Union, a rush every Saturday afternoon for "The Literary Gazette".' In particular, the verse contributions mysteriously initialled L. or L.E.L.

aroused the young men's curiosity. 'We soon learned it was a female, and our admiration was doubled, and our conjectures tripled. Was she young? Was she pretty?' (*New Monthly Magazine*, 32(1831), 546). A female poet who was both young and pretty was already, to their imaginations, an artistic prodigy.

Unfortunately, L.E.L.'s youthful talents, like Hemans', were too soon turned into a financial resource. Her first volume, *The Fate of Adelaide* (1821), was published when she was 19, but it was her second volume which caught the popular imagination and became a spectacular publishing success. *The Improvisatrice* (1824), which she claimed to have written in less than five weeks, went through six editions in the year of its publication. The subject matter, consisting of a series of fatal love stories, supposedly improvised by an Italian woman poet who is evidently another Corinne, strongly appealed to the Byronic tastes of the day and, in the very year of Byron's death, seemed to offer what the new age was wanting: a *Childe Harold* for women. Meanwhile, L.E.L. tasted the financial rewards of such popularity. Her publisher paid her £300 for the volume and, when its success became apparent, offered her £600 for the next. As her father's affairs were proving ever more precarious, such considerable earnings represented a status which was not just poetic. Like Hemans, L.E.L. must have felt the somewhat incongruous connections between her 'natural', improvisatorial effusions as a woman poet and her unnatural responsibilities as a wage-earning daughter. From an early age, the self-advertising poetic glamour of the one offered a cover for the more sordid, disreputable realities of the other; poetic sensibility covered the need for money.

In 1825, when she was 23, Letitia's father died, and the family was left in a state of near penury. His daughter was evidently desolated, and ended her next long poem, *The Troubadour*, with a passionate *envoi* to her childhood idol:

> My own dead father, time may bring
> Chance, change, upon his rainbow-wing,
> But never will thy name depart
> The household god of thy child's heart,
> Until thy orphan girl may share
> The grave where her best feelings are.
> Never, dear father, love can be,
> Like the dear love I had for thee!
> (*PW*: 112)

The compulsive betrayal by men of so many of the heroines in L.E.L.'s poetry hints at a story of desertion older, perhaps, than those of adult romance. Meanwhile, like Hemans, she set herself to remedy that father's absence. Soon, she was earning enough money to support her mother and younger brother, and later helped to pay for that brother's education at Oxford. Not only was this a case of the education 'girls with brothers all must learn / To do without' (*Portraits*: 56), as Augusta Webster puts it, but also of the education girls from impoverished, genteel backgrounds must learn to pay for. Just as Hemans produced innumerable 'desultory effusions' to pay for the education of her sons, so L.E.L. rallied her poetic talents to the economic support of her brother. The verse of both might have benefited incalculably from the leisure and intellectual stimulus they only earned for others. Certainly, there is some truth in Letitia's claim that '"from the time I was fifteen, my life has been one continual struggle in some shape or another against absolute poverty"' (in Blanchard, 1841: I, 56). In the absence of fathers and husbands, both she and Hemans wrote what was required by the market, and in sufficient quantities to keep themselves and their families from the '"absolute poverty"' which was the lot of untrained, unprotected middle-class women.

The fact that Letitia left home at about this time suggests that, without her father, there was little to keep her. Relations with her mother, apparently, were not good. Mrs Hall, one of her closest friends, wrote that she found '"no loving sympathy, no tender care from the author of her being"' (1871: 272), and Barrett Browning, having read Blanchard's biography of 1841, also spotted the absence of daughterly affection: 'Only one letter to her mother, & that of the coldest! There is a mystery somewhere' (*MRM*: I, 252). At first, Letitia lived with her grandmother, but she soon left to become a boarder in Miss Lance's school for girls. There she rented a single attic room which served as bedroom, study and reception room for much of the rest of her life. Grace Wharton hints at a romantic motive behind this move: a desire 'to live, as certain *esprits forts* did, alone; to be a Corinne' (1861: 193). Corinne evidently offered young girls a model for living as well as for writing. However, Mrs Hall also points to more practical motives: '"Miss Landon found there a room at the top of the house, where she could have the quiet and seclusion her labour required, and which she could not have had with her kind-natured but restless grandmother"' (1871: 271). Letitia, it seems, left her mother's and grandmother's homes, not because she was flighty and loose-living, as public opinion promptly assumed, but because she needed that one essential of the professional writer: a room of her own. No doubt the fact that she was supporting her mother and brother financially gave her power to demand what other women might only long for. The literary ideal of 'a very high attic' (G. Eliot, 1954–78: I, 261), like George Sand's in Paris, haunted women writers well into the twentieth century. Yet in London, in the 1820s, such unusual independence cost the young L.E.L. dear, both in literary 'drudgery' and eventually in reputation.

Between 1821 and 1830, L.E.L. published six volumes of poetry. In addition, she undertook vast quantities of casual writing and editorial work for the new literary magazines. These were the years in which the annuals flourished, reaching some two hundred in number in the 1830s, and the name of L.E.L. became one of their strongest selling points. For all the scorn that they provoked, the annuals could afford to pay their authors high fees, and, for example, neither Scott, Southey, Moore, Wordsworth, Coleridge, Landor, Lamb, Hood, Tennyson nor Ruskin were above contributing to them. *Findens' Tableaux of the Affections* paid £5 for a poem (see *MRM*: I, 39 note), while it was rumoured that *The Keepsake* paid Scott 400 guineas for a short story (Crosland, 1893: 95). Evidently, the financial lure was strong, even to the most high-minded. Coleridge admitted that the £50 he was offered to contribute two short poems to *The Keepsake* for 1828 was 'more than all, *I* ever made by all my Publications' (1956–71: VI, 752). On the whole, women were less anxious than men about the taint to their reputations, perhaps because the annuals offered a context for publication which, being largely female, on the one hand presupposed a kind of literary modesty but, on the other, offered a discreetly lucrative living. Both Barrett Browning and Christina Rossetti contributed to them, while Miss Mitford, Mary Shelley, Hemans and L.E.L., for instance, depended for their very livelihoods on the financial rewards they offered. Critics in the major journals often forgot this economic motive. Thackeray, reviewing the annuals for *Fraser's Magazine* in 1837, rebuked L.E.L. for associating with them, on the grounds that: 'An inferior talent . . . must sell itself to live – a *genius* has higher duties; and Miss Landon degrades hers' (16(1837), 763). Geniuses, it seems, especially female ones, are assumed to have husbands, fathers or brothers to free them for 'higher duties' than those of keeping alive. In fact, it was often the other way around. Hemans supported five sons, Miss Mitford a father, Mary Shelley a son, L.E.L. a brother and Barrett Browning, for many years, a husband. Not all geniuses were free to fulfil the 'higher duties' of art.

Meanwhile, the 'picturesque' emphasis of the annuals, which were often named after their engravers – Heath, Fisher and Findens, for instance – dictated the kind of writing, mainly narrative and descriptive, which was expected of their contributors. Very often, the editor chose a picture, which might be a reproduction of an old master, or a contemporary work by Thomas Lawrence, Turner or John Martin, for instance, and commissioned poems on its theme. Such required writing seems to have been particularly attractive to women, who perhaps felt the poverty of their actual lives as subject matter for romance. The engravings themselves probably comprised the annuals' most popular feature, while the accompanying literature was no more than a colourful illustration of a theme. Mrs Gaskell's report of a paper found at Haworth Parsonage containing 'minute studies of, and criticisms upon, the engravings in "Friendship's Offering for 1829"' (1975: 118) points to an enthusiasm for the visual effects of the annuals which was not confined to the young Brontës.

But although this picturesque mode encouraged the writing of minutely specific melodramas of love, despair and death, the reality of writing for the annuals was far from dilettantish. Very often it required hard-headed composition to strict deadlines and, in the case of editors, both a huge correspondence with no secretarial help and an obligation to make up for any shortfall with their own works. When, in 1833, L.E.L. edited the first *Book of Beauty*, she wrote all the stories and poems herself, and Lady Blessington, who took it over in the following year (in a vain attempt to stem the tide of bankruptcy threatening her), included at least seven works of her own (Sadleir, 1933: 218). L.E.L. also wrote most of the letterpress for Fisher's *Drawing Room Scrap-Book* between 1832 and 1839. As Joanna Burch has pointed out, this was regarded as one of the most lively of the annuals, and L.E.L.'s own racy comments and annotations make it distinctly less sentimental than others (1991: 186). In one of them, written to illustrate an engraving of a wedding ceremony, for instance, she tartly offers the following moral:

It is a mistake to be born – another to live – and a third to die. However, there is one other mistake, more absurd than all the three – and that is marrying – and which is made worse by the fact, that the other three we cannot very well help, but the last we can.

She continues in this vein: 'Every year, one sees a young woman in a white gown, and a young man in a blue coat, adventuring on what is called "the happiest day of one's life;" so called, perhaps, as they are never very particularly happy afterwards.' Far from reproducing the soft meanings of the picture, L.E.L. ends with satirical contempt: 'Love has two terminations; it concludes either in profound indifference, or in intense hate' (*Drawing Room Scrap-Book*, 1833, 35). Her prose writings, by contrast to the high-souled misery of much of her poetry, betray a crisp and worldly scepticism.

In 1838, Miss Mitford assumed the editorship of *Findens' Tableaux*, and proceeded to solicit poems from her friends and contemporaries. Her letter to Barrett Browning offers an insight into both the tone of pretty

sentiment and the prompt professionalism usually expected of contributors. 'I want you to write me a poem in illustration of a very charming
group of Hindoo girls floating their lamps upon the Ganges', she
explained, and added, 'I want a poem in stanzas. It must be large enough
for two large pages and . . . I must entreat it within a fortnight or three
weeks if possible' (in *MRM*: I, 37 note). In just over two weeks, Barrett
Browning produced the twenty-three stanzas of 'A Romance of the
Ganges'. For this she refused to accept any fee, 'for friendship's sake'
(*MRM*: I, 38), thus tactfully turning over to Miss Mitford, who was sole
provider for an invalid father, the fee which she herself, as a maintained
invalid in her father's house at this time, did not need. This touching
exchange behind the scenes points to the hard-pressed reality behind
what Thackeray could afford to ridicule as L.E.L.'s and Mitford's
'namby-pamby verses about silly, half-decent pictures' (*Fraser's Magazine*,
16(1837), 758). Throughout her life, Barrett Browning submitted poems
to annuals and magazines, sometimes against the wishes of father,
brothers and husband. 'Don't say the absolute truth – that Robert
doesn't like my writing for magazines' (*Sister*: 98), she whispered to her
sister in 1848. None the less, although she continued to support such
publications, she also knew that, to develop as a poet, she must move on
from the 'rapid' (*AL*: V, 85), improvising fluency of her ballads on
charming 'Hindoo girls' to a more laboured, thought-laden poetry (86),
for which the rewards were less obvious.

By contrast, it was L.E.L.'s fate as a poet to depend for her very
survival on the financial benefits of the popular press. Thus, while it is
tempting to yoke her with Hemans in a bracket of 'silly poets', there is
one crucial fact about their lives which gives pause for thought: unlike
Barrett Browning, and indeed all the other major poets in this book, they
alone were forced to write for a living. Neither of them possessed the
leisure in which to develop their gifts, and both suffered from the slur of
unrespectability which was readily put upon 'unprotected' women.
Barrett Browning may well be remembering the life of L.E.L. in her
portrait of Aurora Leigh, who starts her poetic career in an artistic garret
in London:

> 'And, being but poor, I was constrained, for life,
> To work with one hand for the booksellers
> While working with the other for myself
> And art . . .'
>
> (*AL*: III, 302–5)

However, the real story of L.E.L.'s life suggests that this ideal of independence and well-weighed balance between 'the booksellers' and 'art' was not so easily achieved. Though in constant demand and able to write at an improvisatorial high speed – ' "In prose I often stop and hesitate for a word; in poetry never" ' (in Hall: 268), she admitted – she was rarely free from financial cares or from the petty social intrigues of the literary salons on which she depended for company and amusement. The opportunity of writing ' "for myself / And art" ' never came to L.E.L.

During the 1820s and 30s Letitia was on friendly terms with such openly free-living women as Lady Caroline Lamb and Lady Blessington. Lady Lamb, the one-time lover of Byron, was separated from her husband, and was involved in a series of romantic entanglements with younger men and women, including Bulwer Lytton's future wife, Rosina Wheeler. Lady Blessington, having been married twice, was living during the 1830s at Gore House with the Count D'Orsay, the husband of her stepdaughter. In spite of having no title and little beauty (her snub nose being regarded as a singular defect), L.E.L. made her way in these aristocratic circles with few resources except her poetic reputation and her vivacious personality. The strain of being a drawing-room attraction by night and a hack journalist and poet by day soon told on her nerves. Rosina Wheeler, with whom she formed a passionate friendship for a time and whose beauty she praised in *The Golden Violet* (*PW*: 170), describes how Letitia once ' "insisted on my going to a ball with her" ' (in Sadleir, 1931: 85), though both had influenza. Mary Howitt, the Quaker poet, once described L.E.L., disapprovingly, as 'a most thoughtless girl in company, doing strangely extravagant things; for instance, making a wreath of flowers, then rushing with it into a grave and numerous party, and placing it on her patron's head' (1889: I, 187). Such Corinne-like antics have an insecurity about them which, retrospectively, seems comical.

However, more intimate friends were aware of the real cost of this high-pitched lifestyle. Mrs Hall affirms that Letitia lived ' "a double existence" ', wildly gay in public and sick with anxiety in private, adding that ' "the melancholy was real, the mirth assumed" ' (1871: 270). H. F. Chorley of the *Athenaeum*, who had no reason to like the woman who wrote for the rival journals and whose 'miserably low standard of . . . literary morality' (1873: I, 249) he deplored, none the less also found reason to excuse her. He thought she presented a front of '*bravado* in her intercourse with the public' (I, 250), which concealed a nature that was essentially 'good and real' (I, 253). He describes how, on one visit, he was kept at bay by a stream of inconsequent chatter until, making known the object of his visit, which was to help her brother to a church living, the talk suddenly gave way to 'a flood of hysterical tears' (I, 253). Certainly this suggests a woman living on the edge of her nerves. Out of her family and out of her class, L.E.L. emerges as a sad figure behind the posturing and flirtatious facade she adopted. As Mrs Crosland remembered, she often 'suffered from terrible headaches, but wrote verses, to keep her engagements with publishers, with wet bandages across her forehead!' (1893: 104) – a picture of unglamorous, sweated creativity which is very different from the well-dressed, effortless effusions of her Corinne-like heroines.

During the 1820s and 30s, the names of three men, William Jerdan, William Maginn and Bulwer Lytton, became scandalously associated with L.E.L.'s. Jerdan, who had adopted her as his cherished protégée, was in the habit of visiting her alone in her room at Miss Lance's, and this gave rise to gossip. Given Letitia's circumstances, however, she had little choice as to where to conduct her professional business, and Jerdan was an important publisher as well as, in some sense, a friend of the family. Whatever the truth, the circumstances of Letitia's life did not help matters. The rumours about Maginn were harder to refute. He was a rascally Irish journalist, a drinker and bon viveur, with a streak of malice in him. According to fairly reliable evidence, Mrs Maginn found two letters from L.E.L. in her husband's pocket, '"filled with the most puerile and nauseating terms of endearment"' (in Enfield, 1928: 107). Letitia herself insisted, in a letter to Lady Blessington, that she was never Maginn's mistress and that, although he had made advances, she had rejected him (Sadleir, 1931: 250). It seems most likely that she was really the victim both of a certain 'puerile' naïvety in her own nature and of a vindictive class morality of double standards in those around her. Moreover, her inclination to say 'things for "effect" – things in which she did not believe' (Hall, 1871: 264) may itself have been a source of rich misinterpretation in the treacherous, intrigue-ridden limelight in which she lived. Thirdly, L.E.L.'s name became linked with that of Bulwer Lytton. She was certainly in the habit of visiting Bulwer and Rosina at home, and was observed to be somewhat flirtatious in her manner. It was unfortunate, then, that in 1831 the *New Monthly Magazine* carried, first a glowing review of Lytton's novels by L.E.L. and then a correspondingly good review of L.E.L. by Lytton. A skit published in *The Age* enjoyed the implications of this literary complimenting:

> 'N.   Child of love and Muse of Passion
> Pretty Letty – that is you.
> L.E.L.   Ned, in all *you* lead the fashion
> Neddy mine, indeed you do.'
> (in Sadleir, 1931: 415)

In all probability there is no more substance to the story of their attachment than this satirical scandalmongering of warring journals, and the venomous comments made more than twenty years later by an embittered, separated Rosina.

In the end, however, L.E.L. paid dearly for these indiscretions. In the early 1830s, her friends and acquaintances started to receive anonymous letters, accusing her of being the mistress of a married man. Perhaps if this had happened ten years earlier, or if she herself had been less socially and sexually vulnerable, it might have passed without harm. Evidently, the behaviour permitted to a Lady Lamb or a Lady Blessington was not permitted to an unprotected, unmarried woman, without economic or social means. Letitia herself clearly recognised this difference:

> 'my very soul writhes under the powerlessness of its anger. It is only because I am poor, unprotected, and dependant [*sic*] on popularity, that I am a mark for all the gratuitous insolence and malice of idleness and ill-nature. And I cannot but feel deeply that had I been possessed of rank and opulence, either these remarks had never been made, or if they had, how trivial would their consequence have been to me.' (in Blanchard, 1841: I, 54)

However, the consequence of all the gossip was not 'trivial'. In 1834, she was forced to break off her engagement to John Forster, the future biographer of Dickens. Hearing of the rumours, Forster demanded an explanation, and she, though denying the facts, felt bound to free him. '"The more I think, the more I feel I ought not – I cannot – allow you to unite yourself with one accused of – I cannot write it. The mere suspicion is dreadful as death"' (in Enfield, 1928: 108), she wrote to him. Whether those anonymous letters were penned by an already jealous Rosina (Ashton, 1951: 320), or, as seems more likely, by a mischief-making Maginn (Sadleir, 1931: 425), their effect was to ruin L.E.L.'s reputation. She was now 32, exhausted and often sick with work, and her fame as a poet was on the decline. Her years of success had left her with neither the experience of her own heroines' high romances nor with the domestic security she now craved.

It is not surprising, then, that, when in 1837 she met Captain George McLean, Governor of Cape Coast Castle in West Africa, she was eager for marriage, and no doubt also eager to leave London, the scene of so many miseries. The thought of Africa may also have revived memories of her father's romantic tales and of the brief paternal security he represented. Whether or not it is true, as Enfield rather melodramatically claims, that Captain McLean tried to free himself from a rash proposal only to find Letitia clinging all the more dearly to her hope of escape (1928: 139), in June 1838 the couple were finally married. The Halls recalled 'the chill' at the wedding party when, in returning thanks, Captain McLean only announced curtly: ' "If Mrs. McLean has as many friends as Mr. Hall says she has, I only wonder they allow her to leave them" ' (1871: 278). The couple set sail at the beginning of July and arrived at the notorious, slave-trade post of Cape Castle in mid-August. The dreary solitude of the place – ' "I look upon the vast sea, whose dash against the rock never ceases" ' (in Blanchard, 1841: II, 156) – and the surly character of her husband, must have seemed cruelly different from L.E.L.'s childhood dreams of travel and romance.

During the next two months, she continued work on a series of essays on the female characters in Scott and wrote some apparently quite cheerful letters home. One of them, however, hints at an old frustration. ' "There are eleven or twelve chambers here, empty, I am told, yet Mr. McLean refuses to let me have one of them for my use" ', she complained, and added, ominously: ' "He expects me to cook, wash, and iron; in short, to do the work of a servant. He says he will never cease correcting me until he has broken my spirit" ' (in Hall, 1871: 278). Admittedly, the Halls were more antagonistic to Captain McLean than other friends. Nevertheless, there is a note of disillusioned weariness here which can also be heard in the essays on Scott. For instance, L.E.L. suggestively generalises in one place: ' "I believe that more women are disappointed in marriage than men; a woman gives the whole of her heart – the man only gives the remains of his, and very often there is only a little left" ' (in Blanchard, 1841: II, 151). She then repeats the much quoted cry of Madame de Staël: ' "by whom have we been beloved, even as we have loved!" ' (II, 153). But unlike Hemans, who turns this cry into the creed of faithful womanliness, L.E.L. characteristically probes its politics: ' "an affection too utterly self-sacrificing always meets with an evil return" ' (II, 190), she warns. The reality of life at Cape Castle, with its prisoners in the dungeons, its recollections of some of the worst atrocities of the slave trade, its ' "absolute" ' (I, 198) solitude and its grim Governor, must have been, indeed, a harsh awakening for the sentimental dreamer. Although she had escaped from the ' "envy, malice, and all uncharitableness" ' of the London salons, it was only to find that Africa was unromantic, marriage lonely and love perhaps only a fiction of her imagination. Yet even before marriage, L.E.L.'s work, particularly the verse epigraphs of her satirical society novel *Ethel Churchill* (1837), seem to express a darker realism and scepticism than is found in her earlier poetry, as well as to foreshadow, rather ominously, the course of her own life:

The altar, 'tis of death! for there are laid
The sacrifice of all youth's sweetest hopes.
It is a dreadful thing for woman's lip
To swear the heart away; yet know that heart
Annuls the vow while speaking, and shrinks back
From the dark future that it dares not face.
The service read above the open grave
Is far less terrible than that which seals
The vow that binds the victim, not the will:
For in the grave is rest.

(*PW*: 434–5)

On 15 October, two months after landing, L.E.L. was found dead on the floor of her bedroom, a bottle of prussic acid in her hand. She was 36 years old. The news of her death took several months to reach London, but when it did, an incident was recalled which immediately set tongues wagging again. Before her marriage, Letitia's brother, the Revd Whittington Landon, had looked into certain rumours that Captain McLean was already married to a native woman. He was reassured that, although McLean had had a native mistress, he had never married her. This was sufficient for all concerned, and the customary double standards for men and women passed unquestioned. Certainly, Letitia knew of this previous liaison. She had written to her brother on 27 September, two weeks before her death and presumably in answer to his queries: ' "I can scarcely make even you understand how perfectly ludicrous the idea of jealousy of a native woman really is. Sentiment, affection, are never thought of – it is a temporary bargain – I must add that it seems to me quite monstrous * * *" ' (in Blanchard, 1841: I, 206). There the letter breaks off, censored either by its receiver or by L.E.L.'s biographer. However, Blanchard cannot let the matter rest, and the coy mysteriousness of his language only encourages the fascinated negrophobia of his readers. He writes that 'to those whose minds reverted to the hot blood and the fierce habits of the natives of Western Africa, the dreadful suspicion was presented, that . . . the European lady of the colony, had been sacrificed to a horrible spirit of female vengeance' (I, 217). He then concocts a story about L.E.L. dying from an abscess of the ear, for which she was taking her prescribed medicine, to divert suspicion from the possibility of suicide. Barrett Browning was rightly offended by the way 'Mr. Blanchard presses in his words where we want hers, & his commentaries & explanations where we want none at all' (*MRM*: I, 251). Meanwhile, however, the damage had been done, and L.E.L. continued to be, after her death as in life, the subject of largely salacious rumour and speculation. Two slight and fanciful biographies in the twentieth century, Enfield's (1928) and Ashton's (1951), continued this habit of cheap speculation long after L.E.L. had ceased to be read as a poet.

Thus her life, whatever the true facts, disturbingly and quite shockingly reinforced the conclusions of the Sappho–Corinne myth: ' "the fruits of a successful literary career for a woman" ' are, ultimately, death. Whether or not Letitia killed herself, the shady and much publicised nature of her end only intensified the punishing moral which lies at the core of the myth. Woman's creative success leads to moral and domestic disaster. In a sense L.E.L. lived the story which Hemans only mythologised, and thus, unfortunately, left to later generations an altogether shabbier example of the woman poet as suicidal victim of men's treachery. Sappho may be a tragic heroine in verse; in life, she is simply disreputable. The problem of *being* a woman poet, rather than of just writing about her, is thus handed down, riddled with cautions and contradictions, to the poets of the future. Hemans, as a woman, though not always as a poet, played safe and stayed at home; L.E.L. as both woman and poet, openly embraced the public stage of her professional success, and died. The comparison would not have been missed by their successors.

Yet as a poet, L.E.L. represents an advance on Hemans. She is less pious, less bound in a 'satin riband' of right thinking, less dogmatically sweet. In many of her later works, she seems to be explicitly rejecting her earlier tricks of emotionalism for a new sense of reality as movingly small-scale and unheroic:

> Life's smallest miseries are, perhaps, its worst:
> Great sufferings have great strength: there is a pride
> In the bold energy that braves the worst,
> And bears proud in the bearing; but the heart
> Consumes with those small sorrows, and small shames,
> Which crave, yet cannot ask for sympathy.
> They blush that they exist, and yet how keen
> The pang that they inflict!
>
> (*PW*: 430)

Barrett Browning was right to prefer L.E.L.'s poetry to Hemans': 'I surmise that it was more elastic, more various, of a stronger web', she ventured. 'She might indeed have achieved a greatness which her fondest admirers can scarcely consider achieved now' (*MRM*: I, 235), she declared, on hearing of her death. L.E.L. was not an original poet, but she was, in the end, one who repudiated the high style of exotic melancholia which was the key to her easy, short-lived success, and who eventually faced her own artistic failings with an honesty which is unsoftened by religious or romantic sentiment.

IMPROVISING WOMAN

Woman must write herself: must write about women and
bring women to writing . . . By writing her self, woman will
return to the body which has been more than confiscated from
her, which has been turned into the uncanny stranger on
display . . . (Cixous, in Marks and de Courtivron, 1980:
245)

The cult of sensibility, which in many ways lies behind the rise of
women's poetry at the beginning of the nineteenth century, offers a
highly duplicitous model of creative power. On the one hand,
traditionally a mode of 'display', a performance of extreme emotions on
the stage of the body, sensibility would seem to express above all the
inner self-alienations of female subjectivity: woman is, to herself, a
'stranger', though transparently obvious to others. Yet, on the other
hand, the model of sensibility offers women, both in the 1820s and in the
1980s, a means of recovering a lost 'self', and of returning 'to the body'
as an active subject rather than a passive object. Both Hemans and
L.E.L. promote an aesthetics of physical fluency which, like that of
Cixous, for instance, expresses the special gift of the newly self-assertive,
generic subject, woman. They, too, seek to reclaim woman's poetic
selfhood as a physical identity translated as a kind of writing. 'A
feminine textual body', claims Cixous, 'is recognised by the fact that it is
always endless, without ending: there's no closure, it doesn't stop' (1981:
53). A similar fluency and endlessness is promoted by the popular
nineteenth-century ideal of female improvisation. It, too, asserts an easy
equivalence of body and text, as the one provides a visible motive for the
other. Thus, for instance, Corinne's own singing very often seemed to
issue from a physical spasm: 'she was oppressed by so violent a tremor,
that her voice trembled' (de Staël, 1833: 25). In Hemans, the idea of
such inspiration remained prominent, but always within the morally
restrictive control of her metre and rhyme. It is L.E.L. who finally takes
this whole movement of rehabilitated sensibility to its extreme, in poems
whose language *sounds* improvised, and whose very structureless length
mimes the notion of woman's unstoppable flow of creativity:

> My power was but a woman's power;
> Yet, in that great and glorious dower
> Which Genius gives, I had my part:
> I poured my full and burning heart
> In song . . .
>
> (*PW*: 1–2)

The Improvisatrice (1824) is unmistakably modelled on *Corinne*. In it,

58

L.E.L. strings together a series of little tableaux about long-suffering maidens with Byronic names like Leila, Ida, Zaïde and Cydippe, who experience cruel if indistinguishable betrayals in love. The whole is 'improvised' by an Italian woman poet (who unfortunately betrays her origins by locating St Mark's in Florence), who herself suffers the same fate as her heroines, being rejected, at the end, by the hero, Lorenzo. L.E.L., who translated the songs of Corinne for the most popular English edition of 1833, was familiar with the postures of self-appreciation which that novel had long made popular. Like Corinne, the Improvisatrice is both obsessed with and apologetic about her 'woman's power'. The whole poem is, in effect, an extended advertisement for female genius which, through the first-person narration, is kept constantly before the eyes as well as ears of the reader. Like de Staël, too, L.E.L. enjoys a certain costume-gallery ostentation. Corinne was described as standing at the Capitol as if in a conscious–unconscious charade: 'Attired like Domenichino's Sybil, an Indian shawl was twined among her lustrous black curls, a blue drapery fell over her robe of virgin white, and her whole costume was picturesque, without sufficiently varying from modern usage to appear tainted by affectation' (1833: 20). Such roundabout special pleading reveals all the cracks in its dubious ideology. But it was not only L.E.L. who followed the fashion to be poetic, and rushed into drawing-rooms with a wreath. An article in *Every Woman's Encyclopaedia* recalls how the novel influenced the dress fashions of the time and 'excited the furore for flimsy attire, a rapt expression of countenance, and for playing on the harp!' (2(1911), 1,003). Corinne, who is both Sybil and Virgin Mary, both in costume yet unaffected, is a character split by a duplicity which lies deep in the very idea of the woman poet.

The Improvisatrice similarly is a creature of contradiction. She is both the passionate subject who sings and the visible object that is sung about; she is both subject author and studied *objet d'art*. Her purpose thus constantly rounds on herself, as singing becomes an endless, self-appraising celebration of the wondrous fact that she is a poet: 'I poured my full and burning heart / In song'. Thus the fluid heart becomes a fluent poem, in a short-circuit of epithets which never settles into one thing or the other, into body or text, desire or art, womanly love or womanly power. Where Hemans tends to close off the options with a domestic moral at the end, L.E.L. works the sheer fluidity of meaning (or near meaninglessness) for all it is worth. Language conveys no 'thought-content', but is a 'convulsive' (Clément, 1980: 134) sign of pure feeling which, like a lava-flow of the heart (that recurrent image in Victorian women's poetry), never cools into hard thought. L.E.L.'s songs go on and on, at the edge of the precipice which constitutes the only impending dramatic event through pages of burning verse: that is, death.

Characteristically, the first song that the Improvisatrice sings is a last song by Sappho. This crucial signature is underlined by an illustration by Bell Scott in the edition of 1873, which shows the poet gliding gracefully off her rock, her lyre slipping from her hands, her dress twisting into a shroud round her feet. The hystericised body of the woman poet is thus graphically highlighted in isolation from any social purpose, domestic duty or even human relationship, at the moment when its much-sung fluidity is about to be literally confirmed. Meanwhile, 'Sappho's Song' tells the old story:

> Farewell, my lute! – and would that I
>   Had never waked thy burning chords!
> Poison has been upon thy sigh,
>   And fever has breathed in thy words.
>
> Yet wherefore, wherefore should I blame
>   Thy power, thy spell, my gentlest lute?
> I should have been the wretch I am,
>   Had every chord of thine been mute.
>
> It was my evil star above,
>   Not my sweet lute, that wrought me wrong;
> It was not song that taught me love,
>   But it was love that taught me song.
>
> If song be passed, and hope undone,
>   And pulse, and head, and heart, are flame;
> It is thy work, thou faithless one!
>   But, no! – I will not name thy name . . .
>
> (PW: 4)

These reproachful heavy hints to the 'faithless one' insist on the traditional legend of Phaon. The eye of a hidden male onlooker thus once again justifies and objectifies the emotional abandon of the woman's body, as she displays her misery for all, but especially 'one', to see. However, although the 22-year-old L.E.L. is falling into the familiar patterns of the Sappho–Corinne myth, she also, interestingly, refuses to moralise the relationship between fame and faithlessness. Sappho would have been the same 'wretch' of love if she had never played her lute. The 'Poison' lies in being a woman, not a poet. This small advance on Hemans' anxious denigrations of poetic fame points to L.E.L.'s much more determined and unapologetic sense of vocation. Poetry is the single motive and motif of most of her verse.

At the end of *The Improvisatrice*, the singer dies, unrequited, leaving a repentant Lorenzo brooding over a picture of his lost love:

She leant upon a harp; – one hand
   Wandered, like snow, amid the chords;
The lips were opening with such life,
   You almost heard the silvery words.
She looked a form of light and life,
   All soul, all passion, and all fire;
A priestess of Apollo's, when
   The morning beams fall on her lyre;
A Sappho, or ere love had turned
   The heart to stone where once it burned.
                        (*PW*: 33)

Although this should be a figure of rebuke, in fact L.E.L. uses it as a pretext to return to her favourite, elaborate topography of passion. The picture is not a memorial at all, but an excuse to paint the woman poet, yet again, in all her parts. If the rhymes and images seem slap-happy – with the exception of that 'hand . . . like snow' which is curiously arresting – none the less the general effect is of emotional power building up to a liquefying climax: 'All soul, all passion, and all fire'. This hardly conveys the message either that the Improvisatrice is dead, or that she would have made a good wife. Intended as a reproach, the picture in fact becomes another self-celebration. Moreover, it is suggested, Lorenzo's regret is that he has lost, not his wife, but his inspired sybil or Sappho; he misses her harp and 'silvery words'. The real rebuke which the picture represents at the end is that the man did not listen to the woman's poems.

It is interesting that, although L.E.L. insists on art as an overflow of the female body, she also frequently freezes the woman into a picture, a statue, an art work. No doubt the picturesque emphasis of the annuals contributed to this attitude. None the less, the end of *The Improvisatrice* also suggests two things. On the one hand, the woman has become her own work, her own Grecian Urn, thus underlining the message that femininity itself is the main subject matter of these poems. On the other hand, such frozen postures are also a way of turning the woman into a form of sexual or artistic property for the man. Lorenzo can keep his poet for ever in a picture; in life, she was likely to flow constantly out of his grasp. It is possible to read the end of *The Improvisatrice*, not as an emotional reproach or a self-pitying suicidalism on the part of the woman, but as a comment on the very unsocialised extremism of this female aesthetic. In order for the woman to be loved, owned and kept by a man, she must forgo all her fiery, burning, flowing energy, which cannot be held down, and become a cold, still effigy of herself – in other words, be dead. The picture woman, who has no subjectivity but is entirely an object, best suits the domestic requirements of the man. Lorenzo, at the end, is evidently in love with his picture in a way he was never in love with the woman herself.

Thus L.E.L., for all her formal carelessness, touches on an intriguing complexity in her own sentimentalism. Woman's creativity is an overwhelming Romantic energy which cannot be socialised, but which flows across the boundaries of body and writing, heart and song, self and work. However, in order to be loved, woman must be turned into a single, visually bounded object, fixed and unchanging, and thus fit for domestic use. Christina Rossetti, who is in some ways L.E.L.'s natural successor, may well have been remembering the end of *The Improvisatrice* when, in her poem 'Reflection', the frustrated male lover dreams of finally possessing his beloved by having her 'carved in alabaster' (*CP*: III, 266–8, l.53) after she is dead (see pages 156–7). It is as if Rossetti picks up this distinctive motif of the dead stone effigy, which L.E.L. brings to the tradition of sensibility, but exploits, from the woman's rather than the man's point of view, its playful secret meanings. Where L.E.L. generally simplifies those meanings: 'LORENZO! be this kiss a spell! / My first! – my last! FAREWELL! – FAREWELL!' (*PW*: 32) Rossetti leaves them unguessed and elusive, somehow mysteriously at odds with the romantic patterns of the poem.

At its simplest, then, L.E.L.'s early work repeats the sentimentalist creed that art is equivalent to feeling and that woman's art, especially, lies in her facility for tears. In *The Golden Violet* (1826), the troubadour setting is a pretext for a succession of 'endless' poetry readings by male and female minstrels. The poem, which runs to some eighty pages, bears witness to an insatiable appetite among young women readers of the time, if not for poetry, at least for the idea of being a poet. Such an idea is, of course, equivalent to being a woman:

> For what is genius, but deep feeling
> Waken'd by passion to revealing?
> And what is feeling, but to be
> Alive to every misery,
> While the heart too fond, too weak,
> Lies open for the vulture's beak?
>
> (*PW*: 117)

Feeling, here, is a quivering sort of touchiness, 'Alive', not to a range of emotions, but only to one masochistic 'misery'. Being unhappy is the easiest sign of 'genius', while tears are the body's most spontaneous overflow. Elsewhere L.E.L. proclaims, with Hemansesque pride: 'My songs have been the mournful history / Of woman's tenderness and woman's tears' (*PW*: 221). But mournfulness without wit and grievance without energy are fatal ingredients of poetry, even if they seem the natural condition and consequence, in the early nineteenth century, of being a woman. Although L.E.L. reappropriates the model of sensibility for woman's poetic vocation even more fervently and single-mindedly than Hemans, she is also in danger, to use Adrienne Rich's distinction, of 'viewing physicality' as 'a destiny' rather than 'a resource' (1977: 62). As a 'resource', sensibility can become a powerful, gender-specific motive for verbalising – a means of reclaiming desire from the forbidden subject of the body, *as* a subject for poetry: 'I poured my full and burning heart'. As a 'destiny', however, it becomes a predictable and confining physical vulnerability – a means of returning to the body as a trapped object of desire and pain: 'Alive to every misery'. The young L.E.L. veers from one to the other as she turns her own economic neediness into a theory and practice of woman's improvising heart-inspiration, which is alternately strong and weak, concerned with self-expression or merely concerned to make an impression.

It is Barrett Browning who, with her customary acuteness, points to the problem, not only with much of L.E.L.'s verse, but also with the whole tradition of female sensibility as it is revived in the early nineteenth century. 'And besides, is it not true', she asks,

> that the strength of our *feelings*, often rises up out of our *thoughts* – out of our bare intellectuality, – hard & cold thing as it is, of itself? – It seems so to *me*; & that if she had been more intellectual she wd. have been more pathetic. (*MRM*: I, 18–19)

This touches on a paradox which later poets will struggle to assert in the face of that Victorian sentimentalism which constantly requires of women poets a heart-bare sincerity and extempore simplicity. As Barrett Browning points out, the 'intellectual' and the 'pathetic' are not separate but mutually affirming impulses. The idea of spontaneous expression, that 'A song came gushing, like the natural tears' (L.E.L., 'Erinna', *PW*: 216), which the cult of the improviser encouraged, is likely to result in a pathos which is, in fact, unfeeling. George Eliot may well have been remembering L.E.L.'s 'Erinna' in her own poem of the same name, which begins with the usual icon of suffering femininity, but then starts to develop a self-distance which splits the self, sexually and intellectually, from its bodily pain:

> Hark, the passion in her eyes
> Changes to melodic cries
> Lone she pours her lonely pain.
> Song unheard is not in vain:
> The god within us plies
> His shaping power and moulds in speech
> Harmonious a statue of our sorrow,
> Till suffering turn beholding and we borrow,

Gazing on Self apart, the wider reach
Of solemn souls that contemplate . . .
(1989: 187)

The poet Mary Coleridge is still wrestling in the shadow of this tradition when, some ninety years after L.E.L., she argues:

Poetry is, by its very derivation, *making*, not feeling. But the odd thing is, I think, that what is most carefully made often sounds as if it had been felt straight off, whereas what has been felt carelessly sounds as if it were made. (1910: 252)

The struggle against feeling for its own sake is a struggle against a whole, essentially Victorian ethic of womanhood. The need to keep women weeping and not thinking, feeling and not questioning, suffering and not writing, carries a strong social and moral purpose, which ensures that the trembling, ill-used goodness of the female heart remains part of 'the woman's sway' in purifying the new age.

L.E.L. is interesting, however, because the sheer extremity of her model of sensibility constantly turns its ethical use into a merely aesthetic extravagance. The very undramatic pointlessness of her long monologues makes them morally inapplicable, in a way which Hemans' are not. Her heart-gazing serves no useful purpose – it cannot comfort in the sickroom or uplift on the battlefield. As a result, what Stuart Curran has called 'the void at the center of sensibility' (1988: 205) becomes increasingly open and visible in her work. To go on and on feeling, intransitively and self-reflexively, is to be doomed to die in too many words and without end. Certainly, L.E.L.'s poetry catches a quality of addictive obsession with suffering which, in part, is also the key to her power. Her language of bodily sensation becomes a verbal, ventriloquising end in itself – a formality of speech unattached to the contingent realities of women's lives, but technically self-justifying and self-prolonging. However, it is L.E.L.'s own eventual recognition of the 'void' at the core of her sagas of sensibility which marks the beginning of her too short and too late imaginative development.

SCEPTIC TO THE TRUTH

The work which represents something of a turning point in L.E.L.'s career is the semi-autobiographical 'A History of the Lyre', which was published in 1828. Although it concerns yet another improvising woman poet, it makes some small changes to the old motifs. Certainly, its heroine Eulalie is another mellifluous Corinne who, Italian, orphaned

64

and unloved, ends up dead from despair. However, her story is now framed by the words of a detached male observer, who is not the usual implicated betrayer, but simply a passing visitor. The poem thus opens, not with a tumultuous outpouring of Eulalie's misery, but with the cool, puzzled generalisations of this disinterested onlooker:

> 'Tis strange how much is mark'd on memory,
> In which we may have interest, but no part;
> How circumstance will bring together links
> In destinies the most dissimilar.
> This face, whose rudely-pencill'd sketch you hold,
> Recalls to me a host of pleasant thoughts,
> And some more serious.
>
> (PW: 223)

This distancing register, together with a welcome blank verse which frees the ear from the obvious agreement of rhyme, creates an effect of detached curiosity, reticence and uncertainty at the very heart of the poem. Instead of the monotonous high-volume of despair which marks the earlier verse, 'A History of the Lyre' keeps a sense of perspective, both technical and thematic, on its 'mournful history / Of woman's tenderness and woman's tears'. Rejecting the complicitous identification of reader and heroine, L.E.L.'s language, here, for once permits us also to be merely interested and impartial observers, rather than aggrieved co-victims. The verse has become a frame rather than an open mouth to feeling, and as a result something 'hard & cold' – the man's objective register, for instance – distances and questions the excess of sentiment in the heroine.

'A History of the Lyre' also shows L.E.L. turning altogether away from Hemans' association of art and love. Where Properzia Rossi ultimately castigated her betrayer and blamed her artistic failure on loneliness, Eulalie recognises that failure comes from within, and then scrupulously surveys its inner scope:

> 'Speak not of this to me, nor bid me think;
> It is such pain to dwell upon myself;
> And know how different I am from all
> I once dream'd I could be. Fame! stirring fame
> I work no longer miracles for thee.
> I am as one who sought at early dawn
> To climb with fiery speed some lofty hill:
> His feet are strong in eagerness and youth,
> His limbs are braced by the fresh morning air,
> And all seems possible: – this cannot last.
> The way grows steeper, obstacles arise,
> And unkind thwartings from companions near.

> The height is truer measured, having traced
> Part of its heavy length! his sweet hopes droop.
> Like prison'd birds that know their cage has bars,
> The body wearies, and the mind is worn . . .'
> (PW: 226)

This is a landscape of the soul for once free of self-pity, reproach and romance. The demand to be admired and loved has gone, and in its place there is a sense of inner artistic test and achievement. The small hill of fame turns into an unscalable mountain, the idea of the self proves self-differing and disappointing. Instead of externalising inspiration as a free-flow of feeling into song, the passage internalises it, and then finds it full of discrepancies and blocks: this poet is 'different' from her dreams of self – so different in fact as to be represented by the male pronoun – while her art is not a matter of standing naturally to sing, but of climbing wearily without hope of reaching the summit, where the 'way' is full of 'thwartings' and 'obstacles'. This rough landscape of self-knowledge is quite different from the smooth physiologism of the earlier monologues. Here, subjectivity opens up like an unknown place within.

The passage then culminates in an admission of artistic vanity which is repeated in much of L.E.L.'s late poetry:

> 'I am vain, – praise is opium, and the lip
> Cannot resist the fascinating draught,
> Though knowing its excitement is a fraud . . .'
> (PW: 228)

In lines like these she seems to be confronting the real source of her poetic failure: she has courted easy popularity and has been satisified with it; she has wasted her gifts instead of nurturing them. Perhaps L.E.L. was remembering a review of her poems by Roebuck which appeared in the *Westminster* the year before. In this intelligent piece, he roundly castigates her for encouraging those qualities which keep women in the position of 'useful and agreeable slaves' (*Westminster Review*, 7(1827), 66), for glamourising 'war' (63) and for repeating the same dreary narrative of crossed love and fatal death in all her poems (53). Above all, he warns: 'The merely writing correct poetical lines, is the easiest part of the poet's task' (61). Yet, in spite of these hard criticisms, she is addressed as a serious author and 'as an equal' (51), in strong contrast to the infantilising mode of *Blackwoods* which, four years before, began a review of her poems with 'Now it is not because she is a very pretty girl, and a very good girl, that we are going to praise her poems' (*Blackwoods*, 16(1824), 190). The rather searching honesty of 'A

History of the Lyre' suggests that L.E.L. was indeed taking criticism, rather than praise, to heart. Eulalie regrets having wasted her gifts in attention-seeking displays. Meanwhile, she views her own subjectivity as a little-known landscape, a teasing perspective of heights and depths, dreams and disappointments, instead of as a single, spotlighted object, petulantly rehearsing its own death. It is not only the voice of the monologue which is divided, between woman and onlooker, female and male, but the self is divided as well. As a result, the old improvising monologue gives way to a more dramatic form, in which the self is not unitary and perpetually self-justifying, but unsure, unlike its self, possibly untrue to itself. The gap is not ironised, but it is, for once, just visible.

'A History of the Lyre' also subtly modifies the mythical story of the culpable male betrayer. In her *Life of Rosina*, Louisa Devey quotes a letter from about 1825, in which L.E.L. makes the sudden declaration: '"Experience, as far as mine goes, has read me a lesson of so much disgust, that I really do sometimes lament I have no means of becoming desperately wicked, in order to ensure every advantage of life"' (1887: 141). Something of this sense of disadvantage and lack, rather than of hurt and victimisation, is expressed in the poem:

> 'I have sung passionate songs of beating hearts;
> Perhaps it had been better they had drawn
> Their inspiration from an inward source.
> Had I known even an unhappy love,
> It would have flung an interest round life
> Mine never knew. This is an empty wish;
> Our feelings are not fires to light at will
> Our nature's fine and subtle mysteries;
> We may control them, but may not create,
> And Love less than its fellows. I have fed
> Perhaps too much upon the lotos fruits
> Imagination yields, – fruits which unfit
> The palate for the more substantial food
> Of our own land – reality.'
>
> *(PW: 229)*

In passages like these a new L.E.L. seems to be emerging. The poet of 'Love' is admitting that she has never felt it. Her life has lacked that 'interest' which none the less has been the sole pedantic topic of her poetry. In one of her essays on Scott, L.E.L. hints at the larger social context of this disadvantage. She writes: '"Take the life of girls in general . . . they know nothing of real difficulties, or of real cares; and there is an old saying, that a woman's education begins after she is married"' (in Blanchard, 1841: II, 111). Taken alongside Rosina

Wheeler's passing comment that L.E.L. ' "never was in love in her life" '
(in Sadleir, 1931: 84) and her own longing to be ' "desperately wicked" '
rather than inexperienced in life, the theme of absent rather than
unrequited love in 'A History of the Lyre' is a poignant comment on the
reputation L.E.L. earned in real life. In this later work, she is realising
the advantage of facing the desolation of reality, which, for the woman,
is very often the desolation of a reality she may have simply missed:
' "Had I known even an unhappy love, / It would have flung an interest
round life / Mine never knew." ' The hollowness at the heart of so much
of L.E.L.'s effusive early work is eventually confronted and expressed,
and the poetry, as a result, begins to sound, paradoxically, less hollow,
less imitative and less skiddingly emotional. 'A History of the Lyre',
although still patterned on the Sappho–Corinne myth and still ending
with the heroine becoming her own funeral statue, has none the less also
shed much of the external drapery of that myth: the culpable betrayer,
the display, the singing. Instead, it confronts the poverty of what
remains. It is that poverty, much more than all the pretended wealth of
feeling in the tradition of sensibility, which gives L.E.L. a subject worth
writing about and a loss worth lamenting.

Gradually, her poetry achieves a new realism and self-distrust, which
are expressed as a scepticism precisely about feeling. In one place,
Eulalie considers the career of a young poet who, though imagined as
male, is evidently herself. Having been courted and flattered, ' "What
marvel if he somewhat overrate / His talents and his state?" ' (PW: 228),
she asks, and then explains how, in his new self-understanding: ' "He has
turn'd sceptic to the truth which made / His feelings poetry" ' (229). To
be sceptical of feelings is a new truth which L.E.L. learns towards the
end of her poetic career. In these two lines she seems to acknowledge, by
implication, that ' "feelings" ' are not necessarily a poetic ' "truth" ' at all,
though to lose faith in them is to lose almost the whole basis of her art.
Such a truth was, indeed, for much of the century, the supposed 'true
religion' of women's poetry. L.E.L.'s loss of faith in it is the beginning
of her belated development as a poet, though the void which opens up in
the place of feeling is never filled by any other commitments.

The word ' "sceptic" ', though used cautiously in this context, also
hints at an aspect of L.E.L.'s work and imagination which signals her
main difference from Hemans, and which may have subtly affected her
reputation, especially after her death. In the same year as Blanchard's
biography there appeared a book written by Sarah Sheppard, a friend of
Letitia, called *Characteristics of the Genius and Writings of L.E.L.* (1841).
Sheppard makes one point, discreetly near the end, which offers a crucial
insight into the poet's work. It depicts, she suggests, 'human nature in
its unchanged state, destitute of the light of Christianity' (1841: 164),

adding that it 'represents life unsanctified by religion' (165). This corroborates a comment made by Amelia Opie to Miss Mitford, that L.E.L. ' "had strong feelings, not under the only safe control – that of religious principle" ' (in L'Estrange, 1882: II, 51). Whatever the biographical evidence, it is certainly true that, compared with Hemans, L.E.L.'s poetry is strikingly free of religious conclusions. Death or suicide are her usual outcomes; the suffering faith of 'therefore pray!' is not. In 'A Girl at Her Devotions', for instance, L.E.L. quietly questions the power of religious consolation: 'She was just risen from her bended knee, / But yet peace seem'd not with her piety'. Like many of her later heroines, this one cherishes some dark secret in the 'heart's undream'd, unsought recess' which is not altogether sweet and holy. 'Too dazzling to be scann'd, the haughty brow / Seems to hide something it would not avow' (PW: 264). If ' "secretiveness" ' was the 'bane' of L.E.L.'s own personality, as Mrs Hall affirmed (1871: 263), it is also a dimension of experience – troubling, anarchic and often destructive – which marks out the heroines of the later poems. It is as if L.E.L. eventually rebels against the idea that femininity is a transparently good, hurt, simple object of reproach to men and appeal to heaven, and instead shows it as having depths of knowledge lying out of the eye's easy reach. Unlike Hemans, she dares to write about women who are wicked, secretive or self-deceived.

In *The Venetian Bracelet* (1829), for instance, written a year after 'A History of the Lyre', the betrayed Amenaïde is driven to poison her rival in love. Instead of buying a ruby cross from a passing pedlar, she buys a poisonous bracelet, kills her rival with it and subsequently kills herself, 'The wild eye flashing with unholy light' (PW: 211). In this poem, suicide is a gesture not of reproach and self-pity, but of real moral, if somewhat Byronic despair. This heroine does not only feel, but acts, thinks and sins. The hero, who catches two dying women in his arms, is, by comparison, relatively redundant. The sense of evil, the fear that 'Left to ourselves, all crime is possible' (PW: 450), is more than just a sensational Gothicism in these later works. It points, instead, to hidden forces in human nature, even in female nature – forces which, 'unsanctifed by religion', might sweep the soul out of its picture-book passivity into real chaos and crime.

It is the idea of the 'secret' which, appearing only in L.E.L.'s later poetry, seems to sum up this new, moral and emotional scepticism:

> Life has dark secrets; and the hearts are few
> That treasure not some sorrow from the world –
> A sorrow silent, gloomy, and unknown,
> Yet colouring the future from the past.

We see the eye subdued, the practised smile,
The word well weighed before it pass the lip,
And know not of the misery within:
Yet there it works incessantly, and fears
The time to come; for time is terrible,
Avenging, and betraying.

(PW: 423)

Entitled 'Secrets', this fragment hints at an almost classical tragic perspective, of 'time' as an unredeeming and unforgiving force of destiny. These 'secrets' will not be expiated by any Christian scheme of things, but only by the inner workings of time, 'Avenging, and betraying.' The 'secrets' themselves are ambiguously either forms of 'sorrow' or forms of 'well weighed' deception. Victimisation is thus complicated by crime and guilt. When L.E.L. starts to look inwards, she finds secrets which, like Rossetti's, make nonsense of moral and spiritual values. It is as if, at last, she is probing the negative side of her earlier, over-exposed picturesqueness. Some forbidden knowledge and doubt – the very antithesis of the creed of feeling – has crept into her verse, and given it a certain sharp-edged realism, expressed, significantly, without the reassuring bands of rhyme. The register sounds halting and pedestrian, while the abbreviated form of the fragment, which breaks off in the last line, audibly expresses a disenchantment with the prolonged, effortless *cantabile* of her earlier heroines.

Altogether, a new sense of the trivial, small-scale dimensions of experience informs these late fragments:

Life is made up of vanities – so small,
So mean, the common history of the day, –
That mockery seems the sole philosophy.
Then some stern truth starts up – cold, sudden, strange;
And we are taught what life is by despair: –
The toys, the trifles, and the petty cares,
Melt into nothingness – we know their worth;
The heart avenges every careless thought,
And makes us feel that fate is terrible.

(PW: 448)

This, for instance, seems to have arrived at the same paradox of the 'hard & cold thing' as that advocated by Barrett Browning. The 'stern truth' is 'cold, sudden, strange'. It takes both the complacent and the mocking by surprise, and insists on its own reality against preconceived thoughts or feelings. The abrasive and abrupt rhetoric of these fragments, with their pitiless abstractions and unrhyming, inconclusive conclusions, points to a new-found imaginative honesty in L.E.L. as well as a new, desolating sense of reality. Lovelessness and petty intrigue in her own life at least gave her a truer subject for poetry than the mechanical lamentations of imaginary romance. Having learned to distrust the 'lotos-fruits' of the imagination and finding, in reality, that neither love, marriage nor even womanly faithfulness could compensate for the 'stern truth' of life's unheroic unhappiness, it seems that, as a poet, she had nowhere to go. She had lost faith in the smooth arias of sensibility, but the 'void' which remained could only support a philosophy of 'despair'. The stern truths of money, power and class, of that '"envy, malice, and all uncharitable-ness"' which L.E.L. knew so well in her own life, feature abundantly in her prose, in her contributions to the annuals and especially in her satirical novel *Ethel Churchill* (in which one of the heroines poisons two men!), but in general remain either absent or briefly glimpsed in the verse. It will be for later poets to set such truths explicitly against the powerful, ritualised grain of the heart.

L.E.L. is to be credited, however, with having developed from a garrulous girl prodigy, gifted with a trick of versifying which suited the tastes of the day, into a poet who, looking back over her career, could write honestly and quite sternly about her poetic failings. Her death at 36 ensured that she never achieved much more than the easy fame which she derided in the end. But meanwhile, her retrospectives of her own life point to an imagination more self-critical and perhaps more capable than she had opportunities and leisure to realise. Her fragment 'Gifts Misused' starkly sums up the progress of her own too 'golden' career, while pointing, in its rougher, more awkward, more truly 'natural' idiom, to the possibility, though too late, of better verse to come:

> Oh, what a waste of feeling and of thought
> Have been the imprints on my roll of life!
> What worthless hours! to what use have I turned
> The golden gifts which are my hope and pride!
> My power of song, unto how base a use
> Has it been put! with its pure ore I made
> An idol, living only on the breath
> Of idol worshippers. Alas! that ever
> Praise should have been what praise has been to me –
> The opiate of the mind!
>
> (*PW*: 436)

LAST QUESTIONS

During her journey to Africa in 1838, L.E.L. wrote two poems, 'The Polar Star' and 'Night at Sea'. They were published in the *New Monthly*

Magazine, just as news of her death was reaching England in January 1839. The second is a personal farewell to the friends she left behind and whose company she misses:

> By each dark wave around the vessel sweeping,
>   Farther am I from old dear friends removed,
> Till the lone vigil that I now am keeping,
>   I did not know how much you were beloved.
> How many acts of kindness little heeded,
>   Kind looks, kind words, rise half reproachful now!
> Hurried and anxious, my vexed life has speeded,
>   And memory wears a soft accusing brow.
>   My friends, my absent friends!
>   Do you think of me, as I think of you?
>   (*New Monthly*, 55(1839), 30)

The refrain echoes Hemans' lines from 'A Parting Song': 'When will ye think of me, my friends? / When will ye think of me? (*Works*: VII, 189), thus suggesting the poem's literary as well as personal inspiration. Later that same month, the *Athenaeum* published Barrett Browning's reply: 'L.E.L.'s Last Question'. This, like her formal commemoration of Hemans, contains both sympathy and criticism, both allegiance and revolt. It is particularly L.E.L.'s refrain, with its pitiful self-importance, which the younger poet analyses and rejects. With characteristically brusque philosophical logic she replies:

> 'Do ye think of me as I think of you?' –
> O friends, O kindred, O dear brotherhood
> Of all the world! what are we that we should
> For covenants of long affection sue?
> Why press so near each other when the touch
> Is barred by graves? Not much, and yet too much
> Is this 'Think of me as I think of you.'
>   (*CW*: III, 117–19, ll. 50–6)

Instead of answering L.E.L.'s personal plea to be remembered, Barrett Browning turns the personal into the impersonal, and asks her own larger question instead: 'what are we that we should / For covenants of long affection sue?' The movement from 'friends' to some universal 'brotherhood' puts the personal appeal into a proportionately diminished context. Though saddened by the poet's death, she also hints that such a request to be remembered is a self-flattering demand: it is 'Not much, and yet too much'.

Barrett Browning's poem thus rejects, not only the appeal of L.E.L.'s last line, but also, by implication, the whole romance ethic within which the older poet still seemed to be caught. The narcissistic impulse behind that ethic is brought out in stanza II:

> And little in the world the Loving do
> But sit (among the rocks?) and listen for
> The echo of their own love evermore –
> 'Do you think of me as I think of you?'
> (11–14)

Passive, self-absorbed and self-requiting, 'the Loving' do little 'in the world' except listen for the return echoes of their own love and love-language. Barrett Browning is sufficiently drawn by those echoes to write her own poem of affectionate remembrance, but she explicitly refuses to give L.E.L. the easy answer she requires. Implicitly, she refuses to write the kind of poem which will chime consolingly with those of her two demanding predecessors. Their self-involved echoes are like the calls of powerful sirens, sitting 'among the rocks', and enticing others into their beautiful but dangerous embraces. Barrett Browning, with her intellectualism and political commitments, unequivocally refuses to join the charmed circle of precursors, whose poetry has too many echo-effects for the comfort of this more original daughter. Not sufficiently 'in the world', their imaginations risk becoming, as the refrain suggests, entirely intertextual, echoing each other on an island of love, set well apart from the real world.

'L.E.L.'s Last Question' not only acknowledges the younger poet's anxiety of influence with regard to these poetic mothers, but it also issues a quite searching criticism of L.E.L.'s ideological innocence:

> Love-learnèd she had sung of love and love, –
> And like a child that, sleeping with dropt head
> Upon the fairy-book he lately read,
> Whatever household noises round him move,
> Hears in his dream some elfin turbulence, –
> Even so suggestive to her inward sense,
> All sounds of life assumed one tune of love.
> (15–21)

'The striking of one note does not make a melody' (*MRM*: I, 18), Elizabeth had complained of L.E.L. to Miss Mitford. By contrast to the reviewer who asked: 'How . . . can there be too much of love in a young lady's writings?' (*Fraser's Magazine*, 8(1833), 433), Barrett Browning's poem makes the point that the tune is monotonous, that there is too much 'love and love' and that ultimately such poetry, like the dreams of a child, is a sleepy, self-consoling fairy-tale. She exactly and ruthlessly identifies her precursor's weaknesses: her inspiration is bookish, her fantasy self-centred and her subject matter trivial: 'some elfin turbulence'. Furthermore, the stanza points to another later poem, which may well have been written with L.E.L. in mind. 'The Romance of the Swan's Nest' (1844) tells the tale of a child heroine, Little Ellie, who dreams all day of a chivalrous knight who will snatch her away from her uneventful life, and to whom alone, on the day he marries her, she will reveal her secret of a 'swan's nest among the reeds' (*CW*: III, 141–5, l. 24). The poem plays lightly between the antique register of love troths and tokens and the startlingly sexual, procreative image of the swan's nest. In the end, Ellie's dreams are broken by a reality which turns the courtly gestures of romance into a knowledge rife with implications of rape, violence and faithlessness: 'Lo, the wild swan had deserted, / And a rat had gnawed the reeds' (95–6). The poem's disclosure of the swan's ravaged nest expresses a natural or sexual violence which is subtly related to Ellie's old-world dreams. Barrett Browning, characteristically, uncovers the presence of the sexual at the heart of the domestic picturesque. She uncovers the very thing which is noticeably missing from the heroic love stories of Hemans and L.E.L.

That Little Ellie is in fact L.E.L. is supported, not only by the obvious consonance of their names, but also by the similar, cruel awakening experienced by the child poet in 'L.E.L.'s Last Question':

> And when the glory of her dream withdrew,
> When [k]nightly gestes and courtly pageantries
> Were broken in her visionary eyes
> By tears the solemn seas attested true . . .
> (22–5)

The journey from visions of romance to the truth of real experience is one which Barrett Browning herself will travel, and there is, perhaps, considerable self-recognition in her ambiguous tribute to L.E.L. The struggle of the woman poet to replace the sweet, infantile tune of love with that 'hard & cold thing' which is imaginative truth is a slow and difficult one. The journey towards that truth was never completed by L.E.L. Barrett Browning was luckier and lived longer. None the less, hers too is a long training in antique ballads and old-world melodramas before her prototype, Aurora Leigh, can recognise the difference between merely true feeling and really true poems:

> For me, I wrote
> False poems, like the rest, and thought them true
> Because myself was true in writing them.

74

I peradventure have writ true ones since
With less complacence.

(AL: I, 1022–6)

The example of L.E.L. stands both as a dread warning to the women poets who come after, but also as a figure whose mistakes may become the measure of the possibilities of their own art. In either case, echoes of her life and work reverberate in women's poetry long after her death.

Those echoes are revived most powerfully, not by Barrett Browning, but by Christina Rossetti. It is she who finds a way to 'inhabit' many of the attitudes and registers L.E.L. made popular at the beginning of the century. In 1848, the 20-year-old Dante Gabriel Rossetti wrote to his brother William: 'The only book I have picked up is L.E.L.'s Improvisatrice, for which I gave ninepence. By the bye, have you got her Violet and Bracelet with you? I cannot find them in our library' (1965–7: I, 41). The Rossetti children were evidently familiar with L.E.L.'s works and, ten years after her death, eager to possess volumes of her verse. Two years later, in 1850, Christina wrote a poem which she originally entitled 'Spring', but then changed to 'L.E.L.' It was published in 1863, in the first edition of Emily Faithfull's Victoria Magazine, which was set up with the declared political purpose of providing work and a publishing outlet for women – a role which the now defunct annuals once played. In his note to the work, William Michael asserts that the second title was meant as a decoy, and that the poem 'relates to herself, and not at all to the poetess L.E.L.' (in PW: 482), whom he describes, in 1904, as 'that now perhaps unduly forgotten poetess' (483). But he himself was perhaps forgetting the extent to which L.E.L., like Sappho and Corinne before her, provided a powerfully seductive model of tragic creativity to the first generation of Victorian women poets.

As if in recognition of this inheritance, Rossetti subtitled her poem with a quotation, though a mis-quotation, from Barrett Browning's 'L.E.L.'s Last Question'. Barrett Browning's line 'One thirsty for a little love' becomes, in Rossetti's hands, '"Whose heart was breaking for a little love"'. The reference suggests that, contrary to William Michael's explanation, she was indeed thinking back through her mothers, and writing, like Barrett Browning, against the siren echoes of other poems. But while Barrett Browning rejects L.E.L.'s last question, Rossetti answers it by thinking herself into the by now legendary melancholy of L.E.L.'s life:

> Downstairs I laugh, I sport and jest with all:
>   But in my solitary room above
> I turn my face in silence to the wall;
>   My heart is breaking for a little love.

Tho' winter frosts are done,
And birds pair every one,
And leaves peep out, for springtide is begun.
(*CP*: I, 153–5, ll. 1–7)

In attitude, theme and image, this is highly derivative. L.E.L. herself wrote innumerable poems about the difference between public face and private mask. In 'The Mask of Gaiety', for instance, she scans the facade of cheerfulness which keeps the heart's secrets hidden: 'But mocking words, light laugh, and ready jest, / These are the bars, the curtains to the breast' (*PW*: 449). Barrett Browning's poem 'The Mask' (1850), though more idiosyncratic in its register, seems to be reproducing and re-echoing L.E.L.'s characteristic plight: 'I have a smiling face, she said, / I have a jest for all I meet' (*CW*: III, 190–1, ll. 1–2). The discrepancy between what may and may not be seen has become the conventional condition of the creative woman. She is a creature of doubleness and disguise, of face and mask, secrets and jests. Yet the striking fact about Rossetti's version of the myth is how, in spite of its limpidly obvious emotions of despair and heartbreak, it nevertheless lacks L.E.L.'s self-pity. She has taken this well-worn woman's pose 'to heart', but somehow emptied it of all the cloying appeal of the earlier poet's verse, retaining only the shell – the exquisite, formal shell of rhyme and metre – which holds almost no emotional purpose or petition in it at all. Where L.E.L.'s poems are loaded, tonally and metrically, with the melancholy she cannot hide, Rossetti's most explicitly heart-broken verses verge on being, indeed, insouciant jests.

Thus, the tragic life of L.E.L., which gave blood to the myths of Sappho and Corinne, was not soon forgotten by later poets. Rossetti, in particular, took the myth and made a life's work of it, both in her poetry, and also, in a curiously perverse way, in her life's choices. Silence, death and rejection in love become her own special creative atmosphere, within which she revises and reworks the sentimental myth of the tragic improvisatrice for her own self-sufficiently sensual uses:

I deck myself with silks and jewelry,
I plume myself like any mated dove:
They praise my rustling show, and never see
My heart is breaking for a little love.
(ll. 22–5)

This is in a direct line of descent from the showy emotionalism of *Corinne*. But here, the dichotomy between appearance and reality, between public and private, mask and face, serves some purpose other than that of sexual entreaty. The 'silks and jewelry', which the puritanical Rossetti would never have worn, are a dress of the imagination which she continues to put on, and which whispers in her verse of a passion no real-life love could ever match or satisfy. As a result, the poem turns in on its own fictions and figures, its own 'silks and jewelry', outside of which there is no culpable betrayer or appreciating friend to bind it fast into a strategic drama of romance. Rossetti's great gift as a poet is to make nonsense of romance, not, like Barrett Browning, from without, but, 'secretly', from within.

Elizabeth Barrett Browning
(1806–61)

> Poor Beth had one great misfortune. She was born a
> woman. Now she despised nearly all the women in the world
> except Ma.dme de Stael- She could not abide their littlenesses
> called delicacies, their pretty headaches, & soft mincing
> voices, their nerves & affectations. . . . One word Beth hated
> in her soul .. & the word was 'feminine'. Beth thanked her
> gods that she was not & never wd. be feminine. (*Corr*: I,
> 361)

Barrett Browning's prose fragment about the 10-year-old Beth, who has
ambitions to be a poet as great as Homer and who repudiates feminine
sensibility as a nervous affectation, is evidently a semi-autobiographical
sketch of her own tomboyish girlhood. Elizabeth's scorn of feminine
'littlenesses called delicacies' was apparent from an early age and, in spite
of her later invalidism, remained an attitude of mind for much of her
life. It is interesting, however, that the one woman to escape Beth's
general opprobrium of her own sex is Madame de Staël. *Corinne*, which
Elizabeth read at least three times and, in her twenties, pronounced 'an
immortal book' (*Boyd*: 176), is the one exception to the rule of mincing
femininity which she abhorred. Such a comment suggests the extent to
which the novel was read in the nineteenth century as a daring,
emancipating text, which implicitly rejected the domestic and
physiological restrictions of femininity. Simply its subject matter, of a
woman strong enough to stand in public as an acclaimed poet, seems to
have filled its readers with infectious self-esteem. Elizabeth herself owed
a lifelong debt to this favourite work of her youth, although its influence

on her imagination was not unproblematic, and it would lessen as she matured.

As a child, Elizabeth was indeed precocious and ambitious, and determined from an early age to be a poet. At 8, for instance, her register already ranged from such chatty lines as those to her sick sister:

> Indeed I hope you'll soon get better,
> And I am dearest Henrietta,
> Your very dear Elizabeth Barrett,
> Compared to you, a chatting parot. [sic]
>
> (Corr: I, 12)

to the learnedly melodramatic and macabre stanzas written for her mother on her birthday:

> 'Twas dark – the tempest blew aloud,
> And light'ning flashed from every cloud,
> A wretched Mother, fondly pressed
> Her infant Babies to her breast . . .
> This wretched mother's gone into her wat'ry grave,
> No man can pass – no man can save!
> The waters shook, as there she fell,
> The chilling tempest blew farewell! –
>
> (Corr: I, 11)

As Elizabeth recalled years later, 'I used to write of virtue with a large "V," & "Oh Muse" with a harp – , & things of that sort' (RB: I, 391). The harping manner was rarely, however, even in the earliest poems, unmodified by the wit of the 'chatting parot'. None the less, accustomed to being addressed within her large family circle (she was the oldest of eleven children) as 'Our dear Sapho' (Corr: I, 91), 'The dear Poetess' (I, 92) or 'My dearest Mrs poet' (I, 150), Elizabeth was early impressed by the seriousness of her chosen role. When, in 1820, her father privately published her long, classical epic, The Battle of Marathon, and dubbed her the 'Laureate of Hope End', it might have seemed that she was on the way to becoming another of those girl prodigies, like Hemans and L.E.L., to whom fame came early and easily.

However, Barrett Browning's fate was different. The Battle of Marathon, written in imitation of Pope rather than of Byron, met with a dismissive review and was in no danger of being taken up by the editors of the annuals. Moreover, Elizabeth was under no financial or other pressure to publish more, and was able to continue her wide and surprisingly liberal education at home – an education which included the much coveted classics which, at her own insistence, she was allowed to study in the company of her favourite brother, Bro. Although she read and contributed to Jerdan's *Literary Gazette* in the early 1820s, and recorded her admiration for two poems by Hemans and L.E.L. which appeared in *The Literary Souvenir* for 1826 (Taplin, 1957: 21), her intellectual interests at this time went far beyond the thin diet of the annuals. In particular, her early reading of Wollstonecraft's *Vindication*, which produced 'a steady indignation against Nature who made me a woman, & a determinate resolution to dress up in men's clothes . . . & go into the world "to seek my fortune"' (*MRM*: II, 7), gave her a lingering distrust of the fashionable sentimentalism which passed for creative ability in women. At the age of 15 she was already declaring her dissent: 'My feelings are acute in the extreme but as nothing is so odious in my eyes as a damsel famed in story for a superabundance of sensibility they are carefully restrained!' (*Corr*: I, 354).

It is Barrett Browning who first brings to the somewhat frozen postures of women's poetry in the early nineteenth century a sense of a reality beyond the claims of the heart. Although she is in many ways a true inheritor of the tradition of female sensibility which Hemans and L.E.L. had popularised (Aurora Leigh, with her long, self-conscious disquisitions on the nature of female creativity, is the natural descendant of Properzia Rossi and the Improvisatrice), Barrett Browning also rejects, from an early age, the idea of feeling as a poetic end in itself (Aurora is a poet because she works and writes, not because she suffers and dies). Very simply, Barrett Browning takes the story of woman's creativity out of the self-echoing island of books which her predecessors had inhabited, and sets it in the contemporary world; she takes the woman poet off the stage of isolated self-appreciation, and gives her real work to do in society. No longer a poetry of 'love and love', hers is a poetry which constantly asks about the conventions of power which lie behind love, and which affect the improvised expression of the heart. Her poetry, to use Showalter's words, asserts that 'there can be no expression of the body which is unmediated by linguistic, social, and literary structures' (in Abel, 1982: 19). Those structures, the systems of socialisation represented by sex, class and money, for instance, and the systems of literary meaning, represented by historical and political reference, for instance, everywhere make themselves felt. This is not to say that Barrett Browning rejects her inheritance altogether. The figures of sensibility reappear in her poetry, often with startling explicitness, but never as a self-sufficient end. Instead, the creed of feeling is constantly set against the 'hard & cold thing' of social reality, which sceptically decentres the self's narcissistic egotism. Barrett Browning begins where L.E.L. left off.

FROM SENSIBILITY TO SEXUAL POLITICS

From her earliest ballads, even those written specifically for the annuals, Barrett Browning subtly deviates from the patterns of despair laid down by her predecessors. Her heroines have a habit of walking rather than standing, of talking rather than singing to a lyre. The ambitious Beth, for instance, intends to 'wear men's clothes, & live in a Greek island' when she grows up. She also hopes to be 'a warrior' and, in a more dynamic version of the Corinne myth, to 'sing her own poetry' as she rides into battle to 'destroy the Turkish empire' (*Corr*: I, 361). This Byronic ideal was certainly autobiographical. Elizabeth recalled with amusement her youthful 'resolution to dress up in men's clothes' and make her way in the world. 'I rather leant towards being poor Lord Byron's PAGE' (*MRM*: II, 7), she explained to Miss Mitford. The idea of the poet as a man of action is not, contrary to Ross's argument (1989: 161), confined to men. Nor was Barrett Browning's a particularly original ambition. Byron's *Lara*, which tells of a faithful female page accompanying her moody and cynical master into battle, and which ends with the tantalising line 'Her tale untold, her truth too dearly proved' (1970: 627), seems to have given a number of women writers a figure for their own 'untold' ambitions.

Yet, the idea of the poet as warrior, criminal, libertine and religious sceptic, like Lara himself, seems expressly at odds with the domestic and religious faith required of Victorian women. When George Sand published *Lélia* in 1833, the novel in which the Byronic hero's cynicism and dark *ennui* are transferred to a woman – 'a monster, a Byronic woman – a woman', as one reviewer raged, 'without hope and without soul' (*Athenaeum* (Sept. 1833), 646) – it was widely condemned, and even Barrett Browning herself dismissed it as 'a serpent book' (*MRM*: II, 127). Clearly, the idea of a female cynic touched a nerve of deep-seated anxiety in the age. Yet, paradoxically, Byronism seems to have been especially attractive to women, to the sex which carried the special burden of representing the century's 'hope' and 'soul'. To be Lord Byron's page, or Lord Raymond's Evadne (M. Shelley, *The Last Man*), or Rochester's Jane or even, at some level, the Chamois Hunter's love, suggests a drama of desire in which the woman seeks, not only a lover, but also her forbidden other self – the one who is experienced, worldly wise and, like Lélia, cynically unromantic. Elizabeth no doubt also read in the *Athenaeum*, in 1833, a review which disclosed George Sand's real identity: 'now positively known to be Madame Dudevant, a young lady who, some years back, distinguished herself at the age of thirteen by an indomitable wish to escape from her parents and seek out Lord Byron'

(*Athenaeum* (Feb. 1833), 74). As so often, it is hard to separate real life from literary myths, real desires from second-hand quotations. Byronism evidently offered many of these women writers, not so much the cheap ideal of a dark, handsome husband, but the prospect of a transvestite emancipation from the restricting dress of femininity. Certainly in the early nineteenth century, Byron's entourage of would-be girl pages was a large one.

'My ballad', Barrett Browning wrote in July 1838, 'containing a ladye dressed up like a page and galloping off to Palestine in a manner that would scandalise you, went to Miss Mitford this morning' (*Letters*: I, 62). 'The Romaunt of the Page', which was written for the first issue of *Findens' Tableaux*, is an awkward, pseudo-Spenserian ballad. The story, while accommodating the usual picturesque medievalisms of the annuals, also reworks Elizabeth's youthful Byronic fantasy. The heroine, instead of waiting at home for her husband to return from the Crusades, disguises herself as a boy and goes to fight at his side. The poem's interest lies in the way that the quaintly heroic plot is disturbed by a quite modern sexual politics.[1] Whereas Hemans and L.E.L. turn love, whether lost or found, into the only rationale for any relation between the sexes, Barrett Browning explores, in its place, power, prejudice and deception. A streak of witty worldly wisdom debunks even her own literary myth in this poem, for the knight turns out to be no mysterious betrayer or doom-laden Lara, but an ordinary Victorian husband who entertains certain limited prejudices about women. Implicitly revising the formulas of absolute desire and absolute betrayal which mark the general run of verses in the annuals, Barrett Browning offers a tragedy of love from a new angle. It is not male unfaithfulness which kills this heroine, but male conventionality.

Having told her own story under the pretence of a sister's, the page receives a swift reply from her knight husband:

> – 'Well done it were for thy sistèr,
>   Thou tellest well her tale!
> But for my lady, she shall pray
>   I' the kirk of Nydesdale.
> Not dread for me but love for me
>   Shall make my lady pale;
> No casque shall hide her woman's tear –
> It shall have room to trickle clear
>   Behind her woman's veil.'
>   (*CW*: II, 241–54, ll. 214–22)

At issue throughout the poem is not so much love's constancy but the nature of womanhood. The knight refuses to countenance a wife who has been 'Unwomaned' (196) in her clothes and actions. His own wife, he is certain, goes to the kirk to pray and weeps behind her veil. The idea that there is more '"room"' behind a veil than behind a casque is, of course, only a trick of male perspective. Yet the more emphatically the knight lays down the law of womanhood, the more the poem opens up the gap between his myth and the reality. He finally offers, as conclusive proof of the domestic faithfulness of his wife, the example of a cloud:

> 'Look up – there is a small bright cloud
> Alone amid the skies!
> So high, so pure, and so apart,
> A woman's honour lies.'
>
> (230–3)

He thus defines the honourable wifeliness of his wife as uniquely elevated and safely out of the way.

Elizabeth knew a real-life counterpart to her cloudy-minded knight. Some years later she wrote bitterly to Miss Mitford of a certain Mr Hunter who, particularly after the success of her 1844 volume of poems, 'talks epigrams about the sin & shame of those divine angels, called women, daring to tread in the dust of a multitude, when they ought to be minding their clouds'. She added, acutely: 'It is not the pudding-making and stocking-darning theory – it is more graceful & picturesque. But the *significance* is precisely the same' (*MRM*: III, 81). In both the poem and the letter, men talk 'epigrams' about women and clouds. As Barrett Browning slyly hints, such woolly idealism betrays a quite determined sexual dogmatism. Although a '"woman's honour"', in all its un-avoidable physiological specificity, is '"a small bright cloud"', remote, exalted and distinctly nebulous, nevertheless, behind this woman-cloud is the reassuring figure who will go to church, weep, make puddings and darn stockings as required. The knight's ulterior motives, as well as his ulterior anxieties, show through the conventional rhetoric he espouses. Meanwhile, however, he cannot see, for clouds, the real wife who stands before him.

For all its graceless rhymes and quirky, archaic registers, 'The Romaunt of the Page' is ideologically intriguing. Rejecting the stultified poses of the traditional waiting game of woman's love, Barrett Browning puts her heroine on the road, 'to tread in the dust', as she herself so much longed to do. Furthermore, she puts her in literal pursuit of the husband who, having wedded but not bedded her, has then fled in fear to the more congenial wars. The undercurrent of sexual meaning is given an added, faintly comical impetus from this domestic plot. In the end, however, this heroine is as cruelly betrayed as any Sappho or Corinne. The man she loves has fallen for angels in the clouds, ' "So high, so pure, and so apart" ', while her fate is to die, fighting to save him from a band of Turks. If, on another level, this is also a poem about the woman poet's ambition, her desire to follow in the footsteps of Lord Byron, here too the message is a rebuff. In this Victorian woman's version of the story of *Lara*, epigrams and conventionalities have taken the place of Romantic androgyny, and Lord Byron turns out to be just another Mr Hunter. Not aloof superiority but disappointing conventionality is the reaction in men which blocks women's ambition.

A curious element in the poem, which seems at first to be merely a colourful Gothicism, is the voice of nuns echoing from a distant convent, where they sing a requiem for their dead abbess. The nuns not only provide a background commentary on the virgin fate of the page-wife, by pointing to an alternative life of communal womanhood as opposed to male warfare; they also seem to offer, at the end of the poem, a generalised mourning for the fates of all women, however different or far removed. The technique of counterpointed voices recalls Hemans' gendered metrical divisions:

> Dirge for abbess laid in shroud
> Sweepeth o'er the shroudless dead,
> Page or lady, as we said,
> With the dews upon her head,
> All as sad if not as loud.
>   *Ingemisco, ingemisco!*
> Is ever a lament begun
> By any mourner under sun,
> Which, ere it endeth, suits but *one*?
>   (341–9)

Such an ending distances and generalises the pity of the tale. As in 'L.E.L.'s Last Question', a sense of the universal pushes against the individual story; the 'lament' finds scope beyond the fate of any *'one'* heroine. Barrett Browning is already alert to social and ideological structures, whether of convents or of marriage, which affect the fate of the individual. Instead of giving a sentimental close-up of her dead heroine, or putting her in a sad, funerary picture, she reminds her readers, through the nuns' 'lament', that there are always others dying 'under sun'. The chorus of nuns, which frames the poem, hints at other, larger perspectives outside the embattled mis-recognitions of romance. Yet, paradoxically, this impersonal, open-ended mourning is more in touch with the fate of the unknown page than is her own husband's convention-clouded imagination. Barrett Browning has not only rewritten *Lara* from the page's point of view, domesticating the allure of its gloomy masculinity, but she has also brought to it a politics of gender which points to allegiances outside either marriage or true love. Just such an allegiance, between women, counterpoints and criticises the love story in *Aurora Leigh*.

Towards the end of her life, Barrett Browning wrote a ballad which shows how far she had travelled from the archaisms of sensibility towards the sexual politics of the contemporary world. In 1861, 'Lord Walter's Wife' was rejected by Thackeray as unsuitable for family reading in the *Cornhill Magazine*. 'Thackeray has turned me out of the "Cornhill" for indecency' (*Letters*: II, 443), Elizabeth triumphantly reported. Clearly the 'indecency' of 'Lord Walter's Wife', in which nothing indecent ever occurs, stems from the extra-marital situation it insinuates. The poem, as the very title suggests, is about the emotional property values of marriage. Lord Walter is absent throughout, though he 'owns' both title and wife. The woman who speaks and the friend she addresses are both nameless, known only in their relation to the absent lord. The poem is interesting because, while it sets up the opportunity for an adulterous affair between wife and friend, its purpose is ultimately neither to condemn adultery nor to reaffirm the sanctity of marriage. It is, rather, to expose the double standards of men. 'Why are women to be blamed if they act as if they had to do with swindlers?' (*RB*: I, 341) Elizabeth once demanded of Robert. Lord Walter's friend proves to be not so much a seducer as a swindler. He is corrupt precisely because he does *not* feel the adulterous passion he disingenuously proposes.

The poem opens with the lady asking why her friend must go so soon. She receives, for answer, a series of reasons in which sexual gallantry barely disguises accusation:

> 'Because I fear you,' he answered; – 'because you are far too fair,
> And able to strangle my soul in a mesh of your gold-coloured hair.'
> $\qquad\qquad$ (*CW*: VI, 9–14, ll. 3–4)

He thus plunges the conversation into sexual meanings at the first opportunity. However, instead of receiving the coy protestation of innocence which he expects, and which would have ensured a safe passage for his one-sided game of seduction, the lady answers him with apparently reciprocal interest: '"Oh, that," she said, "is no reason! Such knots are quickly undone"' (5). Both her hair and her marriage, she suggests, are easily unknotted. When the friend starts to protest, '"I value your husband, Lord Walter"' (8), the laws of property making themselves heard in that loaded verb, she precipitates his insinuations into a real possibility of unfaithfulness:

'Oh, that,' she said, 'is no reason. You smell a rose through a fence:
If two should smell it, what matter? who grumbles, and where's the pretence?'
(9–10)

As she crudely literalises each of the hints he has dropped, meeting his proposals more than halfway, the friend suddenly turns on her as the guilty party in a fantasy he had thought entirely his own:

At which he rose up in his anger, – 'Why, now, you no longer are fair!
Why, now, you no longer are fatal, but ugly and hateful, I swear.'
(19–20)

The reasoning is exquisite. The contemporary slang of 'fatal' to mean only sexually alluring and not 'fatal' at all when it comes to it, shows up the selfish level of his thinking. The woman is only beautiful and fatal for as long as she remains innocent and inaccessible. He is another Mr Hunter who 'talks epigrams' of sexual gallantry in the safety of his assumptions that women are not sexual beings in any way, but angels in the clouds or faithful wives in the kitchen.

The contradiction between the man's rhetoric and his feelings is then exposed, word for word, by the lady herself:

'If a man finds a woman too fair, he means simply adapted too much
To use unlawful and fatal. The praise! – shall I thank you for such?

'Too fair? – not unless you misuse us! and surely if, once in a while,
You attain to it, straightway you call us no longer too fair, but too vile.'
(29–32)

Though no more than a verbal encounter in a garden, the episode is rich in the other meaning of real sexual use and abuse. It is the woman who brings into the open ground of straight speaking the double standard which is the very condition of the man's desire. He desires her only as a modest wife and adoring mother, yet at the same time the drift of his speeches is that she might be willing to be something else. ' "You take us for harlots, I tell you, and not for the women we are" ' (50), she accuses. The whole event of seduction emerges as a complacent and self-regarding fantasy of male power (as it does in Doris Lessing's short story, 'One Off the Short List' (1965: 7–33) which it curiously foreshadows). As in 'The Romaunt of the Page', the language of the heart proves wholly mediated by other, socio-political structures of desire.

Thackeray, perhaps, was right in detecting in the poem a subject not fit for family reading. For it is as much a critique of marriage as of adultery, of ownership as of unfaithfulness. As Mary Poovey puts it: 'Modesty announces purity in a virgin, promises fidelity in a wife, and thus will continue to be a reflection of her husband's power' (1984: 22). In this poem, the man's game of seduction relies on the whole structure of marriage, motherhood, title, purity, property and, of course, male friendship, remaining intact. ' "I value your husband . . ." ' is the crucial admission. The object of the friend's attentions is precisely 'Lord Walter's *Wife*'. Adultery, Barrett Browning might almost be hinting, is not so much the threatening opposite of marriage, as its hidden re-affirmation.

As a poet, she learned early to distrust the iconic postures of romance in favour of a socialised and contextualised account of desire. She perceives love, not as a conclusive emotional absolute, but as a mixture of lust, ambition, rhetoric, fear and, above all, conventionality. Hers is thus an essentially politicised poetry, not because politics is its dominant subject matter and not because she shows herself in any sense a political radical (as some critics have complained[2]), but because the tensions between desire and fact, between the individual and the system, can be felt in it. Those tensions were missing in the work of de Staël, Hemans and L.E.L., whose sense of morality was identical with the claims of the heart, but Barrett Browning found them in the novelist who, in a sense, provided her with a much needed counterbalance: George Sand.

Elizabeth lighted on 'the new French literature' (*MRM*: II, 85) comparatively late, in 1842, but thereafter was a confirmed devotee, who tried to convert both Miss Mitford and Robert Browning, though she kept her French enthusiasms secret from her increasingly puritanical father. In particular it seems to have been, as Patricia Thomson points out, not so much the *Corinne*-like *Consuelo* which drew her admiration, but Sand's novels about class and politics (1977: 57). 'Such a colossal nature in every way – ', she exclaimed to Robert, 'with all that breadth & scope of faculty which women want – magnanimous, & loving the truth & loving the people' (*RB*: I, 114). When she visited Sand in Paris in 1852 she was struck, above all, by the novelist's indifference to appearances: 'A scorn of pleasing she evidently had; there never could have been a colour of coquetry in that woman. Her very freedom from affectation and consciousness had a touch of disdain. But I liked her' (*Letters*: II, 56–7). After the narcissistic monumentalism of *Corinne*, the sheer emotional and political variety of Sand's writing must have seemed like an opening into that 'experience of life & man' (*RB*: I, 41) which Elizabeth herself so much craved. The story of *Aurora Leigh*, her long epic poem about the development of the woman poet, contains, among other things, the drama of Barrett Browning's own imaginative emancipation from the self-centred sensibility of de Staël's romance into the 'breadth & scope' of vision she envied in George Sand. Such an emancipation is achieved through sceptically reproducing many of the old figures of female sensibility: the myth of Italy, the figurative anatomisation of the woman's body, the interlocking of the narratives of love and fame, but such devices are now put in the context of a diminishing and sometimes discrediting reality.

As Ellen Moers has shown, the crowning scene in the garden of Book II is a prolonged, literary in-joke about the Corinne myth (1978: 182). Aurora, on her twentieth birthday, persuades herself of her poetic vocation by playing the part of Corinne at the Capitol, and crowning herself poet in her aunt's garden. She is then caught in the classic pose of a statue by the unexpected audience of her sceptical and disdainful cousin, Romney:

> I stood there fixed, –
> My arms up, like the caryatid, sole
> Of some abolished temple, helplessly
> Persistent in a gesture which derides
> A former purpose. Yet my blush was flame,
> As if from flax, not stone.
>
> (II, 60–5)

In this moment of triumph turned silly, Barrett Browning seems to be enjoying a joke against all the Corinnes whose art consisted of standing in attitudes. 'Her arms were transcendently beautiful; her figure tall' (1833: 20), de Staël wrote. At the end of 'A History of the Lyre', L.E.L. reproduced the same posture:

> There was a sculptured form; the feet were placed
> Upon a finely-carved rose wreath; the arms
> Were raised to Heaven, as if to clasp the stars . . .
>
> (PW: 231)

But instead of a tragic funerary monument, Aurora looks like a useless 'caryatid', whose hands are empty and whose arms carry nothing. Purposeless and pretentious, her moment of triumph has the opposite effect to Corinne's, for Romney is not impressed. The temple of the old poetic goddesses has been 'abolished', and the 'former purpose' of uplifted arms, if there ever was one, has somehow been forgotten. Barrett Browning takes the classical imagery of the myth and turns it into an imagery of purely archaeological interest (see Cooper, 1988: 157–8). Aurora's vocation is to be a poet, not a statue.

Yet it is interesting that, in the argument which follows, Romney tries to recuperate the myth for his own domestic purposes. He tells Aurora:

> 'Keep to the green wreath,
> Since even dreaming of the stone and bronze
> Brings headaches, pretty cousin, and defiles
> The clean white morning dresses.'
>
> (II, 93–6)

The ' "green wreath" ' of leaves represents, for Romney, an Aurora who will stay ' "pretty" ' and ' "clean" ' in her ' "white morning dresses" ', and thus be a more picturesque and pleasing wife. Like Gilfillan, who praised Hemans for saving him from 'the ludicrous image of a double-dyed Blue . . . sweating at some stupendous treatise' (*Tait's*, 14(1847), 361), Romney treacherously advises Aurora to avoid the ' "headaches" ' and dirty dresses of real work, and to keep to the pose of creativity which shows her person off to more advantage. To stand still in a wreath is thus turned back into the attitude, not of solitary poetic triumph as Aurora had fantasised, but of sexual and domestic appeal. It is as if Barrett Browning has found out the ideology behind her old favourite novel. By putting a man in the scene, she entirely changes its meaning. It is Romney's eye which both devalues Aurora's pose and then cunningly re-evaluates it in terms of its domestic propriety. The old double purpose of sensibility is thus exposed as Barrett Browning hints that, in the long run, it is Romney, not Aurora, who desires to play at statues. It is he who justifies, but only in his own terms, this standing about in a 'white' dress. Through such a deft reversal, which comments on the whole critical reception of women's poetry, she points out that, in fact, Romney's appreciation is worse than his scorn, for it traps the aspiring poet in the same formulas of romance as her predecessor, who sang to implore 'the protection of a friend' (de Staël, 1833: 21).

However, it is at this point that Aurora makes her break with the whole debilitating collusion of work and love which *Corinne* had encouraged. She tells Romney that she would rather be dead,

> 'than keep quiet here
> And gather up my feet from even a step
> For fear to soil my gown in so much dust.
> I choose to walk at all risks.'
>
> (II, 103–6)

To rise and walk is a gesture full of defiance, not only of all the self-conscious statuary of the myth, but also of all the men in Elizabeth's own life, her father, brothers and Mr Hunter, who had a vested interest in her not 'daring to tread in the dust' (*MRM*: III, 81). Aurora, instead of being rejected, herself rejects the cousin who offers her a wreath as a plaything or an ornament, and goes in search of the real one with all its 'headaches'. *Aurora Leigh* is Barrett Browning's poem of escape, both from the marital home and the Palace of Art (the two often subtly confused by critics) where, as a woman, she risks becoming a permanent fixture, whether angel or art work. In order not to be a Galatea but a Pygmalion, she must '"walk at all risks"'. Her declared aesthetic aim of rejecting 'togas and the picturesque' (V, 209) in order to capture her own 'live, throbbing age' (203) is connected with this rejection of an iconic poetic identity which ultimately only justifies the condescensions of male praise.

The scene of reunion between Aurora and Romney in Book VIII intriguingly parallels this first garden scene. But although it is June again, the place is Italy, Aurora has achieved fame in her writing and Romney is blind. This change is driven home in an image which crucially reverses the old roles:

> he, the man, appeared
> So pale and patient, like the marble man
> A sculptor puts his personal sadness in . . .
> (VIII, 1099–101)

Now it is Romney who is the art object, the statue, and Aurora who walks free. Her reward at the end is not a triumphal crowning in public, but, almost its opposite: an invisibility which the darkness of the garden and the blindness of the man both emphasise. 'He had to be blinded, observe, to be made to see' (*Letters*: II, 242), Barrett Browning explained. Romney, who voices many of the prejudices and epigrams of the men Elizabeth knew and of the reviewers she had read, is deprived of the sense which lies behind the whole aesthetic of sensibility: the sense of sight. The eye of Phaon, for whom Sappho supposedly killed herself, the eye of Oswald, for whom Corinne paraded her art round Italy, the eye of Lockhart, which dissolved in tears at the frontispieces of women's poems, the eye of Mr Hunter, dogmatically fixed on women as clouds, and the eye of Romney himself, who once preferred Aurora to stand prettily in a garden rather than labour in the dust of the real world, are all forms of a controlling, external viewpoint, which turns women's art into a sight for men. Where Hemans and L.E.L. had played to a double audience, encoding a message to other women through their ritual appeals for one man's love, Barrett Browning, characteristically, exposes the contradiction. By blinding Romney, she attacks the whole sexually appreciating voyeurism of the literature she inherits.

To read this episode as part of a developing aesthetics rather than as a crude revenge of the plot is to avoid the embarrassment, either of Aurora seeming to be thus proved 'right' (Tompkins, 1961–2: 19) or of her seeming to be thus turned into another of Milton's daughters (Gilbert and Gubar, 1979: 578). Her triumphant invisibility at the end is, instead, a sign that she has freed herself from the applause of the Capitol. She has learned to write of something other than herself, and Romney's praise, which was once only praise of her looks, is now honest praise of her work. ' "But, in this last book, / You showed me something separate from yourself" ' (VIII, 606), he tells her. To gaze 'on Self apart' (1989: 187), as George Eliot puts it in 'Erinna', is to have achieved the artist's necessary breadth and scope of feeling. Romney's blindness is Aurora's sight, in a symbolic disequilibrium which runs through Victorian women's writing. Aurora has learned to see precisely because she has learned the insignificance of being seen; she has learned to write because she has learned the insignificance of being loved. She gets both love and fame in the end, but only because she has found them to be separate and different, each with their own requirements and their own rewards. Furthermore, she has learned the 'hard & cold thing', that love may be only an elaborate convention of feeling or a flattering fantasy of power. *Aurora Leigh* thus continues the work of the ballads in rescuing the woman from the thrall of being seen, or rather not seen, for all the angels, clouds and statues of men's eyes. It offers a drastic revision of the terms of romance, even if it is a revision for which Romney pays a high and somewhat obvious price.

It is this sceptical awareness of the sexual politics of sensibility which marks out Barrett Browning's poetry from that of her predecessors. Love, in her work, is not a sacred ideal, removed from the contingencies of the world, but is dragged in the dust of that reality which was itself so hard-won an experience and a theme for her. The facts of power and money, which are so singularly absent from the works of de Staël, Hemans and L.E.L., give Barrett Browning an imagery for the larger system of things, which increasingly, in her work, undermines and disproves the inherited sanctities of the heart. If *Aurora Leigh* contains the story of this development, it is in some of Barrett Browning's lesser known political poems that the power of the system makes itself felt.

THE SYSTEMS OF MAN

'None of all these things
Can women understand. You generalise
Oh, nothing, – not even grief! Your quick-breathed hearts,

So sympathetic to the personal pang,
Close on each separate knife-stroke, yielding up
A whole life at each wound, incapable
Of deepening, widening a large lap of life
To hold the world-full woe. The human race
To you means, such a child, or such a man,
You saw one morning waiting in the cold,
Beside that gate, perhaps. You gather up
A few such cases, and when strong sometimes
Will write of factories and of slaves, as if
Your father were a negro, and your son
A spinner in the mills.'

(*AL*: II, 182–96)

These criticisms, which Barrett Browning puts into the mouth of
Romney, are not simply to be dismissed as examples of male prejudice.
His attack on the narrowness, sentimentality and ultimate self-centredness
of women's verse is one which, at the moment of her humiliation in the
garden, Aurora takes to heart. An article in the *Edinburgh Review* for
1841, which discussed some works by Lady Morgan and Mrs Ellis
among others, had made similarly confident assertions about the law of
sexual difference. Women, it claimed, 'are inferior in the power of close
and logical reasoning. They are less dispassionate . . . They have less
power of combination and generalization. They are less capable of steady
and concentrated attention' (*Edinburgh Review*, 73(1841), 193). The 1839
Works of Mrs. Hemans carried a prominent review by Lord Jeffrey,
which proposed that women are 'incapable of long moral or political
investigations' since they are by nature 'averse to long doubt and long
labour' (*Works*: V, 318). In 1833 a reviewer of L.E.L. had asked,
scornfully in her defence, if women could be supposed 'to write of
politics or political economy' (*Fraser's Magazine*, 8(1833), 433) instead of
love. Such comments, which appear continuously throughout the
century, must have impressed the weight of their assumptions on the
consciousness of women poets. Even Elizabeth, though only in secret to
Robert, fell into such comparisons. She comments, for instance, on a
note she has received from one of Felicia Hemans' sons, 'which quite
touched me', and then, as if there were some connection, she ventures a
comparison between men and women: 'there *is* a natural inferiority of
mind in women – of the intellect'. A little later, however, she points to
the one exception which might disprove the rule: 'George Sand' (*RB*: I,
113). As so often in her writings, Barrett Browning takes her bearings
from other women. Hemans and Sand subconsciously represent for her
the difference between a woman's writing which is 'naturally' inferior
and one which may be equal to men's in power and scope.

However, as the reader discovers, the criticisms which Romney issues are only the other side of an even more disabling praise. He concludes his devastating assessment of women's capacity to write with the exclamation:

> 'Women as you are,
> Mere women, personal and passionate,
> You give us doating mothers, and perfect wives,
> Sublime Madonnas, and enduring saints!
> We get no Christ from you, – and verily
> We shall not get a poet, in my mind.'
> (II, 220–5)

In a singularly self-contradicting article on 'The rights of women' in the *Quarterly* for 1845, the writer asserts: 'We hope – nay, we proudly believe – that the honourable freedom of our women may long be made to rest on those only foundations which can keep it secure against change – the purity, the harmony, the genial brightness of our English homes' (*Quarterly Review*, 75(1845), 122). In fact it is not 'freedom' but 'women' who must be kept at home, 'secure against change'. The word 'home', which sums up a peculiarly English combination of wifeliness and property, and which de Staël used in its English form in *Corinne* because she could find no French equivalent, appears rarely in Barrett Browning's poetry. When Aurora finally admits her love for Romney, it is a love specifically free of homes, stately or otherwise. None the less, the ideological swindle in the myth of '"doating mothers, and perfect wives"' is a powerful one, particularly because it invokes a religious fervour hard to disavow. In 1883, Eric S. Robertson pointed to the hidden implication of such a myth. 'The trustfulness that is so characteristic of woman's views of existence may be one great cause of her comparative lack of imagination', he asserts. The double-handedness of his reasoning is like Romney's. The age needs women to be saints not poets. Men in particular need it, for, as Robertson neatly summarises: 'Faith is woman-like, doubt is man-like' (1883: xiii). What he does not consider is the extent to which faith and doubt are qualities of reading as well as of writing, and therefore the extent to which male readers will look to women's writing, as they look to women themselves, for a reassuring statement of faith in a world beset by doubts. Aurora has to contend, not only with Romney's doubt of her poetic abilities, but also with his faith in her as one of the '"Sublime Madonnas"' and, if possible, a perfect wife.

To '"write of factories and of slaves"' with political as well as personal passion is something Barrett Browning learned to do against the odds of all these assumptions. In 1843, she read the Royal Commission's report on the 'Employment of Children in Trades and Manufactures' and, like

Dickens who was 'perfectly stricken down' (1965–88: III, 459) by it, was haunted by its cry. In August of that same year, *Blackwood's* published her poem, 'The Cry of the Children'. It caused something of a stir, and helped rouse many consciences in preparation for Lord Shaftesbury's 'Ten Hours' Amendment' Bill, introduced the following March. 'The Cry of the Children' is a propagandistically tear-jerking poem which, none the less, issues a subtle challenge to certain social alliances and their corrupt nexus of interests. Although not unusual in its subject matter – Mary Howitt's poem on the plight of factory children, 'The Rich and the Poor', appeared in the *Forget-Me-Not* for 1838 – 'The Cry of the Children' stands out from the run of social problem poems by women because its scope is precisely not that of ' "such a child" ', but of a whole system of work and thought. Furthermore, it incorporates that system as the imaginative structure of the poem itself.

The first two stanzas, for instance, set up a family drama of brothers, mothers and fathers which, although starting with a comfortingly sweet scene: 'They are leaning their young heads against their mothers' (*CW*: III, 53–9, l. 3), gradually broadens to include a much larger relationship of powers:

> But the young, young children, O my brothers,
> Do you ask them why they stand
> Weeping sore before the bosoms of their mothers,
> In our happy Fatherland?
>
> (21–4)

There is a family story, here, which has nothing to do with 'the purity, the harmony, the genial brightness of our English homes'. Although the scene has all the emotive simplicity of a moral tableau, these children are caught in a national scandal which the homely 'bosoms' of the 'mothers' cannot prevent. The phrase which swings the poem out of its local homeliness is that finely ironic title, 'our happy Fatherland'. The shift of perspective here is crucial. The phrase ushers into the poem the figure who has been noticeably absent so far: the father. He enters the scene, however, not *as* a father, to complete the family circle of mothers and children, but as a totalising abstraction, an uncompromising, all-inclusive monolith, whose purpose is precisely to take the children out of the home. He is, indeed, a barabaric and brutal Symbolic Order; a 'Father'-thing whose happiness is as hollow as the cliché which tells of it. The idea of the father is the pivot, as it is in much of Barrett Browning's poetry, on which the family system turns into the socio-economic system. The stony abstraction of 'our happy Fatherland' takes the problem out of the home, and into the realm of ideologies and idealisms;

of those monumental, symbolic myths which are the law of real fathers as
well as of imaginary fatherlands.

The poem then goes on to suggest other extensions of this law:

> Now tell the poor young children, O my brothers,
>   To look up to Him and pray;
> So the blessed One who blesseth all the others,
>   Will bless them another day.
> They answer, 'Who is God that He should hear us,
>   While the rushing of the iron wheels is stirred?
> When we sob aloud, the human creatures near us
>   Pass by, hearing not, or answer not a word.
> And *we* hear not (for the wheels in their resounding)
>   Strangers speaking at the door:
> Is it likely God, with angels singing round Him,
>   Hears our weeping any more?'
>   (101–12)

The injustice of this religious solution can be heard in the very terms of
its proposal: that while 'all the others' are blest, these children must pray
for 'another day'. This exactly reproduces the condition in which the
children already live – the condition of having unluckily missed God's
blessing for the day. The injunction to 'pray' thus becomes not a solution
to the problem, but only part of the scandal. Although the poem is
intended to speak to the Christian conscience of Barrett Browning's
readers, it does so by making the children's atheist convictions more
convincing than the speaker's holy advice. The noise of the wheels is
God's as well as the master's strategy for not hearing the awkward
questions of 'Strangers speaking at the door'. The imagery of the poem is
thus catching up all possible exceptions to the rule of exploitation in its
ever more universalist system of 'wheels'.

The surprising sharpness of 'The Cry of the Children' is brought out
in a comparison with Eliza Cook's poem on the same subject. The
Commission's report told of how the factory children repeated the phrase
'Our Father', without understanding its meaning. Cook unashamedly
turns the anecdote into a pious example and exhortation to the rich:

> Then to your homes so bright and fair,
>   And think it good to pray;
> Since the sad children of Despair
>   Can kneel in thanks and say,
>   'Our Father!'
>   (1870: 453)

By comparison, in Barrett Browning's poem the phrase becomes hideously annexed to the figure who, by sex and by authority, most resembles a divine father:

> 'But, no!' say the children, weeping faster,
>   'He is speechless as a stone:
> And they tell us, of His image is the master
>   Who commands us to work on.
> Go to!' say the children, – 'up in Heaven,
>   Dark, wheel-like, turning clouds are all we find.'
>
> (125–30)

This indictment of a male line of mastership subtly connects with the first play on fathers in the 'happy Fatherland'. In the imagery of this poem, God, masters, fathers and fatherland conspire into a single tyrant, who uses children as labour and is cruelly deaf to their cries. The repeated image of wheels turning mimes the repetitiveness of a wholly mechanised universe, in which even angels singing are part of a system of deafening noise. Such singing is, therefore, either a sort of picturesque nonsense (like most of the angel imagery in Barrett Browning's work) or else just another excuse for the children's cry not being heard. By taking the part of the children, the poem quietly challenges the notion both of a benign God and of the protective home, and offers, instead, the picture of a bleak, totalitarian universe, worked by the linked wheels of various fathers in power.

'The Cry of the Children' has many faults. Its metre is wrung out of all recognisable rhythm at times, and its over-insistent, inexact rhymes, like 'stilled in' to rhyme with 'children', 'shower' with 'know her', can sound far-fetched and trivial. None the less, its world-view of wheels extending even to the turning clouds and the singing angels is a potent expression of a system which connects patriotic fervour, family feeling and religious belief in a single, senseless rote of exploitation. The poem itself, with its slippery, yet entrenched imagery of male authority, reproduces this state apparatus of power, this controlling ideology of mechanisation, which affects every area of life: family, country, religion, fable and play. In the end, in lines which recall the baroque literalism of Shelley's 'Mask of Anarchy', all these are shown to uphold the inhuman power of the other Victorian god: 'the mart':

> 'How long,' they say, 'how long, O cruel nation,
>   Will you stand, to move the world, on a child's heart, –
> Stifle down with a mailed heel its palpitation,
>   And tread onward to your throne amid the mart?'
>
> (153–6)

In its web of connected images, 'The Cry of the Children' creates a verbal equivalent to the deterministic nexus of power which it attacks. Homes and fathers, like heaven and Father God, belong within the same machinery of mindless noise. Such imagery only just stops short of being cynically absolutist, by being, specifically, an imagery of the fathers, not of the mothers.

It was during the early 1840s that Elizabeth began to feel the oppression of her own father's irrational 'system' most acutely. His pathological refusal to countenance marriage for any of his children, and his increasingly tyrannical attitude to them, became progressively hard to bear. In 1845, Elizabeth was asked by the Leeds Ladies' Committee to write a poem in support of the Anti-Corn Law League, but her father began to 'murmur' his disapproval, and she was caught in a conflict of loyalties which was agonising: 'to refuse to give . . . a voice to a great public suffering, when I am asked to do it .. & when I recognize the existence of the suffering .. should THIS be refused? – Oh – I wd. not vex Papa for the world' (*MRM*: III, 73), she wrote in distress to Miss Mitford. In the end, the 39-year-old daughter obeyed her father, though she remembered, years later, with some bitterness, that 'Papa . . . wouldn't let me write for the anti-corn law association' (*Sister*: 119). But her fiercest arguments were with her brothers, who, as she put it, 'abused the League & laughed at the ladies' committee, & at the idea of my verses doing good at all, – a woman's verses!' (*MRM*: III, 75). The conventionality of her own brothers gave Elizabeth daily evidence of the prejudices readily adopted by men. 'The secret of the bearing of men towards women, let it be ever so much "made up of adorations" & the like, is just .. contempt' (*MRM*: III, 80), she raged, after another battle about poetry and the Corn Laws. Her own desire to write with the political 'breadth & scope which women want' encountered not only the sentimentality of the reviewers, but also the very real obstructions of her father's political displeasure on the one hand and her brothers' sexual 'contempt' on the other.

However, in the 1840s, she did write another overtly political poem: 'The Runaway Slave at Pilgrim's Point'. This, too, was a commission, and Elizabeth fulfilled it, perhaps significantly, only after she had secretly eloped from her father's house, in 1846. It was published in the Boston anti-slavery journal, *The Liberty Bell*, in 1848, and was subsequently reproduced as a pamphlet. The subject was not, however, one of merely philanthropical interest. Elizabeth's comments about her family's slave-owning past are few and bitter. To Robert she wrote, in 1845: 'I would give ten towns in Norfolk (if I had them) to own some purer lineage than that of the blood of the slave!' (*RB*: I, 333). On the other hand, her reserve did not stem from womanly reticence. In defence of Beecher Stowe, she wrote to a correspondent:

Oh, and is it possible that you think a woman has no business with questions like the question of slavery? Then she had better use a pen no more. She had better subside into slavery and concubinage herself, I think, as in the times of old, shut herself up with the Penelopes in the 'women's apartment'. (*Letters*: II, 110–11)

The relation between slavery and the condition of women lurks in her consciousness like a constant irritant to speech. Elizabeth's own escape from the family home in which, as she once put it, the children were often driven to the ' "vices of slaves" ' (*RB*: I, 169), was recent enough for the comparison to be in her mind. However, if an autobiographical impulse lies behind 'The Runaway Slave', which was written by a runaway daughter, the poem's anger and energy are also characteristically larger than any private grievances.

In some points, 'The Runaway Slave' recalls Hemans' poem, 'The Landing of the Pilgrim Fathers in New England'. Where Hemans, however, strings together an easy necklace of moral values, and then issues a loud clarion call to faith, Barrett Browning ends by putting even faith in doubt. Hemans concludes:

> Ay, call it holy ground,
>   The soil where first they trode.
> They have left unstain'd what there they found –
>   Freedom to worship God.
>   (*Works*: V, 282)

The first stanza of 'The Runaway Slave' similarly focuses on the 'Point' itself, but with a crucial difference:

> I stand on the mark beside the shore
>   Of the first white pilgrim's bended knee,
> Where exile turned to ancestor,
>   And God was thanked for liberty.
> I have run through the night, my skin is as dark,
> I bend my knee down on this mark:
>   I look on the sky and the sea.
>   (*CW*: III, 160–70, ll. 1–7)

This, by contrast, is firmly located in time and place, so that its abstract ideals, those of pilgrimage and 'liberty', are not presented as unassailable universals but as contingent ideas. Above all, they are contingent on a sense of time: both a narrative and a historical time, with a present and a past, and a feeling of the discrepancy between them: between 'God was thanked' and 'I bend my knee'. 'The Runaway Slave' is a dramatic monologue spoken by a black female slave who chooses the once 'holy ground' of the pilgrims' landing place on which to kneel – not in awe, to pray, but in anger, to curse. Between the two events of kneeling, history has intervened. It is this sense of history which, although it does not challenge the 'univocal' (Mermin, 1986: 76) nature of the self, none the less creates the external dramatic ironies of this poem. The suggestively condensed line 'Where exile turned to ancestor' itself contains the paradox of history in miniature: that, even as the Pilgrims landed, there was a subtle transformation and they became, no longer drifting outcasts but powerful originators of a new line. That word 'ancestor' contains a knot of familial and gender connotations which the poem will gradually untie. As in 'The Cry of the Children', the imagery sets up connections which are not simply poetic elaborations, but political complicities. The issue of power and lineage is deeply embedded in the very metaphors of this poem which, when she sent it off, Elizabeth wondered if it were 'too ferocious, perhaps, for the Americans to publish' (*Boyd*: 283).

The slave herself has reached the 'Point' of freedom, ironically, out of terror of the very representatives of freedom:

> O pilgrims, I have gasped and run
> All night long from the whips of one
> Who in your names works sin and woe!
> (12–14)

Unlike Hemans, whose moral positions are shining clear, Barrett Browning introduces this confusion: pilgrims who prayed have become ones who whip, nameless wanderers have bequeathed powerful names. The ideal of liberty has thus given way to tyranny, not fortuitously in the course of time, but by a direct lineage: 'in your names'. This is a poem which is almost entirely free of sentimentality because, for all its emotional rhetoric, it holds nothing sacred. Democracy, religious liberty, family ancestry and even mother love cannot be kept, to use Hemans' word, 'unstain'd'. Barrett Browning's great insight, which Hemans lacks, is that a morality of good and evil cannot be separated from the realisation of that morality in human history. The relativity of the speaking voice thus becomes a means of asserting a relativity of moral values which no authorial voice oversees. Thus the slave, like the children, extends her challenge beyond her immediate persecutors:

> I am black, I am black,
>   And yet God made me, they say:
> But if He did so, smiling back
>   He must have cast His work away
> Under the feet of His white creatures,

> With a look of scorn, that the dusky features
> Might be trodden again to clay.
>
> (22–8)

Like the factory children who project a universe of turning wheels, the black slave projects a universe of segregation from its beginnings. The white God is complicit with the other half of his creation. The slave, who has seen her black lover killed, who has, herself, been flogged and raped, points, with persuasive logic, to those interlocking systems of religious belief, racial authority and simple brute force, which seem to make up the rationale of her pain. The image of male power treading underfoot a weaker creature is a leitmotif of Barrett Browning's poetry which acquires far-reaching, invariably gender-specific connotations by the end of her career. Here, the creator God allows a whole race, in a reverse creation, to 'be trodden again to clay'. Meanwhile, the slave's point of view projects an extended apartheid of the imagination, back to the origins of creation and forwards to the end of time. Such an apparently God-given system, a colour imagery from which nothing, not even the colour of the earth's 'clay', goes free, reproduces the very net of ideology against which the poem itself is written.

The slave's rejection of this system then extends to the most sacrosanct relationship in the Victorian domestic church:

> My own, own child! I could not bear
> To look in his face, it was so white;
> I covered him up with a kerchief there,
> I covered his face in close and tight:
> And he moaned and struggled, as well might be,
> For the white child wanted his liberty –
> Ha, ha! he wanted the master-right.
>
> (120–6)

The English reading public, which objected to the references to prostitutes in *Aurora Leigh* and to the adulterous passions in 'Lord Walter's Wife', seems not to have been troubled by the murder, rape and infanticide of 'The Runaway Slave'. Certainly, Barrett Browning describes the killing of the child with a forbearing impartiality which, while reflecting the exhausted meticulousness of the mother, has the effect of naturalising the act in the reader's consciousness. But this is exactly the point. The slave's terrible mother-right to kill is never morally questioned. What is more, the reasons given for the act are not 'personal and passionate' but coolly political; this is not a *crime passionnel*, understandable and forgivable, but an outcome which has behind it the perfect logic both of historical reality and of the imagination's by now endemic colour codes: 'the white child wanted his liberty'. The word 'liberty', too, is ripe with so many connotations of whiteness, masculinity and racial superiority that the irony is almost lost. Just as 'exile turned to ancestor' so 'liberty' turns to 'master-right'. All values, in this poem, shift from one meaning to another, from good to evil. Ultimately the slave kills her child, not out of love, hate or despair, but in order to break the natural line of mastership he represents. Barrett Browning, like Toni Morrison, refuses to make even motherhood the saving ideal in a corrupt legacy.

Having smothered her infant, the slave then imagines a scene of immortality which is fantastically ironic and strange:

> But *my* fruit . . . ha, ha! – there, had been
>   (I laugh to think on't at this hour!)
> Your fine white angels (who have seen
>   Nearest the secret of God's power)
> And plucked my fruit to make them wine,
> And sucked the soul of that child of mine
>   As the humming-bird sucks the soul of the flower.
>   (155–61)

This cartoon of the afterlife as a banquet of angels sucking new wine is still riddled with the colour scheme of the whole poem. These are, the slave scornfully points out to the reader, '*Your* fine white angels' and this God has a secret 'power' all too similar to the dreaded 'master-right'. Capricious and cruel, God and his angels reproduce the caprices of power on earth; they too are thirsty for blood, however much sweetened into heavenly metaphors of 'wine'. Meanwhile, however, the slave has achieved her purpose of depriving the child of his badge of control: the white skin has become blood-red and the 'white child's spirit' (163) has left a 'dark child in the dark!' (186).

'The Runaway Slave' thus posits a stark choice: morality is either universal and totalitarian or it is historical and relative; it is either a matter of absolute black and white, fixed from the beginning, or it is a matter of white shading into black and one thing becoming another. As in 'The Cry of the Children', Barrett Browning imaginatively reproduces the first, setting up a linguistic equivalent of the grid of power which traps her speakers, in order to issue a silent plea for the second: for history rather than doctrinaire myth, even where that myth consists of her own Christian beliefs. Far from confirming the assumption, then, that 'Faith is woman-like, doubt is man-like' (Robertson, 1883: xiii), she confirms, in these political poems, that doubt is the condition of the poetic imagination and faith too often a colourful justification of suffering. She differs from Hemans in daring to doubt, not only the purity of the victim, 'exile turned to ancestor', and the benevolence of

God who seems to be 'smiling back', but also that there is any authority, either of heaven or of the heart, outside the social and historical systems of men. In these political poems she confronts sexuality, violence and power with few aesthetic sweeteners.

It was in her own home that Elizabeth experienced a system of male domination which threatened to confuse altogether her sense of personal and moral allegiance. In passionate defence of the figure who kept all his children effectively enslaved to his rule, she wrote to Robert:

> But what you do NOT see, what you *cannot* see, is the deep tender affection behind & below all those patriarchal ideas of governing grownup children 'in the way they *must* go!' – and there never was (under the strata) a truer affection in a father's heart.

She added, emphatically: 'The evil is in the system' (*RB*: I, 169). She knew, as well as Engels, that the 'system' of the Victorian family was to blame for its tendency to despotism and enslavement. Although her explanation of the psychology of domestic power has the ring of first-hand experience: 'after using one's children as one's chattels for a time, the children drop lower & lower toward the level of the chattels, & the duties of human sympathy to them become difficult in proportion' (*RB*: I, 514), this too is part of a social system in which 'parental rights' are in a line of power from the 'divine right' of 'the Kings of Christendom' (*RB*: I, 169). In her letters as in her poems, Barrett Browning tracks down the connections.

At the same time, she does not avoid the contradictions. After all, even the patriarchal Mr Barrett was capable of 'a deep, tender affection', while Robert, who was apparently the most tender of men, had to be rebuked for his unthinking chauvinism: 'why how can you, who are *just*, *blame women*', she exclaimed, 'when you must know what the "system" of man is towards them' (*RB*: I, 341). The ' "system" of man', whether of Gods, fathers, masters or even lovers, underlies and corrects the sentimental, idealistic tendencies of her work, and it does so, in *Aurora Leigh* as elsewhere, through a 'system' of imagery which itself, subtly and subtextually, reproduces an alliance of corrupt and insidiously connected (male) powers. Even the story of romance and love is not exempt from this overshadowing reality.

POETRY AND POLITICS: A DOUBLE VISION

'*Marriage in the abstract*', Elizabeth wrote in 1846, when she was contemplating marriage in actuality, 'has always seemed to me the most profoundly indecent of all ideas' (*MRM*: III, 160). She could be as scornful on the subject as the notorious anti-matrimonialist, George Sand. A dream recorded in her *Diary* when she was 25 suggests a temperamental aversion as well: 'I dreamt last night that I was married, just married; & in an agony to [procure] a dissolution of the engagement' (*Diary*: 111). Years later, when she read *In Memoriam*, she wished away 'the marriage hymn at the end' (*MRM*: III, 318). Throughout her life she held to the opinion that 'marriage is more necessary for a man than a woman' (*MRM*: III, 394; *Sister*: 71) and, in Rome in 1853, she was intrigued by the 'house of what I call emancipated women' (*Sister*: 196), consisting of the sculptress Harriet Hosmer and the novelist and translator of George Sand, Matilda Hays. In the years which followed her own marriage, Barrett Browning wrote her epic novel poem about two unmarried women: Aurora the poet and Marian Erle the fallen woman. The delayed 'sistering' of the two is a powerful emotional event in the text (see Rosenblum, 1983; Leighton, 1986: 141–57), and points to an alternative love story, full of pastoral images of flowers and animals by comparison with which Romney's marital cravings seem obsessively money-minded. None the less, it is this sense of money and power, everywhere underlying the romance story of *Aurora Leigh*, which represents Barrett Browning's emancipation from that 'superabundance of sensibility' (*Corr*: I, 354) in her precedessors.

After the wreath crowning in Book II, Romney adds to his many criticisms of Aurora's poetry the final insult of a marriage proposal. He reminds her that, if she marries him, she will legitimately inherit her part of the family fortune which her father had forfeited by marrying an Italian. Legally, of course, she would still not inherit her money because the first Married Women's Property Act, for which Elizabeth herself collected signatures in Paris and which, according to Mary Howitt, was spoken of 'as the petition of Elizabeth Barrett Browning, Anna Jameson, Mary Howitt, Mrs. Gaskell' (1889: II, 116), had not yet been passed. The language of Aurora's refusal clearly brings out the connection between the terms of Romney's proposal and his economic power:

> 'At least
> My soul is not a pauper; I can live
> At least my soul's life, without alms from men . . .'
> (II, 680–2)

The sense of that money, which ought also to be her own, if it were not for the 'master-right' of English inheritance laws, gives Romney's love a buying quality which irks Aurora:

> If I married him,
> I should not dare to call my soul my own
> Which so he had bought and paid for . . .
>
> (II, 785–7)

George Eliot, who read *Aurora Leigh* at least three times and felt a deep 'sense of communion' (1954–78: II, 342) with its author, puts many of Aurora's arguments against marriage into the mouth of her own artist heroine, the opera singer, Armgart:

> I will not be
> A pensioner in marriage. Sacraments
> Are not to feed the paupers of the world.
> If he were generous – I am generous too.
>
> (1989: 140–1)

Marriage, for women, is a state of sentimental pauperism, of continuing gratitude to the charity of men. Both Aurora and Armgart reject the offer of security which is, in fact, a kind of blackmail, though it is interesting that, while Aurora holds out to the end and gets both fame and money of her own, Armgart's pride and power are broken and she accepts, after the loss of her voice, an almost Hemansesque fate of humble usefulness, teaching music in a small town. George Eliot punishes, not her heroes but her heroines, in an anxious swerve away from the female triumphalism of Barrett Browning's poem.

In the parallel garden scene at the end of *Aurora Leigh* there is a curious repetition of this exchange. Romney arrives in Florence and tries to make amends to Marian Erle by once again proposing marriage. The episode is one of those narrative doublings which run through the poem and seem intended to decentre the status of the romance. Romney, in the course of the poem, makes four proposals, two to each of the heroines. Whether this is narrative clumsiness or emotional realism, it is certainly quite different from the simple high peaks of individual faithfulness or betrayal in Hemans and L.E.L. Furthermore, the guilt which evidently motivates Romney's second proposal to Marian suggests another slippage or doubling: between himself and her unknown rapist. In terms of the plot, Romney can have no responsibility for Marian's escape and rape; it was she, after all, who left him on the wedding day. However, his offer of marriage at the end is riddled with subconscious self-justification. Her answer, like Aurora's in Book II, resoundingly exposes and rejects the system of values which underpins his somewhat dubious good intentions. 'Here's a hand shall keep / For ever clean without a marriage-ring' (IX, 431–2), she tells him. Even though Romney is now property-less and blind, he can still make moral and emotional beggars of women. With the offer of '"a marriage-ring"', he can seem to purchase moral cleanness for both himself and Marian, though neither seems to have committed any sin. Her refusal typically rejects the short-cut of his reasoning: he is responsible neither for her fall nor for her rehabilitation. Above all, the etiquette of a marriage-ring is shown up as a form of male power which, even without money to justify it, assumes the pauperising generosity of the powerful and the moneyed.

Romney's sexual assumption of power is thus even more deep-rooted than his actual economic status. In one place near the beginning, Aurora mimics the terms of his proposal. He might as well have said outright:

> 'Come, sweep my barns and keep my hospitals,
> And I will pay thee with a current coin
> Which men give women.'
>
> (II, 539–41)

The '"current coin"' is, politely, marriage. But the bareness of the phrase '"Which men give women"' loudly hints at the thing which is not always given within marriage:

> 'What, what, . . . being beaten down
> By hoofs of maddened oxen into a ditch,
> Half-dead, whole mangled, when a girl at last
> Breathes, sees . . . and finds there, bedded in her flesh
> Because of the extremity of the shock,
> Some coin of price! . . .'
>
> (VI, 676–81)

Marian's angry, articulate description of her rape uses an image of violence which recurs throughout Barrett Browning's work. Male power, whether of gods or men, is very often described as an animal trampling, and thus, even where it is meant as an attitude of mind, it develops the potently physical connotations of rape. It is interesting that, in one of her outbursts against the odious Mr Hunter, Elizabeth explains his constant reproofs of her as 'a sort of masculine rampancy which wd. have a woman under the feet of a man' (*MRM*: III, 85). In *Aurora Leigh*, the classical gods are invoked, as Dorothy Mermin (1989: 211) has shown, as figures both of rape and inspiration. Danaë, in Vincent Carrington's picture, is 'Half blotted out of nature' (III, 132) by the golden rain of Jove. In 'The Runaway Slave' even the Christian God himself seemed to condone the treading down 'to clay' of a whole race. Individual acts of violence are thus associated with the idea of masculinity itself.

Marian Erle points to this larger system of exploitation, when, in a speech which already repudiates the '"marriage-ring"' of the moral law, she asserts her mother-rights according to the other prevailing law of brute power:

> 'Mine, mine,' she said. 'I have as sure a right
> As any glad proud mother in the world,
> Who sets her darling down to cut his teeth
> Upon her church-ring. If she talks of law,
> I talk of law! I claim my mother-dues
> By law, – the law which now is paramount, –
> The common law, by which the poor and weak
> Are trodden underfoot by vicious men,
> And loathed for ever after by the good.'
>
> (VI, 661–9)

Her self-defence consists in making a deliberate connection between the church law of marriage and, punningly, the '"common law"' of oppression, between legalisation of motherhood in a '"church-ring"' and legalisation of poverty in an established system. As '"law"' thus comes to seem, throughout the passage (as well as throughout the poem), less of a moral absolute and more of a social commodity affordable by the rich, the very nature of what is lawful and unlawful blurs. According to the common law of power, 'masculine rampancy' prevails. Thus Marian's own rape, '"being beaten down / By hoofs of maddened oxen into a ditch"', is equated with this more general beating '"underfoot"' of a whole class of '"the poor and weak"'. Barrett Browning's occasional tendency to portray Marian Erle as a sublime Madonna (Kaplan, 1978: 25) is counteracted by this secularising and socialising connectiveness in her imagery. Rape is part of a system of law which has little to do with wedding rings, but which does have something to do with class, power and specifically with '"men"'.

Marian's rape thus gathers a cluster of images of violence, masculinity and money, which send small shocks in many directions through the poem. But it is above all the image of the coin which conveys the social as well as physical reality of the rape itself:

> 'and finds there, bedded in her flesh
> Because of the extremity of the shock,
> Some coin of price! . . .'

This last phrase brilliantly slides away from the expected biblical 'pearl of price', which is the more conventional conclusion. Instead, the image of the coin keeps its reference to the market – literally, the market of prostitution or, figuratively, of sexuality in general – and refuses the usual Christian argument that the purity of the child 'pays for' the sin of the mother. Hester Prynne's child, Pearl, in *The Scarlet Letter* (Hawthorne, 1850),

106

which Barrett Browning had probably recently read, is a 'pearl of price'. This '"coin of price"', however, keeps its stark connotations of the actual (unpaid) prostitution Marian has experienced: '"it shall pay you for the loss"' (VI, 684), she imagines a good man saying. Barrett Browning's 'coined' phrase seems to drive the sexual and monetary argument home, as it were – literally into the woman's flesh – while keeping the hard, unmetaphorical, unchanged meaning of the coin awkwardly and harshly present. '"Some coin of price"', far from being a polite circumlocution, insists on the physical facts of conception, and resists transformation of those facts into moral or emotional compensations. It is, unambiguously, still '"bedded in her flesh"'.

However, yet another meaning can be heard here. The coin recalls, at a distance of several books, the terms of Romney's proposal to Aurora. The narrative doubling between Aurora and Marian, which the plot repeatedly exploits, is emphasised by this imagery. Aurora is offered the '"current coin"' of marriage; Marian gets a crueller '"coin of price"'. But both actions are represented, if subconsciously, as parts of a monetary transaction – a paying for or a paying off – in which both women are victims. Everywhere in this poem sexual relations, whether kind or violent, the aristocrat's or the rapist's, are part of a larger and interrelated economics of power. The Danaë myth, in which the raping god appears in the form of money itself, provides an association deeply and guiltily embedded in the Victorian subconscious. In *Aurora Leigh* the meaning of the 'coin' can be tracked down, through all its social ramifications, in race, class, family and birthright, to the lowest denominator of what '"men give women"'.

Thus symbolising all the other economic legacies in the poem (and there are many), the coin traffics freely between the love story and the rape story, between romance and sexual power, between literary metaphor and social fact. It deliberately breaks down the differences between them. In the poem's market exchange of meaning, it shifts from one signification to another, thus introducing a relativity of meanings which cannot easily be separated out into good and bad, pure and impure, protected and unprotected. But these shifts are not gratuituous or purely playful. Rather, they are part of a larger story, a larger system of violence and money, which shadows the emotional and poetic progress of Aurora's creative self-realisation. That self-financed journey to Italy, unlike the aristocratic, self-advertising tourism of Corinne, ultimately leads towards an art which disproves Romney's criticisms, and shows the poet's capacity to write a love story whose '"personal pang"' is everywhere connected, through a mesh of images, to the impersonal reality of '"the world-full woe"'. Aurora's romance, unlike that of her performing predecessors, is tainted through and through by this 'coin' of socialisation which goes to 'the heart' (or even more literal organ) of love. *Aurora Leigh* is the epic of the woman poet who finds love, not in unique and tragic isolation on a cliff, but in the dust of the real world where it is rarely clean of double standards, power, crime and suffering.

For all her faults, Barrett Browning has succeeded in this poem in turning the woman's lyre of private feeling into an instrument of public conscience, and her improvised epithets of the body into a sexual complexity of desire which denies neither the claims of the body nor the claims of the work of art. All the poured, burning hearts of Hemans and L.E.L., which flowed from them so easily, are transformed by her, in a famous passage in Book V, into a statement of her own distinctive aesthetics: into a lava-flow which is not fluent and univocal, but awkward and 'double' in its commitment both to 'song' and to 'true life', as well as to the differences between them:

> Never flinch,
> But still, unscrupulously epic, catch
> Upon the burning lava of a song
> The full-veined, heaving, double-breasted Age:
> That, when the next shall come, the men of that
> May touch the impress with reverent hand, and say
> 'Behold, – behold the paps we all have sucked!
> This bosom seems to beat still, or at least
> It sets ours beating: this is living art,
> Which thus presents and thus records true life.'
> (V, 213–22)

Yet it is true that, on the level of its plot, *Aurora Leigh* also plays out a struggle between politics and poetry in which poetry wins, hands down. Barrett Browning distrusted socialism, and Romney's socialistic experiments of setting up a 'phalanstery' in his ancestral home are made to look foolish. In 1848, in the midst of ferment and revolution on the continent, Elizabeth expressed her worries to Miss Mitford:

> As to communism, surely the practical part of *that* . . . is attainable simply by the consent of individuals .. who may try the experiment of associating their families in order to the cheaper employment of the means of life .. & successfully in many cases. But make a government-scheme of *even so much*, & you seem to trench on the individual liberty – All such patriarchal planning in a government, issues naturally into absolutism. (*MRM*: III, 235)

Such language suggests that memories of her own experience of the small patriarchy of Wimpole Street are still colouring her views (see David, 1987: 135). 'I love liberty so intensely that I hate Socialism' (*MRM*: III,

302), she writes elsewhere. But although she ultimately shows up Romney's socialistic experiments as another patriarchal scheme, her cherishing of individuality is not to the exclusion of the general good, but remains discrepantly and sceptically juxtaposed with it. In Book V, such a 'marriage' of perspectives becomes, explicitly, a poetic theory:

> But poets should
> Exert a double vision; should have eyes
> To see near things as comprehensively
> As if afar they took their point of sight,
> And distant things as intimately deep
> As if they touched them.
>
> (V, 183–8)

In Barrett Browning's best poems such a 'double vision' involves, not so much an easy equivalence of the near and far, the personal and the general, the poetic and the political, as a sense of the difference between them, of the stress and tension of making the two match.

It is in some of her Italian poems that this doubleness is most clearly confronted. G. K. Chesterton's was one of very few voices, either in her own time or since, to praise Barrett Browning's 'political poems' (1913: 179). Most critics dismissed them as intemperate and unwomanly. At a time when the *Sonnets from the Portuguese* were being universally lauded as the best of her poetry because, as Eric Robertson asserted: 'They are not primarily works of art; they are spontaneous expressions of strong feeling' (1883: 313), Chesterton dared to extol the unnatural, baroque exuberance of her verse, its 'audacity and luxuriance', and its 'hot wit' (1903: 57). But above all, he admired her poetry's cosmopolitan breadth. 'She is by far the most European of all the English poets of that age; all of them, even her own much greater husband, look local beside her' (1913: 178), he declared.

It was Italy which, not only fulfilled Elizabeth's personal need for liberty, but also gave her, during the 1840s and 50s, a living example of the political dimensions of that liberty. She was, much more than Robert, fascinated and tormented by the maddening internal conflicts of the Risorgimento. 'My interest in Italian politics has set me eating my heart lately' (*Sister*: 311), she wrote in 1859. Her poems about Italy are often racked and contorted works, both thematically and metrically, as if the problem of Italy, instead of being an opportunity to harp on the song of woman's creativity, confronted her with the grotesque facts of real, unaesthetic suffering. In 'Mother and Poet' (1862), for instance, the speaker specifically refuses the Corinne-like role of writing a triumphal poem for a liberated Italy, because, as a mother, she has known the personal cost of liberation:

> Dead! One of them shot by the sea in the east,
> And one of them shot in the west by the sea.
> Both! both my boys! If in keeping the feast
> You want a great song for your Italy free,
> Let none look at *me*!
>   (*CW*: VI, 71–6, ll. 96–100)

The very title of the poem opens up that 'double vision', that stress of the political on the personal, which lies at the heart of so much of Barrett Browning's work. Out of the emotional refusal of the 'mother', the political poem of the 'poet' is written, but written differently from the easily improvised 'great song' of liberation.

It is in *Casa Guidi Windows* (1851) that Barrett Browning offers the most extended meditation on Italy, as a poetic image on the one hand and as a contemporary reality on the other, as both myth and history. It is not one of her best works, but its rough energy and forthrightness, its cosmopolitan vision and its grappling concern with certain large questions about poetry make it, in many ways, a summing up of lifelong preoccupations. It is also a retrospective commentary on the tradition of Italianate heroines, who sang and died with neo-classical decorum in a place which was entirely invented by the imagination. By contrast, Barrett Browning's Italy exists *outside* her windows.

In one passage near the start, the poet brings together her long developed distrust of the sentimental mode, her repudiation of images of mournful femininity and her increasing awareness of the difficult relation between poetic beauty and political reality:

> Then I thought, musing, of the innumerous
>   Sweet songs which still for Italy outrang
> From older singers' lips who sang not thus
>   Exultingly and purely, yet, with pang
> Fast sheathed in music, touched the heart of us
>   So finely that the pity scarcely pained.
> I thought how Filicaja led on others,
>   Bewailers for their Italy enchained,
> And how they called her childless among mothers,
>   Widow of empires, ay, and scarce refrained
> Cursing her beauty to her face, as brothers
>   Might a shamed sister's, – 'Had she been less fair
> She were less wretched;' – how, evoking so
>   From congregated wrong and heaped despair
> Of men and women writhing under blow,
>   Harrowed and hideous in a filthy lair,
> Some personating Image wherein woe
>   Was wrapt in beauty from offending much,
> They called it Cybele, or Niobe,
>   Or laid it corpse-like on a bier for such,

Where all the world might drop for Italy
Those cadenced tears which burn not where they touch, –
. . .
Of such songs enough,
Too many of such complaints! behold, instead,
Void at Verona, Juliet's marble trough:
As void as that is, are all images
Men set between themselves and actual wrong,
To catch the weight of pity, meet the stress
Of conscience, – since 'tis easier to gaze long
On mournful masks and sad effigies
Than on real, live, weak creatures crushed by strong.
(*CW*: III, 249–313, ll. 14–35, 40–8)

The poet, here, sets herself against old myths of Italy as a childless mother, a fallen sister or a dead Juliet, picturesque, sexualised and passively ineffectual, and argues, instead, for the brutal, miserable facts of contemporary history: of 'real, live, weak creatures crushed by strong'. Throughout the passage runs a deep distrust of beauty as a gloss for suffering: a distrust of 'music' which hides the 'pang', of 'cadenced tears' which do not 'burn', of the 'personating Image' which conceals offence, of poetry which soothes instead of stirring 'conscience'. Poets, both male and female, have found it convenient to depict Italy as a mythical woman, moralising its plight 'as brothers / Might a shamed sister's'. But while 'Cybele' and 'Niobe' are fine, allegorical images, suitable for statues and sad pictures, they are not real women, with real histories and griefs. The 'personating Image' is an abstract falsification of the individual facts; of what de Beauvoir champions as 'the dispersed, contingent, and multiple existences of actual women' in opposition to the mythical monolith of 'Woman' (1972: 283). Barrett Browning champions the same multiplicity in her 'men and women writhing under blow, / Harrowed and hideous in a filthy lair'. To give offence, even poetic offence (as in some of these strained metres), in the cause of truth, was always one of her aims. Poetry without the 'stress' both of conscience and of contemporary reality is a mere conventionalism of speech, as stiff and ineffectual as funerary statues in a garden.

Casa Guidi Windows is thus a poem which forcefully rejects the lyricism and narcissistic sensibility of the 'older singers', especially, perhaps, the older female singers who turned themselves into artistic spectacles for all to admire and mourn. In place of the old picturesque mode, which was always closely connected with an equally picturesque myth of Italy, Barrett Browning argues for a poetry which puts reality before sensibility, facts before poeticisms, 'since 'tis easier to gaze long / On mournful masks and sad effigies / Than on real, live, weak creatures crushed by strong'. The metre is audibly 'overcrowded' by this jostling

111

of 'creatures' from real life, whose sheer numbers seem to put the rhythm out. In the end, Barrett Browning's best poems are not those which simply protest their politics, but those which keep their 'double vision', their sense of counterpoint between beauty and reality, love and power, to the fore. The Italy which Elizabeth had longed for years to see, 'Am I never never to see Italy with my eyes?' (*MRM*: II, 345), and which Aurora has heard 'crying through [her] life' (V, 1194), provides her, in the end, not with a poetic myth of crowning success, but with a political reality which makes the 'cadenced tears' of older poets seem far too decorous and tidy.

It was at the very end of her life that Barrett Browning wrote the poem which, allegorically, sums up the contradiction of her vision. 'A Musical Instrument' was written in 1860, but its inspiration comes from far back in the poet's career. Almost twenty years before, Elizabeth had written to Miss Mitford about a poem called 'The Dead Pan' (1844) which was composed, she explained, to counter Schiller's 'eloquent Lament for the Gods of Greece & the ancient mythology'. Schiller's highly influential poem 'The Gods of Greece' had recently been 'paraphrased' (*MRM*: II, 205) in Lady Blessington's *Keepsake*. First published in 1788, its message inspired the Romantic movement's great revival of the classical gods as an alternative, more imaginative creed to the truths of Christianity. As Shelley complained in *Hellas*:

> Apollo, Pan and Love,
> And even Olympian Jove
> Grew weak, for killing truth had glared on them;
> Our hills and seas and streams,
> Dispeopled of their dreams . . .
> (1970: 446–82, ll. 232–6)

For the Romantics, Pan was the dreamy, unseen spirit of 'all' nature, who was especially associated with a soporific noon-time atmosphere of sensual desire. To the end of the century, the afterglow of the lost gods of Greece seemed to cast into hard relief the 'killing truth' of the pale Galilean.

In contrast to Schiller and Shelley, however, the young Barrett Browning declared her opposite allegiance: '*I* . . . think the false Gods well gone, & stand up for that best Beauty which is in Truth' (*MRM*: II, 205). In the poem itself, she challenges nostalgic expressions of beauty which are nothing but weeping at an 'antique funeral' (*CW*: III, 147–58, l. 223); and advises that poets should align themselves with the one true God of contemporary history. Yet, in its attempt to propound a creed of poetry which is identical with the truth of Christianity: 'God Himself is

112

the best Poet, / And the Real is His Song' (248–9), 'The Dead Pan' falls altogether dead as a poem.

Pan, however, did not die in Barrett Browning's imagination, but lurked there, making furtive appearances in *Aurora Leigh* (V, 1115–19), and eventually returning, like the repressed, in 'A Musical Instrument', which was published in the *Cornhill* in 1861. This, which indeed has the air of being a 'final statement about the nature of poetic creativity' (Mermin, 1989: 242), is also one of Barrett Browning's most deceptive poems. In 1928, Osbert Burdett greeted it enthusiastically, as marking a 'sudden return from the horizon to the sanctuary of [the poet's] heart, from political to personal sympathies' (1928: 271). Such an explanation, needless to say, has much more to do with the critic's own faith in the 'sanctuary' of the woman's 'heart' than with anything in the poem. Pan, far from being an object of 'personal sympathies', is, as Mermin, like Feit Diehl (1978), has forcefully argued, a figure for that 'sexual violation' which seems to lie 'in a well of silence' (1989: 242) deep within many of Barrett Browning's poems. Without repudiating this gendered interpretation, however, I would overlay it with another: 'A Musical Instrument' is also about that 'double vision' which Barrett Browning spent a lifetime developing, and which remains her most distinctive contribution to the tradition of women's poetry in the nineteenth century.

From the start, Pan is presented, not as some haunting, melancholy spirit of the place, but as a robust, rampant demi-god of sexual and creative pleasure (Merivale, 1969: 83). He is described with a literal-minded relish which counters both Schiller's nostalgia and all the subsequent *Götterdämmerung* of the Romantics. This is a Victorian Pan – a brutal despoiler of the countryside rather than an intensified spirit of it:

> What was he doing, the great god Pan,
>   Down in the reeds by the river?
> Spreading ruin and scattering ban,
> Splashing and paddling with hoofs of a goat,
> And breaking the golden lilies afloat
>   With the dragon-fly on the river.
>   (*CW*: VI, 44–5, ll. 1–6)

What Pan is usually doing is well known. His 'Splashing and paddling with hoofs of a goat' is reminiscent of all those other images of trampling masculine violence in Barrett Browning's work. The clumsy energy of his sexual opportunism causes havoc and destruction all round, and thus expresses something of the sheer obscenity of the original Greek god. However, this is a poem about poetry rather than about gods. It re-tells the story of Pan making his pan-pipes as an allegory of the making of a poem. In Ovid's story, the god's rapacious pursuit forces the nymph Syrinx into a reed to escape his clutches. The echo of that story is embedded in the poem like an unforgotten, though unwritten, female signature, which Barrett Browning herself underwrites. However, there has been a time lag between Ovid's story and the poem – a time lag which will become crucial to the poem's final meaning. 'A Musical Instrument' begins, in true Victorian spirit, somehow long after reeds were nymphs.

Thus, having desolated the pastoral scene, Pan plucks a single, nameless reed among many and starts to make his pipes. Immediately, a contradictory note of regret and pain enters the poem:

> He cut it short, did the great god Pan,
> (How tall it stood in the river!)
> Then drew the pith, like the heart of a man,
> Steadily from the outside ring,
> And notched the poor dry empty thing
> In holes, as he sat by the river.
>
> (19–24)

Pan's craftsmanship is described in meticulous, literal detail: it is a cutting, drawing, notching. But the figurative double-meanings of these actions are also quietly elicited at the same time. Thus 'He cut it short' suggests both actual length and length of life; 'How tall it stood' suggests both height and pride. This duplicity of reference is driven home in the startling, culminating line: 'Then drew the pith, like the heart of a man'. The sense in which it is 'like' remains disturbingly, pivotally ambiguous. On the one hand, this suggestion of a generic, human 'heart' in the reed silently recalls the story of Syrinx, of some earlier life which is being destroyed again. But on the other hand, to 'draw the heart out' also means simply to give inexpressible delight. As in so much of the poem, the literal and figurative senses, though forced together, remain at odds. The one involves pain, the other pleasure; the one involves cost, the other mere play. The two are not easy either to separate or to reconcile, but their double purpose is the theme and meaning of the poem. Thus, just as the reed is briskly reduced to a 'poor dry empty thing', to a purely 'instrumental' object, the language remembers its other life, its 'heart'. In this brilliant double figure, Barrett Browning brings together the two poles of her own difficult aesthetic of poetry: the heartless and the heartfelt. In a single stroke, she both acknowledges the sensibility of the reed – it (or perhaps she) *has* a heart – and also draws it out – leaving only the 'hard & cold thing' of which strong poems are made. To draw out the heart develops, in relation to Barrett Browning's whole literary inheritance, a profoundly important and secretly gleeful meaning.

Pan, certainly, shows no compunction. True to the spirit of the old gods, he laughs:

> 'This is the way,' laughed the great god Pan
>   (Laughed while he sat by the river),
> 'The only way, since gods began
> To make sweet music, they could succeed.'
> Then, dropping his mouth to a hole in the reed,
>   He blew in power by the river.
>
>   (25–30)

Although the poem enacts, with 'excoriating' detail, the death of the reed, it does so against the sound of this careless laughter. The contradiction is a sharp one. Certainly, as Feit Diehl points out, we have only Pan's words for it that this is 'the way' (*Signs*, 3(1978), 585). She herself suggests that there is another, kinder, female way of making music. But this is to import a morality which is foreign to the whole tone of the poem. That tone is irresponsible, free, careless. The sheer, reckless *jouissance* of Pan is a figure for the passions of the imagination, which are anarchic, amoral and yet 'sweet' in spite of all. Out of the literalness of pain, the poem makes an aesthetic of pleasure. Pan laughs because he is able to 'draw out the heart' of any listener to his music.

The sound of that music is then caught in the sound of the poem itself:

> Sweet, sweet, sweet, O Pan!
>   Piercing sweet by the river!
> Blinding sweet, O great god Pan!
> The sun on the hill forgot to die,
> And the lilies revived, and the dragon-fly
>   Came back to dream on the river.
>
>   (31–6)

'Sweet, sweet, sweet' are the first three notes Pan plays. What the poem makes is what it is. In this witty self-reference, the sweetness becomes tangible and self-sufficient; sweet is its own sound, almost. The poem achieves its condition of music by forgoing its responsibility towards reference. 'Sweet, sweet, sweet' is almost pure note, pure 'play'. Such sweetness seems removed from all the clumsy, intemperate, murderous intentions of its maker and from all the lurking disquiet of the poem's buried myth. It is as if Barrett Browning has found a figure for a purely self-rejoicing, self-justifying aestheticism.

However, she is not a *pure* aesthete, and even within this triumphantly celebratory stanza the language seems mindful of something else. 'Piercing sweet' and 'Blinding sweet' are not quite harmless figures of speech. Like most of the figures in the poem, they keep a residual, literal reference to the human effect of Pan's actions. These dead metaphors inevitably start to live again in their proximity to that first, long-drawn-out torture of the reed, which was, after all, itself literally pierced. Like the action of drawing 'the heart of a man', there is a brutal precision about the terms of this aesthetic celebration, as if the effort of the poem were present in the very formal properties of its language. There is something outside form and laughter: a reference, a memory, a 'heart', perhaps, which stops the play of music being simply playful, simply its own end and aim. As Barthes temptingly puts it: 'Writing' is a 'compromise between freedom and remembrance' (1967: 22). Unlike Pan, this poem everywhere remembers the cost of its own freedom. Although the effect of the music is beneficial and revivifying, it cannot save everything. Thus its sweetness is sharpened by the memory of one presence which will never live again: one reed will always be missing, though the lilies revive and the dragon-fly dreams on. At the 'heart' of this apparently careless aestheticism, this art for art's sake, there is a buried memory of pain.

It is this memory and underlying difference in things which the last stanza then eloquently preserves:

> Yet half a beast is the great god Pan,
>   To laugh as he sits by the river,
> Making a poet out of a man:
> The true gods sigh for the cost and pain, –
> For the reed which grows nevermore again
>   As a reed with the reeds in the river.
>   (37–42)

Here, figurative and literal again jostle for attention, as Barrett Browning accuses the 'great god Pan' of being 'half a beast . . . To laugh'. Pan's own double nature of god and beast splits the very meaning of the poem in two: into the creative and the callous. At this point, the poem draws back from his irresponsible, dionysiac pleasure. Such music has indeed seemed free of any moral, ideological or human reference. However, in contrast to Pan, 'the true gods sigh', and their appearance at the end of the poem suddenly swings it into another key. Certainly, these 'true gods' are puzzling. It may be that they represent the Olympians, in opposition to the half-bestial Pan. But if so, it is hard to credit Jove and his company with being particularly considerate of human pain. It may be that they are a variant of the opposition in 'The Dead Pan', between the false gods and the true One – who bore 'the cost and pain' of humanity and found little to laugh about. However, not only does it seem unlikely that Barrett Browning would thus pluralise the God in whom she believed, but also it is clear that, although the 'true gods sigh', they cannot remedy the death of the reed or stop the laughter and the sweet music. Their sighing is ineffectual, though essential. In the end, it is Pan's music and his laughter, not their sighing, which restore the scene to its original beauty, and bring back that suggestively hovering, allegorically uncertain dragon-fly.

What the 'true gods' seem to introduce at the end is the idea of memory. They remember something, across a lapse of time, which Pan has carelessly forgotten or never cared about, but which the poem, until now, has half-remembered and half-repressed. Barrett Browning is finally offering a description of creativity as 'double vision' once again: as heartless laughing and heartfelt sighing, as false and true, artful and conscience-stricken. In this scheme, Pan is the fiction-maker, the creator of substitutions, transformations, music. He cares only for that. By contrast, the 'true gods' are the poem's guilty memory of the natural or social world of suffering. They 'sigh' for what went before: for the reed, the nymph, the woman; for that which the fiction substituted, but also that without which it would have had no 'heart'. These 'true gods', then, are the literalists of the imagination, its ideologists and its historians. They are faithful to the ordinary, local, unaesthetic facts: the reed which was a reed in the river. Without their memory of 'the cost and pain', Pan's play would be frivolous, just as without the poet's memory of the fate of the nymph, her poem would be frivolous.

Thus, at the end of her career, Barrett Browning celebrates an aesthetic which she has been developing throughout her life. It is an aesthetic which rejects the 'mournful effigies' of womanhood perpetuated by Hemans and L.E.L., and rejects, with them, an art of flowing 'cadenced tears' which never catch the 'stress / Of conscience'. Instead, she advocates a sweetness which keeps the contrary grain of truth – a truth which remembers, regrets and counts the cost. At its best, her poetry disproves the notion that the imagination is too doubting and anarchic a faculty for women, and shows that 'sweet music' is neither a matter of female sweet-naturedness nor of easy poeticalness, but of a 'double vision' which sets the false gods against the true, fiction against ideology, freedom against memory. This is her great advance on the merely heartfelt sensibility of her predecessors. In her own best verse, the 'hard & cold thing', whether of the sexual and political system outside, or of a willing, heartless instrumentality within, is what makes even the 'cost and pain' seem 'sweet'.

Christina Rossetti (1830–94)

> It is impossible to go on singing out-loud to one's one-stringed
> lyre. It is not in me, and therefore it will never come out of
> me, to turn to politics or philanthropy with Mrs. Browning:
> such many-sidedness I leave to a greater than I, and, having
> said my say, may well sit silent . . . at the worst, I suppose a
> few posthumous groans may be found amongst my
> remains. (*Letters*: 31)

In 1870, following a request from a publisher for some poems with a
social purpose, Christina Rossetti explained to her brother, Dante
Gabriel, that such writing was not for her. While Barrett Browning's
'greater' gifts might lend themselves to 'politics or philanthropy', her
own lyrical inspiration could not be urged into uncongenial themes or
unnatural activity. Her 'one-stringed lyre', like that of the singing
improvisatrice, is either spontaneously roused to music or else falls
silent. The very monotony which Barrett Browning criticised in L.E.L.
is embraced by Rossetti, half-apologetically and half-boastfully, as her
natural idiom. However, this picture of herself as a minor lyricist was
also calculated to appeal to Dante Gabriel, who habitually cautioned his
sister against Barrett Browning's unwomanly range and tone. Although
Rossetti only claims to sing 'out-loud', like any performing heroine of
love, there is a certain skittish irony about the whole passage, as she both
invokes and mocks her standing model of a singing poetess, and then
plays it out beyond the expected limit: her living tunes might turn to
'posthumous groans'.

In many ways, Rossetti's reputation as a poet has rested squarely on
this self-perpetuated image of the melancholy recluse and other-worldly

mystic – an image subtly reinforced, not only by the whole Sappho–Corinne myth, but also by Tennyson's two influential poems about inspired, dying women: 'Mariana' (1830) and 'The Lady of Shalott' (1842). Both Barrett Browning (*RB*: I, 87; 263) and Rossetti (*CP*: I, 143–5; II, 111) at some level identified themselves with these death-bound protagonists, while the comparison was a favourite one among critics: Barrett Browning was hailed as a 'veritable Lady of Shalott' (Stedman, 1887: 133) and Rossetti as the 'Mariana of Albany Street' (Lucas, 1966: 137). The problem with such models, however, is that they re-emphasise the sentimental suicidalism of women's poetry. After all, Barrett Browning was a Lady of Shalott who got out and lived, while Rossetti, though 'weary' for a lover in her poems, in life banished them all from her door.

Certainly Rossetti found it convenient, in her life and work, to adopt the role of a moated Mariana, permanently estranged from the living world around her. But the psychological and imaginative utility of this myth should not disguise the fact that she also lived her life at the hub of the emotional and artistic storms of the Pre-Raphaelites, and that she was probably in contact with more contemporary poets and artists than any other woman poet of the century. The paradox is deep-rooted. On the one hand, she embraced the pervasive myth of the woman poet as fitfully inspired, sincere and sad, and too sensitive for real life. On the other hand, she is the most calculatingly self-inventing and self-mythologising of poets, whose verse, far from being a 'one-stringed' tune of the heart, is full of obliquities, secrets and riddles. The story of her life is part of the baffling biography of her imaginative writing, with its anachronistic dramas of lost love, missed meetings and highly 'composed' despairs. With Rossetti, the myth of the lovelorn improvisatrice is both lived, outwardly, and disbelieved, inwardly, and the combination is the key to her startling originality and richness as a poet.

*   *   *

Christina Rossetti was the youngest of four children born to an immigrant Italian father and a mother of half Italian descent. Gabriele Rossetti was a poet, a revolutionary and free-thinking Catholic, who had fled into exile after the return of the Bourbons to Naples. Frances Mary Polidori, whom he met and married in England, was, by contrast, a strict high church Anglican who, after her husband's death, burned all remaining copies of his book on Platonic love because it threatened her faith. This mixture of anti-clerical radicalism on the father's side and passionate piety on the mother's seems to have combined with a Victorian sense of separate spheres to produce markedly divergent attitudes in the children. While Dante Gabriel adopted a medievalised aesthetic mysticism, which flowered into the sensual religiosity of the Pre-Raphaelite creed, and William became a free-thinker and confirmed agnostic, the daughters adopted the meticulously disciplined faith of their mother. Maria became a nun in the recently founded Anglican Sisterhood of All Saints, while Christina in some sense internalised the role of nun, living a life of punctilious religious exercises and resorting to religious scruples on each of the two occasions when she received a proposal of marriage. In 1850, she broke her engagement to the Pre-Raphaelite painter, James Collinson, when he decided, after some wavering, to become a Roman Catholic. Then, in 1866, she rejected the kindly, timid scholar, Charles Cayley, ostensibly because he appeared non-committal in faith. Without any acrimony between them, the women and men in the Rossetti household seem to have reproduced the main ideological division between the sexes in society at large: 'Faith is woman-like, doubt is man-like' (Robertson, 1883: xiii). Such a division also hints at a system of spiritual compensation by which the faith of women redeems the doubt of men. Interestingly, in 1890, the poet Edith Cooper (Michael Field) recorded in her journal the rumour that Christina Rossetti was 'striving to work out [Dante Gabriel's] redemption by prayer and denial', adding: 'She is bent on being Love's Martyr for his sake' (*WD*: 115–16). If true, Dante Gabriel's promiscuous and guilt-ridden life, his slowness to marry his model and mistress Lizzie Siddal and his partial responsibility for her suicide, his passions for other women and, in the end, his fatal addiction to chloral, must have weighed heavily on Christina's conscience. However, although she rejected love and marriage for herself and lived with her beloved mother for most of her life, the idea that she was naturally ascetic is not borne out by the facts.

Like Elizabeth Barrett, Christina was a precocious and fiery-tempered child. Far from showing the nun-like control she cultivated in later life, she was, William recalled, 'hardly less passionate than Gabriel' (W. M. Rossetti, 1904: 20). She herself recounted to a niece how: '"On one occasion, being rebuked by my dear Mother for some fault, I seized upon a pair of scissors, and ripped up my arm to vent my wrath."' She added: '"I have learnt since to control my feelings"' (in Packer, 1963: 10). Control is one of the keynotes of her poetry. Pretty, obstinate and passionate by nature, Christina was the focus of admiring attention in a home which, impoverished yet genteel, encouraged artistic expression and was, on the whole, liberal and tolerant. William recalls how, when 4 or 5 years old, Christina wrote her first two-line poem, which she dictated to her mother: '"Cecilia never went to school / Without her gladiator"' (1904: xlix). Such precision of metre and freakish wit are typical of her early verses. At 12 she wrote a mock-melancholy ballad called 'Rosalind' (1843), which energetically sends up the 'deceived maiden' theme of the annuals. A wife, whose husband has been kidnapped by pirates and taken off to sea, sits gazing, Ariadne-like, after him. Suddenly one of the pirates accuses her of betraying him and takes a brisk revenge:

> 'Now for the grief I suffered
> I'll compensated be' –
> He said; and hurled her husband
> Into the raging sea.
> (*CP*: III, 118–19, ll. 25–8)

The Rossetti children's favourite pastime of writing *bouts rimés* sonnets – sonnets composed, in competition, to prescribed end-rhymes – encouraged this quirky, satirical element in Christina's verse. In the short story, *Maude*, the heroine's contribution to a game of *bouts rimés* is typical of the poet's early style at this time:

> Some ladies dress in muslin full and white,
> Some gentlemen in cloth succinct and black;
> Some patronise a dog-cart, some a hack,
> Some think a painted clarence only right.
> Youth is not always such a pleasing sight,
> Witness a man with tassels on his back;
> Or woman in a great-coat like a sack
> Towering above her sex with horrid height.
> If all the world were water fit to drown
> There are some whom you would not teach to swim,
> Rather enjoying if you saw them sink;
> Certain old ladies dressed in girlish pink,
> With roses and geraniums on their gown: –
> Go to the Bason, poke them o'er the rim. –
> (III, 300–1, ll. 1–14)

The streak of caprice and violence in her imagination would never be altogether put under the 'control' of her increasingly exigent conscience.

However, at some point in her teens, Christina suffered a physical, emotional and religious crisis which profoundly changed her. A combination of real physical weakness, emotional melancholy and religious obsession produced her version of that invalidism which affected innumerable Victorian girls in their teens. It was at about this age, for instance, that Elizabeth Barrett, suffering from some unspecific nervous debilitation, became a self-confirmed invalid. Christina, for her part, 'determined never again to enter a theatre', she gave up playing chess because it made her 'too eager for a win' (W. M. Rossetti, 1904: lxvi) and she assiduously cultivated an attitude of self-mortification and self-denial which uncannily reproduced certain pervasive myths about womanhood itself. As William puts it: 'Her temperament and character, naturally warm and free, became "a fountain sealed"' (lxviii). Although Rossetti gives this trauma of self-denial a religious meaning in her short story *Maude*, much of her verse hints that it may also have been a form of imaginative self-protection. To be '"a fountain sealed"', as this image from her own poetry suggests, was to be able to keep the forces of feeling under such pressure of control that the tension remained extreme.

While this attitude of moribund patience was imaginatively productive, however, it should not be taken as the whole story of Christina's life. When Katharine Tynan first visited her in the 1880s, she 'expected to find her in trailing robes of soft, beautifully coloured material' and was 'somewhat taken aback' when she 'entered the room, wearing short serviceable skirts of an iron grey tweed and stout boots' (1913: 158). Tynan, already well versed in the myth of Rossetti as a saintly recluse, evidently expected to find a mixture of Millais' Mariana, 'trailing robes', and a dying ascetic. Christina was, in fact, not nearly so faint-hearted in life as in her poetic self-image. Nor was she as isolated from experience as legend suggested.

Twice, for instance, in 1851 and again in 1853, at a time when her father was dying and Dante Gabriel still studying at art school, Christina and her mother attempted to set up a school – to Christina's relief, unsuccessfully. The role of financially supporting others never fell to her. Twice in her life she went abroad. In 1861, she took a trip to Paris, Normandy and Jersey with her mother and William, and in 1865 the long-dreamed-of trip to Italy was realised, and the three went, through Paris and the San Gotthard, to Milan, Pavia and Verona. Interestingly, however, the Corinne-journey never became a source of self-advertising inspiration, though Christina's southern roots are everywhere felt in her poetry. In England, also, far from being moated at home, she was a frequent traveller, taking trips to Bath to visit her Aunt Polidori, to Hastings for her health, to Penkill Castle in Ayrshire to visit her friends the Bell Scotts, to Newcastle and Bristol to visit the poet Dora Greenwell. Though shy and reticent, Christina is recorded as having been present at many Pre-Raphaelite gatherings, once in '"Syrian dress"' (in Thomas, 1931: 63) for a party. The onset of Graves' disease when she was in her early forties – a disease which caused considerable disfigurement to her face and appearance – was undoubtedly one reason for her increasingly reclusive habits in later years. The sister who used to model for Dante Gabriel's pictures as the Virgin Mary lamented to him, with regret but also with self-irony, in 1881: 'If only my figure would shrink somewhat! For a fat poetess is incongruous especially when seated by [t]he grave of buried hope' (*Letters*: 95).

During her twenties and thirties Christina was in communication with a large number of fellow artists and intellectuals: Patmore, Richard Garnett, Burne-Jones, Swinburne, William and Jane Morris, 'Lewis Carroll', William Allingham, Gerard Manley Hopkins, Edmund Gosse, Arthur Symons, Whistler and Hall Caine (Thomas, 1931: 61–2), for instance. Among many women friends and acquaintances, she counted the poets Jean Ingelow, Dora Greenwell, Adelaide Procter, Augusta Webster and Katharine Tynan. Nor was she altogether oblivious to the calls of 'politics or philanthropy'. In 1854, the year her father died, Christina applied to go to the Crimea with Florence Nightingale, but was rejected as too young. She wrote for Emily Faithfull's *Victoria Magazine*, which was set up specifically to provide work for women. For some years in the early 1860s she became a lay helper at the home for fallen women run by the All Saints Sisterhood. In 1875, in support of a protest movement which drew many women to its ranks, she persuaded Dante Gabriel to sign an anti-vivisection petition (*Letters*: 51). She was interested in Barbara Bodichon's projects for women's education and, in the 1880s, was friendly with Ellen Proctor who worked for one of the Factory Girls' Clubs.

She was also on more or less intimate terms with a number of contemporary women poets. In 1865, she admitted her 'trepidation' (W. M. Rossetti, 1903: 82) at a prospective visit from Jean Ingelow, especially as she was struck with a 'green tinge' (70) of jealousy at the appearance of Ingelow's eighth edition. But she also yearned for the stimulus of a meeting: '*To be tooked and well shooked* is what I eminently need socially' (84). Ingelow, whose poems had become almost as popular as those of Hemans or Eliza Cook, did meet Christina on several occasions, and there is evidence of considerable quiet support among these single women poets, who exchanged information about publishers and read each others' works with professional and sometimes competitive interest. Although William knew nothing about it, Christina belonged to 'The Portfolio Club', started by Barbara Bodichon and Bessie Rayner Parkes in the 1850s as a forum in which women read their poetry and exhibited their sketches to each other (Burton, 1949: 41). Both Ingelow and Adelaide Procter belonged to it. Such a self-consciously female artistic enterprise with, furthermore, distinctly suffragist overtones, was obviously not antipathetic to Christina at this time, although she later expressed opposition to the vote. Certainly, to be a woman poet in the nineteenth century, much more than to be a woman novelist, was to belong to an electively separate female tradition. This was not only emphasised by the reviewers but was acknowledged by the poets themselves. Rossetti invariably looks to other women poets as sources of comparison or emulation.

Of these, probably her closest confidante and the poet for whom she 'cherished a very warm and loving friendship' (in Dorling, 1885: 241) was Dora Greenwell. Dora was also single, lived with her beloved mother and was something of a religious mystic and recluse: ' "a *professed* invalid has many social immunities" ' (Dorling: 77), she once declared. She was also a supporter of the campaign for women's franchise, the abolition of slavery, the education of imbeciles, the anti-vivisection league and the restriction of child labour. Christina visited Dora several times and corresponded with her till the latter's death in 1882. Greenwell's poem 'To Christina Rossetti' expresses an almost adulatory affection for her friend: ' "Thou hast filled me a golden cup / With a drink divine that glows" ' (in Thomas, 1931: 68). In reply, Christina sent a characteristically aloof and impersonal lyric, 'Autumn Violets', which makes no obvious reference to her friend. None the less, Dora's self-professed ' "*liberal*" ' (in Dorling: 55) convictions, her discreet questioning of conventions and untiring support for many political and philanthropic causes, must have kept Christina, however indirectly, in touch with some of the issues of her day. In an article on 'Our single women', for instance, Greenwell argues that women should be paid for their work in hospitals, penitentiaries, prisons and the church, and that society should acknowledge that there are in women's lives 'wider affinities, – relationships yet unrecognised' (*North British Review* 36(1862), 78) beyond the precincts of the home.

Of particular interest is one of Greenwell's comments about religion. She makes the point in one of her letters that: ' "A Christian is too deeply pledged to a foregone conclusion to be bold and fearless in tracking out ultimate truth" ' (in Dorling: 104). Yet by comparison with Rossetti's, her own poetry is much more ' "deeply pledged" ' to the metrical and sentimental expectations of the day. One of her most popular poems, 'Home', for instance, is as sludgy as anything in Hemans:

> Two birds within one nest;
> Two hearts within one breast;
> Two spirits in one fair
> Firm league of love and prayer,
> Together bound for aye, together blest.
> (1906: 55)

'The Gang-Children', which castigates the use of child labour in agriculture, betrays its debt to Barrett Browning's 'The Cry of the

Children', but, unlike its model, this poem eagerly seeks solutions in infantile securities:

> Some things perhaps they miss,
> That other children see –
> The evening chat, and the kiss,
> And the ride on daddy's knee;
> To be tucked in their little beds
> By a mother's loving care . . .
> (167)

Where Barrett Browning ironically identified the family with the injustices of the 'happy Fatherland', Greenwell, like Eliza Cook, finds a sentimental solution in happy families.

One tantalisingly brief glimpse into a subject evidently discussed at length by the two poets is given in a letter which Dora wrote to William in 1867:

> 'I want to write to you upon the Pagan element, which seems to me to enter *inevitably* into all high and free literature and art. Your Sister does not agree with me in this – nor Miss Ingelow, nor anybody; which makes me feel sure I am right. Athanasius against the world!' (in W. M. Rossetti, 1903: 247)

The problem of '"the Pagan element"' in creativity seems to have especially troubled women. Greenwell, for all her faults as a poet, is recognising, theoretically at least, something of the deviant energies of art – energies which cannot be forced into the '"foregone conclusion"' of belief. Christina's disagreement with such notions certainly conforms to the legend of her saintliness. Watts-Dunton, for instance, declared her '"the ideal Christian woman of our own day"', by which he seems to have meant that she was ideally feminine: '"The Christian idea is essentially feminine, and of this feminine quality Christina Rossetti's poetry is full"' (in Hake and Compton-Rickett, 1916: II, 39). The religious and the feminine are thus enthusiastically elided as an artistic '"quality"' of the poetry. With such vested interests all round, it is perhaps not surprising that Christina made a lifelong vow of her faith. Yet the fact remains that it is Rossetti, not Greenwell, who encounters in her poems the temptations of the '"Pagan element"', of the seductively changeable, laughing gods of unseasonal fruits and sensual energy. Greenwell may have been daring in her opinions, but Rossetti was daring, in contradiction of all her opinions, in her imagination.

Another contemporary poet with whom Christina was in communication, particularly in her last years, was Katharine Tynan. Christina was clearly ambivalent about her: 'Miss Tynan is an agreeable young woman enough, and deferential enough to puff me up like puff-paste' (*Letters*: 149), she wrote in 1886. The year before, Tynan had sent a copy of her collection *Louise de la Vallière and Other Poems* (1885) to Rossetti. The title work, a dramatic monologue spoken by the mistress of Louis XIV turned nun, echoes both Rossetti's 'The Convent Threshold' and her verse on the same subject, 'Soeur Louise de la Misericorde'. However, the differences are again revealing. Tynan reproduces the sensuous effects of Rossetti's poetry: 'Rustle and trail of unseen draperies' (1885: 2), but ends with a religious re-conversion and acceptance of 'the Cross' (6). Rossetti's 'Soeur Louise', by contrast, is strikingly restless and tormented, stricken with desires which sound unsatisfied rather than resolved:

> Longing and love, pangs of a perished pleasure,
> Longing and love, a disenkindled fire,
> And memory a bottomless gulf of mire,
> And love a fount of tears outrunning measure;
> Oh vanity of vanities, desire!
> (*CP*: II, 119–20, ll. 6–10)

Christina, as William confirms, suffered from no false modesty about her poetic gifts. She believed herself 'Truly a poetess' and 'a good one' (W. M. Rossetti, 1904: lxix), and this is borne out by her reaction to the increasing numbers of unsolicited manuscripts which she received. She lamented to William's wife, Lucy, for instance, that 'another unknown has presented me with a volume of Sonnets', and added, acidly: 'Don't you ever publish a volume unless you are quite sure you can excel (say) Mr. W. Shakespear' (*Letters*: 149). Her letter of thanks to Tynan for her volume is polite, but devious: ' "I can express my sincere admiration for your poetic gift. But beyond all gifts I account *graces*, and therefore the piety of your work fills me with hopes far beyond any to be raised by music of diction" ' (in Tynan, 1913: 150). Tynan's ' "piety" ' may have been a genuine consolation to the 54-year-old poet, but it is also, evidently, an excuse for not having to praise her poetry overmuch. Christina never uses such language of the poetry she really admires. For instance, when Dante Gabriel gave her a copy of Swinburne's poems, she wrote: 'What a wonderful treasure of beauty the *Atalanta* is, amazing for delightfulness of sheer beauty' (Troxell, 1937: 145). Yet this was the work which contained lines so offensive to her, like 'The supreme evil, God' (Swinburne, 1904: IV, 287), that she covered them over with little strips of white paper. It is characteristic that her praise of 'sheer beauty' should remain unaffected by her religious offence, although her two reactions of praise and censorship point to a split in her own imagination which will often emerge in her poetry. Swinburne, for his part, remained one of her poetry's most devoted admirers.

Of all Rossetti's female contemporaries, there was one poet who always elicited unqualified praise. In 1878, Augusta Webster wrote a short article for *The Examiner* on 'Parliamentary franchise for women ratepayers', which was subsequently issued as a pamphlet. She sent one of these to Christina, with whom she was already in correspondence, and solicited her comments. The pamphlet is a witty attack on the arguments used against women's suffrage, the choice of women ratepayers being, of course, a strategic rather than intentionally limiting move. As Webster points out, it was 'a generally admitted principle that taxation and representation should go together' (1878: 3). The fact that England by now had a large proportion of unmarried women, living alone and paying taxes as individuals, had become a strong argument for the franchise, and one calculated to expose the absurdity of the various myths and moralities invoked against it. As Webster scornfully reports:

> one member of Parliament will . . . defend marriage, another the Bible, another the right of Man to have his dinner cooked by Woman, one will shudder over the feuds the bill's fatal gift would raise between man and wife, another be merry over the influx of lady-bishops to come of it. (2)

Although Rossetti's reply starts with a religious refutation, another kind of reasoning then subtly supervenes:

> 'The fact of the Priesthood being exclusively man's, leaves me in no doubt that the highest functions are not in this world open to both sexes: and if not all, then a selection must be made and a line drawn somewhere. – On the other hand if female rights are sure to be overborne for lack of female voting influence, then I confess I feel disposed to shoot ahead of my instructresses, and to assert that female *M.P.'s* are only right and reasonable. Also I take exceptions at the exclusion of married women from the suffrage, – for who so apt as Mothers . . . to protect the interests of themselves and of their offspring? I do think if anything ever does sweep away the barrier of sex, and makes the female not a giantess or a heroine but at once a full grown hero and giant, it is that mighty maternal love which makes little birds and little beasts as well as little women matches for very big adversaries.'

Her argument, here, quickly outpaces her diffidence. The logic of women's suffrage only becomes surer as she insists on the inclusion of '"Mothers"', and then imagines the entire '"barrier of sex"' being swept away, and all mythical idealisations of woman as '"a giantess or a heroine"' being reduced to a normal equality. It is interesting, too, that her strength of feeling about the rights of animals comes in support of the rights of '"little women"'. Her sympathies, as so often in her writings, run against her religious interests. She concludes, defensively and illogically: '"I do not think the present social movements tend on the whole to uphold Xtianity"' (in Bell, 1898: 112). But meanwhile the grounds of her opposition have slipped from under her racing, forward-thinking pen. Rossetti's admiration for Webster remained constant throughout her life. She rated her poetry 'decidedly higher' (*Letters*: 97) than George Eliot's, and in 1890 complained to William: 'did not Mr. Gladstone omit from his list of poetesses the one name which *I* incline to feel as by far the most formidable of those known to me, Augusta Webster?' (*Letters*: 175). As a poet, Webster is a sharp social critic, not a haunted musician, but it is a sign of Rossetti's impartial perceptiveness that she recognised a good poet, even one whose spirit was so opposed to her own.

Only one woman poet surpassed Webster in Rossetti's estimation: Barrett Browning. In 1863, Christina contributed a poem, 'A Royal Princess', to Emily Faithfull's anthology, *Poems: An Offering to Lancashire*, which was published, as the title explained, *for the relief of Distress in the Cotton Districts*. In this, she met with disapprobation from Dante Gabriel similar to that Barrett Browning had encountered from her own brothers over the Corn Laws. Dante Gabriel conveyed his disapproval more indirectly, but equally strongly, when he objected to poems like 'The Lowest Room', 'Under the Rose' and 'A Royal Princess' for their taint of Barrett Browning's '"modern vicious style"' or '"falsetto muscularity"' (in Packer, 1963: 204). As children, the Rossettis had 'revelled . . . with profuse delight' (W. M. Rossetti, 1906: I, 232) in Barrett Browning's 1844 volume, but the aestheticist creed of the Pre-Raphaelites then set itself against her increasingly political and muscular register. Dante Gabriel's anxious sexualising of her poetic voice as somehow one of castrated masculinity is evidently connected with his assumptions, not only about poetry, but about woman's proper sphere. In 1865, when Christina was preparing her second volume of poems for publication, she once again met with this brotherly resistance to certain topics. 'I endorse your opinion of the unavoidable and indeed much-to-be-desired unreality of women's work on many social matters', she answered, meekly and awkwardly, but insisted none the less on keeping some poems on 'social matters' (Troxell, 1937: 143) in the volume. Christina's declared commitment to her 'one-stringed lyre' may have placated her brother, but her commitment to sensibility was not altogether straightforward or whole-hearted.

Unlike Dante Gabriel's, Christina's admiration for Barrett Browning did not waver, and although she did not 'turn to politics or philanthropy' with the enthusiasm of the older poet, she did learn something from that poet's 'many-sidedness' (*Letters*: 31). When in 1882 John Ingram asked her to write for his 'Eminent Women' series, she offered a volume on Barrett Browning, arguing that ' "I should write with enthusiasm of that great poetess and (I believe) lovable woman, whom I was never, however, so fortunate as to meet" ' (in Bell, 1898: 90). Both Dante Gabriel and William had visited the Brownings when they were in London in 1855, Dante Gabriel, rather typically, with a view to getting 'Lizzy an introduction to them if she goes to Florence' (1965–7: I, 271). Christina, however, never met her great luminary, and William recalls that Barrett Browning herself never expressed any knowledge of Rossetti's work (W. M. Rossetti, 1906: I, 243). Three years before her death, when the two poets were being frequently compared, usually in her own favour, Christina repeated her admiration: ' "I doubt whether the woman is born, or for many a long day, if ever, will be born, who will balance not to say outweigh Mrs. Browning" ' (in Bell, 1898: 93).

Although Rossetti's own poetry seems to be unconcerned with 'the contemporary or social' (Kaplan, 1986: 98) realities which Barrett Browning explicitly dramatises, in fact those realities often lie underground in her imagination, and emerge as riddles and contradictions which unsettle both the message and the metre of her clear tunes. Thus, while on the one hand she returns to the 'one-stringed' lyrical model of women's poetry which Barrett Browning had so vociferously challenged, on the other, she reserves a space within that model for other, surreptitious meanings and energies to play. Where Barrett Browning realises political themes as external systems of power, Rossetti internalises them as moral and emotional games, which threaten the very values she seemed, in life, to exemplify. The public facade of that life provided, in some ways, a persuasive screen of domestic devotion and religious fervour, behind which her imagination had plenty of room to play.

POLITICS AND GOBLINS

During the 1850s, when Christina was in her twenties and still very much a part of the free, artistic atmosphere of the Pre-Raphaelites, she wrote a number of ballads which, in their sexual political dramas, clearly recall Barrett Browning's. However, there is one single difference between them. Where Barrett Browning's imagination is essentially secular, and concerned with the social conventions which masquerade as morality, Rossetti's is essentially religious. Consequently her ballads, while seeming more simply folkloric than her predecessor's, are in fact just as profoundly unsettling and double-dealing, in that a whole system of spiritual meaning is at issue in them. The ' "foregone conclusion" ', as Dora Greenwell put it, of Christian faith is one which her imagination, with its rich load of displaced desires and terrors, its goblin fruits of exotic knowledge, constantly confuses and defers. Sexual politics, for Rossetti, is a game which plays, not only with the heart but also with the immortal soul. Such playing has altogether more to lose.

Interestingly, two of the love ballads written during the 1850s use the name which Rossetti gives the heroine most closely representative of herself in her semi-autobiographical short story: 'Maude' (1850). They thus hint at a personal drama perhaps connected with Christina's rejection of Collinson at this time, but also involving sisterly relationships with other women. The 1850s were years when Dante Gabriel was wavering in his decision to marry Lizzie Siddal, between whom and Christina there was, as observers noticed, some ' "coldness" ' (W. M. Rossetti, 1899: 45). As early as 1852, Dante Gabriel was writing enthusiastically and a little tactlessly to his sister of Lizzie's beauty and gifts. He promises to 'dazzle' her with the sight of one of Lizzie's locks (1965-7: I, 109), and although he encourages her to send him her drawings, he also adds, mercilessly: 'You must take care however not to rival the Sid [Lizzie], but keep within respectful limits' (I, 108). Lizzie, at this time, was being adopted as the artistic protégée of the Pre-Raphaelites, though for reasons which were not always to do with art. As Madox Brown reported in 1854, without a hint of irony, Lizzie was ' "looking thinner and more deathlike and more beautiful and more ragged than ever; a real artist, a woman without parallel" ' (W. M. Rossetti, 1899: 19). To be ' "deathlike" ', even apparently dying, was to seem ' "a real artist" '. Lizzie appeared to embody the moribund beauty of an Ophelia or Mariana, thus proving the validity, not of her own art which is generally meagre and undeveloped, but rather that of her infatuated admirers and painters. Christina's imagination had many reasons to be preoccupied by sisters in the 1850s.

'Maude Clare', which was probably written in 1858, seems to repeat a time-honoured story, about a wedding interrupted by the forsaken true love. Maude Clare arrives at the church and gives to her former lover, as tainted wedding presents, the gifts he had once given to her:

> 'Here's my half of the golden chain
>   You wore about your neck,
> That day we waded ankle-deep
>   For lilies in the beck:
>
> 'Here's my half of the faded leaves

> We plucked from budding bough,
> With feet amongst the lily leaves, –
> The lilies are budding now.'
>> (*CP*: I, 44–6, ll. 21–8)

To Nell, the new wife, Maude Clare leaves her '"share of a fickle heart"' (37). So far, the poem falls into a predictable pattern of constancy on the part of the woman, fickleness on the part of the man (while those lilies, which will return in Rossetti's poetry, hint at a scene deep-set in her consciousness). This is love à la Hemans or L.E.L., with the moral distributed clearly along the grain of sexual sympathy. In the original, much longer manuscript version of the poem, this division continues strong, as Maude, speaking in the unquestionably 'pure voice' of the 'victim' (Elshtain, in Keohane, 1982: 136), accuses her one-time lover of betraying her for status and money (see *CP*: I, 244–7, and Harrison, 1988: 6).

When Rossetti cut the poem to its present length for her 1862 volume, she omitted this accusation and, as a result, completely altered the poem's moral perspectives. Nell, the new wife, now turns on her rival and declares:

> 'And what you leave,' said Nell, 'I'll take,
> And what you spurn, I'll wear;
> For he's my lord for better and worse,
> And him I love, Maude Clare.
>
> 'Yea, tho' you're taller by the head,
> More wise, and much more fair;
> I'll love him till he loves me best,
> Me best of all, Maude Clare.'
>> (41–8)

This stoical and unromantic response unexpectedly switches the moral authority from stately Maude to homely Nell, from, it may be, Corinne to Lucile. Instead of being simply hurt and faithful, Maude Clare now seems vicious, while Nell's willingness to come second and to wear a cast-off love sounds touchingly faithful. The high aristocracy of romantic love is thus scuppered on the humbler virtues of patience and persistence. The convention of being first, beautiful and injured is broken by the genuine alternative of the 'other' woman, who has her own point of view on faithfulness and truth.

'Sister Maude', written about two years later, depicts another holy outsider of the same name. It is spoken by a woman who has been betrayed, not by a lover but by her sister Maude:

> Who told my mother of my shame,
> Who told my father of my dear?
> Oh who but Maude, my sister Maude,
> Who lurked to spy and peer.
> (*CP*: I, 59–60, ll. 1–4)

The usual subject of the woman's 'shame' in the country ballad is quickly passed over in favour of another, subtler sin: that of the killjoy Maude, whose jealousy or righteousness has led to the death of her sister's lover. The Maude of Rossetti's early story was a self-abnegating fanatic; in these ballads she is a corrupt spoiler of the pleasures of others. At the end of the poem, the antique theme of rivalry in love topples into a drama of salvation which damns, not the shamed but the unshamed sister:

> If my dear and I knocked at Heaven-gate
> Perhaps they'd let us in:
> But sister Maude, oh sister Maude,
> Bide *you* with death and sin.
> (19–22)

Rossetti's is not only a sexual but also a moral politics. The larger perspectives of heaven and hell confuse the simplicities of the ballad and strangely mis-align sexuality and sin. Such moral cross-purposes bring to the ballad a possibility of ultimate equivocation which marks a clear advance on her predecessors. If womanly virtue may itself be a vice, then all values risk foundering in the tactical, relative power games of desire.

This sense of equivocation is conveyed in a poem Rossetti never published, perhaps because it bore too close a relation to real life. 'Look on this picture and on this' was written in 1856. Its unpunctuated, metrically jolting triplets rawly express the violent, distorted passions of the speaker. William was evidently perplexed by the poem and, having cut down its forty-six verses to twenty-three, pointed out that its 'singular' (1904: 480) subject matter derives from Maturin's novel, *The Women* (see Rosenblum, 1986: 154–5), while the title echoes the line from Hamlet where Gertrude is shown the pictures of her two husbands. 'Look on this picture and on this', however, is related by a man who is torn between two women. The first, called Eva, is docile and saintly, and dying in his arms; the other, unnamed, is fiery and devilish. The opposition, though deriving from Maturin, is also the old one of Lucile and Corinne. But instead of aestheticised desire, Rossetti conveys pure, untranscended sexual appetite, in language which, lacking the tidy dress of correct metre, seems to approach the naked reality of unpoeticised feeling.

132

The poem opens with an irresolvable comparison:

> I wish we once were wedded, – then I must be true;
> You should hold my will in yours to do or to undo:
> But now I hate myself Eva when I look at you.
>
> You have seen her hazel eyes, her warm dark skin,
> Dark hair – but oh those hazel eyes a devil is dancing in: –
> You my saint lead up to heaven she lures down to sin.
> (*CP*: III, 254–9, ll. 1–6)

The man's monologue swerves with nightmare logic from kind to cruel, loving to hating. Eva appears at first as a 'saint', but then, as his desire veers back towards the other woman, as revengeful and accusing: 'Pale with inner intense passion silent to the end' (32). One minute she is roughly despised, the next invoked as 'my dove my friend' (33). One minute he asks: 'Did I love you? never from the first cold day to this' (97), the next, he contradicts himself, whether from guilty strategy or real feeling: 'For after all I loved you, loved you then, I love you yet. / Listen love I love you' (112–13). Loving, bullying, reassuring, callous, these brilliant changes of register catch the desperation of a mind in a chaos of feeling, outside any social or emotional convention. This is not a poem of marriage versus adultery or of truth versus faithlessness. Both women are mistresses and both are, in different ways, desired. Nor is there a last word of irony to settle the moral grey into clear black and white, or to expose the gap between self-illusion and the self. The speaker could be killing Eva with the cruelty of his words, or reassuring her, at the last, with a vision of salvation. The ambiguity, both of his and her motives, goes to the heart of the poem. Her whiteness, for instance, ought to represent her innocent saintliness but, in fact, in a twist characteristic of Rossetti, might be a repressed 'white-heat' of destructive passion: 'the devil's special taint' (87).

In one stanza, the man turns on Eva with a reproach which is overtly sexual:

> Be still, tho' you may writhe you shall hear the branding truth:
> You who thought to sit in judgment on our souls forsooth,
> To sit in frigid judgment on our ripe luxuriant youth.
> (94–6)

Beneath the religious symbolism of temptress and dove, black and white woman, there is a contradicting sexual symbolism of frigidity and passion, judgment and luxury. In the end, the pale, dying victim seems as much a sinner as the devilish temptress: 'See now how proud you are, like us after all, no saint' (85), the man triumphs. Goodness can be a strategy like any other, and passive, silent victimisation only another form of emotional or moral power. To die is no assurance of purity, as it was for L.E.L.'s many damsels in distress. On the other hand, the strategy may be all the man's, whose egotistical interpretations exclude Eva altogether. Rossetti is a great love poet, not because she idealises love beyond the lies and cruelties of the passions, but because she enters those lies and cruelties with total imaginative abandon. Such abandon has left behind even the secular exposures of Barrett Browning's ballads.

'Look on this picture and on this' thus offers no solution to its double-handedness, no external authority to dispose the reader to one woman or the other and, above all, no absolutes of judgment beyond the many lying arguments of the heart. Yet, it is from such lies that passion, beauty and poetry itself come:

> If you sing to me, I hear her subtler sweeter still
> Whispering in each tender cadence strangely sweet to fill
> All that lacks in music all my soul and sense and will.
>
> (19–21)

Desire is not, for Rossetti, a moral or even an aesthetic solution; it is a moral nonsense. The heart is not an ultimate touchstone of truth and sincerity, but a place of indecipherable secrets and strategies. The speaker ends by invoking the now dead Eva as 'our sister friend and dove' (135), in an attempt to entrammel her in a scene of Christian forgiveness to alleviate his guilt. But the invocation is only another devious and violent protestation of his own needs. Beyond those needs the poem, like the two women themselves, is deathly silent.

Although Rossetti works within the romantic patterns of her predecessors' sentimentalist mode, she riddles their solutions with a sexual politics which not only relativises the issues into 'social matters', like Barrett Browning, but even goes one step further, in suggesting that desire itself is the riddle. In these ballads, she seems to press towards a point where meaning fails, and where the moral or emotional object becomes an elusive conundrum, chased through all the devices of love, reason, despair, possession and power. Choice, in these poems, between one woman or another, one picture or another, even between heaven and hell, begins to seem arbitrary, and the goal of the narrative to vanish between equally weighed opposites. This non-committal playfulness comes close to an absurdity of purpose which, in Rossetti's best poems, is almost pure nonsense. But unlike Carroll's and Lear's, this is 'nonsense' which plays with high moral stakes. Just how high is suggested by the poem which seems to be the culmination of all the devices and anxieties of Rossetti's work in the 1850s.

Goblin Market was written in 1859, between 'Maude Clare' and 'Sister Maude', and it belongs naturally to these sister poems of divided meaning. On the one hand, it seems to offer a moral allegory of feminised temptation and fall, in which one sister plays the role of 'a female Saviour' (Gilbert and Gubar, 1979: 566) to the other.[1] On the other hand, it constantly swerves away from religious meanings in an imagery drawn from the tricks of the nursery or the exchanges of the market.[2] As so often, Rossetti's morality is mismatched with her imaginative desires, her ideological intentions with her verbal energies, her ' "foregone conclusion" ' with a freedom of metre and meaning which waylays it. In her late devotional prose commentary, *The Face of the Deep*, for instance, she piously advises the reader to 'Strip sin bare from voluptuousness of music, fascination of gesture, entrancement of the stage, rapture of poetry, glamour of eloquence, seduction of imaginative emotion' (1892: 399). Yet the more she lists them, the more avid she sounds to imagine all the lovely, deceitful appearances of sin. It is just such an appetite which marks the temptation of the goblins, and just such a failure to 'Strip sin bare' which marks the endless, insatiable fascination of this poem.

Goblin Market was written two years after the publication of *Aurora Leigh*, and bears some obvious similarities to it. It, too, is a poem about two women, about a sexual fall and about money. It tells the story of two sisters, Laura and Lizzie, who, walking late one day at twilight, hear the cries of goblins selling fruit. Laura succumbs to the temptation, pays for fruit with a curl of her hair and subsequently wastes away – not because the fruit is poisonous but because, once met, the goblins cannot be found again, and she sickens with desire. Lizzie, to save her sister, also acquires fruit from the goblins, but neither pays for it nor eats it. Instead, she returns home smeared with its juice, which Laura sucks and is cured. The poem treads a breathtakingly thin line between nursery rhyme, sexual fantasy, religious allegory and social criticism. But thin lines are Rossetti's favourite places.

While many of her contemporaries were able to read *Goblin Market* innocently as, for instance, 'the most naive and childlike poem in our language' (Symons, 1897: 141) or as 'one of the very few purely fantastic poems of recent times' (Gosse, 1893: 215), twentieth-century critics have been troubled by its less childlike social and sexual meanings. For the scene of temptation, here, is explicitly not the mythical garden of Eden, but the contemporary market place, and the goblins, with their familiar street cries, ' "Come buy, come buy" ' (*CP*: I, 11–26, l. 4), are not devils and deceivers, but ordinary 'merchant men' (474), selling imported fruits. Like Barrett Browning, Rossetti plays the socio-economic register off against the biblical register and, like her predecessor, cunningly

135

tricks the one into the other through the same shifting, promiscuous image of the 'coin'. It is money, rather than sin, which becomes the fundamental figure of value in *Goblin Market*, as it is in *Aurora Leigh*.

Thus when Laura, the first sister, meets the goblins, she realises her lack of economic means to buy the fruit she desires:

> But sweet-tooth Laura spoke in haste:
> 'Good folk, I have no coin;
> To take were to purloin:
> I have no copper in my purse,
> I have no silver either,
> And all my gold is on the furze
> That shakes in windy weather
> Above the rusty heather.'
> 'You have much gold upon your head,'
> They answered all together:
> 'Buy from us with a golden curl.'
>
> (115–25)

Not being part of the market economy of goblin men, Laura substitutes herself for the coin which she does not possess and, in a gesture which parodies the favourite exchange of Victorian betrothals, as well as perhaps recalling that dazzling lock which Dante Gabriel once sent his sister, gives 'a golden curl'. In the poem, the moral roles are characteristically reversed. 'Lizzie', the second sister, sets out to save the fallen Laura, but takes care not to make her sister's mistake: she carries 'a silver penny in her purse' (324). She thus obviously enters into a position of economic power in relation to the goblins. The means of payment is shifted, as it were, from the Semiotic Order of the female body to the Symbolic Order of money, and Lizzie makes her entry into the market of male power properly equipped for its games and dangers.[3]

However, Rossetti then takes this power game a step further. Although Lizzie endures the goblins' violent assault (an unmistakable figure for rape as critics have pointed out (Gilbert and Gubar, 1979: 566; Holt, 1990: 55)), in fact she never pays, and returns in the end with her penny intact: 'Bouncing in her purse' (453). The Victorian euphemism of the 'purse' for the vagina, which Hawthorne elaborates in *The Blithedale Romance* (1983: 35) and which Dante Gabriel employs in his own imaginative rewriting of *Goblin Market* in *Jenny*: 'Jenny's flattering sleep confers / New magic on the magic purse, – / Grim web, how clogged with shrivelled flies!' (1913: 62–73, 71), is innocently and yet obviously present in Christina's poem. Lizzie, although she has experienced the same fall as her sister, has avoided paying the price. The 'coin' is explicitly, on one level, her virginity. But it is also, on another level, only a slippery, changing symbol of value – in fact, a coin. Virginity and coins are thus linked as objects which are inherently marketable; parts of a transaction of goblin myth and power.

In this poem, curls and coins, pennies and purses, goblins and men, are figuratively interchangeable in a free market of meaning where one thing constantly shifts into another, and where the rules of trickery, fantasy, or brute force prevail. In this market, everything may be goblinised into something else, while nothing is above being bought. The 'coin', which seems to be the most stable and central value in the poem, being both a physiological sexual object and a social sign of its value, is in fact also the thing which is most easily short-changed or bargained for. In this arena of male power, which is, as the very clash of registers in the title makes clear, an arena not only of economic facts and truths but of myths and magic as well, there is no signifier so secure that it cannot be exchanged at the going rate. The going rate is set by goblins only for as long as the game of sexuality is played according to their laws: the laws of sin and punishment, deceit and force. The law of sisters, however, is different.

Thus, while Barrett Browning tracked down the significance of the coin to its socio-sexual origins, in what '"men give women"' (*AL*: II, 541), Rossetti leaves it equivocally free-wheeling between all her different, conflicting registers. This is where *Goblin Market* brilliantly subverts its own moral as well as social seriousness. The sisters are saved, not by avoiding temptation or by repenting, which would be the logical Christian message, but by tricking the market and beating the goblins at their own games. This is exactly the point made by an outraged contemporary reviewer in the *Catholic World*. The moral of the poem is not, he complained, '"resist the devil and he will flee from you, but cheat the devil and he won't catch you"' (in Thomas, 1931: 61). Other nineteenth-century readers were equally disturbed by this moral illogicality. Alice Meynell complained that 'The moral is hardly intelligible – we miss any perceptible reason why the goblin fruits should be deadly at one time and restorative at another' (*PP*: 147). Eric Robertson gave a paraphrase of the plot and then concluded irritably: 'I do not think this is a pleasant story' (1883: 341). As late as 1920, Oliver Elton was put out by the fact that 'it has no moral, and there is no reason to it' (1927: II, 23). The moral scandal (and poetic brilliance) of *Goblin Market* is that there *is* no reason to it. The fruit is not only evil but also beautiful; the goblins are not only devils but also men, brothers or delightful animals; fallen women are not only streetwalkers and sinners but also loving sisters. Furthermore, sin itself is not a 'naked' fact, which can be stripped bare to its essence, but an elaborate, complicated magic, which derives its significance, not from some original law of God, but from the contemporary market of meaning and ideology run by goblins. As soon as the sisters enter that market, *as* sisters rather than as vulnerable single women like Jeanie, they can counter the goblins' rule of sin and suffering. This is a moral nonsense poem which puts religious myth and sexual temptation into a market economy of language which is endlessly unstable.

The main source of instability in the work is, of course, metaphor – the coin of poetic language itself. It is not so much that the goblins' fruit constitutes that language, as a number of critics have suggested (Gilbert and Gubar, 1979: 568; Conor, 1984: 440; McGillis, in Kent, 1987: 217; Holt, 1990: 61), but that even the fruit is not outside language, and therefore, like everything else in the poem, not outside the metaphorical exchanges of one thing for another. The religious allegory, of a tempted Eve who becomes a saving Christ, is thus also part of this system of metaphorical substitution which leaves everything, coins, fruit, sisters, goblins and markets, open-enddedly interpretable as something else. The links between myth, morality and money in this poem are at once unavoidable and yet arbitrary, as if Rossetti were expressing, in fiction, the pattern of ideology itself. It is a 'market' of power upheld by fairy-tales. The now-you-see-them-now-you-don't effect of the goblins drives this home. Although it seems to possess a moral logic (if you eat the fruit you cease to see goblins), that logic can be cheated (if you can get more fruit, you will not miss goblins). As a result, this morality market emerges as what it truly is: a nonsense which, depending on the point of view, may be either violent or harmless, divine or chimerical, destructive or invigorating – ultimately, there or not there. Such choices leave nothing, neither social power nor even sin as original.

Meanwhile, it is evident that, in spite of the message to avoid goblin fruits at the end, the whole energy and inspiration of the work drive towards more temptation, more fruit and more poetry:

> 'Apples and quinces,
> Lemons and oranges,
> Plump unpecked cherries,
> Melons and raspberries,
> Bloom-down-cheeked peaches,
> Swart-headed mulberries,
> Wild free-born cranberries,
> Crab-apples, dewberries,
> Pine-apples, blackberries,
> Apricots, strawberries . . .'
> (5–14)

This paratactic piling up of noun on noun suggests an aesthetic of pleasure, a sensual art for art's sake, which is, indeed, textually addictive. *Goblin Market* is a feast of appetite – appetite which is contradictorily linked with imaginative inspiration on the one hand and moral depravity on the other. It is the mis-alignment of (at least) these three which is the source of the poem's fascination. The garrulous, nonsensical energies of the imagination play at the expense of the true gods; the pleasure of metaphor at the expense of truth. Like 'A Musical Instrument' (which had not yet been published), *Goblin Market* is tense with the contradictions it sets up, between beauty and truth, pleasure and sin, delight and judgment. Goat gods and goblins are figures which in themselves cross-breed religious meaning and irreligious energy, thus laying down the law of changeability as the law of fiction itself, but hardly, one would suppose, as the law of the sighing true God.

The sign of this irresponsible, pleasure-loving energy is, once again, laughter:

> Laughed every goblin
> When they spied her peeping:
> Came towards her hobbling,
> Flying, running, leaping,
> Puffing and blowing,
> Chuckling, clapping, crowing,
> Clucking and gobbling,
> Mopping and mowing,
> Full of airs and graces,
> Pulling wry faces,
> Demure grimaces,
> Cat-like and rat-like,
> Ratel- and wombat-like,
> Snail-paced in a hurry . . .
> (329–42)

Such language breeds goblins like similes. In this land of nonsense, 'grimaces' might be also 'Demure', 'Snail-paced' also 'in a hurry'. Such a chiasma of rhythm and meaning is characteristic of Rossetti's best work. She, like Barrett Browning, defies her heritage of metrical correctness and womanly propriety, and, instead, suggestively connects the goblins' hobbling, laughing energy with the missed steps of a metre which explores the paths outside the '"foregone conclusion"' of the soul's salvation. '"Twilight is not good for maidens"' (144), the rational Lizzie warns at the start. When Laura encounters the goblins at dusk, she subsequently loses all sense of time, and 'knew not was it night or day' (139). However, twilight is also Rossetti's favourite time. It is the time of fantasy, a time which lies between the pleasure of the past and the judgment of the future, between delightful memory and ascetic goal, between regret and grace. Like all the lagging dead women in her poems, whose consciousness stops short of eternity to go 'dreaming through the twilight' (*CP*: I, 58, l. 13), Laura delays for pleasure and risks missing forever the goal of salvation.

In the end, however, it is interesting to notice that Lizzie has filched, not only the goblins' fruit, but also their sceptical, mischievous laughter; their moral carelessness of cost and pain. As she returns with her saved penny, we are told she 'laughed in heart' (433). *Goblin Market*, in the end, gives women money, fruit, pleasure, children and, above all, a laughter at the heart which defies all the morally punitive connections between them. It gives them the aesthetic playfulness, the freedom of art for art's sake, which had seemed to be reserved for men. Against all the religious logic of her poem, Rossetti has found the thing which was missing in Hemans and L.E.L.: an imaginative scepticism which refuses to obey the laws of sin and punishment, woman-like faith and man-like doubt. Instead of reproducing the true religion of woman's sincere, faithful suffering, Rossetti laughs, daringly, from within, and thus asserts the priority of her art over even her own punishing conscience. Lizzie's 'inward laughter' (463) as she returns with fruit, is, like Pan's, the sign of a sweetness gained at the expense of all the literal-minded, serious, moral interpretations of this exquisitely joking poem.

BROKEN-HEARTED VERSES

Touching these same verses, it was the amazement of every one what could make her poetry so broken-hearted as was mostly the case. Some pronounced that she wrote very foolishly about things she could not possibly understand; some wondered if she really had any secret source of uneasiness; while some simply set her down as affected. Perhaps there was a degree of truth in all these opinions. (*Maude*: 31)

While Rossetti's ballads and narrative poems contain the dynamics of a sexual politics which threatens to disorder all their emotional and religious messages, her lyrical works, for which she has always been better known, seem to fall into a more traditional mould. Musical and melancholy, they have long been acclaimed as examples of a pure, womanly verse which is sexually unambiguous and perfectly sincere. As Arthur Waugh asserted: 'Christina Rossetti was above all things else a woman' (1915: 150) – a characteristic still, in 1915, as clear as water. 'Her poetry, therefore', he concludes, 'has no quality more distinguishing than its sincerity' (151). The model of the spontaneously improvising woman continues to provide a criterion of poetic value, even into the twentieth century. Rossetti is the century's true Sappho because, in her poetry, she sings, loves and dies with effortless, unquestioning spontaneity. Yet although she herself 'lived' this myth with evident self-identification and inspiration, she also probes it from within. The 'broken-hearted' attitude of Maude's youthful verses may, after all, as Rossetti slyly proposes, be as much a matter of studied affectation as of real secret sorrow.

Maude was completed in 1850 before Christina was 20 years old, and at the time of her broken engagement to James Collinson. Unpublished during her lifetime, it offers, as William points out, a rare glimpse into 'her own character' (in *Maude*: 79), and particularly into that 'over-scrupulous' religiosity which he notes as the one defect of her nature (1904: lxvii). Certainly, this portrait of a girl poet who is, by turns, vain and self-abasing, ambitious and awkward, boastful and shy, seems to express some of the contradictions in Christina's own personality. Maude's social ineptitude, her deference to her mother, her religious scruples and her premature world-weariness are all recognisably Rossettian traits. So, too, is the 'broken-hearted' attitude of her verse. In the course of the story, she is confronted with a choice of roles: she may be a wife, a nun or perhaps a poet. In the end, however, that choice is melodramatically avoided, as the confessional mode veers into high fiction and the heroine meets her death as a result of a carriage accident. Such an extravagant conclusion is both fantastically evasive and eerily prophetic.

On the one hand, *Maude* contains many of the familiar outward features of Rossetti's verse: its morbid sadness, religious anxieties, the use of sister women as projections of the self and, above all, the death of the heroine at the end, who is buried with her 'locked book' (72) of poems – an 'unconscious prefigurement' (80), as William puts it, of Dante Gabriel's burial of his own poetic notebook in Lizzie Siddal's coffin. On the other hand, however, *Maude* never answers any of its own questions; in particular, the question of whether the heroine's verse is motivated by foolish ignorance, by a real 'secret uneasiness' or by a mere affectation of grief. 'Perhaps there was a degree of truth in all these opinions', Rossetti teases. She herself was writing melancholy poems about dead or unrequited women long before her own broken engagement. Her first volume of 1847, which was privately published on her grandfather's press when she was 16, contains innumerable examples of that funerary heroism derived from L.E.L., and even the famous song 'When I am dead, my dearest' pre-dates the 'staggering blow' (W. M. Rossetti, 1904: lii) of Collinson's religious defection by more than a year. Critics who have tried to fix on a single biographical inspiration for her poems, whether James Collinson, Charles Cayley or even William Bell Scott, have had to wring their conclusions from the baffling emotional chronology and determined secretiveness of much of her verse. *Maude* suggests the extent to which life and art were always, for Rossetti, only obliquely connected.

One short scene betrays familiar literary origins. The heroine is in the company of two friends, Mary and Agnes, preparing for a birthday party. In a playful moment she allows them to crown her with a wreath sprigged with bay. Although she is humbled by it: '"my wreath is very nice, only I have not earned the bay"', her vanity is also gratified: 'Still she did not remove it; and when placed on her dark hair it well became the really intellectual character of her face' (33). This is, of course, another miniature of Corinne at the Capitol. The scene is typically domestic rather than public, and amounts to little more than a girls' game. Yet, like Aurora, Maude is turned at this moment into a self-conscious spectacle of creative success. A year later, however, she emphatically rejects this role when, called upon to recite her verses at a social gathering, she is struck by 'the absurdity of her position' and, stifling a laugh, refuses to speak. '"I could not think of monopolizing every one's attention"' (49), she explains ineptly.

This suggests a crucial, early revision of the literary model Rossetti inherits. Instead of taking the stage, Maude retreats into tight-lipped silence. The significance of this refusal is brought out when the heroine, already full of religious scruples, suddenly bursts out: '"I am sick of display and poetry and acting"'. Agnes' response to this then consciously poses one of the central problems about Christina's own life and work. '"You do not act . . . I never knew a more sincere person"' (41), she asserts. Like the many reviewers who praise the sincerity of Rossetti's lyrics, Agnes mistakes the surface for the depths. Maude's tactlessness, her puritanism and, above all, her intellectual vanity, suggest a complexity of character which is far from 'sincere', and which may only be controlled by total self-denial. 'No one will say that I cannot avoid putting myself forward and displaying my verses' (53), Maude later declares, in a passionate rejection of the Corinne role. The statement finds an intriguing echo in real life. The year before, in 1848, Dante Gabriel had explained to Holman-Hunt the reason why his sister would not join the Pre-Raphaelite Brotherhood: 'it would seem like display, I believe, – a sort of thing she abhors' (1965–7: I, 45). Thus it seems that, two years before the break with Collinson, Christina had already determined on a course of self-concealing 'mortification' – a course which, judging by the story of *Maude*, had as much to do with her driving poetic vanity and ambition, her desire for a wreath of bay, as with religious scruples. The ending of the story, with its elaborate process of laying out, then gives to that fear of 'display' a crucial, lifelong solution: the poet is dead. By being 'posthumous', this Sappho overcomes the problem of an exhibitionism which is too readily associated with woman's appealing goodness and sincerity. Rossetti needs a place from which to speak which will not be the over-exposed stage of the Capitol or, its real Victorian equivalent, the admiring family drawing-room, and finds it in the grave.

In her teens, the poet wrote two poems about Sappho. The first of these, called 'Sappho' and written when she was 15, seems to delight, in the manner of L.E.L., in a prolonged death-wish and a sense of ineradicable emotional injury:

> I sigh at day-dawn, and I sigh
> When the dull day is passing by.
> I sigh at evening, and again
> I sigh when night brings sleep to men.
> Oh! it were better far to die
> Than thus for ever mourn and sigh,
> And in death's dreamless sleep to be
> Unconscious that none weep for me;
> Eased from my weight of heaviness,
> Forgetful of forgetfulness,
> Resting from pain and care and sorrow
> Thro' the long night that knows no morrow;
> Living unloved, to die unknown,
> Unwept, untended and alone.
>
> (*CP*: III, 81–2, ll. 1–14)

However, although full of the sighing and mourning of the annuals, this poem already seems different from Hemans' and L.E.L.'s last songs of Sappho: its 'forgetfulness' impersonal, its 'long night' of death eerily conscious, and even its reproach, 'Living unloved, to die unknown', curiously detached and self-contained. Even at so early a date, the note of aggrieved resentment, which is so noisy in L.E.L., is muted in Rossetti. Above all Rossetti is fixing, not on a physical trauma of love and suicide, with all its self-conscious anatomical 'display', but on a death-bound state of mind which diminishes rather than exaggerates feeling. This 'posthumous' Sappho, who has gone as it were one step beyond the pose on the cliff top, is 'Unconscious' of others and even 'Forgetful of forgetfulness'. By being already dead, rather than about to die, she is freed from the spectacular sensibility of the earlier poet-heroines, and gains, instead, an eerie afterlife of the imagination, untroubled by weeping or remembering.

Two years later, in 1848, Rossetti wrote a second poem, 'What Sappho would have said had her leap cured instead of killing her', which, in its title at least, quietly satirises the suicidal obsessions of earlier poets. It describes a landscape of sleep and forgetting which, in its limpid and restrained clarity, is already pure Rossetti:

> I walk down by the river side
>   Where the low willows touch the stream;
>   Beneath the ripple and sun-gleam
> The slippery cold fishes glide,
>   Where flags and reeds and rushes lave
>   Their roots in the unsullied wave.
>
> Methinks this is a drowsy place:
>   Disturb me not; I fain would sleep:
>   The very winds and waters keep
> Their voices under; and the race
>   Of Time seems to stand still, for here
>   Is night or twilight all the year.
>   (*CP*: III, 166–8, ll. 19–30)

This Sappho chooses an art of minimal feeling in a drama of death which is not a grand final act, but a prolonged and desired 'twilight' of consciousness. While L.E.L.'s Sapphos are inspired primarily by their own reproachful death-throes, Rossetti's speak from a calm and careless afterlife of love. While death serves L.E.L. as the ultimate in emotional authenticity, it serves Rossetti as the ultimate emotional diversion. This scene of willows and water will become a recurrent figure in her poetry for a displacement of experience beyond the limits of what can be known or remembered, which already signals her difference from her predecessors. Such a scene is, indeed, full of 'voices under', but controlled by Rossetti's register of severe yet ambiguous calm. In this poem, death does not kill the too-feeling poet, but specifically cures her.

Thus, although as Dolores Rosenblum claims, L.E.L. is for Rossetti the 'paradigmatic woman and poet' (1986: 15), it is a paradigm which she does not simply copy and repeat; instead, she challenges it with a kind of humour from within. Some of her most famous songs, like 'When I am dead, my dearest' (1848) and 'Remember' (1849), echo the 'Do you think of me?' strain in L.E.L., but without the gesticulating self-pity which so often mars the earlier poet's work. For instance, L.E.L.'s 'Song' contains all the outward ingredients of a Rossetti poem: forgetfulness, a grave and a broken heart:

> FAREWELL! – and never think of me
>   In lighted hall or lady's bower!
> Farewell! – and never think of me
>   In spring sunshine or summer hour! –
> But when you see a lonely grave,

Just where a broken heart might be,
With not one mourner by its sod,
Then – and then only – THINK OF ME!
(*PW*: 368)

By comparison, however, the casual, shrugging register of Rossetti's own 'Song', 'When I am dead, my dearest', seems, not 'self-pitying and sentimental', as Stuart Curran claims (1971: 289), but strikingly free of any sentiment at all:

When I am dead, my dearest,
 Sing no sad songs for me;
Plant thou no roses at my head,
 Nor shady cypress tree:
Be the green grass above me
 With showers and dewdrops wet;
And if thou wilt, remember,
 And if thou wilt, forget.
(*CP*: I, 58, ll. 1–8)

This cool, witty lyricism almost belies feeling altogether. It will be of no concern to this dead woman whether she is remembered or not. The playful alternatives of the last lines express her indifference to both life and love, remembering and forgetting, as she goes 'dreaming through the twilight / That doth not rise nor set' (13–14). Her own time is characteristically beyond earshot of singing or grieving, imagined in one of those non-committal balancing acts which, so often in Rossetti, are not a choice, but as Dolores Rosenblum puts it, a 'perfect equipoise' (1986: 209). By insisting on 'no sad songs', Rossetti edges her own with humorous irony, and gives, as Barrett Browning did, an implicitly reproving answer to L.E.L.'s demanding last questions.

From the earliest verses, then, Rossetti's imagination seems out of time with its own subject matter and its own feelings. The lapse of time between experience and poem, sensibility and song, life and afterlife, is a discrepancy which specifically challenges the truth of feeling in the sentimentalist tradition. Instead of reproducing the heartfelt immediacy of the Improvisatrice's songs, which allow no break between the spasm of the body and the music of the poem, Rossetti, from the start, explores the 'between-time', precisely the 'twilight', of memory, which intervenes between them. Her version of sensibility is flawed by the thing which both Hemans and L.E.L. metrically and thematically simplified and which Barrett Browning externalised as history: a sense of time.

'The Dream', for instance, which was written before 1847, and therefore before Christina was 16, is already remembering a far distant past:

> Tell me, dost thou remember the old time
> We sat together by that sunny stream,
> And dreamed our happiness was too sublime
> Only to be a dream?
>
> Gazing, till steadfast gazing made us blind,
> We watched the fishes leaping at their play;
> Thinking our love too tender and too kind
> Ever to pass away.
>
> (*CP*: III, 104–5, ll. 5–12)

The speaker of 'The Dream', like the Hardy of 'Neutral Tones', is already old in the imagination, already disenchanted and deserted. Beneath the water into which the lovers gaze is some unknown object or knowledge, barely even named, which then haunts the poem. In one place the speaker turns to ask her lover: 'What found'st thou in my heart that thou should'st break it? –' (31). It is typical of Rossetti to take mere broken-heartedness, that soft subject of women's poetry, and make it brittle again. This heart is an object as tangible as a vase. But the poem probes even deeper than just the heart: 'What found'st thou *in* my heart . . .?' Lurking within the very heart of love, there is something else. Far from being open and true, it contains receding depths of truth.

As Jerome McGann has perceptively pointed out, words like 'it' and 'what' in Rossetti often suggest some 'wholly unidentified referent, something unknown and inexplicable both to speaker and reader', around which meaning none the less takes shape (1980: 244). In 'The Dream' the idea of such a referent is revived in the last stanza:

> Truly love's vain; but oh! how vainer still
> Is that which is not love, but seems;
> Concealed indifference, a covered ill,
> A very dream of dreams.
>
> (39–42)

'Concealed' within love, like a dream within a dream, is lovelessness, 'indifference'. As in many of Rossetti's later poems, 'Memory' and 'Twice', for instance, love shatters at a touch and leaves to the poet an unspecific object buried at the heart, too complex to be named, too distant to be recalled, yet cold and central. Instead of issuing the usual reproach to the heartless lover, 'The Dream' hints that 'indifference' is, in fact, the speaker's own; it is the hidden object which the lover found, and left. This is not the old kind of betrayal. Cold-heartedness, here, belongs to the woman, not the man, and thus opens a new possibility within the whole heritage of sensibility – one which L.E.L. was just beginning to recognise in her later work. Feeling is not identical with truth, especially not poetic truth. Furthermore, as the last line implies, such cold-heartedness is profoundly equivocal. 'A very dream of dreams' may be either colloquial, meaning a quintessential nothing, or else superlative, meaning a dream more precious than dreams. Such ambiguity ensures, however, that 'What' it was is not disclosed: it may be as devastating as 'indifference' or as coolly inspired as 'dreams'.

Eighteen years later, when she was 33, Rossetti wrote a poem which she never published, but which seems to return to the same place as 'The Dream'. 'Under Willows' tells of an encounter between lovers which leaves the speaker chilled by indifference and misrecognition:

> He looked at her with a smile,
>   She looked at him with a sigh,
> Both paused to look awhile;
>   Then he passed by,
> Passed by and whistled a tune;
>   She stood silent and still:
> It was the sunniest day in June,
>   Yet one felt a chill.
>
> Under willows among the graves
>   I know a certain black black pool
> Scarce wrinkled when Autumn raves;
>   Under the turf is cool;
> Under the water it must be cold;
>   Winter comes cold when Summer's past;
> Though she live to be old, so old,
>   She shall die at last.
>   (*CP*: III, 292–3, ll. 9–24)

Beautifully understated, the pattern of meeting, missing and passing is the same as in the earlier poem, and represents a founding motif of much of Rossetti's work. The 'pool', like the one observed by the child in 'Three Nuns' (1849–50), where 'On the waters dark as night, / Water-lilies lay like light' (III, 187–93, ll. 55–6), is a figure for depths of consciousness which go back as if beyond the boundaries of memory. The misrecognition between lovers triggers a self-knowledge which is cold rather than forlorn, dark rather than self-reflecting. In 'Under Willows' the lapse of time, which skips from June to autumn, from summer to winter, from past tense to present and from 'She' to 'I' between the two stanzas, is suddenly halted in the profound familiar otherness of the 'black black pool'. The casual tone of the first stanza keeps the tension close to breaking-point as the personal pronouns, 'She' and 'he', give way at the moment of intensest drama to the self-distanced, impersonal 'one': 'Yet one felt a chill.' It is this 'chill' which then spreads in the second stanza, to become 'cool' and then 'cold', as the mind imagines being not only under 'willows' but also under 'turf' and under 'water'. This is a poem not so much about love, rejection or even death as about the unknown depths of cold of which consciousness is capable. 'I know a certain black black pool' rings with a knowledge which goes back, in Rossetti's poetry (and perhaps life) to some primal scene of desertion which then echoes through innumerable variations. The scene of love's betrayal is remembered, in the repetition-compulsion of the imagination, as a scene almost of the self-separating birth of consciousness itself: 'Water-lilies lay like light'. Such a memory seems immemorial from the beginning; its knowledge, whatever it is, already lost in time.

In the late 1860s, Rossetti wrote a short story, 'Vanna's Twins', which was published in her collection *Commonplace* (1870). It tells of two Neapolitan children, twin brother and sister, so alike in their cleverness and fondness for books that 'they were like one work in two volumes' (228). They die together at the end in a snowstorm, and their intimacy is thus sealed in winter for ever: 'as they had always shared one bed, they now shared one coffin and one grave' (236). Like George Eliot's 'Brother and Sister' (1869) sonnets, which lovingly recall how 'the twin habit of that early time / Lingered for long about the heart and tongue' (1989: 84–90, 90), which Christina may have recently read, 'Vanna's Twins' offers a figure of perfect emotional reciprocity which can only be preserved in death. The motif of burial, here, is evidently meant to protect the twins from loss. In order to continue sharing 'one bed', they must die together. Like much of Rossetti's prose, this sounds loaded with autobiography. Certainly Christina's relation to the brother who was her literary and temperamental equal in the nursery remained imaginatively strong throughout her life. It was Dante Gabriel who first urged his sister to publish her poems in *The Germ*, who made emendations to her work and read her proofs, who managed, and sometimes mismanaged, her financial dealings with publishers and who remained her closest, though not always her best, literary confidant. Yet if the idea of some primal imaginative desertion stems from real life (from the brother who, at some point, replaced Laura with Lizzie), it also serves as a figure for the movements of the imagination itself, which overlays, like lilies, a memory always lying deeper down. Such a memory may be based on some real childhood betrayal, or it may, like much of Rossetti's work, merely echo a literary topos which, like Tennyson, she derives from Romantic myths of incest and lost twins (see Shaw, 1988: 13–35). But it also becomes a technique of anachronistic feeling, which gives to much of her most melancholy poetry its peculiar, hollow effect of echoes. The connection between the echo and the lost twin in many of her lyrics suggests that the theme of betrayal is inherently bound up with the movement of creativity itself. Rossetti turns this woman's motif of being betrayed into an originating condition of writing.

The much anthologised 'Echo', for instance, recalls, across characteristically remote tracts of time, some original, answering companion who is, ambiguously, both an 'echo' revived in the memory and a lover summoned to bed:

> Come to me in the silence of the night;
>   Come in the speaking silence of a dream;
> Come with soft rounded cheeks and eyes as bright
>   As sunlight on a stream;
>   Come back in tears,
> O memory, hope, love of finished years.
> (CP: I, 46, ll. 1–6)

Rossetti was 23 when she wrote this poem of 'finished years'. As always, her imagination exists posthumously to life, and from there recovers an experience of love which seems to belong obscurely to the time of childhood: 'soft rounded cheeks and eyes as bright'. The twinning intimacy of 'Pulse for pulse, breath for breath' (16) keeps an innocence which the long perspective of time encourages, while the echo itself shifts ambiguously between a person and a memory, a lover and an idea. More erotic, in many ways, than Dante Gabriel's famous 'Nuptial Sleep', this poem sidetracks desire into memory, and thus frees it from censorship. Meanwhile, however, the 'come to me' motif, perhaps spoken by Echo herself, who was doomed never to be heard by Narcissus, resonates with permissively unsatisfied desire.

The figure of the echoing 'other' recurs in 'From House To Home', written four years later. Here, Rossetti describes an early 'pleasure-place' (*CP*: I, 82–8, l. 6) of the soul, filled with exquisite tiny animals: 'singing-birds' (23) and 'lizards' (29), 'Frogs and fat toads' (33), caterpillars, snails, slugs, moles and hedgehogs. Christina's love of small animals went back to her childhood visits to the zoo with Dante Gabriel – a passion which he continued in his own home at Cheyne Walk, where the menagerie consisted at one time of a white mouse, an owl, a parrot, a kangaroo, a racoon, an armadillo, a zebu and, of course, that quaint original for Carroll's dormouse, a wombat (W. M. Rossetti, 1906: I, 284). In Christina's poem, the garden of the soul also contains a flamboyant male presence:

> Ofttimes one like an angel walked with me,
>   With spirit-discerning eyes like flames of fire,
> But deep as the unfathomed endless sea

> Fulfilling my desire:
>
> . . .
>
> We sang our songs together by the way,
> Calls and recalls and echoes of delight;
> So communed we together all the day,
> And so in dreams by night.
>
> (ll. 45–8, 53–6)

This angel-muse is remembered as a source, not only of satisfied desire but also of echoing creativity: 'Calls and recalls and echoes of delight'. As in 'Echo', the first love in the primal garden is remembered as a perfectly requiting sound-effect of the speaker's own voice, inspiration and love. Yet inevitably, such fulfilment of her desire cannot last. The companion in 'songs' and 'dreams' is lost, not because he is unfaithful, but because the speaker chooses to leave both him and the garden of pleasure behind. Its 'tissue of hugged lies' (9) is rejected for the poetically arid 'goal' (8) of salvation, a ' "foregone conclusion" ' which puts an end to the free-dallying of the primal imagination with its beloved twin.

That same year of 1858, Rossetti composed the bleakest of all her echo poems. 'Autumn' is Rossetti's 'Lady of Shalott', written, of course, from within rather than from without. Its speaker is trapped on an island strand, from where she can hear the sounds of the world, but cannot herself be heard. In it, the echoes sent from Tennyson's poem meet with others which are more 'familiar':

> Fair fall the freighted boats which gold and stone
> And spices bear to sea:
> Slim, gleaming maidens swell their mellow notes,
> Love-promising, entreating –
> Ah! sweet, but fleeting –
> Beneath the shivering, snow-white sails.
> Hush! the wind flags and fails –
> Hush! they will lie becalmed in sight of strand –
> Sight of my strand, where I do dwell alone;
> Their songs wake singing echoes in my land –
> They cannot hear me moan.
>
> (*CP*: I, 143–5, ll. 7–17)

To be stranded within earshot of her brother's luxurious and artistically productive life was Christina's fate. However, where once the 'echoes of delight' were reciprocal, they now only go one way: 'Their songs wake singing echoes in my land – / They cannot hear me moan.' The idea of having been deserted remains buried deep in the poem. Once, echoes were answered. Yet the idea of her own creativity as echoing sounds from across a barrier of the forbidden or the forgotten is clearly still inspiring. The mis-communications and mis-timings of Rossetti's poems are, paradoxically, like her goblins, also the sources of its erotically delaying, dallying, pleasure-loving rhythms: 'Love-promising, entreating – / Ah! sweet, but fleeting'. By being out of time with pleasure, she can keep a hungry ear on all its licence. By being out of life itself, ghostly and unknown, she can feel its pulses all the more strongly and waywardly. If Dante Gabriel failed to hear her from his love-laden boat of 'gleaming maidens', she, none the less, recorded the constant echo-effect of lost love on her resolutely 'broken-hearted' imagination.

Christina did not publish 'An Echo from Willowwood', perhaps because, once again, the subject was too close to home. It was written to answer and echo Dante Gabriel's 'Sonnets from Willowwood', which were composed a few months earlier, in December 1868, and which seem to express his guilt and grief at Lizzie Siddal's death six years before. The idea of searching for the beloved's face in a pool or stream is present in many of his poems, as well as appearing, with intriguing persistence, in three of Lizzie's own sketches which depict two figures, herself and Dante Gabriel, gazing into a pool or fountain (Marsh, 1991: 50–1). However, Christina's 'Echo' derives from a place which seems to have been hers long before it was Dante Gabriel's. The scene of willows and water was that of her own Sappho's forgetful, curative twilight after her suicidal leap. It was also the scene of the casual desertion of 'The Dream'. Echoes, for Rossetti, are not so much signs of poetic imitation as of hollowed-out memory; they represent something that has been secondary for so long that it has almost lost its literary or biographical origins. As a figure for poetry, the echo points to that element of fiction which is no longer tied to life or feeling, but which sets up its own meaning beyond their gravity. Such a figure marks out the difference between Rossetti's free-playing, light-handed melancholy and L.E.L.'s somehow grasping one.

In Dante Gabriel's 'Sonnets', the speaker meets the reflection of his lost love in a pool:

> Then the dark ripples spread to waving hair,
> And as I stooped, her own lips rising there
> Bubbled with brimming kisses at my mouth.
> (1913: 119–20, 119)

Christina's 'Echo from Willowwood' lacks the baroque and slightly lurid intensity of her brother's sonnets. The allegorical figure of Love has gone, and instead of those Keatsian 'kisses', two lovers look down into a pool, then part:

> Lilies upon the surface, deep below
> Two wistful faces craving each for each,
> Resolute and reluctant without speech: –
> A sudden ripple made the faces flow
> One moment joined, to vanish out of reach:
> So those hearts joined, and ah! were parted so.
>
> (*CP*: III, 53, ll. 1–14)

The depth of the pool with its lilies on the surface (there are no lilies in Dante Gabriel's sonnets) suggest the old perspective of a casual and easily erased loss – a loss specifically related to her brother. However, where he dramatises a calamitous drowning, Christina dramatises a parting as accidental, though 'deep', as a reflection lost in ripples. The sheer lightness of her touch, beside his, emphasises a fragility which is of the very substance of her poems, though below the reflections and the lilies there is that same dark prospect of unknown waters.

One last willow poem, 'In the Willow Shade' (1881), returns to this same scene: 'I sat beneath a willow tree, / Where water falls and calls' (*CP*: II, 106–8, ll. 1–2). 'Calls and recalls and echoes of delight' had passed between the speaker and her angelic muse in 'From House to Home'. Much of this later poem is a conscience-stricken lament for 'work undone' (48) and time wasted. However, in the middle, a somewhat surprising allegory of two larks interrupts the speaker's musings:

> A singing lark rose toward the sky,
> Circling he sang amain;
> He sang, a speck scarce visible sky-high,
> And then he sank again.
>
> A second like a sunlit spark
> Flashed singing up his track;
> But never overtook that foremost lark,
> And songless fluttered back.
>
> (17–24)

In 1880, probably at about the time that she wrote the poem, Christina read an anonymous review of her own and her brother's poetry (in fact written by Alice Meynell), and assured Dante Gabriel: 'Don't think me such a goose as to feel keenly mortified at being put below you, the head of our house in so many ways' (*Letters*: 87). 'In the Willow Shade' hints at a relation of kinship and rivalry between the two larks, who once flew in each other's tracks, but now are separated. The first, specifically male bird soared and sang, but the second could not compete and fell back 'songless'.

As if confirming this separation, the rest of the poem shows the speaker sitting alone by a stream and willows. The scene and the situation is the same as that described thirty-four years before in 'The Dream'. A sudden sense of desertion leaves the speaker, as it did then, solitary, chilled and bereft of meaning:

> Slow wind sighed thro' the willow leaves,
>   The ripple made a moan,
> The world drooped murmuring like a thing that grieves;
>   And then I felt alone.
>
> I rose to go, and felt the chill,
>   And shivered as I went;
> Yet shivering wondered, and I wonder still,
>   What more that willow meant;
>
> That silvery weeping willow tree
>   With all leaves shivering,
> Which spent one long day overshadowing me
>   Beside a spring in Spring.
>
> (61–72)

The unexpected specificity of 'And then I felt alone' hints at a previous companionship which nothing in the poem, except the allegory of the two larks, substantiates. Feeling herself 'in the shade', not only of willows but perhaps also of the 'foremost lark', the speaker feels a 'chill' at a parting which, like all the others, is almost invisible: 'And then I felt alone'. The lover who departed by a stream in 'The Dream' is still departing, in a *déjà vu* which leaves a sort of hidden empty shock in the air. These 'broken-hearted' verses echo with the sound of a break which happened so far in the past that the difference is almost imperceptible, a change with no change, a mere 'chill' in the atmosphere. Yet it makes for this speaker all the difference – a difference between something and nothing, love and lovelessness, then and now. Her imagination, in the Romantic tradition, hovers on this threshold and re-enacts, with the obsession of a trauma, its original, small, yet catastrophic differential of loss.

Something else, however, is associated with this scene of desertion. Although it causes the atmosphere to chill and break, it also creates a perplexity of meaning which then characteristically develops into a playfully unresolved enigma: 'Yet shivering wondered, and I wonder still, / What more that willow meant'. There is something 'more', some unexpressed memory, object or secret behind this melancholy scene. Such a buried reference haunts the poem with a sense of lost meaning, of a solution which lies somehow permanently off-stage. The riddle at the end, 'I wonder still', and the light pun of 'spring in Spring', turns the emphasis away from any drama of love to a play of words, of language suddenly free from the claims of narrative. There is a secret in this poem, as in so many others, which presses against its conventionally sad landscape with distracting, enigmatic, almost whimsical persistence: 'What more that willow meant . . .'

It is this secret reserve of meaning, unidentified yet expressed, which gives Rossetti's 'broken-hearted' lyrics their distinctive tone of emotional riddle, of nonsense at the heart, of wit. The images of the echo and the dark pool suggest that the imagination catches experience across a tract of time or place, rather than directly and spontaneously. As a result, the emotional content of Rossetti's verse seems vague, light, even empty-handed. Far from loading that verse with the proximity of the suffering body, felt in the present tense, she distances suffering into time past, and thus controls, mediates and even 'forgets' it. Where Barrett Browning writes against the heart from without, Rossetti writes against it from within – within an attitude of melancholy which constantly opens up the scope of being heartless. Rossetti is at her best, like her most obvious successor, Charlotte Mew, when catching at the echoes and reflections of experience which she seems almost too calculatingly to have dodged. In the end, the obsessive, apparently traumatised sadness of her verses is not sentimental, because it conceals indifference, chill – something verging on that 'inward laughter' of meaning which, in spite of all her weeping willows, is the secret of her difference from her merely sincere predecessors.

WINTER SECRETS

> I tell my secret? No indeed, not I:
> Perhaps some day, who knows?
> But not today; it froze, and blows, and snows,
> And you're too curious: fie!
> You want to hear it? well:
> Only, my secret's mine, and I won't tell.
> ('Winter: My Secret', *CP*: I, 47, ll. 1–6)

Behind Rossetti's religious attitude of renunciation, which many critics have noted and discussed (Gilbert and Gubar, 1979: 549–54; Blake, 1983: 3–25; Rosenblum, 1986: 175–99; Jones, 1991: 51–88;), it is possible to discern an opposite attitude of secrecy, freedom and caprice. Jerome McGann has suggested that Rossetti 'employs the symbol of the personal secret as a sign of the presence of individuality' (1980: 247), and certainly the element of 'coquetry' (Armstrong, 1987: 124), the playing fast-and-loose both with the reader and with the reference in 'Winter:

My Secret', suggests a self fully in control of its own game. The end of the poem, which promises a disclosure, in fact only offers one of Rossetti's playful alternatives:

> If there's not too much sun nor too much cloud,
> And the warm wind is neither still nor loud,
> Perhaps my secret I may say,
> Or you may guess.
>
> (31–34)

Such a secret comes to almost nothing between these opposites. It belongs to a time when there is neither 'sun' nor 'cloud', neither stillness nor loudness. This verbal balancing trick, like 'Haply I may remember, / And haply may forget', offers a choice which only repeats the riddle of the poem. To be between such opposites is to be on so thin a threshold of sense that it is almost pure nonsense. Yet such thresholds are the key to that flaunted secretiveness which at times seems to be the very subject, rather than just the technique, of Rossetti's poetry.

One such secret poem is 'My Dream', written in 1855 when the poet was 25. It purports to relate the speaker's true dream of a crocodile who eats all his brothers and grows large, powerful and lazy, till, at the end, in a theatrical attitude of repentance, 'The prudent crocodile rose on his feet / And shed appropriate tears and wrung his hands' (*CP*: I, 39–40, ll. 47–8). Whether or not there is any intended family joke, Dante Gabriel evidently relished the poem and gave Christina a Griset drawing of an alligator to commemorate her unbrotherly crocodile. The poem ends with similar tactics of riddling disavowal as 'In the Willow Shade' and 'Winter: My Secret':

> What can it mean? you ask. I answer not
> For meaning, but myself must echo, What?
> And tell it as I saw it on the spot.
>
> (49–51)

In a fit of conscience, however, Christina scrawled in the margins of her 1875 edition of the poem, 'not a real dream' (in *PW*: 479). The poem's small lie of telling it 'on the spot' obviously irked the older woman, whose religious scruples had by now become quite exacting. The ending is thus doubly deceiving: the poem was not a work of 'weighed and sifted truth' (2) as it proclaims, but a conscious invention masquerading as a true dream. Poems, Rossetti knows at some level of her consciousness, evolve from lies, from the 'tissue of hugged lies' which formed the beautiful pleasure garden of the soul in 'From House to Home'. William assures us that Christina had 'the most rigid regard for truth' (1904:

lxvi), and certainly in her later years she could be anxiously finicky in its pursuit. In 1890, for instance, she took the trouble of writing to him to revise her half-truth or perhaps downright lie 'that morning prayer took me (about?) half an hour, – but it did not and does not' (*Letters*: 175). Clearly the difference between the imagination's lie and the mind's strict truth, between, as it were, the laughing Pan and the sighing true gods, worried Christina.

None the less, secrets, with their mischief of reference, fascinated Rossetti, and her poems are full of them. In particular, they belong to women. 'Reflection', for instance, appears at first to be a traditional courtly love poem: there is a woman at her window and a man trying to catch her attention below. But the wild distraction of the one and the increasing irritability of the other seem far from courtly. Failing to read the woman's look of indifference, the man's suspense eventually turns to petulance:

> Now if I could guess her secret
> Were it worth the guess? –
> Time is lessening, hope is lessening,
> Love grows less and less:
> What care I for *no* or *yes*? –
> (*CP*: III, 266–8, ll. 41–5)

As his unrequited love sours into boredom, the 'secret' of the woman dwindles in significance: 'Were it worth the guess?' As a comment on the idealisms of courtly love, the idea that there *is* no secret is devastatingly derisive. Yet in spite of this, the semantic charge, even of nothing, has a strong pull. 'Were it worth the guess?' still draws towards 'it' as towards some hidden, unguessed object at the heart of the poem, or rather, once again, at the heart of the woman, where most of Rossetti's secrets are located. Framed as a love story, 'Reflection', typically, turns into a conundrum. Between its words and its object there is an obliquity which cannot be straightened into a simple account of unrequited love. The woman, through all the man's guesses and interpretations, keeps her 'secret'.

This is emphasised in the last stanza, where the speaker imagines an appropriate ending for his entirely self-invented love story:

> I will give her stately burial,
> Willow branches bent;
> Have her carved in alabaster,
> As she dreamed and leant
> While I wondered what she meant.
> (51–5)

At the end of *The Improvisatrice*, L.E.L. showed Lorenzo penitently in love with the dead heroine's picture. Rossetti, here, draws out the implication of the older poet's innumerable dead women who become pictures or statues, by making this effigy a figment, not of the woman's but of the man's desires. He will 'Have her carved in alabaster', and thus indeed have her in the only way he can. He will be, if not her lover, at least her sculptor of death, and she, by the inevitable logic of his desires, will be as much alive in stone as she seemed dead to him in life. The punitive and acquisitive motives behind this inflicted death-wish are clearly audible. Meanwhile, however, in contrast to the Improvisatrice, this woman dreams on, 'deaf' (37) to all her lover's morbid romancing. The sense of her 'secret' in the poem makes all his speculation irrelevant. 'What' she means is an object outside his frame of reference, intact and inviolable. Such a secret is both the object of the poem and also its negation; its sense and also its nonsense. 'While I wondered what she meant' rings, at the end, with an irresistible double reference both to the woman at the window and also to the woman poet who has played this toying game of meaning within the very house of courtly love.

In one of her best short stories, Rossetti offers a memorable symbol of the secret so many poems display and conceal. 'The Lost Titian', which was first published in 1856, is set in Venice. Titian has just completed the masterpiece of his life, but, we are told, 'its subject was a secret' (*Commonplace*: 147). Rumour abounds that it represents a vintage of grapes or a dance of wood-nymphs, but no one knows for certain. The evening before its exhibition, Titian gambles with his friend and rival, the minor painter, Gianni, and in a reckless moment stakes all on his new masterpiece. He loses, of course, and forfeits the painting. Gianni himself then falls into debt and, in order not to lose the priceless work, paints over it a picture of 'a dragon, flaming, clawed, preposterous' (158). Unfortunately, however, the ruse misfires. His creditor is so enchanted by 'the scaly monster' (160), desiring it as a sign for his wayside inn, that he remits all of Gianni's debt and, instead, takes away his picture. Gianni determines to produce a copy of his dragon and thus retrieve the hidden Titian, but just as it is almost completed, he dies. As Rossetti points out: 'His secret died with him' (161). Somewhere, meanwhile, a flaming twinkling dragon with erect tail hangs on a wayside inn, hiding one of the world's lost masterpieces.

The story is much better than Dante Gabriel's 'Hand and Soul' which it partly recalls, because, unlike that story, it entirely resists allegorical decoding. In fact, its very theme is the impossibility of such decoding. Its meaning is on the one hand as flamboyantly suggestive as the dragon, but on the other, as hidden and secret as the lost Titian. In terms of the plot, the irony lies in the fact that Gianni's covering dragon turns out to be as valuable, at least in the world's eyes, as the masterpiece it hides. But this image of the double painting, the secret masterpiece below and the vivid decoy above, also expresses something of Rossetti's own art: its moral nonsense, whether goblins, crocodiles or dragons, its obliqueness and disguises and, above all, its secret meanings which have been forever concealed, forever lost:

> Or, after all, perhaps there's none:
> Suppose there is no secret after all,
> But only just my fun.
> ('Winter: My Secret', *CP*: I, 47,
> ll. 7–9)

In the end, the secret itself may be only another device of 'fun'. By implication, the idea of some inherent, unlockable meaning at the heart of poetry may be only another of its enticing lies; another of the 'supplementary' flaming dragons, debarring the way to the true original. 'The Lost Titian' is about secrets, both the secret of Titian's subject matter and the secret of the painting's whereabouts. Both of those, however, are permanently lost references, like so many of the secrets in Rossetti's poetry. All that remains in this seductively self-deconstructing story is the difference, never to be resolved but always felt, between the lying decoy and the nostalgically desired authenticity of the lost work, like the difference between the man's interpretation and the woman's dream, the lilies on the surface and the dark pool below. Secrets, for Rossetti, are a figure for that game of reference which, true to the mood of many of her poems, is both a haunting loss and a teasing strategy of 'fun'.

The two come together in that motif which Rossetti, from an early age, made distinctively her own: death. Christina was obsessed by it from an early age. A letter exists, for instance, in which the young girl asks to see her dead grandmother, 'unless the lapse of so many days renders it undesirable'. She was similarly concerned that, at her own death, certain observances should be kept. She left instructions that Mackenzie Bell should be allowed to see her if he called within a reasonable time (Packer, 1963: 407) and she informed her Executor that 'I wish to be buried in the nearest approach convenient to a *perishable* coffin'[4] – a forethought which hints at a peculiarly literal-minded obsession with burial. Yet here too the subject easily slips into comedy. In one of her short stories, 'Nick' (1853), she turns her fascination with being 'posthumous' to comic account when the hero, a curmudgeonly old man who wishes ill to his neighbours, finds his dream of being robbed and killed come true. As he is being buried, 'An utter horror seized him, while, at the same time, he felt a strange consciousness that his hair would not stand on end because he was dead' (*Commonplace*: 178). Being conscious in unconsciousness, which was her early Sappho's expressed wish, inevitably has its edge of 'fun'.

Christina, for all her religious scruples, also seems to have been haunted by doubt. Her widespread reputation in the nineteenth century for being '"a saint"' (Tynan, 1913: 158) or, in the twentieth, for being 'a simple and pious woman' (Curran, 1971: 298) are only justified by the externals of her life. Her brother William, who witnessed her disturbing deathbed terrors, recognised in his sister 'an awful sense of unworthiness, shadowed by an awful uncertainty' (1904: lv). In the penultimate sonnet of her *Later Life* sequence, Rossetti herself gives voice to this uncertainty:

> While I supine with ears that cease to hear,
>   With eyes that glaze, with heart pulse running down
> (Alas! no saint rejoicing on her bed),
>   May miss the goal at last, may miss a crown.
>   (*CP*: II, 138–50, No 27, ll. 11–14)

Rehearsing the attitude of her death for almost fifty years before the event, this poet was, in the end, terrified she would prove 'no saint' and 'miss the goal'.

Yet in many of her poems, missing the goal is precisely the point. The twilight thresholds to which her imagination is drawn are places of disorientation and delay. They open up a vague and obsessional dreamland in which consciousness seems suspended between heaven and earth, remembering and forgetting. Both the emotional cause and the religious goal are liable to be forfeited to that intervening fantasy which distracts the mind's purpose and diverts desire:

> And dreaming through the twilight
>   That doth not rise nor set,
> Haply I may remember,
>   And haply may forget.
>   (*CP*: I, 58, ll. 13–16)

The time of being dead is itself a secret between-time, not a conclusion. Such a time seems liberated from both life and afterlife, both regret and expectation. This most erotic and religious of poets is also, at some level of consciousness, profoundly indifferent to both love and faith. For to go 'dreaming through the twilight' is to suspend in imagination both the call of the heart, on the one hand, and the goal of heaven, on the other. This is the hallmark of many of Rossetti's 'posthumous' women who are dead but unrisen, buried but unhopeful. They are not heavenly Beatrices or Blessed Damozels, whose role is to lead the quester to salvation (Harrison, 1988: 157), but heartless, fixated dreamers, whose attention, like the woman's in 'Reflection', is focused elsewhere.

The work which most fully enacts this drama of missed goals is *The Prince's Progress* (1866), the title poem of Rossetti's second major volume of verse and the natural parallel to *Goblin Market*.[5] This story of a prince's love-quest for a dying princess seems, like much of Rossetti's verse, to reproduce all the courtly arrangements of desire: the man journeys, the woman waits, the man proves himself worthy, the woman is his prize, the man is faithless, the woman dies. Over this, Rossetti sets a religious symbolism of the heavenly Bridegroom come to woo the human soul. As in *Goblin Market*, the discrepancy between the secular and the religious meanings is extreme. If the prince is a Christ figure, he is also a flirtatious laggard, full of casuistries, self-deceptions and bonhomie; if the goal of the quest is salvation, its prevailing atmosphere is one of pleasure-loving distractions and dream-riddled desires. Rossetti's religious patterns of thought are profoundly and disturbingly at odds with the imaginative vagaries of her verse. It is those vagaries, however, which create the essential tension of her writing – a tension which, as always, involves strange perspectives of time.

At the start, the princess asks a crucial question about time:

> 'How long shall I wait, come heat come rime?' –
> 'Till the strong Prince comes, who must come in time'
> (Her women say), 'there's a mountain to climb,
> A river to ford. Sleep, dream and sleep:
> Sleep' (they say): 'we've muffled the chime,
> Better dream than weep.
> (*CP*: I, 95–110, ll. 7–12)

However, the answer she gets is ambiguous. The prince will come '"in time"', which may mean 'in good time' or just 'some time'. Such indeterminacy makes for a frivolous sort of reassurance, while hinting at how much of the subsequent poem will be, as Kathleen Blake has noted (1983: 7), a play on time. The prince's fitful progress is then beautifully captured in the metrical waywardness of the verse itself where, as Alice Meynell points out, the stress falls 'now upon a syllable and now upon a rest' (*New Review*, N.S., 12(1895), 204). Christina herself defended the work's 'metric jolt' (W. M. Rossetti, 1903: 77) to Dante Gabriel who, like many reviewers, preferred women's poetry to be (morally as well as metrically) regular. It is evidently Rossetti's intention, however, to describe, not a fluent progress but one of missed beats and missed steps of the way. Time, both poetic and emotional, is an unreliable quantity in this poem. On the one hand its passing is inevitable, because the prince ' "must come" ', but on the other hand it is incalculable, ' "we've muffled the chime" '. The pressure of the inevitable upon the incalculable creates the intensely uncertain stress of its whole vagrant progress.

The prince's infirmity of purpose is described, from the start, as a mis-calculation of time:

> In his world-end palace the strong Prince sat,
> Taking his ease on cushion and mat,
> Close at hand lay his staff and his hat.
>   'When wilt thou start? the bride waits, O youth.' –
> 'Now the moon's at full; I tarried for that,
>   Now I start in truth.'
>
>   (13–18)

Starting, like Tennyson's Ulysses, when the time is already late, the prince embarks on his nuptial quest with the first lie: ' "I tarried for that" '. Quick to make a pretext of the moon, he is none the less still slow to leave. In fact, he tarries so long to talk about his bride that, some five stanzas later, he sets out, not at the full moon but at dawn. Thus early is already late, desire is already delayed and ' "truth" ' is already a lie. The very lightness of his step as he sets out sounds hollow:

> While the song swept by, beseeching and meek,
> Up rose the Prince with a flush on his cheek,
> Up he rose to stir and to seek,
>   Going forth in the joy of his strength;
> Strong of limb if of purpose weak,
>   Starting at length.
>
>   (43–8)

The skip of the metre suddenly stalls in the last line, as the chiastic effect of 'Starting at length' suggests a faltering stride, a drag of purpose, an uncertainty at the very heart. This is a false dawn of desire and it is a false start.

In the course of his journey the prince dallies with a milkmaid, falls in with an old alchemist who offers him eternal life, loiters with maidens who rescue him from a river and finally arrives at the palace gate ' "Too late" '. Christina may have been drawing on several models for her prince: Collinson's religious wavering, Dante Gabriel's reluctance to marry Lizzie Siddal or Cayley's timidity in responding to her own love. The evidence of much of her poetry, however, is that the image of the dilatory lover, like that of the lover by the pool who carelessly passes by, was a requirement of her imagination long before it became a requirement of her life. Imaginative delay, in time and emotional purpose, is the atmosphere of much of her poetry, and it characterises especially her death-bound women. They die, not because the lover delayed, but because they want that opportunity of 'twilight' dallying for themselves. Rosenblum writes that, in Rossetti, ' "death" is a vehicle for expressing not only profound alienation but self-possession' (1986: 127). Even more than this, death is a symbol for being 'out of time', literally, morally and metrically – all of which are of the essence of her best poetry. Thus, between the princess's time-muffled trance and the prince's wayward progress, with all its stalling oxymorons: ' "bands loosed" ' (117), ' "slackness girt" ', ' "softness quelled" ' (119), ' "slowness fleet" ' (120), there is a sort of perfect complicity: the one requires the other, the dreaming woman requires the lover not to come, the dream itself requires the goal to be postponed. The prince is doomed by something more than just constitutional apathy to miss his goal. The motives of the dreaming woman herself go against him.

Like many Victorian quest poems, particularly Robert Browning's 'Childe Roland' which it recalls, *The Prince's Progress* is an anti-quest, unheroic and late. The prince himself is a dilettante and opportunist who, having made a pretext of the full moon, is constantly distracted by other sorts of moon: ' "You may give the full moon to me" ' (80), the milkmaid taunts, while the girl who hangs over him as he struggles in the river is 'a moon face in a shadowy place' (343). The moon is a figure for all the erotic substitutions of the quest and for all the temporal evasions of the route. The prince substitutes other women for the one, a phoney hope of eternal life for life itself, a vague moon-time for the princess's 'golden' (463) dawn. Perhaps it is because the goal of salvation was so strict and magnetic a fact of Christina's own life that the poetic temptations of deviating from it are so conflictingly strong. *The Prince's Progress* is ultimately neither a lover's quest nor a pilgrim's progress, but a poem about the infinitely seductive substitutions of poetry – substitutions encountered in Rossetti's favourite twilight region of displaced experience and desire. The way to the goal of salvation is beset by idols and simulacra: 'Was it milk now, or was it cream? / Was she a maid, or an evil dream?' (67–8), but these, like the goblin fruits, are the very stuff of poetry. They represent endless metaphorical shifts of one thing into another, 'a tissue of hugged lies', a teasing fantasy. This is not a prince's but a poet's progress, and consequently its object, like all the other secret references in Rossetti's work, is not where we would expect, in the ' "foregone conclusion" ' of faith, but rather in the shifts and devices which seem, precisely, to lose faith in their object. At some level, *The Prince's Progress* is about having nowhere very clear to go.

It is also, for all her appearance of being traditionally betrayed and nearly dead, about a princess's progress. She, after all, is the poem's dreamer out of time. It is she who leaves just as the man arrives, in a cross-purpose which is the recurrent emotional drama of Rossetti's work. Her 'posthumous' women are not dead from pique or self-pity, like L.E.L.'s ill-used Sapphos, nor are they dead from waiting too long. Instead, their death is a kind of capricious and determined choice. They, too, seek to miss 'the goal' of a woman's life. Against the heavy heritage of the heart, Rossetti writes love poems which are full of caprice and coldness, of casually missed encounters and coincidental deaths. The princess at the end of this poem dies, like the woman in 'A Pause' (*CP*: III, 215–16), almost triumphantly, as the prince arrives at the gate, while her women sing:

> 'Ten years ago, five years ago,
>   One year ago,
> Even then you had arrived in time,
>   Tho' somewhat slow;
> Then you had known her living face
>   Which now you cannot know:
> The frozen fountain would have leaped,
>   The buds gone on to blow,
> The warm south wind would have awaked
>   To melt the snow.'
>
>   (491–500)

If Christina herself remained, in William's words, '"a fountain sealed"' (1904: lxviii), it was from the sealed place, the coffin or the winter snow, that she wrote her most powerful and passionate love poems. The winter secrets of her life are not explained by this poetry, but they are uncannily repeated and echoed in it, till what looks like personal tragedy begins to appear as a highly worked invention and device. To miss life itself is to gain, in its place, the free time of the dream.

Dead women, then, are one more figure for that element of caprice and nonsense which runs through Rossetti's poems. Their teasing secrecy presses against the old structures of romance and betrayal, and suggests an ulterior motive, a hidden, colder wisdom in the woman's traditionally exposed and broken heart. To 'miss the goal', whether of love, salvation or life itself, is to find, in their place, another time, place and meaning in her poetry: the 'muffled', wayward, delighting time of fantasy, the haunted, lily-covered place of memory, and the flaming, fork-tailed dragon of all her mischievous cover-ups, her declared winter secrets which are, after all, perhaps no more than 'just my fun'. After Rossetti, only Charlotte Mew will show such a determined wintriness of the imagination in the face of the woman's 'natural' subject of love.

Augusta Webster (1837–94)

A sad thing is the morbid and artificial melancholy which the
sickly-sensitive so often prize and parade as a high proof of
high imagination. A sad thing is the life that gives itself up to
dreams, and calls weakness strength, as if the misty
purposelessness that too often mars genius were itself
genius. (*HO*: 217)

Augusta Webster's poetry, although nearly contemporary with Christina
Rossetti's, marks a decisive shift away from the model of sensibility
which still haunts and shapes the work of the younger poet. Her
rebellion against 'the morbid and artificial melancholy' of the 'sickly-
sensitive' is conducted, not like Rossetti's, by elaborating a lifelong,
teasing drama around it, but by repudiating it altogether. A sharp
exposer of 'misty purposelessness', whether in life or art, Webster is,
even more than Barrett Browning, a determined literalist of the
imagination. Her concern is not with the myth of the woman poet, but
with real, live women; not with 'genius', in all its prized and paraded
sensitivity, but with ordinary, unheroic men and women, whose lives are
determined by the solid facts and prejudices of contemporary society.
Where Rossetti is lyrical and introspective, Webster is prosaic and
dramatic; where Rossetti's imagination is out of time with reality,
Webster's is entirely of her own time. An outspoken feminist and social
critic, her verse finds its distance from the 'artificial melancholy' of the
heart by turning altogether away from self, and dramatically adopting the
voices of others.

★   ★   ★

It is interesting that when, in 1890, Rossetti criticised Gladstone's failure to include the name of Augusta Webster in his 'list of poetesses', she wondered about his motives: 'I did not notice the omission at the moment, but suspect it in retrospect' (*Letters*: 175). Evidently her suspicion is that Gladstone's well-known opposition to women's suffrage coloured his judgment. Rossetti's own impartial admiration for her poetic contemporary was already, in the 1890s, going against the tide. In 1895, William Michael Rossetti prefaced Webster's unfinished sonnet sequence, *Mother & Daughter*, with a highly laudatory review of her work, but acknowledged that her 'true rank' had not yet been 'fixed' (in *MD*: 14). Far from being fixed in any rank at all, her fate as a poet is to have disappeared almost entirely from literary history. In 1914, Theodore Watts-Dunton wrote to Hugh Walker to complain: 'It is a monstrous thing that such poetry as Augusta Webster's should be unknown. Her name is not even mentioned in the *Encyclopaedia Britannica*' (Hake and Compton-Rickett, 1916: II, 18). Nor is she mentioned in, for instance, Marjorie Bald's *Women-Writers of the Nineteenth Century* (1922), Oliver Elton's *A Survey of English Literature: 1830–1880* (1927) or Ifor B. Evans' *English Poetry in the Later Nineteenth Century* (1933), all of which devote space to other women poets. Evidently by this time, the stylishness of the aesthetes and the milky lyricism of the Georgians had conspired to oust such socially committed voices as Webster's. When, in 1929, Vita Sackville-West searched for some biographical information about her, she could find little more than 'so much orange-peel and spume' (1929: 123), and the situation has changed little since then. The letters which passed between Webster and Christina Rossetti seem to have disappeared (see Bell, 1898: 111), and the little that is known about this poet amounts to a few, unsensational paragraphs.

Augusta was born in Dorset, in 1837, and her earliest years were spent on board the *Griper*, of which her father, George Davies, was Vice-Admiral. Later, he became Chief Constable of Cambridgeshire, where Augusta was evidently given a good classical education, for in 1866 she published much-acclaimed translations of *Prometheus Bound* and *Medea*. She attended the Cambridge school of art and made brief educational visits to Paris and Geneva. Perhaps it was at this time that she also gained admission to the South Kensington Art School. In one of the few personal anecdotes about her, Ray Strachey recalls that Augusta 'nearly dashed the prospects of women art students for ever by being expelled for whistling' (1978: 96). In 1863 she married Thomas Webster, Fellow and law lecturer at Trinity College, Cambridge, by whom she had one child, a daughter. Whatever the reasons for it, the fact of having only one child is overtly defended and celebrated, against the prevailing fashion, in her sonnet sequence *Mother & Daughter*:

Since first my little one lay on my breast
I never needed such a second good,
Nor felt a void left in my motherhood
She filled not always to the utterest.
The summer linnet, by glad yearnings pressed,
Builds room enough to house a callow brood:
I prayed not for another child – nor could;
My solitary bird had my heart's nest.
But she is cause that any baby thing
If it but smile, is one of mine in truth,
And every child becomes my natural joy:
And, if my heart gives all youth fostering,
Her sister, brother, seems the girl or boy:
My darling makes me mother to their youth.
                                        (*MD*: 41)

This daughter later became an actress and performed in one of her mother's plays, *In a Day*, at Terry's Theatre, London, in 1890 (*Dictionary of National Biography*: under Webster).

Webster's first two volumes of poems were published in 1860 and 1864 under the pseudonym 'Cecil Home'. In 1864 she also published a novel, *Lesley's Guardians*, but thereafter published under her own name. It seems that, in the late 1860s, Augusta persuaded her husband to resign his partnership and move to London so that she could pursue her literary career (Hake and Compton-Rickett, 1916: II, 17). There she became increasingly involved in the women's suffrage movement. Frances Power Cobbe mentions her as being a member of one of the suffrage committees in the 1860s (1904: 586), which suggests that she may also have known John Stuart Mill, who was one of the prime movers of women's suffrage at this time, and who is clearly one of the models for her own liberal philosophy. Augusta also served on the London School Board where, Mackenzie Bell claims, 'her influence was considerable' (in Miles, 1891–7: VII, 499), no doubt particularly in the promotion of education for women. She wrote for *The Examiner* during the 1870s, and was, for some years in the 1880s and 90s, the regular poetry reviewer for the *Athenaeum*.[1] Apart from these sparing details, two footnotes to poems tell that she was in Italy in 1881 and 1882. When she died in 1894, Watts-Dunton wrote an obituary in the *Athenaeum*, quoting an earlier article of his own which referred to ' "the noble band represented by George Eliot, Mrs. Webster, and Miss Cobbe, who, in virtue of lofty purpose, purity of soul, and deep sympathy with suffering humanity, are just now far ahead of the men" ' (*Athenaeum* (15 September 1894), 355). Whether or not Webster was personally acquainted with George Eliot as well as with Power Cobbe, such company is, intellectually and politically, the right one. She belongs in the liberal, humanitarian tradition of the high

Victorians, with its social responsibility and philanthropical concern – the very thing which the aesthetes, as Yeats would recall, rebelliously 'denounced' (1936: xxvi) at the end of the century.

In her own time, by contrast, Webster was much acclaimed. In 1871 Buxton Forman affirmed that 'I have more than once seen claimed for her the first place among the women-poets of England' (1871: 183), and Edmund Stedman proclaimed her verse 'nearly equal . . . to that of the best of her sister artists' (1887: 281). The virtue which was most often extolled in Webster's work, but which also sent her critics into a flurry of sexual anxiety, was her 'strength', by which they seem to have meant an intellectual, socio-political content. A contemporary review of her play about Caligula, *The Sentence* (1887), described it as 'masculine and vigorous', while another asserted that 'No other Englishwoman has done work of such masculine strength' (in *Sel*: 11). Eric Robertson praised her poetry for its 'man-like reserve of expression' (1883: 354–5), while Mackenzie Bell, writing for Miles's anthology *The Poets and the Poetry of the Century*, turns somersaults of sexual praise and blame in his effort to define the precise nature of that strength. He points out that the 'quality which distinguishes her from all the other women poets of her time is concentrated strength', or, as he confusingly explains, 'that quality which, as it is generally deemed the specially masculine quality, is called virility' (in Miles, 1891–7: 500). He then hastily retracts:

> Virile, however, as is the strength of the writer, her sex is constantly declaring itself by a discernment of the most secret workings of the heart of Woman such as is far beyond the reach of masculine eyes, and a passionate, almost it might be said, a biassed sympathy with the cause of Woman in her relation to Man. (502)

He seems, at first, to repeat the conventional description of women's poetry as tenderly open-hearted. However, his praise then runs into another problem: too much interest in the woman's heart, that notoriously soft subject of women's verse, may become 'a biassed sympathy'. Between the feminine and the feminist there is a thin line, as the heart may cease to be an open secret and become a 'cause'. Bell skids from admiration to reproof, from male 'virility' to female feeling, in a clumsy effort to extricate himself from his own anatomical values. In the anthology itself, Webster is represented, not by her best, politically explicit poems about 'Woman in her relation to Man', but by a selection of disappointingly innocuous lyrics. Her most famous work on 'the cause of Woman', *A Castaway*, does not appear.

Webster's journalism, and particularly her articles for *The Examiner*, which were collected in a volume called *A Housewife's Opinions* in 1879, help to eke out this scanty information. These essays range from homely advice on domestic servants, gossip, hobbies and the wearing of mourning, to political commentary on the latest controversial parliamentary debates. Women's employment, suffrage and education provoke some of Webster's most saucy criticisms. In 1847, partly as a result of the conscience-stirring of poems like Barrett Browning's 'The Cry of the Children', the Ten Hours Bill was passed, to limit the working hours of women and children to ten a day. In 1873, a Home Office report recommended the further reduction of women's hours of work from sixty to fifty-four a week. Ironically, the cause which had once seemed a matter of ordinary humanity, now threatened to become a source of unjust discrimination in an increasingly competitive market. The report roused the ire of many in the women's movement, and was, in the end, rejected by the House. However, Henry Fawcett's attempts, in 1874 and again in 1878, to free women even from the restrictions of the first Ten Hours Bill were defeated.

Webster, like many women at the time, is quick to point out that such differentiating legislation enslaves more than it protects. She writes that women's lives, as a result of it:

> will be a slavery, not to work, but to laws which forbid them to work. They will be able to starve, for no law can forbid that, but they will not be able to be weary with labour: they will be free to battle against poverty by help of vice, but not to injure their healths by long and exhausting tasks, and their feminine dignity by coarse and mannish occupations . . .

As she forcefully concludes: 'Some women would like a choice' (*HO*: 173). Her reasoning cunningly elides the issue of labour with that of sexual attraction. Male MPs, she suggests, are more concerned about the 'coarse and mannish' appearance of women who work than about the resource of 'vice' to which women might turn for lack of work. Prostitution, she hints, seems to them less objectionable than mannishness, 'vice' less objectionable than loss of sexual appeal. It would be preferable, she continues, to enforce Protection Orders, by which women who suffer domestic violence should be granted a legal separation from their husbands, with alimony (178), rather than to forbid women to work if they need to. Those Orders in fact came into being in 1886, when the Married Women (Maintenance in Case of Desertion) Act was passed. She ends by objecting to the way in which parliamentary legislation increasingly controls women's lives, while excluding them from representation. 'At present', she writes, 'it is the blind leading the dumb' (178).

In 1865 John Stuart Mill was elected to Parliament, and he took the opportunity to introduce a suffrage amendment to the 1867 Reform Bill. In 1866, the first Women's Suffrage Committee, on which Webster almost certainly served, was set up to rally support for Mill, while many others were subsequently established throughout the country. Mill's amendment was defeated, and in 1870, Jacob Bright's Suffrage Bill, which was carried by the House, was defeated at committee stage when Gladstone expressed his opposition to it. Webster gives a gleeful summary of the parliamentary arguments used against the franchise:

> There are fears that [women] will make matrimony illegal, suppress cooking, and have the Prime Minister chosen for his good looks and his skill at lawn-tennis. It is also apprehended that they will at once throw off all their present customs, tastes, virtues, and attractions – which, as is well known, are the compensations bestowed on them by nature for the absence of a vote – and will become coarse-featured un-mannerly hybrids, men-hating and hateful to men. They will wear coats and trousers, they will refuse to sew on shirt-buttons, they will leave off *poudre de riz* and auricomiferous waters, they will be Bishops and Judges, and will break all the commandments. (*HO*: 273)

She whisks through religious, social and culinary arguments to suggest, not only a panic-stricken confusion of male values, but also, cunningly, that the argument from the Ten Commandments is much on the same level as the one from '*poudre de riz*'. The sanctity both of marriage and of feminine perfumery is threatened by the vote. The holy duties of cooking and sewing are similarly under the gravest threat, while the whole moral law is likely to be overturned by the wearing of 'coats and trousers'. The whole passage enjoys the implicit double nature of the myth of womanhood. Within the domesticated, powdered and perfumed angel of the hearth lurks an ambitious, immoral, trousered monster waiting her turn. Such a creature, if let loose from the home, will evidently overturn all the laws of society, which essentially depend on one: the law of marriage. In 1841, an article in the *Edinburgh Review* had confidently asserted:

> we assume that it is never contemplated that the right of voting should be claimed by married women during their husbands' lives: or for unmarried women living under the protection of their parents. The divisions which would thereby be created in the heart of families, and the extensive injury consequent therefrom to domestic peace, are objections too obvious to require discussion. (*Edinburgh Review*, 73(1841), 203)

Domestic angels keep the peace by keeping quiet, and the harmony of the home rests on the acquiescing agreement of wives with their husbands. Given such arguments, it was tactically advantageous for the suffrage movement to leave wives and mothers for the moment out of account. However, the extent to which the Victorians hung their sexual morality on cooking, shirt-buttons and silence gave women, particularly in the last decades of the century, a strong cause for revolt against the whole system of men and matrimony. As Webster herself hints, in a sly double irony at the start, the sanctities at stake are considerable: 'There are fears that [women] will make matrimony illegal . . .'

The education of girls was another cause which she strenuously championed. The Education Act of 1870 made primary education compulsory for girls as well as boys, while in 1872 the establishment of the Girls' Public Day School Trust made secondary education available to some girls. Meanwhile, Girton College in Cambridge had been founded in 1869 and Newnham in 1871. Oxford followed a few years later with its own women's colleges. However, neither Oxford nor Cambridge allowed women to receive degrees. They could attend classes and sit examinations; they were even told their degree results informally by sympathetic examiners. But officially they remained without qualification. The absurdity of this 'polite attention on the part of the examiners' and 'voluntary heroism' (*HO*: 92) on the part of the women students, as Webster points out, turned girls' education into a 'caucus-race' (101) – a sort of all-win, all-lose intellectual caper. It was only when London University opened its degrees to women in 1879 that they were given 'that great boon of life, a fair field and no favour' (95). Irish and Scottish universities quickly followed suit, but Oxford did not give degrees to women until 1920 and Cambridge not until 1947. Education, in some cases, proved an even harder bastion to storm than the vote.

Not only does Webster insist on the value of the degree itself, but also on the wider dignifying of women's time which it entails. Generally, as she puts it, a woman's time is regarded as 'needless to the owner and free to whoever takes it, like blackberries in a hedge' (160). This promiscuous free-for-all of the middle-class girl's leisure is much more disabling than hard work. A proper vocational education will ensure, not only that women will be capable of earning their own living, but also that they will not suffer from that weariness of a life given over to 'the aimlessness and drifting and fussy futility' (96) of protected domesticity. Webster's arguments recall Florence Nightingale's in her prose fragment, 'Cassandra', which was privately printed in 1859. Mill, among others, advised her not to publish it more widely, but it seems likely, from the similarity of their arguments, that Webster saw the private edition. In it, Nightingale also rails against society's theft of women's time: 'Women never have an half-hour in all their lives (excepting before or after anybody is up in the house) that they can call their own . . . it is laid down, that our time is of no value' (in Strachey, 1978: 402). At least a respected education, Webster urges, will free girls from this dutiful availability in the home, and ensure that their 'time will be considered to have some value' (*HO*: 96).

Education alone, however, would not bring about this change of attitude. Alice Meynell, writing in the 1890s, explained to a correspondent how a precious evening's work had been lost '"because three men called after dinner. One wanted to talk literature, the other wanted to talk of religion, and the third was burning to tell me of his engagement . . ."' This hard-pressed mother of seven, poet and journalist was not surprisingly '"sometimes . . . on the verge of crying"' (in Badeni, 1981: 101). In 1928, Virginia Woolf was driven to despair by the freeloading assumptions of a particular male visitor. As she wrote in her diary:

> Is there a woman of my acquaintance who could sit in my arm chair from 3 to 6.30 without the semblance of a suspicion that I may be busy, or tired, or bored; & so sitting could talk, grumbling & grudging, of her difficulties, worries; then eat chocolates, then read a book, & go at last, apparently self-complacent & wrapped in a kind of blubber of misty self satisfaction? (1977–84: 137–8)

Evidently the problem lay deeper than the enlightened, social cure for it offered by Webster.

Elsewhere in these essays, she probes the tangle of myth and prejudice behind many social attitudes. In 'Husband-Hunting and Match-Making', for instance, she points to the contradictory romantic attitudes expected of marriageable girls:

> People think women who do not want to marry unfeminine: people think women who do want to marry immodest: people combine both opinions by regarding it as unfeminine for women not to look forward longingly to wifehood as the hope and purpose of their lives, and ridiculing or contemning any individual women of their acquaintance whom they may suspect of entertaining such a longing. This is hard upon marriageable women. . . . They must wish and not wish; they must by no means give, they must certainly not withhold, encouragement; they must not let a gentleman who is paying attention think them waiting for his offer; they must not let him think they . . . are not waiting for his offer . . . (*HO*:234)

As she wryly summarises, 'the position of our multitude of fresh unpremeditating girls with no particular office in life except to be marriageable may be likened to that of the spell-bound princess waiting . . . for a husband', although, she adds, 'it is not possible to assert that in all marriages the bride believes her bridegroom is the prince' (230). She may be remembering Rossetti's own 'Spell-bound' princess, who fails to wake when her prince arrives, and thus deprives him for ever of his role of husbandly arousal. However, it is characteristic of Webster to reject such fairy-tale formulas altogether. Sleeping beauties, in her works, are only ordinary girls who are waiting, while appearing not to wait, hoping while appearing not to hope. Their sleep is a figure, not for poetic dreams, but for the hypocrisy and resulting mental paralysis of trying to do and think two contradictory things at once; for being both dedicated sexual objects and innocently blank sexual subjects. Webster's journalism, like her poetry, is ultimately concerned with the political truths behind life's pleasing myths, with the real, listless, ill-educated girls behind the spell-bound beauties of fairy-tale.

This scepticism of the poetic and respect for the secular reality is everywhere apparent in her writing. The main cause of women's emancipation, for instance, is recognised, not as an intellectual 'enlightenment' of the age, but as a demographic 'necessity' (241). The census of 1851 showed that there were already half a million more women than men in Britain, and the figure increased throughout the second half of the century. As Webster points out, most legislation assumed that every woman would be in the legal and financial charge of a man, whether husband, father or brother. It was only the stark unreality of this ideal which encouraged the better training and education of women. 'It was seen by all', she writes,

> that persons who have to fend for themselves must not be trained merely to the adherent clingingness which may be very seemly and loveable when there is the due somebody to cling to, but which is looked on as inappropriate, to say the least of it, in women unattached. (241–2)

As Ray Strachey points out, from 1870 onwards women were employed in most of the light trades and industries, usually 'at half or less than half' (1978: 239) the wages of men. Their 'emancipation' was due, not to moral progress, but to greedy market forces.

Thus, under the guise of homely wisdom, A Housewife's Opinions ironically mocks many of the cherished opinions of the day. Webster advocates, for instance, a more rational dress for women, including the wearing of 'trousers' (45), and criticises both the show and the expense of 'mourning' (in 1912 it was still possible to buy corsets respectfully threaded with black lace!); she argues the virtue of 'talking shop' (179), if only to challenge the social requirement that women should always 'talk companionably of what they know nothing about' (180), and she advocates the reading of light literature if only because novel-writing keeps many women in work (192). Of the subject generally assumed to be the special prerogative of women, she has little to say. 'Love, with the wooing left in it, is a sensitive and fault-finding passion', she declares, and proposes that a happy marriage requires, not love, but 'a certain healthy indifference' (201). She is careful, too, to specify that there are other kinds of marriage than the usual one between the sexes: 'there are persons', she writes, 'spinster sisters for instance, no less linked together, although there is no law to enforce the bond' (202).

Altogether, the writer who emerges from these casually provocative writings is an unsentimental social critic, a questioner of grand certainties and a debunker of romantic myths. Not an out-and-out radical, Webster's opinions grow out of a middle current of liberal thinking in the nineteenth century: her scepticism is less angrily polemical than amusingly implicit, her feminism is essentially practical and her views are usually disguised, but not blunted, by ironic humour. Hers is the spirit of pluralist truth-finding best represented by Mill's *On Liberty* (1859), with its insistence that 'the interests of truth require a diversity of opinions' (1974: 114). Like him, Webster uses such 'diversity' to challenge smug or conventional creeds and to insist on a liberal pluralism which refuses to marshal reality into an idealised shape. As a poet, hers is a critical and not a myth-making voice – a voice more concerned with opinions, facts and ideologies than with unsocialised feelings and introspective fantasies. Her plain-speaking register of worldly wisdom and political demystification emerges in works which represent yet another challenging alternative to the singing sincerity expected of women poets.

TOWARDS MANY TRUTHS

Webster's mundane sanity finds its most successful poetic expression, not in the self-conscious musicality of the lyric but in the conversational immediacy and contemporary reference of the dramatic monologue, for which her main model is Robert Browning. Her concern to speak, not passionately and personally from the heart, but, detachedly, from the feelings and thoughts of others, is yet another version of the 'hard & cold thing' women poets needed to challenge facile warm-heartedness. Where Rossetti found the needed detachment within, in a lapse of time which puts the heart itself at a distance, Webster bypasses the self, and looks to the truth in society outside. She thus represents the artistic attitude which was already, in the 1870s and 80s, being challenged by the first aesthetes. Pater, in 'The School of Giorgione' (1877) for instance, is already calling for a poetry which rejects social realism of any kind. 'Art, then', he asserts, 'is thus always striving to be independent of the mere intelligence, to become a matter of pure perception, to get rid of its responsibilities to its subject or material' (1910: I, 138). Webster, however, remains quintessentially a poet of the 'intelligence' and of social 'responsibilities'. This is both her 'strength' and, admittedly, her limitation. Humanitarian and sceptical, she is concerned to earth idealisms and myths in the anonymous driving force of material conditions which cannot be refined into 'pure perception'. In fact, perception is never 'pure' in her work; it is always modified by a reflection from outside. Her verse, therefore, keeps few reserves of meaning, few secrets which are superfluous to its subject matter. It lacks the free play of 'sweet music' for its own sake, but, at the same time, its social and sexual ironies create another kind of play: the play of ideology 'at work' in the poem. Her attention to the social structures of power is not diverted by inner laughter, by that careless freedom of reference which, in Barrett Browning, was set against the social 'cost and pain' and which, in Rossetti, became the secret at the heart of all emotional and moral meaning. Instead, she recognises external reality as the basic matrix, or rather market, of all perception. Hers is, in a sense, a poetry of the market, without any goblins.

However, she too has to make the journey out of the seductive house of romance before she can find her true voice. In 1860, at the age of 23, she published her first volume, *Blanche Lisle, and other Poems*. This consists mainly of short lyrics and ballads, most of which strike an attitude of routine pathos. Poems like 'Cruel Agnes', 'Forsaken', 'Edith' and 'The Fisherman's Betrothed' follow the tragic patterns of love with rather dull and competent assurance. The title poem itself is a creaking romance, full of Gothic terrors and second-hand poeticisms. Blanche, the orphaned, aristocratic heroine who lives with her uncle and aunt, distrusts the affections of her lover. To put her anxieties to the test, she goes at midnight to the family chapel where she witnesses a macabre funeral procession, headed by her dead father and mother. In lines which seem to convey a terror of motherhood similar to Barrett Browning's in 'Bertha in the Lane' (1844), the ghostly mother summons her daughter to look in the bier. There Blanche meets her own dead face:

> *It* slumbered very beautiful and white,
> A pallid face like a carved angel's fair,
> Framed in rich chestnut tresses soft and bright,
> Lovely in the deep calm of death's undreaming night.
> (*BL*: 30)

True to the obvious premonition of the scene, the poem then tells how the lover is faithless and the heroine dies of grief. The patterns of female desire are still caught in the posing self-pity of death.

However, even in this early poem there is a streak of ironic realism which contradicts its 'morbid and artificial melancholy' (*HO*: 217). The description of the old park and mansion clearly point to the influence of that most seductive of poems to Victorian women poets: Tennyson's 'Mariana':

> Far back the old red house seems all asleep,
> No hum of being stirring through its walls,
> It frowns like some enchanted ancient keep
> Where drowsiness on whoso enters falls,
> And with the might of sloth its captives thralls;
> Two cedar giants, glooming at each side,
> Throw dull dark shadows on the dull dark walls . . .
>
> (*BL*: 3)

This, evidently, is a variation of the moated grange, ancient, silent and shadow-struck. Yet Webster's language already betrays an edge of resistance to the enticements of the place. The house, although 'enchanted', makes 'captives' of its inhabitants; the shadows of the cedars, although gigantic, are also 'dull'. Where Tennyson finds the decayed mansion of courtly romance rich in echoes and whisperings of the past, Webster finds it soporific and uninspiring: trees 'Throw dull dark shadows on the dull dark walls'.

This hint of irritation is then given voice in the next passage. Unlike Mariana, who is enthralled within the house of weariness and desire, Blanche has escaped a little way outside, and looks back:

> She gazes at it, resting in the shade
> Of a wide-branching many-belted oak –
> Its huge-zoned trunk with thick green moss enlaid –
> Tracing the coilings of the slow blue smoke
> With dreamy wistful eye of discontent,
> Such as the vague complaint may best express
> Of a young spirit in its yearnings pent,
> Too curbed for joy, too care-free for distress,
> Wearied of all things, most of its own weariness.
>
> (*BL*: 3)

Here, Webster has reduced the pervading ache of expectation in the mythical Mariana to the petulant boredom of an adolescent girl with nothing to do. Like many women poets she takes Mariana's part, but finds in it, not a haunting *Weltschmerz*, but a specific grievance of the female soul. Blanche looks 'With dreamy wistful eye of discontent' – the dreaminess and wistfulness thus acquiring an ulterior emotional purpose which is not present in Tennyson. Within this derivatively poetic atmosphere, Webster, like Blanche, seems to fret. 'Too curbed for joy, too care-free for distress' is a double-bind which realistically expresses the rich girl's lot of repression and indulgence, captivity and leisure. The future advocate of women's education and right to work is not impressed, one feels, by pining maidens or (their real originals) bored girls. The 'morbid and artificial melancholy' of 'the sickly-sensitive' is an inheritance which her imagination already, at some level, rejects.

Then, in a line which cunningly diminishes the grand *ennui* of Mariana's refrain ' "I am aweary, aweary, / I would that I were dead!" ' (Tennyson, 1969: 187–90, ll. 11–12), Webster catches the sound of the girl's real frustration: 'Wearied of all things, most of its own weariness.' Although *Blanche Lisle* ends by repeating the old story of funerary heroinism, it does so without conviction; it is weary of weariness. As Webster writes of Blanche herself: 'She tired of the old legends of her race, / Tired of a life that seemed spent with the dead' (*BL*: 4). The whole story is, in many ways, an old legend of 'the dead', dead parents and dead poets, within whose rattling cupboard of ghostly images Webster already moves with a certain restless scepticism.

Lilian Gray (1864), the title poem of her second volume, takes this rebellion a little further. Here, Webster uses the old narrative patterns of the 'sister' ballad. Margaret tells her younger sister Amy about her love for a certain local aristocrat, Walter Hope, who had seemed to return her feelings but then fell for a country girl, Lilian Gray. Torn between the two women, Walter marries Lilian at Margaret's generous instigation. Within this framework of a man and two women, Webster, like Barrett Browning and Rossetti before her, mis-aligns the reader's sympathies. The very title puts its emphasis off-centre. Lilian Gray is technically the 'other' woman. But she is no evil schemer or cold-hearted usurper; rather she is a kind of 'woodland sister' to Margaret, as Marian was to Aurora Leigh. Walter is not a treacherous double-dealer, but a man genuinely divided: 'Torn by two loves, unlike, yet each a crime' (*LG*: 22). The sheer ambiguity of this doubling is brought out by Margaret herself, when she tells him:

> 'And now I surely know
> Your love for Lilian often moved your heart
> When most you loved me.'
>
> (33)

This contradiction of loving most with the inspiration of another at heart is never emotionally solved.

However, while her predecessors might leave the emotional ambiguity hanging, Webster drives it home in a surprising scene in which Margaret goes to visit Lilian, pining on her sick-bed, and asks forgiveness for unwittingly depriving her of Walter's affection. With an intensity reminiscent of the meeting of Aurora and Marian, the two women come together in a long-delayed embrace: 'Sudden she drew me to her, as I bent, / And clung to me with sobs, and kissed my cheek' (46). At the same moment Walter makes his appearance and, taking Margaret's hand, closes the triangle: 'He took my hand – / One moment only so we three were linked' (47). Such a configuration of three for a moment challenges all the played-out rivalries and fatal conclusions of romance. In this briefly linked threesome, there are no villains or victims, but only three people trapped in a new kind of truth. This scene carries the main emotional conviction of the poem, and is, in a sense, a culmination of all the 'sister' ballads which precede it. However, it has nowhere to go, and after it Webster seems to return to the more traditional arrangements: Lilian dies, and becomes another 'dead maiden sculptured on a tomb' (38). Yet even this is not quite the expected conclusion, which should resolve the triangle into the 'right' partnership. For Lilian dies *after* marriage, and implicitly, therefore, of something more realistic than pining. Nor does Margaret then snatch her chance of getting the man she loves, but decides to remain single and leaves him to his widowhood. Such emotional inconclusiveness is characteristic of Webster's demystifying imagination.

Her real potential as a poet is realised when she abandons the ballad romance altogether, and discovers the dramatic monologue. The form became generally named and recognised after the publication of Robert Browning's *Men and Women* in 1855 – a volume which finally established the form's association with 'abnormal mental states' (Faas, 1988: 51), usually morbid and criminal, and of course with religious scepticism. Not only does the dramatic monologue, as Langbaum has influentially argued, evoke split responses of 'sympathy and judgement' (1974: 91) in the reader, but it also opens up a split in the subject speaker. The modernity of the form derives from its exploitation of a discrepancy which lies at the very core of subjectivity. Instead of being self-consistent, the self is a thing of inner strata and differences, of overlaid repressions and deceptions. By setting the author and speaker at odds, as Joseph Bristow argues (1991: 57), the dramatic monologue allows a space for irony both ways. As a result, the inherent 'empiricism' (Langbaum, 1974: 91) of the form, its rooting of personality in secular realities, is at the same time undermined by an irony which also challenges that empiricism and shows up the ultimate power of language. As Paul de Man writes: 'Language thus conceived divides the subject into an empirical self, immersed in the world, and a self that becomes like a sign in its attempt at differentiation and self-definition' (1983: 213). The dramatic monologue proper thus overtly expresses what the lyric disguises: that the heart itself is another (or several others), and that language already mediates it.

However, for all her indebtedness to Robert Browning, Webster's monologues differ in some crucial ways. Their speakers are not so much victims of an irony which exposes their double standards or double dealings as they are victims of historical and social double standards outside themselves. Especially when those speakers are women, the element of morbid criminality, which fascinates Tennyson and Browning, gives way to more ordinary inconsistencies of the self, as it gazes in the mirror of external expectations and ideals. In some ways more benign, these monologues are also more determinedly secular and everyday than Browning's; their speakers not saints, artists or charlatans, but real men and women, with altogether smaller sins and guilts. Womanhood, while not simply victimised as it is in Hemans, appears self-divided in these poems, not because of disingenuousness within, but because of reflections and myths without. If Webster's speakers lack Browning's more darkly introspective dramas of the soul, this is also because many of them are too humble, inarticulate or simply too tired to trouble much about the soul.

It is clear, none the less, that the form gives Webster an opportunity to express that 'man-like' doubt which motivates much of her writing. Such doubt was already very much in the air, as the 1850s and 60s saw the beginning of those controversial and far-reaching debates about biblical authority which would altogether change the climate of Victorianism. In 1851, Harriet Martineau and Henry Atkinson published their *Letters on the Laws of Man's Nature and Development*. Mary Howitt described it as '"the most awful book that was ever written by a woman"' (in Cruse, 1935: 91), and Charlotte Brontë, admitting that it was '"the first exposition of avowed atheism and materialism"' she had read, similarly could not overcome her '"instinctive horror"' (1932: III, 208) of the subject matter. George Eliot, however, acclaimed it as 'the boldest' work 'in the English language' (1954–78: I, 364). The subsequent publication of both Darwin's *Origin of Species* and Mill's *On Liberty* in 1859 fired the controversy for the next two or three decades. Webster's place in this debate emerges as a quiet but consistently sceptical one. Far from accepting faith as the woman poet's special responsibility, she is openly fascinated by intellectual doubt.

She first published her dramatic monologue, 'Pilate', in 1867. The work takes a theme which was immensely popular at the time: that of Pilate's wife having a prophetic dream of Christ's divinity, and which was generally invoked to 'endorse the Christian message' (Faas, 1988: 171). Webster may possibly have known Charlotte Brontë's poem, 'Pilate's Wife's Dream', published in the 'Bell' volume of 1846. In it,

Pilate's wife ends her monologue with an almost Hemansesque assertion of true faith:

> Ere night descends I shall more surely know
> What guide to follow, in what path to go;
> I wait in hope – I wait in solemn fear,
> The oracle of God – the sole – true God – to hear.
> (1984: 3–8, ll. 153–6)

In contrast to this determined monologue of belief, Webster, interestingly, takes the man's part, and writes in the person of that first questioner of Christian 'Truth'. Defending his actions to his wife, Pilate, here, argues for a duty to the general good rather than to the particular man:

> It means a man, a ruler as I am,
> Must look beyond the moment, must alloy
> Justice with prudence. Innocence is much
> To save a man, but is not everything
> Where a whole province is at stake for Rome.
> How many lives think you had cost this life
> Refused to these hot zealots?
> *(Sel*: 18)

Like Robert Browning, who finds in those first-century pagans, Karshish and Cleon, an innocent-seeming opportunity to challenge Christianity, so Webster sets her monologue at a crossroad of culture. The dramatic tension thus stems from a cross-purpose of ideas and opinions, of ideological points of view, rather than from any inner torment of the soul. Here, it is not Pilate, the hand-washing coward, who speaks, but Pilate the secular politician, the representative of older, classical values of judicious expediency and worldly wisdom. As John Stuart Mill pointed out in *On Liberty*: 'What little recognition the idea of obligation to the public obtains in modern morality is derived from Greek and Roman sources, not from Christian' (1974: 113). For Webster, Pilate is not only the upholder of just such 'public' responsibilities, but he is also the representative of another value in her poetry: the value of doubt. It is he who asks the crucial question, 'What is Truth?':

> Truth!
> He claimed to know Truth, which no man yet knew.
> Was that his meaning? Truth is real life . . .
> *(Sel*: 27)

Pilate's sense of the practical requirements of 'real life' comes close to

Webster's own sense of historical contingency. She, like him, is faithful to the facts, to the social and economic truths of 'real life', and rejects visions which claim transcendent allegiance.

In a passage which seems to glance specifically at the contemporary disputes about biblical authority, Pilate argues forcefully for some better evidence for a creed than hearsay and enthusiasm:

> Let the sage live and give us his own gold,
> That's something: we are all disciples then
> After a fashion. For at least we're sure
> That what we hear him speak he speaks – or thus,
> The sounds he makes have such results on ears
> Which are our own, and so we say we're sure,
> Though in true sense we're sure of nothing.
>
> (28)

Significantly, even the testimony of 'the sage' himself is not foolproof for, although 'The sounds he makes have such results on ears', between the speaking and the hearing falls the shadow of subjectivity, device, desire. Even to hear may be to mis-hear. Thus Pilate comes to his repeated Socratic conclusion, 'Aye, / We're sure of nothing' (28). Truth, like everything else, is at the mercy of wilful or unwitting strategy. Although the poem ends with the wife's intimations of new knowledge to come, its general level tenor is clearly more in sympathy with Pilate's values of common sense and 'real life' than with any dream of revelation. As a poet, Webster consistently keeps saints, martyrs and Christs at a sceptical arm's length, judging them through the eyes of the disbelieving, the worldly, the fair-minded rationalists. Her speakers are, by and large, not the convinced visionaries and prophets of the world, but its disinterested onlookers, who are 'sure of nothing'.

Two poems from her best collection of dramatic monologues, *Portraits* (1870), take up the theme of religious doubt again. 'A Soul in Prison' is spoken by a sceptic who has been sent a religious tract to cure his doubt. Whether or not Webster was remembering Hemans' poem, *The Sceptic*, which famously brought about the conversion of an unbeliever who turned up to thank her, her own poem deliberately refuses the role of 'woman-like' faith which Hemans propagated. Its use of a male speaker no doubt helped to achieve the necessary self-distance. As he peruses the catechisms sent to convert him, this speaker finds that his regretful doubt is not eased but confirmed:

> My author here,
> Honest at heart, but has your mind a warp –
> The zealot's warp, who takes believed for proved;

180

The disciple's warp, who takes declared for proved;
The teacher's warp, who takes defined for proved,
And cannot think 'I know not'?

(Portraits: 79)

The problem, he realises, is that those who are strongest in faith are liable to be the least strong in truth. Zealots, disciples and teachers all have a 'warp' of conviction which too readily turns their own needs and feelings into proof. The honesty of the author's own 'heart' is no surety for there being no 'warp' in his writing. In fact, Webster suggests, the 'warp' is most likely to come precisely from the unquestioned sincerity of the 'heart'. For this speaker, as for Pilate, truth is found, not in enthusiastic certainty, but in being able to 'think "I know not"', without reaching false conclusions.

In a fine, doubly ironic passage, she then issues one of her strongest attacks on the easy satisfaction of faith's uplifting speeches:

> Well, learned man,
> I thank you for your book. 'Tis eloquent,
> 'Tis subtle, resolute; I like the roar
> Of the big battling phrases, like those frets
> Of hissing irony – a book to read.
> It helps one too – a sort of evidence –
> To see so strong a mind so strongly clasped
> To creeds whose truth one hopes. What would I more?
> 'Tis a dark world, and no man lights another:
> 'Tis a dark world, and no man sees so plain
> As he believes he sees . . . excepting those
> Who are mere blind and know it.
>
> (79–80)

This is not Tennyson's doubt, yearning to believe a revelation which might strike like poetic vision at dawn, but an intellectual doubt which refuses to forgo the level of its reasoning for the dream of faith. The poem never rises to any climax either of hope or despair, but remains consistently in the middle grey register of uncertainty – an uncertainty beautifully caught in that suggestive phrase, 'whose truth one hopes'. Hoping for truth proves only the hope, though it may be that hoping is the nearest one can get to truth. Certainly, this 'Soul in Prison' never gets out, but at least he is not duped by the easy freedoms of 'the big battling phrases' and the 'hissing irony'. Such rattling effects of rhetoric are not for this soul, or for this poet. Webster's cautious register of common sense constantly asserts the minor keys, while her wiry syntax can lead, quite surprisingly, from the deceptive sureness of ' 'Tis eloquent' to that dubious 'truth one hopes'. The real prison and the real blindness, she declares in the end, belong to those who believe themselves outside and able to see.

These, then, are neither the charlatans and cheats nor the saints and martyrs of life, but the honest, clear-sighted middlemen, who have no great message to propound. As a result, the interest is turned outwards, away from psychology, towards ideas and principles. In 'A Preacher', for instance, the speaker is a priest who, writing his sermon for the next day, fears he has lost his faith, though his wife and congregation fervently believe him to be a saint. Unwilling to disabuse them, he is forced to continue like a clever 'actor', 'a heartless common hack' (*Portraits*: 136), to play to their convictions. He is a more generous and honest type of 'Sludge the Medium', who is neither so afraid of disbelief nor so deeply entranced by wordy self-deceptions as the other. For, as this preacher asserts:

> Better one should lose
> The present peace of loving, nay of trusting,
> Better to doubt and be perplexed in soul
> Because thy truth seems many and not one . . .
> (133)

The idea that 'truth' may be multiple 'and not one', perplexing and not comforting, is a quietly agnostic challenge to the monoliths of religious conviction and of heartfelt enthusiasm, both of which lie like heavy weights on women's writing. Webster's attention to 'real life', to its historical moment and conflict of interpretations, finds in these unassuming, heroic questioners its true representatives. The sceptical and the disenchanted have one virtue in common in her work: their honesty is not fooled by other-worldly hopes, but remains trained, like Mill's, on the 'many' varieties of truth.

The dramatic monologue, with its relative, historicised speech and its saving distance between the author's and the speaker's voices, gives Webster her own form of resistance to the idea that women poets 'feel all they write' (*HO*: 153). In one of her rare essays on poetry, she points out that such feeling is the most easily acted or conventionalised of experiences. Very often, she argues, poets only feel after the writing is finished: 'the dirge has had to wait for a death to make it relevant; the love poem has had to be antedated to give it an appropriate motive. Byron's most Byronic heroes were certainly less a portrait of him than he of them' (154), she declares. Like Barrett Browning and Rossetti, she rejects the idea of poetry as a transcription of life into art, of the suffering body into the spontaneous text. She proposes, instead, that art antedates life, the love poem invents a lover and the hero forms a poet.

In her own monologues, emotions are assiduously framed by the rational intelligence, so that a space is created between them, and the fanatical gospels of feeling, which mar the work of Hemans and L.E.L., are avoided. The poet's obligation is not to feel truly, but to invent truly, so that, as Mary Coleridge remarks, 'what is most carefully made often sounds as if it had been felt straight off' (1910: 252). Whereas Robert Browning embraced his own mode of oblique dramatisation by putting the burden of truth squarely on Elizabeth: 'You speak out, *you*, – I only make men & women speak' (*RB*: I, 7),[2] thus, like many Victorian reviewers, retaining his faith in the essentially 'effusive' spontaneity of women, Webster, as a woman poet, forgoes that faith altogether. In her best work, she does not 'speak out' from the heart, but speaks against the heart, distrusting its conventions of feeling and the beautiful effortlessness of genius it upholds. In a poem expressly about art, she confronts the theme which Robert Browning seemed to have made especially his own, but from a quietly different perspective.

'A Painter', which originally appeared in *Dramatic Studies* (1866), clearly recalls 'Andrea del Sarto' and 'Pictor Ignotus'. However, unlike Browning, who searches the psychology of his famous, if flagging artists, Webster turns the focus outwards, and looks to the material obstacles in her truly 'unknown' painter's life. She thus gives a vivid and moving description of the lesser art he practises and the real hardships he has to bear:

> Ah well I am a poor man and must earn;
> And little dablets of a round-faced blonde
> Or pretty pert brunette who drops her fan,
> Or else the kind the public, save the mark,
> Calls poem-like, ideal, and the rest –
> I have a sort of aptness for the style –
> A buttercup or so made prominent
> To point a moral, how youth fades like grass
> Or some such wisdom, a lace handkerchief
> Or broidered hem mapped out as if one meant
> To give a seamstress patterns – that's to show
> How 'conscientious,' 'tis the word, one is –
> And a girl dying, crying, marrying, what you will,
> With a blue-light tint about her – these will sell:
> And they take time, and if they take no thought
> Weary one over much for thinking well.
> A man with wife and children, and no more
> To give them than his hackwork brings him in,
> Must be a hack and let his masterpiece
> Go to the devil.
>
> (*Portraits*: 138–9)

Webster's artist is not an arch-Romantic, driven by high ideals which never count the cost, but a humbler sort, whose domestic responsibilities weigh heavily on him. The material conditions of his life, 'I am a poor man and must earn', leave little room for high aesthetic principles. This painter cannot afford to labour at a masterpiece or wait for inspiration, 'when waiting means to starve!' (141). So he works for the market, and produces the sentimental little pieces which perfectly satisfy the popular tastes of the day: girls 'dying, crying, marrying', as Webster pointedly summarises, with an angelic, deathly 'blue-light tint'. In her sympathetic reminder of the basic context of leisure and money demanded by high art, she might be remembering some of her own predecessors too, who wearied themselves in supplying enough 'poem-like' poems of 'dying, crying' heroines for the only market that would pay: that of the despised annuals. Meanwhile, her painter imagines how, in other conditions, he might have been great: if he had no wife and children, if he already had a name in the artistic world, if he had more time. It is characteristic of Webster to give full scope to the argument from circumstance and economic conditions.

Thus while her poem may seem shallower than Browning's, whose second-rate artists have time to search the depths of their souls for the flicker of genius, the shallowness also perfectly conveys the unaesthetic, cramped conditions of the man's life. Victorian rather than Renaissance, market-bound rather than patronised, this painter has no option but to be 'a hack' and stay alive. Webster's commitment to the contemporary, like Barrett Browning's, gives her a language, colloquial, relaxed and familiar, which perfectly reproduces the inartistic, necessarily materialist conditions of the age. If this poem lacks the 'historicism' (Dale, 1977: 4; Bristow, 1991, 67–127) which opens up the scope for irony in Browning's dramatic monologues, it also lacks the metaphysical idealism of his theories of art. Where Browning ultimately believes in the true genius, a Raphael or Michelangelo who rides above circumstance, Webster, writing about post-industrial, post-Marxist England, movingly confronts the possibility that the economic substructure of the market dictates the artistic consciousness itself. The poor man's (or woman's) art cannot afford to be above that market, which is still, in the 1860s, one of picturesque, religiose, feminine sentiment, with its fans, buttercups and handkerchiefs to 'point a moral'. The clutter of contemporary reality in her poem seems to drown out any 'higher' arguments about the nature of art.

However, in the end, an element of doubt creeps in. This speaker loves his wife, yet wishes her away; he despises the fashionable cliques of the art world, yet wishes he might have been patronised by them; he ardently defends the artistic power within him, yet blames circumstance

184

for its extinction. The materialist argument, in the end, for all its poignant persuasiveness, does not quite carry the day. The painter's last words to his wife, as he uncovers the 'masterpiece' he hopes will prove his gifts to the world, sound a false note:

> Come, stand there
> And criticise my picture. It has failed,
> Of course – I always fail. Yet, on the whole,
> I think the world would praise it were I known.
> (147)

The last line, with its vain desire at least to be 'known' if not to be great, sounds suddenly petulant and frivolous. Webster thus swings the whole drift of the poem back to an idealist statement. Although she gives full credit to the argument from socio-economic necessity, ultimately she too insists on some other power, some total conviction which this painter lacks. The terrible honesty of 'I always fail' is spoilt by the hope that 'the world would praise it'.

Thus, for all her sympathy with the doubting, humane, ordinary voice of truth and reason, for all her demystifications and attention to material reality, Webster, when it comes to art, still acknowledges some other power of creativity. She is herself a poet of the many truths of 'real life', who rarely falls for metaphysical myths and dreams, and who gives full dues to the substructural context of money, class and opportunity. None the less, she also recognises the place of dream and revelation: of a subjective force which may readily distort into pious fanaticism, but which also feeds the imaginations of the greatest artists. It is part of the intelligence and honesty of her own work that she generally describes such a force, not as fluent, easy and sincere, but as largely missing.

A WOMAN SURE

> And now it seems a jest to talk of me
> As if I could be one with her, of me
> Who am . . . me.
>
>   And what is that? My looking-glass
> Answers it passably; a woman sure,
> No fiend, no slimy thing out of the pools,
> A woman with a ripe and smiling lip
> That has no venom in its touch I think,
> With a white brow on which there is no brand;
> A woman none dare call not beautiful,
> Not womanly in every woman's grace.
> (*A Castaway*, in *Portraits*: 36)

It is the nature of womanhood, its mystique, its clichés, its self-reflections and self-divisions, which inspires some of Webster's best poems. Just as the Castaway tries to piece together the broken history of herself by scanning the face in the mirror, so Webster searches the mirror of ideology and myth to find in it, among the fiends and slimy things of moral fable, 'the dispersed, contingent, and multiple' (de Beauvoir, 1972: 283) histories of real women. She uses the monologue, not to divulge the moral and emotional inconsistencies of the inner self, but to probe the borderlands between its social construction and its unknown potentiality, between its past and its present, between 'me' and 'me'. The inconsistencies are not tragic inner flaws, which therefore open up the profundities of psychology, but small, almost reductive contradictions, between the woman's desires and the world's opinions, between, as it were, the soul and the face. The mirror – that most female of Victorian images – gives Webster a figure for the social and ideological frames which trap women in conventional, incompatible pictures, but from which she also refuses to offer any introspective escape. The identities of her speakers 'surface' in their interpreted, external appearances; the 'woman sure' is reflected in 'the pools' of men's imaginations, although the gap between them also remains visible. The self is thus presented as essentially a creature mirrored in the looking-glass of society, and Webster's poems do not try to break that glass; they only set it at different angles.

'By the Looking-Glass' (1866), for instance, is spoken by a plain girl who, returning to her room after a ball, sadly traces her features in the mirror. The poem takes up the same theme as Eliza Cook's 'Song of the Ugly Maiden':

> I know full well I have nought of grace
>   That maketh woman 'divine;'
> The wooer's praise and doting gaze,
>   Have never yet been mine.
> Where'er I go all eyes will shun
> The loveless mien of the Ugly one.
> (1870: 303)

This is the bland, over-rhyming voice of much minor women's poetry of the time. While Webster similarly questions the proverbial equation of woman and beauty, she does so, not in lilting, correctly metrical generalities, but in the halting, prosaic voice of the girl herself:

> A girl, and so plain a face!
> Once more, as I learn by heart every line
> In the pitiless mirror, night by night,

186

> Let me try to think it is not my own.
> Come, stranger with features something like mine,
> Let me place close by you the tell-tale light;
> Can I find in you now some charm unknown,
> Only one softening grace?

But this attempt to find something other than the plainness which she sees in 'the pitiless mirror' quickly collapses into truthful self-recognition: 'Alas! it is I, I, I, / Ungainly, common' (*DS*: 150). From this tragedy of being 'I' there is no inner escape. For all her articulate intelligence, the girl is imprisoned in the conventional–cruel reading of her face. She cannot fool herself with 'some charm unknown' which the world's eyes cannot see. She refuses to set her own subjective desires against the rigid 'tell-tale' truth of the mirror, although that truth seems to split her into two: herself and a 'stranger'. There is no escape from the hammer-strokes of what is ordinary and self-evident: 'I, I, I'.

The poem does not go on to tell a Jane Eyre story; there is no Byronic hero to recognise the plain girl's emotional depths. Instead, she remains hurt, touchy and self-conscious, imagining scorn in every smile and mockery in every look of kindness. It is characteristic of Webster not to reject the evidence of the mirror, but to acknowledge its pervasive blight on a girl's life: 'how a woman's lot / Is darkened throughout!' (154). Identity belongs in the world's eyes. Furthermore, the 'I, I, I' of the girl, like the Castaway's 'me' and 'me', suggests that the self is not an inviolable inner sanctuary, closed to the outer world, but a staggered reflection of history, opinions, moralities and prejudices. The ironic gap in the monologue is thus not one between reader and speaker, but rather between the speaker and her broken other selves. Webster's, unlike Browning's, remains a ruthlessly socialised poetry, even while it protests against the superficial conventions of that socialisation.

A second mirror poem, 'Faded' (1870), is like a companion piece to 'By the Looking-Glass'. Here, an older woman remembers her own younger face, and addresses it in the mirror: 'Fair, happy, morning, face who wast myself, / Talk with me, with this later drearier self' (*Portraits*: 63). Between the two, lies not only the mirror, but the whole social history of her life, dividing the fair and happy girl from the dull and dreary spinster. This history is no *Bildungsroman*, however, but a set of incompatible picture images. As the faded, older woman tries to recover her past self, she touchingly imagines the broken parts meeting once again:

> While now we two a little time are one,
> Elder and girl, the blossoming and the sere,
> One blended, dateless, woman for an hour –

Thou and I thus alone, I read from thee
My lesson what I was; which (ah, poor heart!)
Means trulier my lesson, bitter to learn,
Of what I cease to be.
(63–4)

This coming together of the two selves has the furtive intensity almost of a love encounter. The old maid steals a meeting with her lost girlhood, and relishes 'an hour' of self-communion with the stranger in the glass. It is only when alone, and free from the world's scorn, that she can become one with her own history: 'One blended, dateless, woman', and thus escape the divisive categories of being young or old, beautiful or faded, marriageable or old-maidish; categories which mean, in effect, being either something or nothing in the world. The older woman must win her self-coherence from her absolute loss, in the public eye, of social significance – of being, negatively, only 'what I cease to be'.

As in 'By the Looking-Glass', identity is viewed, not as a precious subjective power at odds with the world, but as an image of the world's approval and disapproval, its dates and its conventions of desire. 'Myself has faded from me; I am old' (64), the woman laments. It is not only her beauty which has 'faded' but her very self, which the world reads either as beauty or as nothing. This residual nothing is then imagined as having a cruel sort of afterlife:

But we in our utter loss, outlawed from life,
Irretrievable bankrupts of our very selves,
We must give ruin welcome, blaze our fact
Of nothingness – 'good friends, perceive I am old;
Pray laugh and leave me.' We are fools, we sin,
Abjectly, past all pardon, past all pity,
We women, if we linger, if, maybe,
We use our petty melancholy arts
And are still women some filched year or two –
Still women and not ghosts, not lifeless husks,
Spent memories that slink through the world and breathe,
As if they lived, and yet they know they are dead.
(66)

Rossetti's favourite imagery of woman's ghostly existence has here been emptied of its imaginative possibilities. This is no posthumously poetic death, full of secrets and inner compensations, but the social death of a being who has forfeited all use and relevance in the world. By comparison with Rossetti's homeless ghosts, who press against the world from a timeless place of dreams, the ghostliness of the faded woman is abject and futile. Characteristically, Webster has demystified death and reproduced it as an image of imposed social insignificance. By writing, not about the single, lyrical 'I' of the poet, but about the 'I, I, I,' of ordinary, other women, she takes the dramatic monologue on to the streets, as it were, where it functions, not as an individualist opportunity for self-expression, but as a source of harsh double vision, which puts the individual under the cold eye of the world. Like the ugly girl, the faded woman is what she sees in the mirror, with very little left over from the public losses of her face: 'And are still women some filched year or two – / Still women and not ghosts . . .' Being alive or dead, a woman or a ghost, is a simple matter of the fresh or faded appearance of her face.

'Faded', though written in 1870, was not published until 1893, and therefore could not have been known to Alice Meynell when, in 1875, she published her own poem on a similar topic: 'A Letter from a Girl to her Own Old Age'. Meynell's work is, intriguingly, like an inverted version of Webster's. In it, a young girl speaks across time to her imagined older self, and begs that self to remember her:

> Listen, and when thy hand this paper presses,
> O time-worn woman, think of her who blesses
> What thy thin fingers touch, with her caresses.
> (*Poems*: 17)

The same impulse of wanting to re-connect and remember a history likely to be self-forgetting lies behind this strangely passionate poem. For Meynell, too, a woman's identity is something precarious, to be imaginatively rescued from the dislocations of time. The girl asks for the coherence of a life in which beginning and end are in touch with each other, rather than, as Webster's poem suggests, fragmented into sexually defined mirror-phases. She thus writes to her own old age, not fearfully but lovingly, from a wish to be known and remembered in her turn, and thus save, at least in her imagination, the unbroken, historical process of who she is. The last stanza, which envisages old age as a beloved mother and lover, enacts a meeting, like the one in 'Faded', between two permanently estranged, yet self-related women:

> The one who now thy faded features guesses,
> With filial fingers thy grey hair caresses,
> With morning tears thy mournful twilight blesses.
> (19)

The two poems, in their rejection of the self-denial which is both expected of women and implicit in the very social structure of being a woman, find in the quest for self-coherence something akin to a thwarted love story. The dramatic monologue thus becomes a dialogue with the self – the self who is indeed an 'other', but not, in Rimbaud's sense, because of some grand Romantic flaw in subjectivity, but because of the social construction of that subjectivity. Woman is a creature of shallow social images, reflected from a sexual mythology which deals life or death, significance or insignificance, to its objects. The mirror is, at once, an external dictator and an internal divider. These ugly or faded women, who seek their self-coherence and self-value in solitude, find that the mirror of the world has entered their private rooms, and refutes their wishes to be, in spite of appearances, 'One blended, dateless, woman'. Webster, even more than Meynell, conveys the pathos of being without a self and without a life, not from any moral choice or inner failing, but simply from a trick of physical dullness. The dramatic monologue, in her hands, conveys the rigidity of social convention and the poverty of hope in Victorian women's lives.

The mirror of the external view is also present in the monologue, 'Tired' (1870), although here it is embodied in the male speaker who frames and verbally dominates the poem. He is a liberal-minded philanthropist and intellectual who, in his Rousseauistic idealism, married a young, uneducated country girl, Madge. At the start of the poem, he is urging Madge to attend a social evening on her own because he is too 'tired' to go. 'There, go to don your miracles of gauze, / And come and show yourself a great pink cloud' (*Portraits*: 81), he cajoles. His meditation then takes place as he waits for her to dress. During this interval, he thinks with regret about the way that his innocent wife has been corrupted by society. Webster puts into his mouth some of her own persuasive objections to society's waste of women's time. He imagines how, in public, she will be:

> prepared to talk
> In the right voice for the right length of time
> On any thing that anybody names,
> Prepared to listen with the proper calm
> To any song that anybody sings . . .
>   (80)

He thus conducts his armchair feminism from the superior, agreeable solitude of his study. His own boredom with the social round feeds his resentment of its treatment of women, but being also, as he thinks, an honest man, he confesses to having taught Madge society's tricks himself. Ashamed of her ungrammatical speech, as well as of her ignorance of domestic tasks, he taught her to talk, listen and arrange flowers, thus turning his prized 'wood violet' into a 'formal rose-box at a show' (82).

So far, the poem has seemed to be about the husband's searching self-knowledge, his guilt and double standards. However, as his monologue continues, at some length, his theoretical right-thinking begins to pall. The more he protests with righteous indignation at the world's mis-use of women, the more absolutist do his theories sound:

> For she loves that round
> Of treadmill ceremonies, mimic tasks,
> We make our women's lives – Good heavens what work
> To set the creatures to, whom we declare
> God purposed for companions to us men . . .
> Companions to each other only now,
> Their business but to waste each other's time.
>
> (95)

This 'new man' has read his John Stuart Mill, and knows the correct formulas for equality: wives are not slaves or servants but 'companions'. Yet his eloquent anger about women's roles seems designed to comfort his solitude and confirm his liberalism rather than to address the specific situation of Madge. Furthermore, a note of self-satisfied superiority begins to emerge from the increasingly loaded masculinity of his pronouns: 'We make', 'we declare', 'us men', 'our' women. This implicit grand collaboration of the male sex builds up a grammatical stronghold of power which dictates not only the facts of 'women's lives', but also their feelings: 'she loves that round'. Alone in his study, with leisure to survey the wrongs of the world, he elaborates a theory which subtly confirms the domination and prejudice he appears to attack. His arguments for equality in fact only provide a reassuring confirmation of the better judgment of men and the frivolity of women: 'Companions to each other only now, / Their business but to waste each other's time.' Webster cleverly turns the liberal's arguments against him: the more clearly he sees the wrongs of woman, the more efficiently does he blind himself to the reality before his eyes. His worthy theories become an elaborate, rigid screen, which saves him looking at the truth about his wife. As the unconverted sceptic proclaimed: 'no man sees so plain / As he believes he sees' (80).

It is only at the very end, when Madge reappears, dressed for her party, that the speaker's capacity for self-delusion becomes clear. As he addresses her, his tone of political seriousness suddenly switches to one of infantilising patronage:

> Ready, love, at last?
> Why, what a rosy June! A flush of bloom
> Sparkling with crystal dews – Ah silly one,

You love these muslin roses better far
Than those that wear the natural dew of heaven.
I thought you prettier when, the other day,
The children crowned you with the meadow-sweets:
I like to hear you teach them wild flowers' names
And make them love them; but yourself –

(97)

Thus he launches into yet another theoretical formulation of Madge's character, setting her in a tableau of flowers and children worthy of the hack painter's talents. The tactics of his praise, 'what a rosy June!' are still calculated to prove his superior tastes and her unemancipated silliness.

Then, just as he starts on another long disquisition about flowers, and the difference between nature and art, she interrupts him. At first, self-deafened, he does not hear her. 'What's that?' he asks. Without stopping to consider, he swiftly ropes her answer into yet another confirmation of his own theories:

'The wild flowers in a room's hot stifling glare
Would die in half a minute.' True enough:
Your muslin roses are the wiser wear.
Well, I must see you start. Draw your hood close:
And are you shawled against this east wind's chills?

(97)

Madge's comment about the 'wild flowers' is thus made to prove, once again, her frivolous accommodation with society. She has fallen for its artificial values, and forgotten her endearingly primitive origins. Meanwhile, however, her continuing and increasingly audible silence becomes charged with dissent, irony and perhaps warning. Deep down, it suits this 'tired' liberal to send his wife into society so that he can pursue his intellectual meditations in peace and, what is more, find those meditations constantly confirmed by her actions. But her response, that '"The wild flowers in a room's hot stifling glare / Would die in half a minute"', is loaded with other meanings. If Madge is a wild flower, then she must find a way not to '"die in half a minute"' in the life her husband has chosen for her. Her reasons may be those, not of compromise or frivolity, but of intelligent, desperate survival in the face of his controlling and dogmatic conventionalism.

In this poem, Webster once again frames the woman as an idea trapped in the mirror of ideology and men's eyes. Madge herself remains invisible behind the violets, roses, children and tittle-tattle her husband confidently and liberally prescribes for her. She remains, like other angels, hidden in a 'great pink cloud' of required femininity. None the less, the dramatic monologue makes room, within the very narrowness of its dominant perspective, for others. Unlike the lyric, which asserts a single, univocal world-view, even if untrue 'at heart', the very controlling loquacity of the dramatic monologue is a world-view imposed as a power structure on others. Not a private speech but a public one, it inevitably enters into a political relationship with other speeches, however silent they may be. The nature of woman, as Webster shrewdly knows, far from validating some residual inner truth and authenticity, is the most strategically and self-servingly fabricated of Victorian ideals. As she puts it, in one of her *Mother & Daughter* sonnets:

> 'Tis men who say that through all hurt and pain
>   The woman's love, wife's, mother's, still will hold,
>   And breathes the sweeter and will more unfold
> For winds that tear it, and the sorrowful rain.
> So in a thousand voices has the strain
>   Of this dear patient madness been retold,
>   That men call woman's love. Ah! they are bold,
> Naming for love that grief which *does* remain.
>
> (*MD*: 25)

What 'men' say about women is one of the most powerful determinants of society's general chorus of 'a thousand voices'.

Webster's monologues thus probe, not metaphysical and psychological depths of character, but the flat mirror of social ideology and public opinion which reflects character from the outside. She is not a Romantic, in the sense that she does not set the depths against the surface of the self. Instead, she explores its social shallows, its construction in terms of the 'thousand voices' of opinion, conventionality and myth. The very level tenor of her language reproduces this trap – a trap which, in a sense, catches her characters, especially her female characters, in a social formula of ugliness, fadedness or frivolity, against which they may protest but from which they cannot fully escape. The truth may be different from what the 'thousand voices' declare, but it remains bound within the power structure of those voices, without the poetic escape routes of dream or the social escape routes of outright protest.

It is in one of her classical monologues that Webster turns the mirror against its controllers. In 'Circe' (1870), she takes the classical myth of the sorceress who held Ulysses' men captive on her island, and re-writes it from Circe's disenchanted point of view. The poem echoes and challenges Tennyson's version of the story in 'The Lotos-Eaters'. There, the atmosphere of spoiling sensuousness points to an enchantment which is essentially debilitating and dangerous:

> All round the coast the languid air did swoon,
> Breathing like one that hath a weary dream.
> Full-faced above the valley stood the moon;
> And like a downward smoke, the slender stream
> Along the cliff to fall and pause and fall did seem.
> (1969: 429–38, ll. 5–9)

Webster's, however, is not a poem about passive, male seduction, but about active female desire; it is not about being bewitched, but about being the witch.

It opens with an invocation of the storm which will break the boredom of Circe's unsatisfied longings:

> The sun drops luridly into the west;
> Darkness has raised her arms to draw him down
> Before the time, not waiting as of wont
> Till he has come to her behind the sea;
> And the smooth waves grow sullen in the gloom
> And wear their threatening purple; more and more
> The plain of waters sways and seems to rise
> Convexly from its level of the shores;
> And low dull thunder rolls along the beach:
> There will be storm at last, storm, glorious storm!
> (*Portraits*: 14)

Unlike the reluctant weariness of Tennyson's language, Webster's is charged with expectation and desire. The landscape enacts a wish-fulfilling sexual encounter in which female 'Darkness' draws down the male sun into her bed of storm. Pre-empting the proper time and 'not waiting', she seduces him with unrestrained passion, till 'more and more / The plain of waters sways and seems to rise'. With this pathetic fallacy of sexual appetite, the stifling beauty of enchantment becomes stormy from within. Unlike Tennyson, who finds in the heavy-scented *ennui* of the island a sensuous invitation to dream, Webster finds in it an irritant and restriction. For the woman, such an atmosphere is too literally familiar; it is a 'sickly sweet monotony' from which Circe begs for 'change' (15). As in *Blanche Lisle*, the Mariana condition seems too true of women's lives to be embraced as a privileged aesthetic haven.

Tennyson's addictive, repetitive descriptions of the weary air are then brusquely parodied by this bored enchantress:

> I am too weary of this long bright calm;
> Always the same blue sky, always the sea
> The same blue perfect likeness of the sky . . .
> (15)

This woman does not want to keep Ulysses in a realm of emasculating female sensuousness, from which he must protect himself if he is to continue on his expedition; she wants the thrill of change and experience for herself. Instead of the enervating sultriness of 'The Lotos-Eaters', 'Circe' is full of quite homely frustrations: 'Always the same blue sky, always the sea'. In this poem, the real victim of enchantment is not Ulysses but Circe, who cries, like Florence Nightingale's Cassandra (in Strachey, 1978: 398), for less easy pleasure and more suffering, less sunshine and more storm:

> Give me some change. Must life be only sweet,
> All honey-pap as babes would have their food?
> And, if my heart must always be adrowse
> In a hush of stagnant sunshine, give me, then,
> Something outside me stirring; let the storm
> Break up the sluggish beauty, let it fall
> Beaten below the feet of passionate winds,
> And then to-morrow waken jubilant
> In a new birth; let me see subtle joy
> Of anguish and of hopes, of change and growth.
>
> (16)

Webster's speaker is evidently yet another nineteenth-century woman begging for that most elusive of rights: the right of experience. Such experience includes sexual passion as well as real human 'anguish'. Trapped in her condition of idealised and feared enchantment, Circe dreams of a liberating storm of feeling to break her life's trance, her 'honey-pap' existence. She dreams of thus escaping from the fantasy of sexual allure and danger which keeps her islanded, like so many women, in an old myth.

Buxton Forman's comment that Circe is 'a woman waiting and longing for the arrival of some master-man, who shall claim her by virtue of superiority' (1871: 179) misses the whole point of the poem, which is that such 'superiority' is non-existent. This is not another story about the enchanted princess waiting to be rescued by the explorer prince, as Buxton Forman hopes; it is about the total improbability of princes. For, as Webster pointedly reminds us, there are other presences on the island:

> Oh, ye gods,
> Will he not seek me? Is it all a dream?
> Will there be only these, these, bestial things
> Who wallow in their styes, or mop and mow
> Among the trees, or munch in pens and byres,

> Or snarl and filch behind their wattled coops;
> These things who had believed that they were men?
>
> (17–18)

The irony of this last line is double. The men whom Circe turned into pigs, according to the myth, were never really men, in the positive sense of men as opposed to beasts; yet, they are also still the kinds of men they always were: bestial. Homer's cup of female enchantment becomes, in Webster's hands, the cup of female truth. By drinking from it the men become simply themselves. 'Change? there was no change; / Only disguise gone from them unawares' (21), Circe expostulates. The cup reflects the men as they are, in a punishing reversal of ideology's many reflections of women. The poem enjoys the joke at the heart of the story: men are pigs, not through any trickery of female wiles, but through their honest reflection in the 'cup of Truth' (21).

This figure for truth also points to the inherent purpose of Webster's own art, driven, as it is, by the principles of clarity, realism and demystification:

> 'Oh my rare cup! my pure and crystal cup,
> With not one speck of colour to make false
> The entering lights, or flaw to make them swerve!
> My cup of Truth!'
>
> (20–1)

This is an art which seeks to expose the mythical distortions in the cup, and to give back the smooth, unbiased reflection of reality. For a change, in this poem, the mirror is turned on men, as Circe reflects them in the simplifying evidence of her cup and, in one sweeping generalisation, sums them all up as 'false and ravenous and sensual brutes' (22). She is, indeed, the man-hungry woman, racked with frustrated desire; but she is not, Webster emphasises, hungry for anything less than man.

If the feminist spirit of 'Circe' is humorously disguised in myth and implication, in the best of all Webster's monologues, A Castaway (1870), it is not. Spoken by a relatively high-class courtesan, the poem is a magnificent, panoramic indictment of many of the cherished values of Victorian England. But most significantly, it breaks the silence on a number of obvious, if also closely guarded, secrets. During the 1850s and 60s, prostitution was one of the most discussed social problems of the day. W. R. Greg's pioneering article in the *Westminster Review* in 1850 set the tone of a debate which was to continue for the next three decades and more. Yet it is interesting that in most literature the focus is almost exclusively on the prostitute herself. She is a figure of magnetic fascination and allure, haunting the dimly lit streets and troubling the

196

Victorian conscience with the confusion of values she represents. However, although due attention is paid to the social conditions which create her and the suffering which she endures, rather less is paid to the self-evident 'market' demand for her.

Webster's Castaway, by contrast, points a finger, not only at her silent clientele of married men, but also, even more scandalously, at the hidden, sacrosanct presences behind them:

> The wives? Poor fools, what do I take from them
> Worth crying for or keeping? If they knew
> What their fine husbands look like seen by eyes
> That may perceive there are more men than one!
> But, if they can, let them just take the pains
> To keep them: 'tis not such a mighty task
> To pin an idiot to your apron-string;
> And wives have an advantage over us,
> (The good and blind ones have) the smile or pout
> Leaves them no secret nausea at odd times.
> Oh, they could keep their husbands if they cared,
> But 'tis an easier life to let them go,
> And whimper at it for morality.
>   (*Portraits*: 39–40)

Her intimate and disdainful knowledge of 'fine husbands', like Circe's of her pigs, is one which sees through the disguises of 'morality' to the worth of real men. In this, Webster makes a break with the whole tradition before her. Most of the fallen women in Victorian literature are only variations on the real theme. Seduced, raped, betrayed or fickle, they tend to be either innocent girls led astray or sensational adulteresses. Their actions thus remain connected, however negatively, to romance and love. By contrast, Webster writes about the professional. The Castaway's lovers are not the heroes of literary romance, dark seducers or reckless rakes, but, quite simply, other women's husbands for whom the illicit is routine. Meanwhile, her sheer, straight-talking intelligence is a welcome change from the ostentatiously fastidious manner in which the subject was often treated. W. R. Greg, for instance, claimed that he ventured only 'with hesitation and many misgivings' to write of 'so dismal and delicate a subject' (*Westminster Review*, 53(1850), 448), while William Lecky, in his *History of European Morals* (1869), was still hedging his subject about with elaborate cautions and epithets: 'That unhappy being whose very name is a shame to speak' (1955: II, 283). Webster's style is notably free of such roundabout hints and suggestive metaphors. Her Castaway discusses, not her fall but her trade, with a broad forthrightness which leaves no aspect of it shrouded in biblical myth.

Certainly, by the 1870s, the subject was less taboo than when Barrett Browning caused an outcry by referring to harlots and the stews in *Aurora Leigh*. Webster not only refers to them, but connects them closely with the other women at home:

> Oh! those shrill carping virtues, safely housed
> From reach of even a smile that should put red
> On a decorous cheek, who rail at us
> With such a spiteful scorn and rancorousness,
> (Which maybe is half envy at the heart)
> And boast themselves so measurelessly good
> And us so measurelessly unlike them,
> What is their wondrous merit that they stay
> In comfortable homes whence not a soul
> Has ever thought of tempting them, and wear
> No kisses but a husband's upon lips
> There is no other man desires to kiss –
>
> (40)

This subversively accuses the wives of feeling more 'envy' than true indignation, more sexual frustration than injured faithfulness. Far from being figures of ill-used virtue, they either connive at their husbands' vices or actually envy their husbands' mistresses. Like Barrett Browning, but even more plainly, Webster connects morality to sexual politics, and thus exposes a system of complicity which goes far beyond the guilty players. Furthermore, the Castaway's jibes at the myth of marital bliss suggestively propose an even more scandalous possibility: that sexual pleasure is to be found, not from the one 'idiot' husband, but precisely from having 'more men than one'. Virtue born of 'comfortable homes' and lack of opportunity is not worth the name. Beneath it lies the unspoken reality of women's sexual desire: that restless, amoral energy which Rossetti figuratively displaced onto goblin fruits, but which Webster dares to literalise as a forbidden, subconscious appetite among the wives, for the 'other man'.

A Castaway is, in a sense, Webster's *Goblin Market*, but without the myths and magic which take the other poem, at least verbally, out of the market. Instead, it makes the market a symbol, both of the courtesan's professional trade and of the socio-economic context of that trade. The market provides the underlying rationale of the value system of the whole poem. The fall, here, is not caused by moral choice, by walking at twilight or buying forbidden fruit, but by social and sexual disadvantage from the start: by penury, poor education, an imbalance of the numbers of women against those of men and a shortage of work for both sexes. By comparison with Rossetti, Webster is almost deterministic in her explanations. Thus the Castaway muses on the domestic purposelessness of her girlhood: 'New clothes to make, then go and say my prayers, / Or carry soup, or take a little walk' (35), on her stinted education: the education 'girls with brothers all must learn, / To do without' (56), on her lack of training for any useful work, her financial reliance on a brother who casts her off and on the punishing dreariness of the penitentiary she endures for a week. The problem of her 'vice' is the problem of a pervasive social inequality which leaves women simply out of account in the economic market of survival:

> But I say all the fault's with God himself
> Who puts too many women in the world.
> We ought to die off reasonably and leave
> As many as the men want, none to waste.
>   (48)

Women are commodities in a market even more primary than that of power and money: the market of sheer numbers. According to this sexual Malthusianism, to be 'As many as the men want' is the only hope of survival, in a world where women's sole purpose is to answer to those wants. In this market, the soul itself is saved or damned by numbers:

> But where's the work? More sempstresses than shirts;
> And defter hands at white work than are mine
> Drop starved at last: dressmakers, milliners,
> Too many too they say; and then their trades
> Need skill, apprenticeship. And who so bold
> As hire me for their humblest drudgery?
> Not even for scullery slut; not even, I think,
> For governess although they'd get me cheap.
> And after all it would be something hard,
> With the marts for decent women overfull,
> If I could elbow in and snatch a chance
> And oust some good girl so, who then perforce
> Must come and snatch her chance among our crowd.
>
> Why, if the worthy men who think all's done
> If we'll but come where we can hear them preach,
> Could bring us all, or any half of us,
> Into their fold, teach all us wandering sheep,
> Or only half of us, to stand in rows
> And baa them hymns and moral songs, good lack,
> What would they do with us? what could they do?
>   (47)

In 'the marts' of human life, the difference between 'some good girl' and a bad, between 'decent women' and indecent ones, is a matter of economic balance. So many of the one will create so many of the other, so many 'dressmakers' and 'milliners' create so many sluts and whores. The chances for salvation, in this system, are rigidly demographic. Goodness is allotted by the mart. Once the homes are full of chaste wives, the other women must go on the streets. Beside this ruthless supply and demand of human fates, the Church's rescue of baa-ing sheep seems naïvely picturesque. Morality itself depends, not on 'hymns and moral songs', but on the rules of money, power and exchange; on a market which, in its hazardous, fantastic *laissez-faire*, might as well be run by goblins.

Thus the Castaway ranges over the ills of her society and, in a plain 'prose' of verse, full of wit, common sense and straight-speaking dissent, offers her view of the human mart from within. Webster takes the subject which both *Aurora Leigh* and *Goblin Market* made central, but sheds the creative self-justifications of the first and the myth and magic of the second. What remains, characteristically, is a stark and literal portrait of a woman, neither especially gifted nor especially sinful, whose life has no bearing on poetic genius or Christian morality, but which is simply the product of a set of determining, material circumstances. The market is the Victorian word for that secular determinism, and Webster's poem leaves very little free from its ruthlessly literal 'accounts' of the self.

The problem of womanhood, however, remains. The difference between the innocent girl, who wrote her diary 'with its simple thoughts' (35), and the experienced courtesan who reads it, is still figured, in the loaded mirror of society, as an unbridgeable gap, an incoherent history:

> So long since:
> And now it seems a jest to talk of me
> As if I could be one with her, of me
> Who am . . . me.
>
> (36)

For all her clarity of perception, the Castaway cannot see *herself*. She is split into 'me' and 'me'; into a self-division which is not only a difference in time but also, in the eyes of society, a moral contradiction in terms. The history which leads from the innocent girl to the worldly courtesan – though the poem explains its socio-economic reasons clearly enough – is still baffling, 'a jest'. Such a route seems, morally, impassable, creating a break in sense and speech themselves: 'Who am . . . me.' Woman's subjectivity, according to Webster, opens onto a social mirror which may also be a gulf.

Womanhood thus continues to be figured in terms of sexual and moral opposites: beautiful or ugly, youthful or faded, violet or rose, virtuous or vicious. The mirror of public opinion cannot be turned aside, but remains trained on these ordinary, unpoetic speakers, whose lives are lived, not in some other introspective country of the imagination, but in the real harsh world of economic and sexual survival. The Castaway herself, in a last tragicomic gesture of needy identification with that world outside, welcomes the friend, whoever it may be, who rescues her from herself: 'Oh, is it you? / Most welcome, dear: one gets so moped alone' (62).

Webster's poetry thus presents its own challenge to the sentimentalist mode which she inherits. Her emancipation from its narcissistic atittudes of love and death comes about largely from her adoption of the dramatic monologue – a form which gives her a structure of self-distance which, by its very nature, undermines the notional simplicity of the woman's voice. Although she lacks the verbal exuberance of Barrett Browning and the haunting musicality of Rossetti, her steady, realist vision, so rare among Victorian poets, offers something else instead: a demystifying, agnostic honesty in the face of the many beliefs and ideals of her day. Her version of 'the hard & cold thing' which all these poets set against the soft-heartedness of their first poetic mothers is that 'cup of Truth' which, like Circe, she holds up to her contemporary society in order to reflect, without the ripples of conscious aestheticism or metaphorical play, the values of her world. Such poetry may lack the finer nuances of the lyrical voice, but none the less it puts in their place a 'strength' of conception and purpose which, in its own way, is surprising and original. The omission of Augusta Webster from the list of major women poets of the nineteenth century has gone unchallenged for too long since Christina Rossetti, in 1890, first challenged it.

Michael Field

Katherine Bradley (1846–1914)
and Edith Cooper (1862–1913)

> But I write to you to beg you to set the critics on a wrong
> track. We each know that you mean good to us: and are
> persuaded you thought that by 'our secret' we meant the dual
> authorship. The revelation of that would indeed be utter ruin
> to us; but the report of lady authorship will dwarf and
> enfeeble our work at every turn. Like the poet Gray we shall
> never 'speak out.' And we have many things to say that the
> world will not tolerate from a woman's lips. We must be free
> as dramatists to work out in the open air of nature – exposed
> to her vicissitudes, witnessing her terrors: we cannot be stifled
> in drawing-room conventionalities. (*WD*: 6)

Thus wrote Katherine Bradley to Robert Browning in 1884. Some
months before, he had replied with enthusiasm to a volume of plays,
published under the name of Michael Field, and sent to him by an
unknown correspondent, Edith Cooper. In answer to his curiosity, she
had explained the dual authorship behind the pseudonym: 'My Aunt and
I work together after the fashion of Beaumont and Fletcher. She is my
senior, by but fifteen years. She has lived with me, taught me,
encouraged me and joined me to her poetic life' (*WD*: 3). It seems,
however, that Browning had been indiscreet because, six months later,
the 'Aunt' herself, Katherine Bradley, wrote in dismay, begging him to
disguise the truth which someone had leaked to the *Athenaeum*. Public
knowledge either of their 'dual authorship' or even of their 'lady
authorship', as she puts it, would be 'utter ruin', both in terms of their
reputation in the eyes of the world and also in terms of their inner
freedom to ' "speak out" '. In a phrase which ought to have appealed to the

heart of the poet who had been married to Elizabeth Barrett Browning, she concluded emphatically: 'we cannot be stifled in drawing-room conventionalities.'

Unfortunately, however, something in this comment caused Browning to react with the very outraged conventionality Katherine most feared from the world at large. His reply has not survived (Katherine probably destroyed it), but it is clear from her answer that he had taken fright at some supposed impropriety. She was forced to put him right. 'I did not speak of combating "social conventions"' (8), she pointed out, and repeated, word for word, the phrase she had used. The difference between 'combating' and refusing to be 'stifled in . . . conventionalities' was evidently significant enough to assuage the fears of the elderly poet. Katherine explained, with laborious and pointed emphasis: 'It is not in our power or desire to treat irreverently customs or beliefs that have been, or are, sacred to men' (7–8). Such anxiety about ' "social conventions"' in the poet who had been married to one of the most socially combative women poets of the age and who had recently recognised 'genius' (2) in their own writing, must have sadly confirmed all Katherine's worst fears. Moreover, she herself had already experienced a certain personal hostility after the revelation that Michael Field was not a young man but, quaintly and unfashionably, an aunt and her niece. As she explained to Browning, a certain reader, 'whose earnest praise gave me genuine pleasure, now writes in ruffled distress; he "thought he was writing to a boy – a young man"' (6).

Katherine's fears may have had some foundation. According to their biographer, the general 'neglect', even 'boycott' of Michael Field's work between the 1890s and 1920s was largely due to the 'obscurely repellent' fact of a 'collaboration' (Sturgeon, 1921: 29). Whether the term carries a purely literary or also sexual significance, certainly the idea of a 'collaboration' seems to have threatened some notional sanctity of authorship, as an article by Walter Besant 'On literary collaboration' suggests (*The New Review*, 6(1892), 200–9). Katherine and Edith not only wrote under the same pseudonym; they also often composed collaboratively, each supplying passages or even individual lines to the same work. As Edith explained to Browning: 'Some of the scenes of our play are like mosaic work – the mingled, various product of our two brains' (*WD*: 3). The pseudonym not only disguised their sex, drawing on the two women's private nicknames of Michael (Katherine) and Field (Edith), but also disguised authorial differences between them. Their work, like their lives, was a shared enterprise, defying individualisation. By the 1890s, however, both their sex and their dual authorship were widely known – a fact which, together with their insistence on publishing largely unperformable verse tragedies, probably did hamper their reputation. They themselves increasingly sensed a conspiracy of silence about their work, and others, too, were surprised at this public neglect. As early as 1920, Harold Monro of the Poetry Bookshop observed that the work of Michael Field remained 'strangely unknown' (1920: 21). When, in 1924, Pearsall Smith published an essay on them, he too was puzzled by the continuing silence, and expressed his hope that the verses of 'these bewitched Princesses, these inspired, autocratic, incredible old maids' (1936: 93), might receive due recognition at some future date (88). In 1923, Sturge Moore tried to stir up interest by publishing a selection of their poems and, in 1933, published extracts from their joint journal, *Works and Days*. Meanwhile, Arthur Symons included ten poems by Michael Field in his *Anthology of 'Nineties' Verse* (1928: 56–69) and Yeats, in his *Oxford Book of Modern Verse*, included nine (1936: 68–73). Evidently fellow writers, Browning, Symons and Yeats as well as others, knew and respected their work. But after this brief flurry of revival, the poetry of these two extraordinary, determined, eccentric women disappeared from view for much of the rest of the twentieth century.

Michael Field, in many ways, belongs altogether outside the tradition of Victorian women's verse. As poets, they lack both the socio-political commitment of Barrett Browning and Webster and the sentimental attitudes of desire and repression which characterise Hemans, L.E.L. and Rossetti. Perhaps because of the essential freedom of their lives – a freedom particularly from the conventions and conclusions of heterosexual love – their poetry seems to belong indeed 'out in the open air of nature', and far from all the homes, far countries and graves of their predecessors. It is at once a strength and a limitation of Michael Field's poetry that 'the cost and pain' of women's experience, with all its forbidden fruits and sexual falls, is hardly ever counted. Meanwhile Katherine's and Edith's lives, passed in the more open climate of the rebellious Nineties and in communication with many of their famous contemporaries, are themselves a lesson in the freedoms which came hard or not at all to earlier poets.

* * *

Katherine Bradley was born in 1846. Her father, a tobacco manufacturer, died of cancer when she was 2, and she was subsequently reared by her mother and an older sister, Emma. The profits from the factory were sufficient to keep the family in reasonable comfort, and provided Katherine with a small private income for life. In 1861, after Emma's marriage to a certain Mr Cooper, Katherine and her mother moved with them to Kenilworth. Six years later Mrs Bradley also developed cancer. Katherine, who was 20 at the time, marked the event by starting a diary: 'it will comfort me to write down what happens, & what my darling says & does in these days'.[1] In this sad document, she records her mother's slow decline, and assesses, against that gloomy background, her own spiritual and temperamental failings: 'the graces I most lack are *meekness*, patience & humility',[2] she laments. These pages also express a passionate but generally thwarted desire for experience: 'I feel the desolation of my life here – of my pent-up youth. I thirst for love for communion, for contact with kindred human souls'.[3] She yearns for some life beyond the fixed boundaries of the sick-room and the church, and frequently regrets her lack of opportunity: 'I feel I was made for something nobler than to be an old spinster aunt'.[4] Loving, tactless and headstrong, Katherine was also, judging by one or two agonised comments, highly sensual. She writes in one place that 'Sin is as much a part of us, & as inescapable from us as our blood',[5] and elsewhere admits, intriguingly, that 'Wild gusts of passion sweep over me, & leave me desolated in body & spirit. At such times, I feel evil as a stray man within me'.[6] This is hardly the expected confession of a Victorian girl. Her 'passion', like a 'stray man' in the blood, is a force inherently contradicting the very nature of her sex. Unlike Rossetti, who at about the same age determined to seal her desires in a coffin of self-renunciation, Katherine, both in her poetry and in her life, will be able to release the 'stray man' of passion from the controls of imposed womanhood.

In 1868, her mother died, and Katherine was able first of all to get some of the education she had missed. She attended courses at Newnham College, Cambridge, recently opened to women, and at the Collège de France in Paris, where she also fell in love with the brother of a French friend. His unexpected death left her loveless once again, and, in January 1875, with no prospects of any future from an education which was still, for women, largely honorary, she was back at home. It was at this time that, in her domestic isolation, but showing her usual determination to escape from it, she subscribed to John Ruskin's newly formed Guild of St George. This nostalgic, dictatorial enterprise, intended to promote a pre-industrial lifestyle of intellectual work and manual labour, had resulted in the construction, by Ruskin and some undergraduates (Oscar Wilde among them), of the Ferry Hinksey Road outside Oxford. Members of the Guild, of which there were twenty-four in 1874 (and never many more than that) were expected to donate a tenth of their income, and to agree to a set of rules which included holding some form of religious belief (though of any creed), loving one's neighbour, not hurting any form of life and obeying, without question, the authority of the 'Master' or 'Tyrant', as Ruskin denominated himself. The whole enterprise grew out of a doomed mixture of vaguely socialistic principles and a quirky, desperate egomania which points to the beginning of Ruskin's long and tragic mental collapse. 1875 was also the year in which Rose la Touche, whom he had first idolised when she was 10 years old, died suddenly in her twenties, having become increasingly prone to fits of religious mania bordering on insanity. In the years which followed, Ruskin became more and more unpredictable in his behaviour, filling his lectures with accounts of his dreams, attending seances and, in 1878, risking his own precarious mental balance by entering into the legal absurdity of the Ruskin–Whistler trial. These events form the troubled background to his correspondence with Katherine.

At first, he merely offered advice about her handwriting, made suggestions for investing her income, enquired about her poetry and advocated, when she asked for advice, an open-minded scepticism on the subject of Christian belief: 'let children read the story of Christ – as any other history' (WD: 144), he proposed. However, this smooth beginning was not to last. In 1875, under the pseudonym of Arran Leigh, Katherine published her first volume of verse, *The New Minnesinger and Other Poems*. This already shows something of the religious scepticism and feminist energy which mark the later work. In 'Trompetenruf', for instance, she imagines a scene of world-wide misunderstanding when, at the Last Judgment, 'the long-lost obliterate dead' will be 'All startled, all deafened' (NM: 163) by the last trump, and the 'brain-budding beasts of the ages of Stone' suddenly have to mix with the enlightened races which followed (164). Wryly literal, the poem brings an evolutionary perspective to the contemporary theological debate about soul-sleep – the theory that the soul remains in a state of earth-bound torpor until the end of the world. The sheer scope of evolutionary history, here, threatens to make nonsense of Christianity's small, rather local homecoming of the saved soul.

The title poem, in which Katherine declares her imaginative allegiance to her own sex, also foreshadows the later work:

> Yes, Woman, she whose life doth lie
> In virgin haunts of poesie, –
> How have men woven into creeds
> The unrecorded life she leads!
> What she hath been to them, oh, well
> The whole sweet legend they can tell;
> But what she to herself may be
> They see not, or but dream they see.
>   (2–3)

She sent Ruskin a copy of *The New Minnesinger*, and received in return

206

the grudging reply that his life was 'much too serious . . . to be spent in reading poetry'. Perhaps to encourage her, he added: 'I did accidentally open the *Minnesinger* and liked a bit or two of it – and I don't think I threw it into the waste-paper basket' (*WD*: 147). Yet in this same year he found time to write to Alice Meynell's mother, lavishly praising her daughter's first volume, *Preludes* (1875). The brusque disingenuousness of his reply to Katherine sounds odd beside this evident interest in another's poetry, while also hinting at the problems Michael Field's more robustly sceptical and feminist verses would encounter from the world at large.

Nothing daunted, however, she continued to send him occasional poems and his responses became more generous. 'The verses are very good' (153), he conceded a year later. An altercation developed, however, over his public denunciation of the suffragist and social critic Frances Power Cobbe. In *Fors Clavigera*, the journal of the Guild, Ruskin had sentimentally contrasted 'the ductile and silent gold of ancient womanhood' with the 'bronze, and tinkling . . . saucepan' (1903–12: XXVIII, 621) of the modern woman, epitomised by Cobbe. It seems that Katherine protested at this denigration, to which Ruskin answered irritably: 'I only called her a clattering saucepan – a saucepan is a very good thing in its place' (*WD*: 149). He then justified his opinion of woman's place with a quotation from the Bible: 'It is not the wrongness of her views, but her insolence in proclaiming them – contrary to St. Paul's order "I suffer not a woman to teach"' (148–9). Such responses no doubt helped to feed the spirit of rebellion in his young follower.

The break came at the end of 1877 and, surprisingly, it was caused neither by the issue of poetry nor of women's rights, but of religious belief. The man who had advised reading the New Testament as history, who had himself, in the 1860s, admitted his loss of belief in the afterlife (Evans, 1954: 267) and then troubled his beloved Rose with his '"heathenism"' (275), none the less readily resorted to quoting St Paul when it suited him and, when faced with Katherine's provocative confession of atheism, fell back on simple outrage. No doubt it was the tone as much as the substance of her comments which offended him. 'Your letter telling me you have lost God and found a Skye Terrier is a great grief and amazement to me' (*WD*: 155), he exclaimed. Gods and dogs, like some slippery inversion, will continue to have a curious connection in Katherine's life, even if, at the time, the apparent whimsicality of the choice was calculated to offend Ruskin. For a young girl to espouse atheism so cheerfully was more than even the liberal, agnostic Ruskin could bear. But Katherine, who had been reading some of the contemporary arguments on the subject, persisted in her new allegiance, to the fury of her mentor:

to write to me that you had ceased to believe in God – and had found some comfort in a dog – *this* is *deadly*. And of course I have at once to put you out of the St. George's Guild – which *primarily* refuses atheists – not because they are wicked but because they are fools. (157–8)

He added, as sound proof of his reasoning: 'I know many men of splendid faculty among Atheists. Not one of perfect health of brain' (158). The sad irony of this, in the man whose own sanity was already faltering, would have been lost on Katherine. However, it was probably Ruskin's petulant retraction of his previous literary praise which most hurt her: 'you thought yourself very clever – and are astonished because I think nothing of your poetry – and less than nothing of your power of thought' (158), he ranted. When, seven years later, she started to correspond with Browning, Katherine had already had some experience of the deep-rooted 'customs or beliefs' which are 'sacred to men'.

For a time, the correspondence with Ruskin continued, still eager and provocative on Katherine's side, tetchy and defensive on Ruskin's. One last letter from him, probably written in 1880 and ending: 'Few whom I have ever cared for at all – have been so little worthy', is marked 'FALSE' (168) by her, and it concludes the correspondence. When, thirteen years later, Katherine and Edith went to Brantwood in search of their old 'Master' and, on a 'tragic' (170) day, found him walking alone, looking 'as if freedom had been murdered in him, and as if despair were all he knew of life' (172), he answered their questions by saying he ' "did not remember Katherine Bradley . . . at least not distinctly" ' (171).

By 1880, Katherine had entered into a lifelong partnership with her niece, Edith Cooper, whom she had adopted as a child when her own mother was permanently invalided. ' "I speak as a mother; mothers of some sort we must all become" ' (in Sturgeon, 1921: 75), she once declared. The mothering role remained hers for life, but it also developed into others. In 1878, when Katherine was 30 and Edith 16, they attended classes together in classics and philosophy at Bristol University; thus, like many women of the time, snatching at that forbidden fruit of male knowledge. They also supported the movement for women's suffrage and actively promoted a cause which was always dear to them: the anti-vivisection league. It was probably at about this time that they sealed their friendship with something akin to a vow. Theirs was both a professional partnership of dedication to poetry and also a love affair in which, as Katherine put it, they felt *'closer married'* (*WD*: 16) even than the most romantically married Brownings. Although Lilian Faderman (1985: 210) describes this relationship as one of romantic friendship, Christine White has argued persuasively that, in spite of 'the plurality of ways' in which the two women refer to love in their journals, it remains a sexually, rather than romantically, conceived idea (1990: 206–7). Certainly, to put poems by Michael Field against love poems by other women poets is to be struck by a new language of desire: one which is surprisingly open, sensual and without any overlay of moral virtue or moral guilt.

The poem 'Prologue' (1893), for instance, records the two poets' pact of love and work with a free and informal openness which, while it disarms censor, also discourages a purely innocent reading. Simply the reference to 'lovers' – a word which hardly ever appears in Victorian women's poetry – alerts the reader to new implications:

> It was deep April, and the morn
>   Shakespeare was born;
> The world was on us, pressing sore;
> My Love and I took hands and swore,
>   Against the world, to be
> Poets and lovers evermore,
> To laugh and dream on Lethe's shore,
> To sing to Charon in his boat,
> Heartening the timid souls afloat;
> Of judgment never to take heed,
> But to those fast-locked souls to speed,
> Who never from Apollo fled,
> Who spent no hour among the dead;
>   Continually
>   With them to dwell,
> Indifferent to heaven and hell.
>   (*UB*: 79)

For once, this is a love poem not split into a subject within and an object observed without. It is not an address to the absent listener, but an agreement between partners. Futhermore, it joins the two women in a gesture of love, 'took hands and swore', which is also a gesture of rebellion 'Against the world'. In particular, it is a rebellion against the world's Christian conclusions of 'heaven and hell'. The defiance of such a union is unmistakable. Theirs will be a life and art which go beyond good and evil, in an aestheticism which shows no sign of any struggle with the old creeds of sentimentalist inspiration. It is as if Michael Field begins where Barrett Browning ended, with the careless Pans of laughing creativity. 'To laugh and dream on Lethe's shore' sums up a pagan *jouissance*, even in the place of death, which marks out much of Michael Field's best poetry. Casual and pleasure-loving, their music grows out of the free sensuousness of the pagan gods, invoked, from the start, as an alternative to the moral reckoning of 'heaven and hell'. This poetic testament of having lost God and found Apollo suggests that Katherine's earlier atheism was not just a young girl's whim to provoke her mentor, but already something of a developing imaginative creed. This is a love poem which is also a testament of religious scepticism.

The sexual significance of 'Prologue' becomes clear in its intriguing echo of another poem. Baudelaire's 'Lesbos', from *Les Fleurs du Mal* (1857), contains the following lines:

> Que nous veulent les lois du juste et de l'injuste?
> Vierges au coeur sublime, honneur de l'archipel,
> Votre religion comme une autre est auguste,
> Et l'amour se rira de L'Enfer et du Ciel!

[What use to us the laws of right and wrong? / Virgins of sublime heart, honour of the archipelago, / Your religion like any other is august,/ And love will laugh at hell and heaven!]

Some lines later, Baudelaire refers to Sappho herself as 'l'amante et le poète' (1987: 303) [lover and poet]. Katherine and Edith certainly knew Baudelaire's work well; they translated one of his poems and they remained, in many ways, more in sympathy with the French than with the English tradition. Whether consciously or not, 'Prologue' recalls the sentiments of Baudelaire's poem: its challenge to heaven and hell by the energies of love and laughter, and its resonant appellation of Sappho as the first lover and poet. When they themselves vowed to be 'Poets and lovers evermore' it seems likely that they had in mind the first lover and poet of 'Lesbos', who would be a lifelong poetic model. This was less the legendary Sappho of suicidal leaps than it was the historical woman who wrote love poems to and for her maidens, who was known to have a daughter of her own, whose brother married an Egyptian courtesan and who almost certainly died at home of old age. As J. A. Symonds tactfully put it in his *Studies of the Greek Poets* (1873), which he recommended Edith to read in 1881 (1967–9: II, 683): 'There is enough of heart-devouring passion in Sappho's own verse without the legends of Phaon and the cliff of Leucas' (1920: 194). From Baudelaire and Symonds, but probably also as a result of their own classical learning, Katherine and Edith helped to recuperate a long-suppressed knowledge of Sappho as the lover of women and as the poet who dared express that love.

In this, they were indebted (see *LA*: 130) to the publication, in 1885, of Henry Wharton's highly influential edition of Sappho. This was the first translation of the poet's works in which the 'Ode to Aphrodite' was made to refer explicitly to a girl lover (see DeJean, 1989: 248): ' "*For even if she flies she shall soon follow, and if she rejects gifts shall yet give*" ' (Wharton, 1895: 50). Like Natalie Barney who, in the early 1900s, lit on the Wharton text and turned it into something of a ' "pagan" ' (DeJean, 1989: 279) gospel, inspiring much of her own verse, Michael Field also found in its homosexual meanings an inspiration for a love poetry which seemed never to have been written before. In their own translations and elaborations of the Sapphic fragments in *Long Ago* (1889), Michael Field dares, almost for the first time since Sappho herself, to write love poems addressed by an older woman to younger girls. It was no doubt significant that Katherine's and Edith's first joint collection of verse under their shared pseudonym should have been written in honour of the mother of women poets who was also a lover of women. The double purpose of being 'Poets and lovers evermore' thus becomes, not a costly and fatal association, ultimately dedicated to death, but a laughingly sexual and rebellious one, dedicated to life and pleasure. Michael Field rescues Sappho from her cliff-edge of despair and, with her, the female imagination itself from all its chronically miserable effusions of the heart.

In all, Katherine and Edith published eight volumes of lyrics, many of them in limited, expensive and beautifully produced editions – a *fin-de-siècle* fashion which no doubt also contributed to their early disappearance from circulation. *Long Ago* (1889), for instance, was limited to 100 copies, *Sight and Song* (1892) to 400 and *Underneath the Bough* (1893) to 150. Huysmans' ideal of an edition of Baudelaire limited to one copy only (1959: 146) was an all too well-founded joke. In addition, their joint journal, *Works and Days*, runs to thirty-six foolscap volumes and covers the forty or more years of their life together. The gossipy energy and wit of the journal and the strange, if erratic originality of the poetry, point to, if not exactly *'genius'*, as Browning put it, at least to poets of considerable dedication and gift.

Browning himself, having overcome his initial fear of impropriety, remained a faithful supporter and friend. The poets first met him in 1885 when, as Edith reports, he was full of avuncular affection, and 'stood fondling our hands, with a touch that conveyed what he could not speak, then said, "How nice it is to have you standing one on each side of me" ' (*WD*: 11). On a later visit he showed them, alongside the 'ninepenny' original of *The Ring and the Book* which he had bought in a Florentine market, 'the first book he bought as a boy': 'Mrs. Hemans' *Commonplace Book*.' He also showed them some of Barrett Browning's annotated classics, 'full of her notes and still breathing her love' (15). His evident admiration for his wife's poetry was made clear to Edith: ' "Do you care for her? I hope so," he said, giving me such an emotional push that he nearly hurt me' (16). In fact, Katherine and Edith very rarely mention other women poets in their journal, and perhaps Browning's 'push' was intended to be a sharp prod. In the many visits which followed he took to addressing them as his ' "two dear Greek women" ' (20), suggesting

211

that at least some of his anxieties about '"social conventions"' had been set at rest. 'His limitless belief in us is appalling' (21), Katherine noted with misgiving.

Another friend and admirer was George Meredith, who warmly praised the poems in *Long Ago* (1889) for their 'faultless flow' and 'classic concision' (*WD*: 66). Thereafter, Katherine and Edith were frequent visitors at his house, though they, for their part, found his very inconcise conversation, with its 'grim copiousness of burlesque' (99), fatiguing and chilling after a while. In the 1880s and 90s, they were also friendly with Havelock Ellis and probably knew Olive Schreiner, both of whom were for a time members of the 'Fellowship of the New Life' – a society started in 1883 to promote the ideals of Thoreau and Whitman, but part of which then became the Fabian Society. In 1887, Yeats expressed his wish to meet Katherine and Edith at one of the gatherings of the New Life society. (Evidently their joint authorship was already well known, in spite of their efforts to keep it secret.) Yeats had written a favourable review of some of their early plays, and it is interesting that he rated Michael Field at this time as 'a bird of a [*sic*] another feather from these London literators whom I cannot but rather despise' (1986: I, 18). In the event, they did not meet until 1901.

Meanwhile, Katherine and Edith had embarked on a life of writing and travelling together, the railways playing no small part in this visible emancipation of women's lives. In 1885 they were in Italy, visiting Pen Browning at Asolo, and in 1890 in Paris, making that very Victorian pilgrimage to the morgue, in order, as they explained, to confront face to face the literal facts of death: to 'look deep into birth and death – unflinchingly – accepting all the physical repulsion' (*WD*: 111). Another journey was undertaken in 1891, when they planned a trip round the art galleries of Germany as part of their research for a volume of poems on subjects taken from pictures. By the time they reached Dresden, however, Edith was sick with scarlet fever and, as Katherine refused to leave her, creating a noisy scene in the entrance to the hospital, both women were admitted.

The journal entries during these weeks show something of their exuberance and courage, even in the face of death. Edith herself describes her feverish fantasies in surreal detail in these pages, delirium working like inspiration on her brain. Lying on her moonlit bed, the shadow of Tennyson's 'Mariana' inevitably falls across her memory, but she enters the part with a very unTennysonian energy and humour:

> I feel the outside beauty has an ominous calm about it. I am fervidly hot; the white beams lie on my brain and provoke it – they enter it clear, quiet, precise, they make it vague, distracted, visionary. They evoke their

contraries. I create phantasies that come so fast that they form an element round me in which I sink, sink – then float along under them and then sink again. . . . The moonlight through the blind becomes more powerful – delirium is glorious, like being inspired continuously . . . forms of art and poetry swim round and into me. Every moment is plastic. . . .

A vast dromedary comes along, with red trappings and trophies, in the midst are set the words *Two weeks at Dresden*!! The ironic beast passes. . . .

Vast Bacchanals rush by, Rubensesque, violent . . . I fall into an attitude of sleep like an Antinous on the ground. I am Greek, Roman, Barbarian, Catholic, and this multiform life sweeps me toward unconsciousness – only the shine through the blinds tortures me so that I cannot lose myself. I beg my Love to keep a candle lighted to put out the moon with all its terrible spectral frilliness and to obliterate the white cavern-arch of the door – Death's Door – that I keep approaching, that I cannot pass, for as soon as I am near it, the brilliant swirl of images is round me and I am caught back to life. (*WD*: 53–4)

These feverish hallucinations contain many of the key notes of Michael Field's later poetry. For instance, just when delirium threatens to engulf the mind in solipsistic imaginings, the 'ironic' camel walks on, and catches the nauseous sway of fantasy into self-mocking wit. The idea of the 'Vast Bacchanals' points to the poets' favourite god of inspiration, who had a special power over women. Then, in the middle of this orgy of picturesque visions, Edith imagines herself as Antinous, the beautiful catamite of Hadrian, which suggestively hints at the role of boyish seductiveness she adopted in real life. She then goes through a chameleon change of character: 'Greek, Roman, Barbarian, Catholic', which reproduces the freedom from fixed creeds both women sought in real life. Katherine once wrote to Havelock Ellis, fiercely denying the charge of being ' "orthodox" ', and proclaiming herself, instead, ' "Christian, pagan, pantheist, and other things the name of which I do not know" ' (in Sturgeon, 1921: 47). The need to be, if not exactly atheists, at least promiscuously pluralist believers, was central to their poetic creed during the 1880s and 90s, although the dream sequence, culminating as it does in Catholicism, also points in the direction their lives will take.

The pictorial vividness, the hint of orgiastic physical pleasure, the sexual ambiguity and exuberant adoption of multiple systems of belief, are all elements which will appear in the verse, and they tell how far these poets had travelled from the muscular moralities and gender-specific taboos of high Victorianism. Edith subconsciously turns the moon-shadowed figure of Mariana into a wild, Bacchic dreamer who, far from dying, is constantly 'caught back to life' by the compellingly erotic 'swirl of images' round her. Her imagination, far from being decayed and weary, is rife with images of sexual desire. The passage makes its own small comment on the heritage of the dying poetess, as this living poet finds imaginative ways, it seems, specifically not to die.

While in the hospital, Edith was forced to endure the piety of one nurse and the sexual advances of another. The effect of Bible readings by the first was to drive her into ever more rebellious thoughts of pleasure:

> my whole nature grew elfishly wicked as she read. I determine I will have as much pleasure as I can. I dance at balls, I go to Operas, I am Mars and, looking across at Sim's [Katherine's] little bed, I realise that she is a goddess, hidden in her hair – Venus. (*WD*: 56)

The classical imagery, here, is quite explicit. She desires her lover as Mars desires Venus, and the enforced biblical readings of the Sister only increase her lust. The ideal of 'pleasure' for its own sake, sexual and pagan, is the impulse behind much of Michael Field's best work. Although 'pleasure' is also one of the popular catchwords of aestheticism, for these women poets it has an energy and freedom, a sense of commitment to real life, which is more emancipating than decadent, more active than introspective.

The sexual advances of the second nurse, however, were as unwelcome as the Bible readings, although Edith's clear-sighted explanations of the situation are singularly free of either intrigue or horror. She reports that 'while my Love is in the garden, [she] embraces me bodily' and 'throws herself about me and kisses me with the persistence of madness' (64). She was in no doubt as to the nature of this motherly, yet smotheringly sensual infatuation: 'she is under the possession of terrible fleshly love, [which] she does not conceive [of] as such, and as such I will not receive it' (63). Knowing more, at least about 'fleshly love', than her clumsy admirer, she speaks in the mature tones of worldly experience. The slight, intense, boyish Edith must have been aware of her attractiveness to other women, and certainly she was aware of the nature of this 'fleshly love' which the nurse herself was unable to 'conceive'. The whole section of the journal describing the Dresden hospital is supercharged with a lustful imaginativeness which barely disguises its real-life inspiration in the poets' love for each other. It seems far removed from the spiritual and social complexes of earlier poets.

One of the pictures Katherine and Edith had seen in Dresden was Giorgione's 'The Sleeping Venus'. The poem which they subsequently wrote on it, and which they published in *Sight and Song* (1892), shows the strong influence of that erotic, pictorial quality which Pater had already made fashionable. 'The Sleeping Venus', like many of the poems in the volume, has a luscious descriptiveness about it, a fleshly detail which, although not resulting in very good poetry, shows the extent to which art for art's sake, with its implication of pleasure for pleasure's sake, had freed Michael Field from a female heritage of repressed or displaced eroticism. The sexual clarity of the descriptions is, indeed, in Pater's sense of the words, 'serene' and 'blithe' – full of that '*Heiterkeit*' which, as early as 1867, he had noted as one of the two 'supreme characteristics of the Hellenic ideal' (1910: I, 213):

> Her hand the thigh's tense surface leaves,
> Falling inward. Not even sleep
> Dare invalidate the deep,
> Universal pleasure sex
> Must unto itself annex –
> Even the stillest sleep; at peace,
> More profound with rest's increase,
> She enjoys the good
> Of delicious womanhood.
> (*SS*: 101–2)

Though forced in its syntax and rhymes, this none the less has a self-delighting physical literalness which marks an extraordinary freeing of the female imagination. Indeed, 'delicious womanhood' is a welcome, sexualised description of an ideal too long associated with hearths and angels, while the word 'sex' hovers tentatively between a merely generic and a suggestively erotic meaning. The sensuousness of the human body is given full exposure in these poems of sleepy goddesses and prurient fauns, quivering St Sebastians and gory *Pietàs*. Published by John Lane and Elkin Matthews who, two years later, brought out the first volume of the *The Yellow Book*, *Sight and Song* shows Michael Field, not only employing some of the stock poeticisms of the age, but also drawing on the adventurous and permissively sensual experiences of their own lives together.

During the 1890s, Katherine and Edith became acquainted with many of their eminent contemporaries, whom they describe with a quirkily perceptive relish in the pages of their journal. In 1889 they met Pater, whom they had long admired and who seems to have been the single most important influence on their writing. Pater's famously shy lecturing manner which, in Wilde's phrase, was to be overheard rather than heard, led them to conclude, affectionately: 'Wouldn't one give much to surprise the Bacchant in Walter Pater!' (*WD*: 120). Meanwhile, they deplored his prudishness in striking out the 'Essay on Aesthetic Poetry' from *Appreciations*, in deference to 'the moral weaknesses of everybody' (119). They stayed with the poet Vernon Lee (Violet Paget) in Florence, and they met George Moore in Paris. In London, they encountered Oscar Wilde several times, on one occasion describing him, with mischievous incongruity, as beaming 'with the "Heiterkeit" of a Greek God that has descended on a fat man of literary habits' (139). On another occasion they fell into agreement with him on the Pateresque principle that 'the whole problem of life turns on pleasure' (136). However, when they appeared one day 'not well dressed' and somewhat bedraggled from having walked in the rain, Wilde snubbed them and they were indignant. 'When he shows himself as a *snob* he is disgustingly repulsive', they asserted, and added, perceptively: 'The artist strain in him is crossed with the vulgar respectable – Gods and women cannot endure such a cross' (140). Wilde thus lost two more friends who might have rallied to his support in 1895.

With Havelock Ellis they lunched, true to the spirit of the times, at the 'Vegetarian', and it seems likely that they contributed to some of his theories about lesbianism, or 'Sexual Inversion', as he called it in his pioneering *Studies in the Psychology of Sex* (1897). In 1893 they attended, along with many of their contemporaries, a reading given by Verlaine, the arch-fiend of decadence, at Barnard's Inn. They evidently relished the spectacle of the poet-criminal-homosexual himself, sitting among his polite English audience, most of whom were more than willing to be scandalised. Edith's description of the poet and the occasion is rich in *fin de sièclisms*:

> The skin has the appearance of parchment drawn by fire, and every now and then a smile rises that is full of the innocence of hell, I mean the 'naïveté' of habitual wrong-doing. It is quite delicious. Indeed Verlaine is so necessarily criminal that it has done him little harm to fulfil himself, and the religious fervour that is the accompanying ecstasy of his sin, grows out of it almost as a reward. . . . He sat, his legs stretched out – his vagabondism covered by clean and middle-class garments; he looked like the giant of Bohemia brought out to be seen by Philistia, and he was very, *very* judicious in the choice of his poems . . . It was such an English scene – Satan in a frock-coat, reading religious poetry and darting pitch-spark glances at a company incapable of understanding the tragedies of hell . . . still less its bouts of free revel. (*WD*: 189)

Although she repeats the stock *frissons* of the age: 'the innocence of hell', the 'ecstasy of his sin', 'the tragedies of hell', it is with a sympathetic and lightly mocking humour which enjoys the element of stage-set in the whole event. Verlaine was brought out for London viewing by 'his young neophyte Symons' (188) not, primarily, to read his poems, but to scandalise the philistines. When, in 1895, the 'Philistia' of Victorian England took their revenge, and sentenced Wilde to two years' imprisonment with hard labour for sodomy, the merely *risqué* pose became an actual criminal offence, taking many of the aesthetes, like Wilde himself, by surprise. The effect on Katherine and Edith was probably similarly unexpected and subtly inhibiting.

In spite of their admiration for Verlaine, however, they were always antagonistic towards the more extreme forms of decadence. A streak of dissenting puritanism runs through their comments on contemporary art. About some of Beardsley's illustrations they expostulated: 'Faugh! one must go to one's Wordsworth & Shelley to be fumigated'.[7] For themselves, they expressed 'the one prayer / From decadence, Good Lord deliver us!'.[8] In 1894, passing by the front window of John Lane's Bodley Head, which was exhibiting the new *Yellow Book* with accompanying lurid effects of yellow masks and disembodied heads, they expressed a mixture of quite inventive fascination and outright disgust:

> As we came up to the shop we found the whole frontage a hot background of orange-colour to sly, roistering heads, silhouettes against it – half hiding behind masks. The windows seemed to be gibbering, our eyes to be filled with incurable jaundice . . .
> But the infamous window mocked & mowed & fizgiged, saffron & pitchy, till one's eyes were arrested like Virgil's before the wind of flame.[9]

That same year they requested the return of one of their poems which had been accepted by *The Yellow Book*, in protest at its style. For all their daring in real life, they could be solemnly censorious about art, their commitment to Pater's 'clean' aestheticism resulting in high-minded disapproval of the more perverse forms of decadence. Their rebuff to *The Yellow Book* is in striking contrast to Charlotte Mew's willingness to be published in it, even though, in life, Mew appears much more conventionally inhibited than they. Decadence created strange conflicts of theory and practice in the artists of the time; indeed, it thrived on such conflicts. It was the Wilde trial which finally put an end to such discrepancies, and to the double standards of pose and passion, book and life which, in a sense, buoyed up some of the more outrageous experiments in the illicit. The punitive literal-mindedness of the philistines in 1895 brought to a premature end the 'free revel' of the Nineties (Ellmann, 1987: 288), and left the age poised for an inevitable, full-dress act of repentance.

The poets' distrust of decadence no doubt also derived from their sex, however. As they knew, to their cost, the aesthetic fashions of the day were self-consciously and self-admiringly male. Pater's Hellenising essays of the 1860s and Huysmans' *Against Nature* (1884), that elaborate manual of the macabre and the precious, together served as gospels of a creed which ranged from a philosophy to a pose, a religion to a fashion in house decoration. But in both Pater and Huysmans the standard-bearer of values was male. Katherine herself once told Wilde that she felt much pain at a comment by Pater in his essay on 'Style', 'where he speaks of the scholarly conscience being male' (*WD*: 137). Three years later, in 1893, Edith met Lionel Johnson at a concert, and feeling overwhelmed by the 'brow domed like the British Museum Reading Room (and as full of literature)' (191), she chattered nervously about her influenza. Sensing his disdain, she realised that she was confirming his worst suspicions, and not only his, but those of the age in general: 'I spoil all. I shake from my person all poetry, I demonstrate that woman cannot have the scholarly conscience. I am an occasion for cynicism – a stumbling-block to youth, the sensibility of male youth: a dream turned into a nightmare, perchance!' (192). She is quick to see the reasons for Johnson's contempt, real or imagined: she is, in Pater's sense, not a scholar, not young and not a 'male youth'. At a time when woman was indeed being turned very much into a figure of sexual 'nightmare' in innumerable paintings of Sphinxes, Medusas and Circes (see Dijkstra, 1986), Edith's sensitivity to her own, inherently unpoetic nature is understandable. None the less, she took a small revenge in her journal when she described Johnson, with delicate diminutiveness, as a 'learned snow-drop'.[10]

Envy of the intellectual advantages of men is frequently expressed in the journal: 'What good times men have, what pipes, what deep communings! . . . Yet if women seek to learn their art from life, instead of what the angels bring down to them in dishes, they simply get defamed' (*WD*: 202). Murdering those angels was, even in the liberated Nineties, a hard task. When, in 1893, one of their plays was produced in London and met with fiercely antagonistic reviews, 'like a lot of unchained tigers' (181), they welcomed the humiliation. Explaining to a friend that she 'would go through the whole experience again', Edith pointed out: ' "But then, you see, I am a woman, and to bring out a play is experience of life – just what women feel so crushingly that they need. You men get it like breathing" ' (184). Mary Wollstonecraft's old call to women to ' "Gain experience – ah! gain it – while experience is worth having" ' (1976: 124) seems to ring on down the century. Sheer appetite for life drives Edith to embrace even the public fiasco of their failed play. It is not possible for women to donate 'living' to their 'servants', in the true spirit of decadence, because women have not yet had the experience of living. *Ennui* is for those who have already known too much of life, and can thus afford the ultimate luxury of embarking for Cythera or the various lands of the lotos-eaters. Like Webster, and even to some extent the later L.E.L., Michael Field rejects the hallucinogenic weariness of those imaginative tropics. In repudiation of a reported comment by Sarah Grand, for instance, that she cared 'for nothing but literature', Katherine replied indignantly: ' "I should think a writer who was worth reading would care most of all for life" ' (107). Like Augusta Webster, though perhaps for different reasons, Michael Field also resists literary weariness – Baudelaire's delicate monster 'ennui', of a sensuality spoiling at the core. Instead, theirs are poems which, for all their faults, are vibrant with a newly discovered, still enlightened sensuousness, embraced with the delight of ' "life" ' itself. In 1901 Katherine, interestingly, invoked the figure of the new king 'to keep us genial, simple and humane – to preserve us from being literary' (261). Such a plea is not an about-turn, but a statement consistent with their whole approach to art. Though they adopt many of the ideas and attitudes of the aesthetes, they also remain, as women, outsiders; their imaginations, not weary, cynical and criminal, but 'genial, simple and humane'.

Not long after this comment, Edith describes a visit by Yeats. She observes his nervousness, the way he clutches at a book 'in his shyness', and talks too much. She also notes, with an edge of mockery, his aesthetic appearance. 'His hair dribbles in a Posthlethwaite manner on his brow', she writes, referring to the well-known cartoon of the aesthete poet by du Maurier, and she goes on to describe how 'The hands flap like flower-heads that grow on each side a stem and are shaken by the wind. At first the gesture spells one; then it irritates, because it is a gesture and is not varied' (*WD*: 262). She is more amused than impressed by the poet's modish appearance, though pleased that 'He knows our plays well and seems to care for them with insight. I was not prepared for this, but Dowden fired him with them in youth' (262–3). Two years later, Yeats politely rejected one of their plays for the Irish National Theatre, adding that 'frankly I do not like it as well as your other work' (1954: 408). Nevertheless, he remembered and liked their poetry well enough to include nine poems of theirs, mainly Sapphic lyrics from *Long Ago* (though not any addressed to women) in his *Oxford Book of Modern Verse* (1936).

Meanwhile, a private tragedy marred the later 1890s for them. In 1897, Edith's father was killed on a climbing expedition in Switzerland. He had set out alone one day, and never returned. His body was not found for some months, during which time Edith was obsessed by the idea that he had been murdered. She wrote a number of sonnets about his death, one of which, 'Invocation', describes the place where the body was eventually discovered and which the two poets visited that same year. Characteristically, even this elegy turns into a love sonnet:

Ah me, but what a trysting place is here
Upon the trail of thy mortality!
Still am I found beside thy forest bier;
O lingering ghost, still keep thy tryst with me!
Thou art, I know, long since a soul in bliss,
There should I look for thee – yet stay awhile!
I would remember me how thou did'st kiss,
And part upon the pressure of thy smile.
I love, ah, not thy shadowy Paradise,
I love the very ground where thou hast lain,
This herbage that took record of thine eyes;
And where they faded there would I remain.
Love, leave thine azure heaven, the woods are brown,
Wizard, tempestuous, sheltering, full of night – come down!

(WH: 145)

The last two lines set up a deliberate opposition between the pale security of 'heaven' and the mysterious, wild, yet nurturing darkness of the woods. The sudden energy of that last line: 'Wizard, tempestuous, sheltering, full of night' springs from a deep commitment to the demigods of life, with all their contradictions of tempest and shelter, the living and the dead. Trees, in much of Michael Field's poetry, are figures of secrecy, sex, freedom and pleasure, suggesting a pre-Christian lurking-place of fauns, dryads and rough Pans – of energies which cannot be controlled by the decrees of heaven and hell. As the ascetic Macrinus, from a later poem, cautions:

'. . . trees must have soft dampness for their growth,
    And interfold
Their boughs and leaves into a screen, not loath
To hide soft, tempting creatures at their play . . .'

(PA: 57)

The danger, exhilaration and Dionysiac sensuousness of the woods is a better place for meeting the dead than among the 'azure' consolations of the sky. Edith invokes the ghost of her dead father almost as she might invite a lover to sport in the shade.

By the turn of the century, however, some of this zest for life begins to fade. The death of Victoria in 1901 drew from Katherine some surprisingly passionate remarks: 'She sweeps away with her into the locked land, my life, my youth, my breathing.' The age, which had long called itself 'Victorian' (WD: 237), was over, and those who lived on felt that their moment had passed. At a performance of Wilde's Salomé in 1906, Edith observed how the gathered company, which included Hardy, George Moore, Arthur Symons, Bernard Shaw and Max

220

Beerbohm, looked 'all gray' (249). By this time, she and Katherine felt increasingly snubbed by the literary world, and took refuge in a haughty sort of eccentricity which did not encourage friendship or recognition. Pearsall Smith recalled his visits to their home at about this time as memorably strange occasions. The two 'incredible old maids' (1936: 93), who seemed at first like characters out of Cranford, would gradually turn into 'Pythonesses' and 'Bacchic Maenads' (92) as their conversation became progressively inspired and wild, and Katherine would 'speak of the soul of their sacred dog, or of a flower . . . or of a precious adjective' (91). He himself wished, in later years, that he had been more generous and conciliatory, especially on the occasion when the poets, having stayed in his family cottage, appropriated one of his favourite pictures, on the unquestioned assumption that 'objects of beauty belong to those who love them most' (93). His ungracious insistence that it be returned incurred a displeasure which lasted for several years. For their part, they felt the intellectual and personal isolation of their idiosyncrasies quite bitterly and uncomprehendingly.

Then, in 1906, their beloved dog, Whym Chow, died. The large numbers of letters of condolence received from friends and acquaintances point, rather quaintly, to the passion they cherished for the creature, although the cost to those friends is also made comically clear by Logan Smith's recollection of how he and his sister exhausted themselves 'in agonies of commiseration for the death of Chow', she staying up till four in the morning to compose an adequately grief-stricken letter. However, like many others, they found that their efforts were in vain and they were regally 'cast off . . . for cold-hearted worldlings' (92). Meanwhile, the two elderly Maenads mourned the death of their beloved animal in passionate verse. The growth of the anti-vivisection movement had resulted in a considerable protest literature about dogs. Frances Power Cobbe's *The Friend of Man*, for instance, quotes such popular verses as Emily Pfeiffer's 'The Dog' and Barrett Browning's 'To Flush, My Dog' (1889: 120–2). Michael Field's poems, however, which were privately published in an edition of twenty-seven under the fiery title of *Whym Chow: Flame of love* (1914a), have none of the domestic sentiments that were common to the movement. Their dog is not a friend of man, but a fierce-souled Bacchus of inspiration, power and unfettered lust:

> And from thy glinted eye what lust of eye,
> What joy in having joy to thy desire,
> What potency out of thy gold to fashion
> Thy slaves to aptness for each regal passion.
> What ambush and what ease of rampant fire!
> What somnolence of ancient cruelty!
>
> (*WC*: 20)

More like Blake's *Tyger* than the faithful household dog of anti-vivisection literature, Whym Chow's death was like the death to them of their own pagan, unreckoning past. Beautiful, cruel and lusty, he is also a symbol of their own 'Liberal Love' (*WC*: 46) for each other – a love which seemed set apart from the materialistic strategies of heterosexual desire: 'Magnificent, taintless of scheme or plan. / So was thy love, O little heart, complete' (*WC*: 46). Whym Chow, in these poems, becomes a living metaphor of their own 'lust of eye' for each other. It was perhaps no wonder that letters of commiseration from more conventional friends seemed stintingly dispassionate.

According to Edith, it was the death of Whym Chow which brought about their eventual conversion to Roman Catholicism (*WD*: 273). Just as, almost thirty years before, Katherine had 'lost God and found a Skye Terrier' (155), so in 1906 the poets lost their Chow and found God. The exchange seems to have been the same. The free life of the animal, which gave Katherine her first reason for atheism, was exchanged for a new accountability to heaven and hell. Having lost their Bacchus, the poets turned back to God. They were also, however, taking a well-trodden, literary path from revels to repentance. The Catholic Church, with its erotic rituals and emphasis on chastity, was the natural home of the aesthetes. 'The Bacchic joy of Benediction was shed on me years and years ago' (*WD*: 272), Edith recalled, eccentrically. Their conversion in 1907 had its compensations, but there was also a high price to be paid for this new commitment. As Edith writes, in a rare explicit mention of her own sexuality: 'Since I have entered the Holy Catholic Church, I have never fallen into fleshly sin'[11] and, more specifically, 'When I came into this Church a year ago [I gave] a gift that was a vow of chastity'.[12]

Faith, however, was not good for their poetry. The works in their two last major volumes, *Poems of Adoration* (1912) and *Mystic Trees* (1913), are largely exuberant, versified expositions of doctrine, embraced with the fervour of the convert but not converted into art. Like much of Rossetti's religious poetry, they sound like exercises for salvation, though they have a lush and baroque formlessness which is very unlike her controlled structures. In 'O Trinity, that art a Bank of Violets' (1913), for instance, the attempt to reproduce the Metaphysical voluptuousness of Crashaw simply sounds confused:

> O Trinity, that art a bank of violets,
> Of thy first breath
> Came the long sigh for death!
> While Mary pondereth
> What may the Angel's Salutation be –
> Where there is no more Time, in Trinity,
> The Holy Ghost begets,

> Breathing as from a bank of violets,
> That sweetness blowing through the Word
>   By which Christ is transferred
>   From Man unto the spotless Host,
>   That to His Father offereth
> Himself from the deep spiceries of death.
> (MT: 13)

All the serenity and clarity of the early pagan verse has gone from these over-perfumed and erotic obeisances. Only in the occasional poem remembering the free passions of the past does the language come to life: in the seductive stanzas of 'Macrinus against Trees' (*PA*: 57–8), for instance, or in the first part of 'Descent from the Cross' (1912):

> Come down from the Cross, my soul, and save thyself – come down!
> Thou wilt be free as wind. None meeting thee will know
> How thou wert hanging stark, my soul, outside the town.
>   Thou wilt fare to and fro;
> Thy feet in grass will smell of faithful thyme; thy head . . .
> Think of the thorns, my soul – how thou wilt cast them off,
> With shudder at the bleeding clench they hold . . .
> (PA: 96)

Occasionally, the desire to shake off the 'bleeding clench' of sin and suffering results in a celebration of the old natural pleasures. Here, Michael Field briefly escapes from the plush sanctities of doctrine which spoil many of the late poems. However, unlike Wilde's pre-conversion poem 'Humanidad' (1881), which ended with 'Loosen the nails – we shall come down I know' (1990: 784), Michael Field's answer, thirty years later, is 'O soul remain with Him, with Him thy doom fulfil!' (98). Faith did not re-energise their poetry, but turned it, paradoxically, towards the very flaccid and flowery decadence which they had largely avoided before.

There may, however, have been other reasons for this falling-off. In 1911, Edith, who was 49, was diagnosed as having cancer. The two weeks during which the disease was ascertained were, as she bravely describes them, 'the greatest in experience of my life' (*WD*: 301). She then writes with moving sharpness and simplicity about the events which followed: the visit to the specialist, in which 'everything said about one's disease is a jagged nail driven through one's pride' (302), the increasing pain over the next two years (she refused to take opium in order to keep writing to the end) and the deepening sense of Katherine's 'passionate love' (324) for her. During the last months she received a letter from Alice Meynell, who wrote to express her admiration for their poetry and her wish to meet the two authors – a wish never to be fulfilled. The old spirited self-detachment seems to return in the writings of these last months, as Edith records every detail of her decline. It is as if she has learned, in life, the message of the early poem: 'To laugh and dream on Lethe's shore'. Three weeks before her death, for instance, she writes with humorous surprise: 'I was speaking . . . when suddenly I hear a sound like that of a dove that fights against choking corn. I had to realise it came from my throat and that other spasms were there to choke me, till I let their strange noise grind themselves out' (326).

On the strange sound of that pain, Katherine wrote a poem. 'She is Singing to Thee, *Domine*!' (1913) touches, like Edith's own image of the dove, the edge of the grotesque in its bravely aestheticised metaphor for pain:

> She is singing to Thee, *Domine*!
>   Dost hear her now?
> She is singing to Thee from a burning throat,
> And melancholy as the owl's love-note;
> She is singing to Thee from the utmost bough
>   Of the tree of Golgotha, where it is bare,
> And the fruit torn from it that fruited there;
> She is singing . . . Canst Thou stop the strain,
>   The homage of such pain?
> *Domine*, stoop down to her again!
>
>   (*MT*: 145)

With the same commitment to experience shown throughout her life, Edith met death with clear-eyed attention. One of her last comments is a hope that she will not 'drowse into death when it comes' (*WD*: 326–7), and to within a few days of it she was writing in passionate rejection of the 'merely mortal atmosphere of dereliction' (328). She died on 13 December 1913.

Soon after, Katherine wrote the poem 'Fellowship' (1914) which, in a sudden release of energy, fervently reclaims their old pagan style of passion and art:

> In the old accents I will sing, my Glory, my Delight,
> In the old accents, tipped with flame, before we knew the right,
> True way of singing with reserve. O Love, with pagan might,
>
> White in our steeds, and white too in our armour let us ride,
> Immortal, white, triumphing, flashing downward side by side
> To where our friends, the Argonauts, are fighting with the tide.
>
>   (*Ded*: 123)

'Fellowship' marks a return to the other 'way of singing', not that of the 'True' gods, full of 'reserve' and repression, but that of 'pagan might', energetic, combative and fiery. The poem recalls, across the distance of more than thirty years, the early 'Prologue', with its vow 'To laugh and dream' whatever the cost, and be 'Indifferent to heaven and hell'. 'Lethe's shore', or now 'the tide' embraced by the 'Argonauts', was a place both poets knew in real life, and faced with stoical honesty. The 'old accents' return at the end, as the laughing spirit of a Pan or a Bacchus drowns out 'the right, / True way of singing'. As Katherine herself explained to a correspondent: ' "I have written a poem or two – one pagan. I am reverting to the pagan, to the humanity of Virgil, to the moods that make life so human and so sweet" ' (in Sturgeon, 1921: 57). Those moods were not entirely repressed by the new faith in God. Their subconscious, like that of many of these women poets, remained essentially pagan.

Two days after Edith's funeral, Katherine suffered a haemorrhage. She had kept her own cancer hidden from her lover, unwilling to give her any more pain. In fact, she herself lived on for only another eight months. Having compiled a volume of Edith's early verse and the Whym Chow volume, she died in September 1914, as the world around her was entering a new era. That era would not readily remember two eccentric women whose poetry, even in their own time, seemed calculated to offend against the canons of true womanliness on the one hand and of true decadence on the other. Yet their best poems contain a serene and blithe sensuousness which is, in its way, unique in late Victorian poetry.

WHEN A GIRL BECOMES A LOVER

Michael Field's best poems are love poems. Throughout their lives, Katherine and Edith wrote verses about and to each other, celebrating their love as a sensual and sexual end in itself. Strikingly free of the morbid penalties and self-denying mischances of much Victorian women's love poetry, they write in a voice which is forthright, requited and relaxed. The exhibited melancholy of sentimentalism, the scarlets and whites of Christian morality and the coins of the socio-sexual market are all missing from their verses. It is as if these poems exist in an atmosphere altogether outside the moral and ideological structures of the age. Idiomatic, witty and informal, they are cheerfully defiant both of the literary heritage of the heart and of the heterosexual bargains of the fall. They thus open up a pagan subtext which has lain in 'reserve' in much previous women's poetry, and make it freely and unproblematically accessible. It is true that their poetry therefore lacks, like Webster's, though for different reasons, the imaginative advantages of that 'reserve' – the sense of a residual depth of metaphor which plays against the poem's moral and narrative patterns and, therefore, the sense of language itself as a forbidden fruit snatched from the world of punishing experience. This is a poetry which altogether misses that stress of truth against pleasure, conscience against desire, which constitutes the main tension of other Victorian women poets.

A short, untitled verse from the early volume *Underneath the Bough* (1893) expresses the underlying principle of this new-found freedom:

> How sweeter far it is to give
> Than just to rest in the receiving,
> Sweeter to sigh than be sighed over,
> Sweeter to deal the blow than bear the grieving,
> That girl will learn who dares become a lover.
>
> The songs she sings will have the glee,
> The laughter of the wind that looses
> Wing and breaks from a forest cover;
> Freedom of stream that slips its icy nooses
> Will be her freedom who becomes a lover.
>
> (*UB*: 131–2)

Christina Rossetti also pleaded for passion in, for instance, 'The heart knoweth its own bitterness':

> To give, to give, not to receive,
> I long to pour myself, my soul,
> Not to keep back or count or leave
> But king with king to give the whole . . .
> (*CP*: III, 265–6, ll. 25–8)

However, where Rossetti's register remains open-endedly teleological, duplicating heavenly and earthly desire, even though at cross-purposes, Michael Field's is sturdily, if less musically, literal. The girl, here, must not just 'pour' her love, with all its emblematic significance, but, more practically and strategically, 'become a lover'. As in 'Prologue', the word 'lover' carries a startlingly secular and anti-romantic charge. Where Rossetti craves reciprocity, Field craves self-assertion; where Rossetti waits, like a 'fountain sealed' (44), for the other lover who may come, Field advocates free-flowing 'songs' and 'laughter', whether he comes or not. The explosive self-repression of the one is in strong contrast to the relaxed self-expression of the other. It is not surprising that Edith was nonplussed by Christina's life of 'prayer and denial', and by the rumour that she was determined to be 'Love's Martyr for [Dante Gabriel's] sake' (*WD*: 115–16). By comparison with Rossetti's tormented depths of meaning and evasive cross-purposes, Field's poems seem light and obvious. They assert a connection between creativity and sexual pleasure, art and laughter, which Rossetti buries deep in the tactical ambiguities of metaphor. In Michael Field those connections are embraced as the very public manifesto of their inspiration. The woman poet who 'dares become a lover', and does not merely hope, wait, yearn or call for one, is the poet who has freed her imagination from the 'icy nooses' of faithful expectation and repressed desire, and who can thus speak with the free-spirited, careless 'laughter of the wind'. As Adrienne Rich puts it, in relation to a much later lesbian poet, Judy Grahn: 'The word *lover*, purged of romantic-sentimental associations, becomes a name for what human beings might mean to each other in a world where each person held both power and responsibility' (1980: 251). The girl, in the nineteenth century, 'who dares become a lover' dares, paradoxically, to be also free of love, in a world where too much love and love is woman's one compensation for having no 'power and responsibility'.

This carefree passionateness runs through the Sapphic verses in *Long Ago*, 'a little collection of poems by a great genius' (1985: 95), as Robert Browning called it. When, during the early 1890s, Katherine and Edith were feeling especially aggrieved by the critical silence which met their work, and felt that their publisher was pushing younger poets ahead of them,[13] they may have been thinking in particular of Dollie Radford. John Lane's edition of her *Songs and Other Verses* was published in 1895, and it shows the extent to which minor women's poetry continued to fit the sentimentalist model. Although Radford wrote some comical feminist poems, like 'A Novice' (to her cigarette) and 'From Our Emancipated Aunt in Town', these are categorically headed 'Other Verses', while the 'Songs' themselves fall into a disappointingly familiar rote of rhymed lyricism. The frontispiece drives home the message of the whole collection: it shows the woman poet in a state of improvising abandon under her large lyre. The poems themselves then coyly insist on this epithetical imagery in mournful set-pieces:

> The little songs which come and go,
> In tender measures, to and fro,
> Whene'er the day brings you to me,
> Keep my heart full of melody.
>
> But on my lute I strive in vain
> To play the music o'er again,
> And you, dear love, will never know
> The little songs which come and go.
> (1895: 20)

By comparison with this furtive, miniaturist passion, blandly addressed to the observing reader, Michael Field's poems in *Long Ago* sound daringly assertive and specific. Their Sappho is not the old sad lutanist of death, but an urgently prosaic speaker, whose love poems to her girls, as well as to gods and men, are free of any morality of faithfulness or idealism. This Sappho is not tied to one object, but sings variously of desire, jealousy, maternal love and friendship. Even when, at the end, she leaps from her cliff (an event for which Wharton expressly finds no 'firm historical basis' (1895: 15)), she thinks as much of 'Damophyla, the lovely-haired' and of 'Eros' (*LA*: 127) her goal, as of Phaon, the betrayer. Meanwhile, the many poems addressed to girls: Anactoria, Gorgo, Atthis, Mnasidica, Gyrinna, Erinna, Dica, bring into English poetry a homosexual strain which, at least in women's poetry, is quite new.

For instance, poem XXXV in *Long Ago* is addressed by Sappho to another woman who has been distracted from real pleasure by a ring. The original fragment consists merely of the line: '*Foolish woman, pride not thyself on a ring*' (Wharton: 93). Around this tantalising hint, Michael Field develops a flirtatiously suggestive little scene:

> Come, Gorgo, put the rug in place,
>   And passionate recline;
> I love to see thee in thy grace,
>   Dark, virulent, divine.
> But wherefore thus thy proud eyes fix
>   Upon a jewelled band?
> Art thou so glad the sardonyx
>   Becomes thy shapely hand?
>
> Bethink thee! 'Tis for such as thou
>   Zeus leaves his lofty seat;
> 'Tis at thy beauty's bidding how
>   Man's mortal life shall fleet;
> Those fairest hands – dost thou forget
>   Their power to thrill and cling?
> O foolish woman, dost thou set
>   Thy pride upon a ring?
>
> (*LA*: 56)

The casual, homely voyeurism of 'Come, Gorgo, put the rug in place, / And passionate recline'[14] shows none of the self-appreciating poses of the older Sapphos. This one has indeed become a lover, able to appreciate a body which is not her own and which is not hysterically traumatised by death. The poem is not a plea for sexual attention from some disembodied male eye, whether the reader's or the imagined unfaithful lover's, but an attentive, half-playful, half-erotic verbal caress, with no ulterior motives of reciprocity, rings or religious idealism. Furthermore, Michael Field's description of love between women has none of the allure of disease and sin which made it fashionable among the decadents. By comparison with this clarity of passion and style, Swinburne's steamy sensationalism in his lesbian poems seems oddly artificial. 'Anactoria', for instance, becomes yet another unspecifically aggressive fantasy of pain:

> I would my love could kill thee; I am satiated
> With seeing thee live, and fain would have thee dead.
> I would earth had thy body as fruit to eat,
> And no mouth but some serpent's found thee sweet.
> I would find grievous ways to have thee slain,
> Intense device, and superflux of pain . . .
>
> (1904: I, 58)

This decadent's Sappho is as much a self-indulgently unnatural invention as the sentimentalist's.[15] In fact, the one is very much the reverse side of the other. Both insist on an extremity of feeling which only betrays its own failure to feel.

By comparison, Michael Field's Sappho has an authentically light-hearted, classical intensity. Around the fragment *'To you, fair maids, my mind changes not'* (Wharton: 80), for instance, they elaborate the stanzas:

> Maids, not to you my mind doth change,
> Men I defy, allure, estrange,
> Prostrate, make bond or free:
> Soft as the stream beneath the plane
> To you I sing my love's refrain;
> Between us is no thought of pain,
>   Peril, satiety.
>
> Soon doth a lover's patience tire,
> But ye to manifold desire
> Can yield response, ye know
> When for long, museful days I pine,
> The presage at my heart divine;
> To you I never breathe a sign
> Of inward want or woe.
>
> When injuries my spirit bruise,
> Allaying virtue ye infuse
> With unobtrusive skill:
> And if care frets ye come to me
> As fresh as nymph from stream or tree,
> And with your soft vitality
>   My weary bosom fill.
>
> (*LA*: 52–3)

This Sappho is no masochistic martyr to love. The verbs are active, 'I

229

defy, allure, estrange', 'I sing', and the gender difference between men and maids knowledgeably sexual. 'Soft as the stream beneath the plane' is a description of an unhampered woman-to-woman's language as suggestively labial as any Irigarayan writing of the body ('When our lips speak together', *Signs*, 6(1980), 69–79). By contrast to the changeable power games of her love for men, this Sappho acknowledges the other 'refrain' of her tender and consoling love for women, with its gratifications of much more 'manifold desire'. The sheer colloquial lucidity of these verses, with their forthright invitations and their plurality of love objects, is in striking contrast to the possessive, fixated idealism of both the courtly and the decadent modes. The register shifts easily from the lustful to the protective, the sexual to the maternal, thus projecting an innocence of purpose which half disguises the subject matter. Unlike Swinburne's swampy declarations of sadistic passion, the naturalness of Michael Field disarms censorship from the start. Their verse shows up the extent to which decadence relies on an endemic and even loudly advertised sense of sin. Without that sin, it loses much of its effect. By contrast, their poetry is genuinely 'Indifferent to heaven and hell'; its Pateresque paganism never a bogey for frightening the philistines. Furthermore, by being simply not interested in sin, they seem to have escaped the scandalised disapproval Swinburne is eager to court.

Evidently, then, so long as Browning's ' "two dear Greek women" ' did not seem to combat ' "social conventions" ' (*WD*: 8) in any obvious way, they caused no offence. His admiration for the poems in *Long Ago* suggests that such conventions are rigidly defined ideas, which cannot be recognised unless they appear, precisely, in conventional forms. The Victorian imagination was, perhaps, singularly free *not* to imagine, at least until Freud named them or the law incriminated them, areas of experience not 'conventionally' immoralised. Although terms like 'Sapphism' and 'lesbian' were current in France at least since the 1840s, they only started to appear in English in specialised medical dictionaries at the beginning of the 1890s (Hallett, 1979: 451). The theory of lesbianism found its permitted expression, in France, in the language of decadent aesthetics, but in England, in the much more regulatory language of psychology. When, in 1883, J. A. Symonds published his essay, *A Problem in Greek Ethics*, ten years after it was written, he dared print only ten private copies. Even in 1908 the work, which contains a most tactful account of Greek sexual mores, was only published privately. Symonds glances passingly at 'feminine homosexual passions', and then only to affirm their social invisibility: they 'were never worked into the social system' (1908: 70), he explains. The difference between Michael Field's uninhibited life and writings and Charlotte Mew's anxious reticence may have had as much to do with the two ages' different conventions of naming and not naming, ignoring and illegalising, as with the poets' own different temperaments.

In general, then, this is a love poetry which focuses on physical desire as an enlightened, innocent end in itself. Such desire has no metaphysical or moral goals. It is not a metaphor for some other drama of salvation or inspiration, neither is it an exquisitely managed hedonism which, like the far-fetched pleasures of the decadents, substitutes sexual artifice for art, pain for passion, sin for love. When Katherine and Edith agreed with Wilde that 'the whole problem of life turns on pleasure' (*WD*: 136), they were speaking as eager novices rather than as weary *cognoscenti*. For them, the idea of pleasure involves an exhilarating recall of woman's subjectivity from the moribund misery of the old Sapphos, as well as a new and explicit demand for real sexual experience in a girl's life.

The poem, 'A Girl' (1893), which was almost certainly written by Katherine for Edith, is, like 'Prologue', a personal testament to their union. In some ways, it recalls one of the two complete poems by Sappho to survive the ravages of time and the deliberate book burnings of the Middle Ages (see Foster, 1958: 21): 'To a Girl' or 'To Brochea'. Its description of female passion as a physical response of blushing, sweating and being tongue-tied was much translated and imitated, notably by Tennyson, though, of course, he radically alters the meaning of the original by writing as the observing male, not as the female lover herself. Although Michael Field's verse does not reproduce Sappho's description of physical passion, its subject draws on this literary tradition of love-addresses to girls, while subtly reintroducing the original homosexual context which had been lost:

> A girl,
>   Her soul a deep-wave pearl
> Dim, lucent of all lovely mysteries;
>   A face flowered for heart's ease,
>   A brow's grace soft as seas
>   Seen through faint forest-trees:
>   A mouth, the lips apart,
> Like aspen-leaflets trembling in the breeze
>   From her tempestuous heart.
>   Such: and our souls so knit,
>   I leave a page half-writ –
>   The work begun
>   Will be to heaven's conception done,
>   If she come to it.
>   (*UB*: 68–9)

The wave effect of the metre here subtly reproduces the very tentative outline of the girl herself, who is seen, as if underwater, like a creature still finding shape. Each specific feature, her face, brow, mouth and lips, is described in such a way that it blurs into distantly imagined prospects of the landscape. 'A face flowered for heart's ease' hovers between its two meanings, of easing the heart and of being, itself, like a pansy, 'heart's ease'. The idea of her brow then opens into another hazy vista, of distant seas shadowed by trees. Far from being a list of the coy mistress's attributes or even a list of the dying woman's wasted attractions, these details capture the sense of unknown potential in the girl, of far possibilities not yet clearly envisaged, of an identity still fluid and shifting. Like some Venus emerging from 'the deep-wave pearl' of seas, she takes shape in a language still, as it were, rippling with the uncertainty of her reality in the speaker's life. Half a love poem and half a poem almost, it feels, of verbally giving birth – ' "I speak as a mother; mothers of some sort we must all become" ', Katherine once stated – it catches the fathomless and free quality of the girl's very nature in the wavering rhythms of its lines. This poem of coming to birth and to consciousness keeps the tone of ambiguous desire and motherliness of Sappho's poems. Michael Field's pagan imagination is not at odds with anything, any system of man or God, but inhabits another land, 'in the open air of nature'. At the end, the invitation to the girl to 'come to it' remains like a delicate, open-ended *double entendre* of love and poetry together.

Such a love poem, like many others by Michael Field, simply avoids the literary figures which, since the Middle Ages, had dictated the terms of love. While Barrett Browning re-appropriates that courtly imagery, though making it as foreign a language to the woman's heart as any 'Portuguese', and while Rossetti re-animates it, in her own quizzical way, by being always, at the last minute, dead, Michael Field has no truck with any of its suing and pleading, buying and denying. All the courtly clutter of desire: gloves, curls, rings, flowers, lutes and letters, has gone, and instead the intonations of real speech come cleared of the dust of literary self-reference:

> I love you with my life – 'tis so I love you;
>   I give you as a ring
> The cycle of my days till death:
>   I worship with the breath
> That keeps me in the world with you and spring:
> And God may dwell behind, but not above you.
>
> Mine, in the dark, before the world's beginning:
>   The claim of every sense,
>   Secret and source of every need;
>   The goal to which I speed,

232

And at my heart a vigour more immense
Than will itself to urge me to its winning.
                    (*WH*: 71)

Instead of that bookish and rather dusty exchange of goods, which the courtly model substitutes for desire, the natural imagery of Michael Field's love poetry insists on an alternative perspective. The motivation for love is a force which pushes darkly from 'before the world's beginning'. The superstructures of desire are thus reduced to a basic life force, which has no ulterior 'goal' beyond the 'claim of every sense'. Vigorous rather than hurt, 'winning' rather than to be won, the 'heart', here, is not a trembling instrument of sensibility, waiting to be struck, but part of an anonymous compulsion of lusts and needs. There is no wrangle for this 'ring' of love because it has no marketable, social value; it is simply the 'cycle of my days till death'. On the one hand, this natural imagery seems unengaged with the complex myths and ideologies of the real world; but on the other hand, its very remoteness is a challenge to those myths. Where Rossetti goblinised them from within and Barrett Browning and Webster boldly mocked them from without, Michael Field has moved out of their range altogether. By taking human love out of the context of courtship and marriage, as they naturally do, and putting it in the context of life's ancient, evolutionary forces, they strip it of all but its own inner rationale of 'sense' and 'need'. In some ways, this is not an escape from the contemporary world, but another kind of engagement with it. In the place of sentimentalism, Michael Field offers a kind of literal, elemental Darwinism of the heart.

The language of this unsocialised love draws especially on the active 'drive' of verbs:

> The love that breeds
>   In my heart for thee!
> As the iris is full, brimful of seeds,
> And all that it flowered for among the reeds
> Is packed in a thousand vermilion-beads
> That push, and riot, and squeeze, and clip,
> Till they burst the sides of the silver scrip,
> And at last we see
> What the bloom, with its tremulous, bowery fold
> Of zephyr-petal at heart did hold . . .
>   (*UB*: 77–8)

Such reproductive imagery packs the poem with a Keatsian sense of elemental reality. 'That push, and riot, and squeeze, and clip' turns the heart, not into a vessel of outpouring tears, but into a crammed and seedy flower head, bursting with new life. Elsewhere, the verbs seem even more sexually assertive:

> I love her with the seasons, with the winds,
> As the stars worship, as anemones
> Shudder in secret for the sun, as bees
> Buzz round an open flower: in all kinds
> My love is perfect, and in each she finds
> Herself the goal . . .
>
> (WH: 173)

Once again, love is an activity not an abstraction, a deed not a religion, a matter of lovers rather than of loving to death.

Other love poems, however, show a streak of fantastical wit. The quirky sonnet, 'The Mummy Invokes his Soul' (1908), for instance, which obviously derives from an idea in the Egyptian *Book of the Dead*, is addressed by the trapped, mummified body to its own free soul. But the direction in the poem, unlike its original, is far from spiritual and transcendent:

> Down to me quickly, down! I am such dust,
> Baked, pressed together; let my flesh be fanned
> With thy fresh breath; come from thy reedy land
> Voiceful with birds; divert me, for I lust
> To break, to crumble – prick with pores this crust! –
> And fall apart, delicious, loosening sand.
> Oh, joy, I feel thy breath, I feel thy hand
> That searches for my heart, and trembles just
> Where once it beat. How light thy touch, thy frame!
> Surely thou perchest on the summer trees . . .
> And the garden that we loved? Soul, take thine ease,
> I am content, so thou enjoy the same
> Sweet terraces and founts, content, for thee,
> To burn in this immense torpidity.
>
> (WH: 88)

The poem evidently has its roots deep in Katherine's past when, at the age of 21, she worried over the theological doctrine of soul sleep, and wrote in her diary: 'it seems to me a strange almost ghastly notion, – that of our Lord having dominion over thousands of torpid souls – Of the buried centuries, that he could quicken with a breath'.[16] Unlike the early 'Trompetenruf', however, 'The Mummy Invokes his Soul' has shed all its Christian anxieties about salvation, and turns the idea of interminable death into a conceit for heightened sexual desire. The positioning of phrases like 'I lust', 'I feel thy hand', 'and trembles just', lets the meaning hang, suggestively, in undecided expectation of the pleasure to come. In spite of the incongruity of the mouldering mummy quickening with new desires, the poem enacts, in its language, the barely disguised climax of physical pleasure. The 'come to me' motif carries no theological promise; only the sheer delight of a touch which rifles the mummy's hard-baked dust for the 'heart' which is touched as literally as by a 'hand': 'Oh, joy, I feel thy breath, I feel thy hand / That searches for my heart . . .' Such rummaging for the heart, in this reductively literal-minded context of a dead body, seems grotesque, a grim mockery of all the emblematically bared hearts of other, more soulful lovers. Yet, the rising excitement of the phrases also metonymises the heart into a more practically responsive organ of desire. The anatomical specificity of 'flesh', 'breath', 'hand' and 'heart' allow the airy soul and the dusty mummy to consummate, at least in the mummy's imagination, the pleasures of their long-dead senses.

The poem is a nonsense, but it is also a prolonged joke against the metaphysical or merely macabre connotations of the title. For all the Neoplatonic imagery of the soul as a bird in the 'trees', this is a love poem of the body, which invokes its soul, not as a principle of spiritual freedom or new life, but as the lost pleasure principle of its own material reality. Bound in mummy cloth, this absurdly passionate, dry-as-dust lover never seeks anything else than the hand to move its heart. In the end, however, with generous forbearance, it grants the soul 'ease' and enjoyment in the pleasure gardens of the afterlife, while it continues to burn in the 'immense torpidity' of lustful sleep and heat which are its eternal lot. No trumpet of the resurrection or bird of artistic immortality ever diverts the poem from its eccentrically insistent physical invitation. Out of the unresurrected tomb comes a posthumous consciousness still obsessed with its physical, fleshly life.

Another burial poem, 'Embalmment', similarly explodes the traditional motifs which it seems to invoke:

> Let not a star suspect the mystery!
> A cave that haunts thee in the dreams of night
> Keep me as treasure hidden from thy sight,
> And only thine while thou dost covet me!
> As the Asmonaean queen perpetually
> Embalmed in honey, cold to thy delight,
> Cold to thy touch, a sleeping eremite,
> Beside thee never sleeping I would be.
>
> Or thou might'st lay me in a sepulchre,
> And every line of life will keep its bloom,
> Long as thou seal'st me from the common air.
> Speak not, reveal not . . . There will be

In the unchallenged dark a mystery,
And golden hair sprung rapid in a tomb.
(*WH*: 26)

This queer conceit of being embalmed beside her lover, cold and chaste and perpetually awake, is imagined by the speaker as a figure, not of repression and self-denial, as in much women's poetry, but as a figure for being perpetually desired. The origin of the conceit comes from the story of Mariamne, the 'Asmonaean queen', who was Herod's first wife and whom, suspecting her of adultery, he had executed and embalmed in honey. However, nothing of the (heterosexual) horror of that story remains in Michael Field's poem. Instead, the embalmment (perhaps by way of the notion that mummia was an aphrodisiac, as in a nearly contemporary poem by Rupert Brooke[17]) serves as a figure for an entirely responsive and accessible sexual desire. The speaker asks to be buried where she will remain invisible except when actively coveted. Death is invoked, not as a state of cold-hearted abstraction from the world or of punishing inaccessibility to the lover, but as a perpetual, unfailing physical attentiveness: 'Beside thee never sleeping'.

In the second part, this metaphysical conceit is extended even more elaborately and absurdly. If sealed 'in a sepulchre' the lover will not fade or pale, but remain, in that air-tight atmosphere, as if freshly loved and cherished. Furthermore, in such a sealed place she will even thrive, like any 'mystery' that is 'unchallenged' in the 'dark'. The last line then invokes an idea which runs through Victorian literature, and which, in 1869, became a real-life legend. One of the observers at Lizzie Siddal's exhumation spread the rumour, which haunted a whole generation of writers, that her hair had continued to grow after her death and had filled the coffin with its gold. Dante Gabriel Rossetti refers to the event in the last lines of his sonnet 'Life-in-Love': ' 'Mid change the changeless night environeth, / Lies all that golden hair undimmed in death' (1913: 115). In 'Embalmment', all the controlled, delayed expectancy of the speaker's wish to be preserved in her lover's dreams suddenly climaxes in that disconcertingly lively image of 'golden hair sprung rapid in a tomb'. It is as if Michael Field has taken a figure for woman's repressed sexuality – a sexuality which flowers only in the grave – and turned it into a figure of comically prompt, live and 'rapid' responsiveness.

The Rossettian myth of burial is thus turned into a fantastical, mock-heroic simile of which the tone of secret mystery-mongering: 'Let not a star suspect the mystery!' 'Speak not, reveal not', is only part of a long-drawn-out strategy of seduction, audibly culminating in that flowering hair. Such an image is no more than a far-fetched, shared joke, and a 'mystery' only if it remains in 'the unchallenged dark' of innumerable airless Gothic vaults of desire. Ultimately, 'Embalmment' mocks its own macabre conceit of love, and challenges the very unenlightened morbidity of the Pre-Raphaelite myth which it has enjoyed. With a certain tasteless but witty exuberance, the poem takes the figure of the dead woman, embalmed and mummified, and brings her energetically back to life as a figure of speech for the unwilled, uncontrolled pleasure of sexual love.

The fascination with mummies in *fin-de-siècle* literature was partly encouraged by accounts of real archaeological excavations at the time. During the 1890s, the *Athenaeum* carried regular features on the discoveries of new tombs and cemeteries in Egypt, not so much for their own interest, but because they were rich sources of classical writings. The papyri which were used as mummy wrappings were frequently covered in classical texts, many of them new. One of the most important finds was at Oxyrhynchus where, among other things, new fragments of Sappho's poems were brought to light, and these explicitly proved the female sex of many of her lovers (Foster, 1958: 19–20). In 1894, Pierre Louÿs published his *Chansons de Bilitis*, a set of mildly pornographic verses, allegedly written by one of Sappho's girl lovers, which he claimed to have discovered in Bilitis' real tomb in Egypt (1949: 21). The connection, which Louÿs exploited, between mummies and Sapphic love poetry may lie bedded deep in the 'cryptic' (Stimpson, in Abel, 1982: 21) imagery of Michael Field's own sonnet. Out of the crypt of women's repression and morbidity they bring, not a dead Lizzie with such hair, but a real, live lover who has only been waiting her time: at some level, another Sappho, 'sprung rapid' from the mummy cloths of sealed tombs.

Such, then, is Michael Field's strange, sometimes excessive and baroque, but also witty and sceptical contribution to the tradition of Victorian women's love poetry. In mockery of all the metaphorical vaults of death and repression as well as of all the spiritual goals of heaven and salvation which haunt their predecessors, they assert their alternative creed of self-justifying physical pleasure. To celebrate such pleasure as a female right – the right of 'a girl' not only to love but to 'become a lover' – is to break one of the most deep-seated silences in nineteenth-century women's poetry. Sappho has finally been recuperated for women as a model of poetry and of love together, with no social or metaphysical (death) penalties to be paid for either.

THE ANCIENT LAW OF PLEASURE

Apart from these love poems to or for women, Michael Field also wrote a number of poems about the law of desire in nature. These bleaker, impersonal verses portray a universe cleared of religious or human purpose, and driven only by the anonymous, evolutionary forces of life itself. It is in these that Michael Field's earlier pagan creed is most movingly and sometimes quite awesomely expressed. Such a creed accepts the harsh realities of the natural world without judgment or sentimentality, and reproduces them in a sparing, depersonalised style which is quite unlike any other contemporary verse. Meredith's Darwinian perspectives, in 'The Woods of Westermain' for instance, are much more long-windedly deliberate and spooky, while Mathilde Blind's, in 'The Ascent of Man', are more philosophical and abstract. Michael Field's sense of nature, by comparison, is largely free of imported human significance. Neither socially combative nor metaphysically comforting, their best nature poems continue their own creed of looking 'deep into birth and death – unflinchingly' (WD: 111), and accepting those elemental realities without protest or distortion. Being 'out in the open air of nature' (6) also means, for them, being outside the drawing-room conventions of Victorian women's lives. Their imaginative scepticism is rooted in that ideologically outdoor place.

The sonnet 'Eros' (1908), for instance, searches both the harshness and the scope of this natural law of life:

> O Eros of the mountains, of the earth,
> One thing I know of thee that thou art old,
> Far, sovereign, lonesome tyrant of the dearth
> Of chaos, ruler of the primal cold!
> None gave thee nurture: chaos' icy rings
> Pressed on thy plenitude. O fostering power,
> Thine the first voice, first warmth, first golden wings,
> First blowing zephyr, earliest opened flower,
> Thine the first smile of Time: thou hast no mate,
> Thou art alone forever, giving all:
> After thine image, Love, thou did'st create
> Man to be poor, man to be prodigal;
> And thus, O awful god, he is endued
> With the raw hungers of thy solitude.
>
> (WH: 142)

No baby philanderer with bow and arrow, 'Eros', here, is the older, Homeric god of love, associated with the germinating force of life itself. Such love is no more than a tyrannical and lonely 'drive', a lust to live, as ancient as the universe itself. Such a pleasure principle is not benign, discriminating or moral. Neither is it decadent, extravagant and immoral. Man, who is explicitly made in the 'image' of Eros rather than in the image of God, is a creature of both unfulfillable and wasteful desires, of need which is both starved and squandered, both 'poor' and 'prodigal'. In the end, the characteristic of Eros is not a warm ripeness of the senses, but rather 'raw hungers' – a phrase which sharply summarises lust's crude, impersonal, plural appetites. This is the bleak side of Michael Field's creed of pleasure. It is not, like Huysmans', an exquisite, indoor sampling of multiple sensations, but an ancient, universal, almost deterministic law, in which love remains immemorially tied to some essential, ancient hunger of the planet.

Far from being a source of regret, as it is for Tennyson, this vast, pre-historic backdrop to human life is welcomed and celebrated. 'Nests in Elms', for instance, proposes that the very indifference of nature is comforting:

> The rooks are cawing up and down the trees!
> Among their nests they caw. O sound I treasure,
> Ripe as old music is, the summer's measure,
> Sleep at her gossip, sylvan mysteries,
> With prate and clamour to give zest of these
> In rune I trace the ancient law of pleasure,
> Of love, of all the busy-ness of leisure,
> With dream on dream of never-thwarted ease.
> O homely birds, who know not anything
> Of sea-birds' loneliness, of Procne's strife,
> Rock round me when I die! So sweet it were
> To die by open doors, with you on wing
> Humming the deep security of life.
>
> (*WH*: 62)

The sound of the rooks is a language of the past: 'old music', sleepy 'gossip', 'prate and clamour', strange 'rune' or final 'Humming'; it is a natural ur-language which expresses nothing human, but also, for that very reason, 'nothing sad'. The 'ancient law of pleasure' which is also, inseparably, the law of 'love', is an idea which runs through much of Michael Field's work, and gives to its human purpose the harsh association of nature's post-Darwinian insouciance and age. The paradoxes at the end typically offer no consolations beyond the material facts themselves: the homeliness of the rooks is found through 'open doors'; death is a return to 'the deep security of life'. This nature is no nurse or guardian of human desires, but simply a free, open-doored reality, which continues irrespective of all the living and dying around it. The keening cry of 'sea-birds', with its Anglo-Saxon melancholy, is thus rejected for this cheerfully common 'cawing', which, in its crowded and unliterary homeliness, offers a rough, oblivious sort of home to the imagination. After all, whoever dies under these trees, there will always be more 'Nests in Elms'.

Michael Field's is thus essentially an outdoor aestheticism, sharpened by a Darwinian perspective of life's impersonality. Their best poems have an emotionless detachment and a verbal casualness which is in strong contrast to the sensational, wordy artifices of their contemporary decadents. Something of this almost devastating impersonality of nature is caught in one of the rare poems Michael Field wrote about a contemporary event. 'After Soufrière' (1908) is about the destruction of a town in Guadeloupe by a volcanic eruption. Its tone is in marked contrast to Alice Meynell's poem, published five years later, about the earthquake which destroyed Messina. 'Messina, 1908', in attempting to explain the event as an act of God, sounds both reductive and sickly cruel: 'Lord, Thou hast crushed Thy tender ones, o'erthrown / Thy strong, Thy fair' (*Poems*: 111). By contrast, 'After Soufrière' describes the eruption as an act of nature, involving no crime, no retribution and no moral meaning of any kind. The language itself perfectly conveys the catastrophic simplicity of the event:

> It is not grief or pain;
> But like the even dropping of the rain,
> That thou art gone.
> It is not like a grave
> To weep upon;
> But like the rise and falling of a wave
> When the vessel's gone.
>
> It is like the sudden void
> When the city is destroyed,
> Where the sun shone:
> There is neither grief nor pain,
> But the wide waste come again.
>
> (*SP*: 31)

The idiomatic simplicity of this is much more expressive of the reality than Meynell's frantically moralising gestures. The human reactions of 'grief or pain' or of weeping on 'a grave' are made irrelevant by this cataclysm of nature which happens as 'naturally' and as meaninglessly as 'the even dropping of the rain' or the 'rise and falling of a wave'. The sheer inhumanity of the event is caught in the emotionless, forgetful quiet of the verse. Nature is heartless and indifferent, its eruptions as ordinary as 'rain' or 'sun', and its destruction of a city simply a return of things to the old order of what was there before: 'the wide waste come again.' The metrical irregularity of the poem, its unexpected rhymes and understating brevity and ease, movingly convey the awesome surprise and effortlessness of nature's own movements.

It is this register of utter clarity which the baroque ingenuity of the later poems, especially the religious poems, misses. Such simplicity seems essentially connected to a world-view which Katherine and Edith held before their conversion: that of a bleak yet bracing paganism, 'Indifferent to heaven and hell', but, in itself, exhilaratingly sensual and pleasure-loving. Furthermore, they can express such a world-view, not regretfully, protestingly or on behalf of some new-age morality of brave atheism, but with an almost shrugging naturalness:

> Death, men say, is like a sea
> That engulfs mortality,
> Treacherous, dreadful, blindingly
> Full of storm and terror.
>
> . . .
>
> Death's a couch of golden ground,
> Warm, soft, permeable mound,
> Where from even memory's sound
> We shall have remission.
>
> (*UB*: 8–9)

During her last illness, Edith was visited by the Indian poet, Rabindranath Tagore. Her rejection of his, as she sees it, sentimental pantheism is interesting for the light it throws on the two poets' own development. 'Pantheism ignores sin, evil, suffering, or vaguely trusts in nature – in sunrises, sunsets, rushing seas, air full of birds and suchlike pleasurable things', she complains. But she does not dismiss pantheism out of hand, even in 1911, four years after her conversion. Instead, she only rejects Tagore's optimistic pantheism, which, as she explains, 'demands passion for nonenity [*sic*] – for, to the heart, to ask it to love a vague all – a Pan, who has never had his Syrinx – is to ask it to love non-entity' (*WD*: 318). The comment recalls Michael Field's many poems about Pan, particularly the strange, heavy-aired 'Penetration',[18] which suggestively reworks Barrett Browning's 'A Musical Instrument' by reversing the roles and having Syrinx seduce and penetrate her clumsy, animalesque lover with sweet music:

> I love thee; never dream that I am dumb:
> By day, by night, my tongue besiegeth thee,
> As a bat's voice, set in too fine a key,
> Too tender in its circumstance to come
> To ears beset by havoc and harsh hum
> Of the arraigning world; yet secretly
> I may attain . . .
>
> (*WH*: 13)

In the journal, then, Edith is not repudiating, but reasserting the basic aesthetic of their own verse: Pan must have his Syrinx, or rather, Syrinx her Pan. Sexual desire is the main, motivating impulse of the imagination as it is the impulse of life itself. The law of life, like the 'law of pleasure', is not separate from hunger, destruction and suffering, and, indeed, in the best of Michael Field, the pantheism is neither rosy-coloured nor God-scaped. Instead, it is harsh and exact. Even if such poetry does not always speak overtly for the cause of woman, it always speaks, 'secretly', in a woman's voice which, like Syrinx's, penetrates by its different 'key'. As the poets once protested in their journal:

> And here is the *Athenaeum* saying that women only have sentimental experiences – & that they cannot approach the fires of Eros, they who are his priestesses by fate & experience, if only rarely in song . . . but [they conclude triumphantly] Sappho has sung her sensations, and Christina Rossetti her suffering.[19]

★   ★   ★

In one short poem, placed towards the end of the *Wild Honey* volume, Michael Field seems finally to acknowledge the strength of their 'old accents' of pagan freedom, and the comparative weakness of their 'new right way of singing'. 'A Palimpsest' describes two writings, old and new. In their journal, Edith had described their conversion to Catholicism as a dethroning of the old gods: 'Demeter and Dionysus (our lord Bacchus) yield themselves up as victims to the great Host' (*WD*: 273). However, the poem tells a different story:

> . . . The rest
> Of our life must be a palimpsest –
> The old writing written there the best.
>
> In the parchment hoary
> Lies a golden story,
> As 'mid secret feather of a dove,
> As 'mid moonbeams shifted through a cloud:
>
> Let us write it over,
> O my lover,
> For the far Time to discover,
> As 'mid secret feathers of a dove,
> As 'mid moonbeams shifted through a cloud!
> (*WH*: 180)

The act of writing 'it over' is, paradoxically, also a way of preserving the 'golden story' of the past. The overlay of truth keeps the fiction 'secret', a thing obscured, like clouded moonlight. But the relation between the two is not, as the journal version suggests, one of simple supersession, but of palimpsestic doubleness. The new writing may be more true, but

242

the 'old writing' was certainly 'the best'. The new gods may sigh for the cost and pain of salvation, but the old gods had the advantage in always being able to 'laugh and dream'.

It is that laughter – the imagination's daring and free recognition of woman's sexual pleasure, accepted as an ancient, impersonal law of nature – which inspires the best of Michael Field's poetry. They were right in surmising, sadly but also surely, that it would take 'the far Time' a long time to 'discover' it.

—7—

Alice Meynell (1847–1922)

'If these nerves are tolerably in tune with one another [a girl]
becomes a great woman – a writer, say, famous for laying bare
the melancholy secrets of the female heart to the curious gaze
of material-minded man; if the chords jar, she dwindles into a
miserably self-conscious melancholy which feeds upon itself,
or the struggle is sharper, the pain shorter, and she dies.' (in
Badeni, 1981: 28)

Thus wrote the 18-year-old Alice Meynell, as she surveyed the prospect
of her future life and summed up the choices open to a girl. The old
poetic cliché of woman's open-hearted sensibility is ironically revived and
confronted. A woman's lot, whether in art or in life, is a '"melancholy"'
one. Her '"nerves"' may be tuned for art or jar in self-conscious
introspection, but in either case woman's heart is a too highly strung
instrument which, sooner or later, breaks down. Unlike Rossetti,
however, who at about the same age made her symbolic choice of death,
and enacted her own imaginary burial in *Maude*, Meynell finds in the
melancholy options of womanhood a cause for anger and protest. Instead
of accepting the condition of her sex, she is quick to name the culprits
who enforce it: '"Of all the crying evils in this depraved earth . . . the
greatest, judged by all the laws of God and of Humanity is the miserable
selfishness of men that keeps women from work"' (28).

   This defiant accusation points to some of the choices Alice will make
in her own life. Rejecting '"melancholy"' altogether as a conventional
badge of femininity and poeticalness, she opts, in life, for constant hard
work in the world of men and, in her art, for an impersonal, intellectual
register which avoids, almost too studiedly at times, the secrets of the

heart. But at 18, the conventions of womanhood weigh heavily on her: ' "But whatever I write will be melancholy and self-conscious as are all women's poems" ' (29), she complains. It was not only an over-prized tradition of self-conscious sadness which these women poets, in their different ways, struggled to overcome, but also, and even more inhibiting to their art, the melancholy realities of their very lives.

*　　*　　*

Alice Meynell was born in 1847, the second daughter of Thomas and Christiana Thompson. Her father, according to the wishes of his grandfather, followed no profession, but lived on an inheritance bequeathed him from the family estates in Jamaica – an inheritance which in fact connected the Meynells with the Barrett Browning family. Her mother was a concert pianist, whose career was cut short by marriage. Alice and her older sister Elizabeth were largely brought up in Italy, where the family rented a number of houses in the district of Genoa. This other country of childhood, with its different tongue (the children spoke Genoese dialect) provided Alice throughout her life with an alternative perspective on the attitudes of Victorian England, as well as, perhaps, a restlessness of spirit which for much of her life had to be curbed. She herself returned to Italy with the passion of a pilgrim many times during her later years. ' "Nothing but Italy could have drawn me away from all I love" ' (in V. Meynell, 1929: 280), she wrote to her family on her last visit there in 1913.

The two girls were educated by their father who was, by all accounts, an enlightened, liberal, but reticent man, and the object, to Alice, of a deep and troubled love. The correspondence between them has not survived, but the evidence of her poems and prose points to one of those imaginatively charged relationships which often developed between Victorian parents and the daughters whom they educated. In her biography of her mother, Viola Meynell recalls only one occasion when Alice's 'habitual reserve' about her father was broken: 'she was found by one of her children weeping in contrition for what? – a day long ago when her father had wanted her company for a walk and she had refused him' (1929: 33). Years later, Virginia Woolf recollected a similar occasion for guilt when, after her mother's death, she hid in the garden to avoid keeping her father company, only to find that the freedom thus won from daughterly duty was 'without delight' (1976: 31).

In one of her essays, 'A Remembrance' (1893), Meynell gives a portrait of her father which tells more about his influence on her own imagination than about his actual character. 'The delicate, the abstinent, the reticent graces were his in the heroic degree', she wrote, adding: 'Where shall I find a pen fastidious enough to define and limit and enforce so many significant negatives?' (*PP*: 226). If one of the faults of Meynell's poetry is precisely its fastidiousness, certainly one of its strengths is its resonant resource of silence.[1] The reserve of character which she shared with her father is turned, in the poems, into a language loaded with the 'significant negatives' of the unsaid. As she summarises in her essay: 'his personality made laws for me' (227). Those laws, of metricality, impersonality, exactness, but also of a certain meagre and precious dispassionateness, became a lifelong poetic creed:

> Dear laws, come to my breast!
> Take all my frame, and make your close arms meet
> Around me; and so ruled, so warmed, so pressed,
> I breathe, aware; I feel my wild heart beat.
>
> (*Poems*: 173)

The family finally settled in England, in 1864, when Alice was 18. She attended some balls and had a few brief affairs of the heart, disconcerting one young man who was sweet-talking in her ear by preaching '"women's rights energetically"' (in Badeni, 1981: 24) to him. But evidently, as the diary tells, she was listless and unhappy, and suffered from various debilitating illnesses. The poems she wrote at this time sound melancholy with a conventional, though no doubt heartfelt conviction. 'In Autumn', for instance, turns on a quite Hemansesque burden of womanly tearfulness:

> The low winds moan for dead sweet years;
> The birds sing all for pain,
> Of a common thing, to weary ears, –
> Only a summer's fate of rain,
> And a woman's fate of tears.
>
> (*Poems*: 15)

Then, in 1868, Alice went with her mother to Malvern for a rest cure, where she took the step which her mother had taken secretly years before: she became a Roman Catholic. 'Why is it that we see so many women carefully educated going over to the Roman Catholic Church?' Mrs Jameson had asked (1855: 94), some ten years earlier. In Alice's case, Catholicism seems to have given her a pattern of discipline and control otherwise lacking in her life. In one account of her conversion, she describes it as the logical end of a distinctly poetic road:

'In quite early childhood I lived upon Wordsworth. . . . When I was about twelve I fell in love with Tennyson, and cared for nothing else until, at fifteen, I discovered first Keats and then Shelley . . . It was by no sudden counter-revolution, but slowly and gradually that I returned to the hard old common path of submission and self-discipline which soon brought me to the gates of the Catholic Church'. (in V. Meynell, 1929: 42)

As for Rossetti, faith was less a form of imaginative escape from the world than of self-imposed discipline within it. Like the 'laws' of her father, the laws of the Church emphasised constraint rather than freedom, control rather than range – virtues which, for good or for ill, Alice made peculiarly her own. It was precisely the useless freedom of a woman's life to which she had objected in her diary. The Church offered both a moral and, one suspects, artistic solution to the problem of that free-for-all of a middle-class girl's existence, fiercely decried by Augusta Webster.

In an article published in 1896, Alice reiterated this lifelong creed, and touched on its political extension: 'I do not understand why there is so much fear of outward control. Individualistic as is my Faith in regard to thought and Art, I am politically rather inclined towards Socialism than towards Individualism' (*Woman* (12 August 1896), 7–8). Like Rossetti, she yearned for 'control', both in her life and in her work, although, like Rossetti too, the requirement also suggests a mind otherwise inclined. The novelist Phyllis Bottome, who met Alice in Italy in 1913, thought she caught a glimpse of this other self:

I felt that I was watching a magnificent, wild creature – a tethered angel – suited for enormous distances and stately freedoms, closed into a narrow space behind the iron bars of a cage. The sense of this disciplined self-control was so severe, and yet so impassioned, that it hurt me. I wanted to break down the bars and I knew that I never could. I knew that Alice Meynell meant never to have the bars broken down. (1952: 364)

Those 'iron bars', whether of religious faith, of poetic form (the 'fetter' of 'metre', as she called it (*PP*: 102)) or of temperamental reticence, are the very condition of Meynell's art.

This sense of 'bars' must have been reinforced by Alice's first serious love, for the young priest Father Dignam who received her into the Church, and with whom she formed a friendship which was both durable – they continued their correspondence for many years to come – but also hopeless. Renunciation remains, in much of Meynell's poetry, like an unbreakable imaginative bar to passion. Yet, where Rossetti keeps the contradiction between bars and passion sharp and explosive, Meynell's poetry risks becoming impassioned *about* the bars. The much antho-logised sonnet 'Renouncement', for instance, which Dante Gabriel Rossetti, who knew it by heart, recommended to Hall Caine for his *Sonnets of Three Centuries* (1882), was written at about this time, and it suggests the extent to which denial shaped both her experience and her early poetic inspiration:

> I must not think of thee; and, tired yet strong,
> I shun the thought that lurks in all delight –
> The thought of thee – and in the blue Heaven's height,
> And in the sweetest passage of a song.
> O just beyond the fairest thoughts that throng
> This breast, the thought of thee waits hidden yet bright;
> But it must never, never come in sight;
> I must stop short of thee the whole day long.
> But when sleep comes to close each difficult day,
> When night gives pause to the long watch I keep,
> And all my bonds I needs must loose apart,
> Must doff my will as raiment laid away, –
> With the first dream that comes with the first sleep
> I run, I run, I am gathered to thy heart.
>
> (*Poems*: 69)

For all the praise bestowed on it, as one of the greatest sonnets written by a woman (Noyes, 1924: 6) – itself a comment on the still oppressively sentimental assumptions of the age – 'Renouncement' singularly lacks the verbal passion of Christina Rossetti's 'Echo', which it recalls. In comparison, it sounds stiff and coy. 'Must doff my will as raiment laid away', for instance, ostentatiously circumvents, in abstractions and archaisms, the underlying idea of being undressed, while the over-niceness of 'I am gathered to thy heart' sounds innocently girlish rather than, as she would have us believe, unrestrained and sexual. Alice once admitted, towards the end of her life, that her besetting sin was a '"failure of love to those that loved me"' (V. Meynell, 1929: 122), and certainly after 'Renouncement', with its rather too tasteful dream of passion, she wrote very few love poems.

Meynell's first volume, *Preludes*, was published in 1875 when she was 28. It was illustrated by her sister Elizabeth who, two years before, had gained sudden renown when her picture, *The Roll Call*, was exhibited at the Royal Academy to huge and curious crowds, and was subsequently bought by the Queen. Under her married name of Elizabeth Butler, she became famous as a painter of vigorous, panoramic battle scenes, full of the muscular flare of horses and the tragic, heroic energy of wounded men. Although somewhat academic in their realism, they are also a striking challenge to the domestic decorativeness thought appropriate to women's art. In 1876, Tennyson, who had expressed his admiration for *Preludes*, invited the two sisters to visit him. The meeting was not a success, however, as Elizabeth gleefully recorded in her diary. There were long pauses in the conversation, which she attributed to the Laureate's slow-wittedness in taking in '"the meaning of a remark"' and, when Alice asked him to read 'The Passing of Arthur', which he did in a dreary monotone, he grumbled at her choice. But in particular he seems to have taken exception to his visitors' dresses, sizing them up as they walked in the garden with a peculiarly insolent flirtatiousness. As Elizabeth put it: '"He pinned Alice against a pillar . . . to watch my back as I walked on with his son, pointing the *walking-stick* of scorn at my skirt, the trimming of which particularly roused his ire."' If Alice was overawed, Elizabeth was certainly not. '"I was much bored and longed for the hour of our departure"' (Butler, 1922: 157), she declared.

In January 1877, Alice became engaged to Wilfrid Meynell, a Catholic journalist whom she had met the previous year. Her father was opposed to the match, and there followed some months of stormy negotiation before his support was won. The couple, however, were married later that same year, and Alice thus embarked on a life of wearying, unremitting journalistic work – work she had cried out for as a girl, but which must often have exhausted her spirit. She and Wilfrid edited the Catholic periodical, *The Weekly Register*, which they wrote almost single-handed, as well as a literary magazine *Merry England* and the short-lived *The Pen*. She also contributed to innumerable other journals, including a much praised weekly column for women in the *Pall Mall Gazette* during the 1890s. In the meantime, she bore eight children, one of whom died in early infancy, and 'mothered' a number of men, including the poet Francis Thompson whom Wilfrid rescued from his life of drug addiction and destitution, and who was given free access to the house. Not surprisingly, during these difficult years Alice wrote no poems at all.

Nor was she a whole-heartedly dedicated mother. The children soon learned that the work which kept their parents occupied much of the day and night, particularly as the weekly deadline for the *Register* loomed near, was immune from domestic interruption. 'We were', Viola remembers, 'at once the most befriended of children, yet the most slighted' (V. Meynell, 1929: 89). Accustomed to being indiscriminately addressed as '"Child"' (91), when names could not be remembered, they learned to make a joke of their parents' distraction, wrote their own journalism under the table and, in an attempt to waylay a small piece of Alice's love, insisted that she should visit their rooms at night and leave a sign of her presence. One of them recalled how, once, to test their mother's powers of observation, they dressed a regular visitor to the house in some of her own clothes (not specifying which!) and sent him in to her. But she noticed nothing strange and conversed with him as usual (in Badeni, 1981: 144). Other visitors were less forgiving than the children themselves at what looked like domestic chaos. Alice's agent reported his shock when 'two of her little girls came in unaccompanied out of the pouring rain, and stood drenched to the skin'. Alice exclaimed remotely: ' "Darlings – how wet!" ' but continued her literary discussions with barely an interruption (in Bottome, 1952: 365). Nor was the house free of childhood disasters: two of the children, at different times, caught pneumonia, while Viola, the most prone to accidents, one day fell thirty feet over the hall banisters. By her own admission, Alice nursed her children badly. Yet if she was, both by temperament and by necessity, a distant mother, she was also a curiously respectful one, as Viola remembered, and when, years later, her youngest son Francis not only went to prison for conscientious objection but then also, as editor of *The Communist*, helped to smuggle diamonds to subsidise the *Daily Herald*, she never allowed her disapproval to interfere with her respect for his convictions. Meynell's poems about motherhood and parenthood are, paradoxically, some of her best, perhaps precisely because they lack the gratifications of total emotional commitment.

During these years of harrowing responsibilities, Alice was also responding to the difficult demands of three men who were all, in one way or another, in love with her. Francis Thompson, who came and went as one of the family, except on the few occasions when he relapsed into his addiction and was banned from the house, evidently idolised her. His first collection of 1893 contains a section entitled 'Love in Dian's Lap', which is addressed to Alice, and is full of that disturbingly sacralised sexuality which marks much of his work. These poems, for all their fascinated, erotic praise of her, also hint at the high emotional demands being made of one whom, as he puts it: 'The man in me calls "Love," the child calls "Mother" ' (1925: I, 101). To be a muse, lover and mother all in one must have been a trying role for a woman whose domestic and journalistic duties already took a high toll of her creative energies. Thompson's poems insist, with unswerving pertinacity, on the saving role he has allotted to her:

> Lady who hold'st on me dominion!
>   Within your spirit's arms I stay me fast
>   Against the fell
> Immitigate ravening of the gates of hell;
> And claim my right in you, most hardly won,
> Of chaste fidelity upon the chaste:
> Hold me and hold by me, lest both should fall . . .
>   (I, 82)

Like many of the men who knew Alice, he seems to have been especially attracted by the silence which had turned her into a living, rather than a working poet. She thus came to embody, in his eyes, the beauty of her own unwritten poems: 'Yea, in this silent interspace, / God sets His poems in thy face!' (80).

In 1892, Alice met Coventry Patmore, who was then 69 and married to his third wife. This friendship proved more thorny than Thompson's. Patmore evidently fell in love with her, and there are indications that, although she continued to stay with him at his home in Lymington, she had to rebuke him for some indiscretion. Nor was their literary relationship an easy one. Patmore objected strenuously to some passages in Meynell's essay, 'The Leg', which offended his sense of propriety, while she, for her part, informed him that '"some passages"' in his new collection of essays elicited '"no interior assent"' from her, adding pointedly: '"They are all about women"' (in Badeni: 95). Whether or not she assented to some of the adoring poems Patmore wrote to herself remains unknown. One of the most troubling of these is 'Alicia's Silence', in which he ominously proposes that the girl's natural development is to become the poem she once only wanted to write:

> 'A girl, you sang, to listening fame,
>   The grave that life might be,
> And ceased when you yourself became
>   The fulfilled prophecy.
> Now all your mild and silent days
>   Are each a lyric fact,
> Your pretty, kind, quick-hearted ways
>   Sweet epigrams in act.
> To me you leave the commoner tongue,
>   With pride, gaily confessed,
> Of being, henceforth, sole theme of song
>   To him who sings the best,'
>   (in V. Meynell 1929: 117)

Meanwhile, her life of harassed motherhood and incessant work, much of it financially necessary hack work, is blithely poeticised into 'mild and silent days'. The compliment of being a poem rather than of writing poems, of being 'a lyric fact' rather than a living poet, evidently derives from Patmore's own famous idealisation of woman as a luxuriously leisured 'angel of the house'. The truth, that Alice suffered from blinding migraines, slept badly, felt desperate at losing an evening's work to three men who wanted to talk and who also felt a constant underlying 'distress and agitation' (V. Meynell: 251) at being unable to write her own poetry, does not feature in these literary tributes. For both Thompson and Patmore, her poetic silence only added to her erotic potency as a muse.

Meanwhile, an intense and almost paranoid jealousy had developed between the two men. Thompson implied to Alice that her friendship with Patmore was the cause of his new lapse into addiction, while Patmore, for his part, became increasingly sulky and irrational, finding cause for jealousy in any man she happened to mention. As the situation became increasingly bitter, the ever patient and supportive Wilfrid advised his wife, for her own sake, to distance herself from Patmore, and she was no doubt relieved to do so. The ironic consequence, however, was that the two men, both feeling themselves obscurely betrayed and victimised, struck up a somewhat malicious and self-comforting friendship with each other. ' "I think she treats us both very badly!" ' Patmore wrote to Thompson, and in another letter made the interesting comment that ' "Her one abiding passion is for literary fame" ' (in Badeni: 117). The woman he had cast as the perfect muse was proving, not only fickle in her bestowal of inspiration and friendship, but also not entirely muse-like in her own desire for fame. The hidden power game of poetic idealisation becomes all too apparent in this triangle of creative interests. Alice may have been recognising precisely this when, in one of her regular columns for the *Pall Mall Gazette* at about this time, she casually comments, concerning rivalry among actors: 'the thing to pause upon is not the jealousy of women among themselves, but the curious fact of jealousy between man and woman' (*Pall Mall Gazette*, (11 August 1893), 5).

Meanwhile, the wounded feelings of both Patmore and Thompson had found a new exacerbation in Alice's friendship with another elderly man of letters, George Meredith. By the early 1890s, after a silence of more than thirteen years, she was writing poetry again, and Meredith, for all his convoluted garrulousness which so irritated Michael Field, perhaps seemed like a rock of common sense and support after the inquisitional vulnerabilities of Thompson and Patmore. Yet here too, she met with a form of praise which seems more debilitating than encouraging. Meredith, who was also in love with her, named a blue Iris after her, and sent some verses in explanation:

> For reasons known to us we give the name
> Alicia Caerulea to that flower,
> Sweet as the Sea-born borne on the sea-wave:
> That Innocent in shame where is no shame;
> That proud Reluctant; that fair slave of power,
> Who conquers most when she is most the slave.
> (1970: III, 1,237)

Even this theoretical champion of women's rights and of marital freedom (more theoretical than practical, for Meredith never forgave his first wife for taking his ideal of an open marriage literally, and left her to die in poverty with the child she bore her lover) could not resist the popular analogy, which Wollstonecraft had condemned a century before, between woman's power and the slave's. This literary complimenting, which imagines Alice innocently naked as a 'Sea-born' Venus, cannot have been entirely welcome to the woman who was prudishly modest and who, moreover, was becoming increasingly involved in the women's suffrage movement, who wrote for the suffrage papers and would be at the forefront of the large suffrage rallies in the early years of the twentieth century.

In 1897, Alice was elected President of the Society of Women Journalists, and thus became something of a figurehead for the women's rights movement in general and for the cause of women writers in particular. One suspects that she was glad to escape from the poetic sweet-talking and touchy rivalries of her three admirers. Certainly, during the 1890s, she seems to have turned more and more to friendships with women. Katharine Tynan was one of the closest of these, and it was to her that Alice wrote, in about 1914: 'nothing has ever brought pain into my feelings for you. Of no other friendship now existing can I say this'.[2] By now, Thompson, Patmore and Meredith were all dead. None the less the note of wearied disappointment and perhaps self-recrimination is clear. Alice may have felt acutely her own '"failure of love"' to others, but the love demanded of her also seems to have been exorbitant.

In 1900, after twenty-three years of unremitting shared work which always kept one or both of them at home, Alice and Wilfrid had their first holiday together, and went to Italy. In the years which followed, Alice could begin to indulge a restlessness which had always been in her nature. Her longest absence from home was a six months' trip to the United States in 1901–2. She had been invited to give a lecture tour (a sign of her well-established reputation across the Atlantic) and her friend, the American poet Agnes Tobin, offered her hospitality. At 54, Alice describes spending six hours in the saddle in the mountains of the Yosemite Valley, sitting up overnight in crowded trains, taking seven-mile walks and giving lectures across the length and breadth of the country to help the domestic budget at home. This was no frail and ethereal angel, but a woman whose adventurousness had perhaps been controlled for too long. Energetic and resilient, she saved up her experiences for future columns in the ever voracious journals.

Later, in 1905, she went with friends to Paris, Munich and thence to Italy, and in the next ten years made almost as many trips abroad, mostly to her beloved Italy – the land, as she presents it in 'The Watershed', of her own heart's lifelong double allegiance. Here, she describes travelling south as a form of inner rebellion and opposition to the prevailing currents:

I seemed to breast the streams that day;
I met, opposed, withstood
The northward rivers on their way,
My heart against the flood –
My heart that pressed to rise and reach,
And felt the love of altering speech,
Of frontiers, in its blood.
(*Poems*: 106)

As well as travel, political activity was increasingly a part of Alice's later life. She was present at many of the suffrage demonstrations, alongside Ethel Smyth, Evelyn Sharp, Cicely Hamilton and May Sinclair, for instance. In 1910, she marched as a member of the non-militant Women Writers' Suffrage League, in which, as the main suffrage paper reported: 'Each carried a goose-quill and a black-and-white banneret bearing such familiar names as George Eliot, Fanny Burney, and Elizabeth Barrett Browning' (*The Vote* (25 June 1910), 101). Since the age of 18, when she had invoked Shelley in the grand cause of redeeming ' "my trampled and polluted sex" ' (in V. Meynell: 38), she had been quick to defend women against chivalrous or derogatory comments. In 1912, a three-column letter appeared in *The Times*, written by a prominent physician, who argued the case against women doctors on the score of modesty. Meynell's answer, like many others, was quick to expose the inconsistency: ' "The different modesty assigned to the woman doctor who is to be condemned and to the nurse who is to be used, must be explained by difference of social caste" ', she declared. In answer to his other anxieties about woman's ' "physiological emergencies" ', she pointed out: ' "It is a fact of human life that 'sex' troubles man at least as much as it troubles woman, but it does not disfranchise man" ' (in V. Meynell: 266). Interestingly, in one of her columns for the *Pall Mall Gazette*, she considered the issue of a woman painter (probably her own sister Elizabeth) who, in submitting a picture to the Royal Academy, requested an extension because she was giving birth. The objection that she was thereby gaining an unfair advantage is roundly repudiated: she was only coming 'nearer to that equality of conditions which can never really be attained' (*Pall Mall Gazette* (16 June 1893), 5).

The issue of the vote seems to have roused the feelings of the whole Meynell family, Everard and Francis, much to their mother's disapproval, supporting the militant wing from which she largely held aloof. She herself expressed her feelings in a rare, political poem which is the title work of her 1917 volume: 'A Father of Women'. Published in the middle of a war which seemed, in her own words, to have 'changed the world!'[3] and at a time when she was losing all hope of votes for women,[4] it succeeds in being at once a war poem, a suffrage poem and a personal testimony to her own father. It ends, however, by calling on the generalised fathers of the land to bequeath a legacy of justice to their daughters:

> Come then,
> Fathers of women with your honour in trust,
> Approve, accept, know them daughters of men,
> Now that your sons are dust.
> *(Poems*: 148)

The harsh irony of having to wait for the 'sons' to become 'dust' was precisely, of course, the irony of historical reality. The vote was won, a year after the poem's publication, only after the daughters had earned their inheritance by working in the place of the dead sons. The final line of the poem, with its punishingly hard last word, contains the suggestion of a price cruelly commensurate with the right it buys.

By the time of her death in 1922, and in spite of her generally meagre output, Meynell was still considered one of the foremost women poets of the day, as well as a prominent and well-respected voice in the campaign for women's emancipation. Yet, in the subsequent attenuation of her reputation, she became, like many of these women poets, a figure in poetry anthologies, remembered only for one, and that probably the worst, of all her poems: 'The Shepherdess'.

In general, however, unlike Barrett Browning's or Augusta Webster's, Meynell's poetry tends to occupy a separate sphere from her political activities. No doubt she was influenced by the climate of late Victorian aestheticism and the general reaction against humanitarian seriousness in the last decades of the century. She was also, for all her feminist sympathies in real life, unduly harsh in her judgments of other women poets, and often unduly lavish in her praise of Patmore and other men. It was Alice Meynell who wrote the review in *The Pen* which Christina Rossetti read, comparing her unfavourably with her brother. The point is made again in her introduction to a collection of Christina's verse for the Red Letter Library. 'Christina Rossetti's highest honour is that she is the sister of a great and doubtless an immortal poet' (1906: 3), she asserts without qualm, though she acknowledges that 'The Convent Threshold' contains 'more passion than in any other poem written by a woman' (4). Her objection to *Goblin Market* on the score of its moral illogicality is also characteristic of a certain prissy literal-mindedness, particularly where religion was concerned. Her comments about Barrett Browning reflect both the tastes of the day and her own preference for a prettily trimmed lyricism to any epic volubility. Like most late Victorian critics she praises the *Sonnets from the Portuguese* (1903: vii) above all the rest, and predictably omits *Aurora Leigh* from her selection. Her criticism of it, interestingly, betrays political rather than poetic anxieties. 'The blank verse of "Aurora Leigh" is defiant almost throughout, and the phrase has a turn of assertion and of menace' (n.d.: ix), she writes. It is Barrett Browning's 'violence' (vii) and 'too resolute originality' (ix), as she contradictorily puts it, which spoil her poetry, as if 'violence', as in the case of the militant suffragists, were by its very nature improper and 'originality' somehow lacking in restraint.

Meynell's own sense that poetry exists in a rarer atmosphere than reality is one of her greatest shortcomings. She saves herself for some too exquisite, too perfectly formalised statement and, as a result, though her poetry always shows, as Chesterton wrote, 'the rib of a strong intellectual structure; a thing with the bones of thought in it' (*Dublin Review*, 172 (Jan.–March 1923), 1), it sometimes lacks the flesh and blood of passion. Her prose writings, for which she was even more famous in her day, as Arthur Symons grudgingly acknowledged (in Beckson, 1987: 208), now seem quaintly dated in their style, showing, as one critic put it, 'the effect of too conscious research, the triumph of a phrase too choice for its need' (Tuell, 1925: 61). This sometimes pretentious scrupulosity inevitably supplied a welcome target for the modernist reaction against the past. In a letter to Ethel Smyth in 1931, Virginia Woolf revelled with delight in her new-found freedom from the constraints of female reticence, particularly from what she calls the 'Meynell claustrophobia – no word not cut on Miltons tombstone . . . and all that hard boiled aridity' (1975–80: IV, 361). None the less, for all the meagreness of her output (there are not many more than a hundred poems altogether), and in spite of her faults of 'tombstone' preciosity and choiceness, Meynell's best work has a sparing, chiselled, intellectual lyricism which is, in its way, quietly original.

SHE WHO BEARS

One of the working women who contributed to Llewelyn Davies' collection of women's writings from the co-operative movement, *Life as We Have Known It* (1931), named as her two favourite poets Ella Wheeler Wilcox and Alice Meynell (1977: 122). Although the two poets share a simplicity of style which speaks to the common reader as well as a direct thematic appeal to women, the comparison also brings out certain differences. Wilcox's is the poetry of the 'agony aunt'; its language, like Hemans', is overloaded with moral messages offering advice and commiseration to women. Meynell's, on the other hand, is not consoling. It is particularly on the subject which generally inspired bad poems in the best nineteenth-century women poets that Meynell rises above the norm. She writes almost the first, serious, adult poems, by any poet, about biological motherhood. The experience to which she dedicated some thirteen years of her own life, but about which she felt considerable emotional ambivalence, elicits from her a number of unsentimental poems about mothers and children which are unrivalled in their unobtrusively suggestive scepticism.

Perhaps the fact that Victorian motherhood very often entailed infant mortality was part of the problem. The tragically ordinary event of losing a child seems to lie somehow outside the literary interests of the day, or rather, to belong more to children's literature than to adults'. Victorian children's books are full of dying babies. Christina Rossetti's verses for children in her collection *Sing-Song* (1872), for instance, are inclined to make death, although ubiquitous, diminutively palatable to the child reader:

> Baby lies so fast asleep
> That we cannot wake her:
> Will the Angels clad in white
> Fly from heaven to take her?
> (*CP*: II, 50, ll. 1–4)

In adult poetry the subject similarly tends to elicit a picturesque religiosity. Wilcox herself is fully in this tradition of minor consolatory verse for women:

> A baby went to heaven while it slept,
> And, waking, missed its mother's arms, and wept.
> Those angel tear-drops, falling earthward through
> God's azure skies, into the turquoise grew.
> (1909b: 91)

By contrast, Meynell's short poem 'Maternity' (1913) never eases the tragedy of a child's death into religious prettiness. Furthermore, it is unusual in turning its attention away from the child towards the suffering mother:

> One wept whose only child was dead,
> New-born, ten years ago.
> 'Weep not; he is in bliss,' they said.
> She answered, 'Even so,
>
> 'Ten years ago was born in pain
> A child, not now forlorn.
> But oh, ten years ago, in vain,
> A mother, a mother was born.'
> (*Poems*: 119)

257

Alice herself, when one of her children died in babyhood, wrote in unconsoled reproach: ' "We have something to forgive God for" ' (in Badeni: 75). The mother in 'Maternity' tacitly rejects the conventional offers of comfort in heavenly 'bliss'. It is she who, after all, remains unrewarded for her pains; more than the child's, her own birth has been 'in vain'. Even in so slight a poem, this shift of interest suggests a new seriousness, a depth of grief which resists the emotional baubles of consolation so easily won from the thought of babies in heaven. Heaven, here, has nothing to offer the empty-handed mother.

Even where the subject is not bereaved but fulfilled motherhood, the tendency to infantilise the subject is strong. Motherliness is presented as a prompt reflection of babyishness, and mother love as a reaction entirely and only comprehensible to babies. As Rossetti writes, though with her own inimical charge of emotion:

> I know a baby, such a baby, –
> Round blue eyes and cheeks of pink,
> Such an elbow furrowed with dimples,
> Such a wrist where creases sink.
>
> 'Cuddle and love me, cuddle and love me'
> Crows the mouth of coral pink:
> Oh the bald head, and oh the sweet lips,
> And oh the sleepy eyes that wink!
> (*CP*: II, 50, ll. 1–8)

The popularity of such verses, for adults as well as children, is evident throughout the century. Edith Nesbit's baby poems, for instance, were acknowledged to be 'very sweet' (in Miles, 1891–7: VII, 580), one of the best known being:

> Oh, baby, baby, baby dear,
> We lie alone together here;
> The snowy gown and cap and sheet
> With lavender are fresh and sweet;
> Through half-closed blinds the roses peer
> To see and love you, baby dear.
> (581)

Dollie Radford, similarly, writes lyrics about babies which fatally imitate the jingle of baby-speech:

> Sleep my little dearest one,
> I will guard thy sleep,
> Safely little nearest one,
> I will hold thee deep,

In the dark unfathomed sea
Where sweet dreams are made for thee.
(1895: 40)

The mannerism of pretty babbling, appropriate to a real lullaby, was unfortunately thought all too appropriate an expression of woman's own sweet and simple nature. Motherhood, in much of this verse, inspires a poetry of 'sing-song' obviousness and unqualified, unrelieved sincerity of feeling. It is as if the subject is the last to get free of that sentimentalism of the heart which weighs heavily on women's poetry as a whole. The child, in these verses, is rarely older than a baby (Augusta Webster's *Mother & Daughter* sonnets make an interesting exception) and the mother rarely expresses any feelings beyond those of absolute love or grief.

In contrast, Meynell writes with a new restraint and sceptical distance about a subject which has conventionally lain outside the sphere of serious literature. Motherhood, for her, carries a troubling knowledge of separation and difference, of love which is not necessarily satisfied and of birth which cannot be dissociated from death. She quietly turns this last Victorian certainty: that the mother's heart, if nothing else, is holy, and in her muted way suggests that the truth may be less dependable, less reassuringly transparent. 'Those who loved her were unusually powerless to interfere with her griefs, she was so private, so unapproachable, so convinced' (V. Meynell, 1929: 48), Viola wrote of her. Some of the privacy and emotional distance of Alice's own nature seems to inform her poems about a subject which too readily turns to emotional treacle in other hands.

'Cradle-Song at Twilight' (1895), for instance, would seem, by its title, to be yet another soothing, sleepy lyric. However, from the start, its unsinging rhythm and abrupt abstractions suggest something else:

The child not yet is lulled to rest.
Too young a nurse, the slender Night
So laxly holds him to her breast
That throbs with flight.

He plays with her, and will not sleep.
For other playfellows she sighs;
An unmaternal fondness keep
Her alien eyes.
(*Poems*: 86)

This odd, deceptively simple little poem does not ever clarify the problem of its multiple reference. In the first stanza, the main subject seems to be the 'child', who cannot sleep because the night is still 'Too young'. So far this falls into the expected pattern of a cradle song. But in the second stanza, the 'Night' becomes the subject of the poem, and is then progressively humanised as a literally 'Too young' nurse or mother who, far from being devoted to her child, yearns for 'other playfellows'. The register totters between the abstract and the literal, the childish and the sexual. The nurse may be a young child or a young woman, and the 'playfellows' may be real other children or longed-for other lovers. The last two lines then confirm, with the force of an imperative, this 'unmaternal fondness' with its 'alien eyes'.

The slip of reference through several registers: nurse, Night, lover, mother, makes this jolting 'Cradle-Song' oddly devious and hardly motherly. Unlike most such lullabies, the attention of the reader is not focused on the child, but goes outwards, to imagine the unknown, tempting alternatives of the 'other playfellows', for whom the nurse or night 'throbs with flight'. The child's wakefulness is thus due to the restless inattention of this 'unmaternal' minder, who is reluctantly bound to an unwanted duty, and whose 'alien' thoughts are the real, though tantalisingly unspecific, objects of the poem. Meynell's refusal to explain the identity of this child cradler leaves it open both to a socio-political interpretation: she is a too young 'single mother' with an illegitimate child, or even to a larger philosophical interpretation: she represents that other, darker side of motherhood, whose real thoughts, contrary to all the conventions, are 'unmaternal' and 'alien'.

'Separate and alien life is hers to do what she will with', Meynell wrote of 'the mother' in one of her *Pall Mall* articles which, although cloaked in discretion, is in fact about child abuse: about, as she puts it 'the offence of the mother trusted, unwitnessed, unjudged, who is unkind' (*Pall Mall Gazette* (9 June 1893), 5). Motherhood never evokes raptures of delight in her writing, but unease, distrust and, above all, detachment. The word 'alien' conveys both the unknown otherness of the child and the separate, complex desires or unkindness of the mother. In a later work, *Mary, The Mother of Jesus* (1912), Meynell offers what seems to be a celebration of motherhood in the figure of the Madonna, whose role she traces in art and Christian belief. However, many of her statements betray an edge of ambiguity. In one place, she hints that, far from being perfect, motherhood involves actual moral limitations. 'Perfect self-less love would perhaps be distributed through the multitude', she writes, 'but a mother is not perfect; nature has so much use for her – separate, family use – that she cannot let her go free from irrational, indispensable partialities and limitings, even injustices' (*PP*: 213). Here, instead of presenting motherhood as the highest womanly virtue and as a moral absolute, responsible for righting the injustices of the world, she quietly implies that it is, by necessity, an imperfect, limited, less than 'self-less' love, which (to reverse her own cautious double negatives) keeps the mother from the freedom of more rational, impartial, universal and just commitments. This is certainly less than whole-hearted devotion, and, by contrast to the usual litanies, seems to acknowledge an alternative, freer scope for women's energies in the world outside, among 'the multitude'. It was her daughter Viola who suggested that the work 'had its interlacing' (V. Meynell: 263) in her mother's mind with the cause of women's emancipation.

Thus, instead of reproducing the moral values and emotional gratifications of motherhood, Meynell's poems hint at boredom, misrecognition and unsatisfied desire. 'The Modern Mother' (1900), for instance, declares its difference from what has gone before in its very title. The poem then opens with a scene of domestic love which is, from the start, more unsettling than reassuring:

> Oh, what a kiss
> With filial passion overcharged is this!
> To this misgiving breast
> This child runs, as a child ne'er ran to rest
> Upon the light heart and the unoppressed.
>
> (*Poems*: 91)

This mother meets her child's embrace with a less than full-hearted attention. Like the nurse of 'Cradle-Song', she is distracted by other anxieties, which weigh at her oppressed and 'misgiving' heart, and make it inaccessible to the child. Such 'filial passion' is therefore all the more unexpected and complex. Between child and mother, there is a drama of separate interests and separate needs, which the kiss cannot altogether overcome. Once again, the poem itself faces outwards, away from this 'overcharged' scene of affection, to the unknown realities of the modern mother's own life. A sense of other perspectives, other pressures of the 'heart', complicate the love which should be primary and all-engrossing. This woman is, as it were, surprised into motherliness, rather than faithfully embodying it at all times.

The following two stanzas then startlingly suggest that the unease and oppression of the speaker are not even external ills, to be cured by the panacea of the child's kiss, but in fact are inextricably tied to it:

> Unhoped, unsought!
> A little tenderness, this mother thought
> The utmost of her meed.
> She looked for gratitude; content indeed
> With thus much that her nine years' love had bought.
>
> Nay, even with less.

> This mother, giver of life, death, peace, distress,
>   Desired ah! not so much
> Thanks as forgiveness; and the passing touch
> Expected, and the slight, the brief caress.

Meynell, here, expresses something about motherhood which seems entirely new: its guilt. Motherhood gives, not only life and peace and love but, logically, their opposites as well. The mother is a giver of 'distress' and 'death', and in return for those terrible gifts the best she can expect from her child is 'forgiveness'. The shock of that word after a century of uplifting mother-morality is profound. Instead of being the ultimate protector and guardian, the source and sign of virtue itself, the mother kills, and, in a reversal of values which strikes at the very sanctuary of the Victorian home, deals mortality to her own child. Mothers, in these poems, are guilty, whether of life or death, of being unmaternal, as in 'Cradle-Song', or, even more disturbingly, as here, of being maternal. The anxiety is not, ultimately, about commitment or competence, social legitimacy or illegitimacy, but about the 'act' itself. To give life is to give death, in the long term. The screen of verbal simplicity in these poems cunningly disguises notions which are far from acceptable commonplaces of women's poetry.

A strange, late poem, which was apparently not published in Alice's lifetime, seems to offer another version of 'The Modern Mother', but this time addressed specifically to a daughter. 'The Girl on the Land' appears at first sight to be one of Meynell's inconspicuously simple lyrics, confirming her belief that 'obscurity' in poetry is 'unpardonable and difficulty a great offence'.[5] However, once again, other meanings press on the poem's clean-cut outlines and characteristically abstinent emotions:

> 'When have I known a boy
> Kinder than this my daughter, or his kiss
> More filial, or the clasping of his joy
>   Closer than this?'
>
> Thus did a mother think;
> And yet her daughter had been long away,
> Estranged, on other business; but the link
>   Was fast to-day.
>
> This mother, who was she?
> I know she was the earth, she was the land.
> Her daughter, a gay girl, toiled happily,
>   Sheaves in her hand.

> (*Poems*: 194)

The intimacy of the first stanza, with its deceptively colloquial present tense and effect of physical closeness: ' "Closer than this" ', is then lost in the temporal and spatial distances of the second stanza, in which another voice displaces the mother's into the past: 'Thus did a mother think . . .' As in 'The Modern Mother', the idea of a filial ' "kiss" ' is associated, not with union but separation: 'yet her daughter had been long away, / Estranged . . .' This daughterly affection, which seems more intimate than a son's, is remembered, paradoxically, in terms of something at a distance, even at an emotional distance. 'Estranged' carries the uneasy connotations of forgetfulness and misrecognition. The sense of time's dispersals is felt through these several, layered past tenses in the poem: already, for the mother, 'her daughter had been long away', but then even the mother herself is remembered as 'away' in the past: 'Thus did a mother think'. The notion of motherhood, like all Meynell's accounts of the nature of the self, is not a goal but a process, and therefore subject to all the estranging differences of time and chance which life brings.

In the third stanza, this effect of distance is taken even further. The mother who speaks at the beginning was, apparently, not a human mother at all. 'I know she was the earth', the impersonal speaker tells. As in 'Cradle-Song', an abstract and mythical dimension diverts the human scene of love. The mother has become Mother Earth, and her daughter, a solitary reaper who is elsewhere, yet invisibly and unconsciously tied to 'the land' she reaps. Although alone, she remains in the lap of the ever-present mother. The classical figure for Mother Earth is Demeter, the goddess of the harvest, of corn and 'Sheaves', which means that her 'gay girl' is, at some level of Meynell's consciousness, Persephone – the daughter who, while she wandered happily in the fields, was kidnapped by Hades, the god of the underworld, and was taken away to be his wife. The anxiety which underlies so many of these poems thus develops into a vague, half-hidden story, of motherly fear and loss which no love can prevent. Here, too, the giver of life is the giver of difference, separation, danger. The protection this mother represents is both as wide and nourishing as the 'earth', but also, ultimately, as helpless.

It is this lurking sense of mistrust and culpability which lies behind one of Meynell's best poems, about motherhood and fatherhood together: 'Parentage'. First published in 1896, it was the one poem which Meredith did not like, in a small volume which included the simpering 'Shepherdess'. 'It is not the voice of her soul' (III, 1223), he hinted, grandiloquently, to Alice. With such advice about the nature of her 'soul', both from her trusted poetic contemporaries and from the world at large, it is perhaps surprising that Meynell wrote as many good poems as she did. Meredith evidently preferred the mincing sickliness of the poem which would be reproduced, like Hemans' 'Casabianca' and Barrett Browning's 'How do I love thee?' in innumerable school anthologies, as a usefully memorisable example of Victorian women's verse:

> She walks – the lady of my delight –
> A shepherdess of sheep.
> Her flocks are thoughts. She keeps them white;
> She guards them from the steep;
> She feeds them on the fragrant height
> And folds them in for sleep.
>
> (*Poems*: 79)

'Parentage', on the other hand, offers a distinctly unfeminine and unconventional protest at the moral assumptions behind procreation. Written to an epigraph which quotes Augustus Caesar's proclamation that '*unmarried citizens*' are '*slayers of the people*' (*Poems*: 84), the poem strenuously and succinctly asserts the opposite:

> Ah! no, not these!
> These, who were childless, are not they who gave
> So many dead unto the journeying wave,
> The helpless nurslings of the cradling seas;
> Not they who doomed by infallible decrees
> Unnumbered man to the innumerable grave.
>
> But those who slay
> Are fathers. Theirs are armies. Death is theirs –
> The death of innocences and despairs;
> The dying of the golden and the grey.
> The sentence, when these speak it, has no Nay.
> And she who slays is she who bears, who bears.

As in 'The Modern Mother', the dealers of birth are also the dealers of death. The general doom of mortality falls on the 'helpless nurslings' from the start of their 'journeying'. This picture of mass mortality is not simply universal, however. It pivots round the political connotation of 'Theirs are armies', which incriminates the fathers in a more specific scene of slaughter than that of 'the journeying wave', and then includes the mothers in responsiblity for this male 'sentence' of death. The result of this shifting from social to universal meaning is that the two are implicitly connected. The fathers' armies conduct indiscriminate massacres of 'the golden and the grey', but the mother is an even more intimate and original killer: 'And she who slays is she who bears, who bears.' The pun on bearing, to mean both birth and endurance or forbearance, keeps a political intentionalism hidden within this general scene of devastation.

Women bear 'nurslings' for the fathers' armies, and this, of course, is precisely the drift of Augustus' utilitarian edict. The mothers are thus doubly guilty, for bearing in the first place and then for tolerating, or 'bearing with', the armies which men create, causing the 'death of innocences and despairs'.

The poem's deep-rooted sense of gender institutionalises the slaughter round the two complementary roles of mothering and fathering, while also being able to offer no alternatives to the indifferent, life-squandering march of fate. Meynell's understanding of parentage cannot be extricated from political collusion, on the one hand, and universal destruction, on the other. Her sense of the ruthless connections between all three give this surprising poem an almost tragic breadth of scope.

In all these poems about motherhood, restrained and simple as they seem, Meynell issues a quiet challenge to the still-standing icon of the sublime Madonna and perfect mother of much popular women's poetry. She rejects the tricks of baby-speaking or angel-speaking which so often characterised the subject before. Her mothers are neither infantile babblers nor perfect nurturers, but anxious, distracted, bored or guilty women, whose lives are shadowed by other dimensions of desire or oppression. As a result, these are in some sense the first 'feminist' poems about motherhood. They neither belittle it into a kind of second babyhood nor idealise it into a moral virtue. Instead, mothers are seen through the 'alien eyes' of her observant, mistrustful imagination. Through it, motherhood appears no longer as a sacred and self-satisfied virtue, but as a double-edged gift, riddled with moral and emotional failure, and requiring, profoundly, not 'Thanks' but 'forgiveness'.

This is Meynell's own small version of that inward play, that self-scepticism and self-difference, which marks the best of these women poets. Even the mother's heart cannot be trusted to hold the truth, and Meynell, with apparently casual, light-handed but determined distrust, writes against it. The 'alien' perspectives of her own temperamental dispassionateness, on a subject that is too often awash with conventional passion, result in poems which, beneath the clear surface of their verbal simplicity, express a quite unique sense of the foreboding and misgiving in giving life itself.

Charlotte Mew (1869–1928)

> My heart went home. The dear place was desolate. No echo of its many voices on the threshold or stair. My footsteps made no sound as I went rapidly up to a well-known room. Here I besought the mirror for the reassurance of my own reflection. It denied me human portraiture and threw back cold glare. As I opened mechanically a treasured book, I noticed the leaves were blank, not even blurred by spot or line; and then I shivered – it was deadly cold. . . . The things by which I had touched life were nothing. Here, as I called the dearest names, their echoes came back again with the sound of an unlearned language. I did not recognize, and yet I framed them. What was had never been!
>
> My spirit summoned the being who claimed mine. He came, stretching out arms of deathless welcome. As he reached me my heart took flight. (*CPP*: 71–2)

Although she did not die until 1928, in spirit Charlotte Mew is one of the last Victorians. Untouched, in life, by the sexual and political emancipations of the twentieth century or, in her art, by the obvious thematic freedoms of modernism, she remained imaginatively tied to the symbols of a past age. This moment of visionary desolation in her short story 'Passed' (1894) hints at the ambiguous nature of that literary tie. The speaker, who has been enticed into the house of a poor girl whose sister has died, hallucinates a scene of her own posthumous return to the 'dear place' of 'home'. But in her imagination, home has lost its welcome, and she cannot find herself among its well-worn symbols of identity: her 'footsteps' are soundless, her 'mirror' empty and her 'treasured book' blank. Not only has she become an invisible ghost of the past; she is also, in a stunning double negative of herself, a ghost of what 'had never been!' The fantasy of having once been at home, loved, echoed and mirrored, is unreal, and the speaker finds only hollow frames of reference, empty signatures, an 'unlearned language' which should have been full of 'dearest names'. This drama of influence in relation to some imagined house of familiars is absolutely disowning and displacing. The very title of the story sums up a sense of belatedness in Mew's writing which is of the essence of her sensibility. 'Passed by' in life itself, she was also, as a poet, tied to a 'past' which, though her 'heart went home' to it, was also strange and cold. An outsider both of the present and of the past, this ghosted speaker haunts the scene, not of her own death, but of her own simple absence: 'What was had never been!'

Yet it is noticeable how the 'names', the 'echoes', the 'language' of that past continue to haunt her, and she to frame them with desire and meaning. Mew is a poet who inhabits a house of echoes, and although she finds in it only a scene of devastation, without purpose or place for her, she is also obsessed by its 'dearest names'. The one particular name which rings through her poetry, and which the whole passage brings to mind, is that of Christina Rossetti. 'As he reached me my heart took flight.' Such swerving away from passionate meeting reproduces the situation of innumerable poems by Rossetti: 'The Dream', 'A Pause', 'Under Willows', *The Prince's Progress*, where, to lose the object of the heart's desire becomes the woman's secret triumph. Like Rossetti's, Mew's is a fantasy not so much of being cruelly 'passed by' but, in a cunning twist of the sentimentalist tradition, of dodging the very thing that she craves. 'My spirit summoned the being who claimed mine', she asserts. But as soon as that 'being' is found, she flees at heart. The Rossettian mis-alignment between object and desire, goal and dream, recurs in Mew, but with an absoluteness of self-denial and desolation of spirit which are new. 'As he reached me my heart took flight' turns the old theme of desertion, so well worked over by Hemans and L.E.L., into a coldly chosen destination – a destination which lies far from home, self, familiarity and love. Out of the essentially Victorian conditions of her life, with its moats and towers of enforced self-repression, Mew develops an aesthetic of poetry bleaker even than the mid-winter secrecy of her great predecessor.

*   *   *

Born in 1869, Charlotte was the third of seven children born to Frederick Mew, an architect from the Isle of Wight, and Anna Maria Kendall, a querulous, sickly woman, who was for much of her life an invalid. More vividly than her parents, however, Charlotte remembered the women who ruled in the nursery: the children's nurse, Elizabeth

Goodman, with her puritanical values and cold baths, and the little sewing woman whom, in an article written years later, Charlotte called 'Miss Bolt' (1901). Nurse Goodman, with her vigorous insistence on cleanliness and righteousness, no doubt provided some security in an increasingly bereaved and insecure childhood. Miss Bolt, on the other hand, gave the young Charlotte a glimpse into the murky London underworld of poverty and crime which would always fascinate her. Miss Bolt told her stories about her ne'er-do-well brother, who worked intermittently in the theatre and who found a short-lived success when, as she put it, an actress took '"a fancy for 'im, making 'im stay at 'er 'ouse frequent, and permitting 'im to lie on any of the droring-room sofias"' (*CPP*: 340). Charlotte also got to know about Miss Bolt's niece, Fanny, who went '"where many's gone before 'er, and where many'll go after 'er"' (346). Such mysterious hints became the 7-year-old child's first intimation of the figure who would haunt her imagination for the rest of her life: the prostitute. Years later, she wondered if '"I and the unhappy girl, who was once such a real and well-known person to me, have since passed each other with a cold unmeaning stare"' (in Fitzgerald, 1984: 21). Fanny was evidently the source for the incident in 'Passed', where the homeless speaker meets the 'void incorporate stare' (*CPP*: 77) of the prostitute who no longer recognises her, and thus experiences another proof of her own 'unmeaning' existence. By contrast to Elizabeth Goodman, Miss Bolt was 'unflinchingly agnostic', and this too seems to have left its mark on Charlotte. She recalls the little woman's angry retort to a nephew who tried to persuade her of the existence of an afterlife: '"they must 'ave a fine time of it, to be that eager to do away with the notion of a bit of rest!"' (*CPP*: 343). In Mew's 'Old Shepherd's Prayer' (1929), the speaker asks for a similarly restful afterlife: 'And if I may not walk in th'old ways and look on th'old faces / I wud sooner sleep' (*RS*: 25).

Death came early to the Mew household, and took its customary Victorian toll of infant lives. Three of the four boys died in childhood: Frederick, aged 2 months, and then in 1876 (a date Charlotte would not forget) both Christopher, aged 1, and Richard, aged 5. Charlotte was 7 at the time, and it fell to her to explain to Miss Bolt what had happened to her favourite charge, Richard. When the 3-year-old Anne piped up to ask what '"dead"' meant, Miss Bolt gave a reply which Charlotte remembered all her life:

> 'It jest means as you go out like the candle or the fire or a noo piece at the theater wot 'asn't took. It don't matter much to anybody but them as wants the fire to warm 'em, and 'im wot perduced the play.' (*CPP*: 345–6)

In a poem Mew never published, 'An Ending', the speaker replies to a preacher's warning about 'the Judgment Seat' that, without the woman he loves:

> my soul goes out
> 'Most like a candle in the everlasting dark.
> And what's the odds? 'Twas just a spark
> Alight for her.
>
> (*CPP*: 56)

During her life, Charlotte wrote a number of poems about the deaths of children. One in particular, 'To a Child in Death', poignantly catches the sense of bemusement in the children left behind, for whom the future now feels like a purposelessly long time on their hands:

> What shall we do with this strange summer, meant for you, –
> Dear, if we see the winter through
> What shall be done with spring?
>
> (*RS*: 34)

In 'The Changeling', too, the child speaker who has been turned into a changeling by fairies remembers how 'dearly I loved the little pale brother / Whom some other bird must have called away' (*CPP*: 14). The idea of being changed into a fairy creature, who would 'feel no pain' and 'always, always be very cold' (14), was an imaginative reaction to loss which marked Charlotte for the rest of her life, and almost certainly began in childhood. These deaths left three girls, Charlotte, Anne and Freda, and one boy, Henry, to live on into adulthood.

In 1879, at the age of 10, Charlotte was sent to Gower Street School for girls, which was run by the energetic educationalist and suffragist, Lucy Harrison. Three years later she became, at her own insistence, one of Miss Harrison's chosen group of girls, who boarded in her own house and were given extra lessons in English literature in the evenings. About two years later, however, Lucy Harrison fell in love with a new teacher, Amy Greener, and the two of them moved to Yorkshire, where they lived together for the rest of their lives. Whatever the personal effect of these years, the intellectual influence was profound. Lucy Harrison was a devoted admirer of the poetry of Emily Brontë, the Brownings, Christina Rossetti and Alice Meynell. In particular, her pupils remembered her highly emotional readings of one of her favourite poems: Meynell's 'To a Daisy':

> Slight as thou art, thou art enough to hide
> Like all created things, secrets from me,
> And stand a barrier to eternity.

269

And I, how can I praise thee well and wide
From where I dwell – upon the hither side?
Thou little veil for so great mystery,
When shall I penetrate all things and thee,
And then look back? For this I must abide,

Till thou shalt grow and fold and be unfurled
Literally between me and the world.
Then I shall drink from in beneath a spring,
And from a poet's side shall read his book.
O daisy mine, what will it be to look
From God's side even of such a simple thing?
(*Poems*: 56)

This knife edge between the macabre and the philosophical, the morbid and the religious, appealed strongly to Victorian readers (Ruskin had praised the same poem when it appeared in 1875), and no doubt Charlotte was steeped, from an early age, in this half-metaphorical, half-literal female grave lore. The idea of being buried but still alive enough 'to look' would haunt her imagination as a literary figure which threatened, at times, to get out of psychological control. Where Meynell turns such looking into a philosophical vantage-point, Mew, with her naturally sceptical agnosticism, is more questioningly literal.

Her own poem, 'Do Dreams Lie Deeper?' clearly echoes and answers Meynell's, thus characteristically finding its own voice through negotiation with another's. Here, she does indeed take the 'poet's side' of the world, but this burial is distinctly earthier than Meynell's, and lacks the other poet's rather coy, spiritual epiphany at the end:

His dust looks up to the changing sky
Through daisies' eyes;
And when a swallow flies
Only so high
He hears her going by
As daisies do. He does not die
In this brown earth where he was glad enough to lie.

But looking up from that other bed,
'There is something more my own,' he said,
'Than hands or feet or this restless head
That must be buried when I am dead.
The Trumpet may wake every other sleeper.
Do dreams lie deeper – ?
(*RS*: 14)

By comparison with Meynell's stiffly didactic optimism, Mew's poem possesses her own halting, idiomatically 'speaking' register. Not bound by the formal rules of verse, her rhymes chance against the altering metre, so that the effect of couplets is lost in the much stronger intonations of real speech. The sense of uncertainty, of a mind following casual trains of thought, inconsistent, wavering and doubting, is her poetry's true note. The daisies no longer represent a special, privileged perspective from the grave, but something too delicate and evasive to be ordered into moral meaning. Although the imagery of burial, daisies and poetic vision is the same as Meynell's, for Mew these cannot be caught up into salvation. Some dreams lie too deep for God, and some sleepers (like Miss Bolt) would prefer to go on sleeping.

In 1888, when Charlotte was 19, the family moved to Gordon Street, in Bloomsbury. The young poet, with her passion for literature, must have been aware of the presence, nearby, of the elderly Christina Rossetti, who lived in Torrington Square, almost a continuation of Gordon Street, until her death in 1894. For a time, too, Charlotte attended the older poet's church, Christ Church, Woburn Square, and may well have seen Christina there, generally at the front and lingering in prayer after the end of the service. It is even possible that she was present at Christina's funeral, which took place in Christ Church in January 1895. The proximity of the poet who will have the most profound influence on her own work seems like a coincidence Charlotte's imagination would not have missed. The coincidence, too, that her own life follows a pattern of renunciation and self-concealment as obsessive and yet as poetically nourishing as Rossetti's, is too obvious to ignore. Between the two poets, whose lives crossed each other for a few years, there is a quite disturbing psychological as well as poetic similarity. Those Victorian vaults of self-mortification, which Webster and Michael Field avoided and mocked, re-open, in Charlotte Mew, in one of the last literary expressions of woman's buried passions.

Meanwhile, however, there were other tragedies in the Mew household. Henry, the only remaining son and the oldest of the children, began to show signs of mental breakdown in his twenties and, as a result, was confined in Peckham hospital where he remained for the rest of his short life. Then, in the early 1890s, the beautiful, brilliant Freda, the youngest girl and darling of the family, began to show similar symptoms of mental collapse. She was to spend the next sixty years of her life in an asylum at Carisbrooke on the Isle of Wight. Thus, by the time they were in their early twenties, Charlotte and her younger sister Anne were the only survivors of this family devastation. They had lost four brothers and a sister, and it is perhaps no wonder that they clung to each other and to the remaining securities of their lives with frightened tenacity.

In addition, they had to contend at this time with the spread of popular theories of eugenics. During the 1890s and the early decades of the twentieth century, insanity, as well as other diseases, were increasingly being described as inherited deficiencies which it was the duty of individuals not to pass on. The notion of responsibility towards the race became a fashionable morality, which was used to justify the incarceration of the insane and which put considerable pressure on those related to them. For instance, *Everywoman's Magazine* for 1912 not only insisted on 'the control of the mentally and physically defective', but also argued, with terrifying vagueness, that 'there are immense numbers of people who are relatively unfit, people who are tubercular, dangerously neurotic, who have some taint in their family history which makes it desirable for the sake of the race that they refrain from marriage' (*Everywoman's Magazine*, 7(1912), 5086). The 'family history' of the Mews must have left Charlotte and Anne in no doubt of their duty to 'the race', while the moral stigma of insanity became another source of secrecy and paranoia. Mew's poem 'Ken' (1916), which was turned down by one editor because it seems to question the justice of incarceration, imagines with repressed horror the inside reality of the two asylums which housed a brother and a sister. Ken, the idiot boy, is taken away to the unknown house on the hill, leaving the speaker to see something the poem dare not name:

> Do roses grow
> Beneath those twenty windows in a row –
> And if some night
> When you have not seen any light
> They cannot move you from your chair
> What happens there?
> I do not know.
>
> So, when they took
> Ken to that place, I did not look
> After he called and turned on me
> His eyes. These I shall see –
> (*FB*: 29)

In 1898, Frederick Mew died of cancer, leaving his two daughters to look after an invalid mother and pay the private nursing expenses of Henry and Freda out of a small inheritance. With the prospect of considerable hardship before them, Charlotte and Anne decided to take lodgers without their invalid mother's knowledge, and meanwhile hoped that Charlotte's short stories and Anne's paintings might bring in a small income. Then, in 1901, there was another death. Henry died of pneumonia in Peckham hospital, and it fell to Charlotte to make the arrangements for his burial in Nunhead Cemetery. As always, she remained silent about the tragedies which struck deepest; few of her friends even knew of the existence of Henry and Freda. Their lives, like so much else for Charlotte, were buried deep in the place of denial and dreams.

Yet the poem, 'In Nunhead Cemetery', spoken by a callow clerk who gradually loses his sanity as he stands by the new grave of the woman he loved, hints that Henry's death was yet another blow against Charlotte's hard-won mental survival:

> There is no one left to speak to there;
> Here they are everywhere,
> And just above them fields and fields of roses lie –
> If he would dig it all up again they would not die.
>
> (*FB*: 21)

The last stanza, she explained, expresses ' "a lapse from the sanity and self-control of what precedes it" ' (in Davidow, 1960: 302) – a ' "lapse" ' which is conveyed metrically, as speech pushes the line out to an extreme of desperate fantasising. Her own need for control, both as a woman and as a poet, should be set against this background of deeply feared insanity and repeated bereavement. The emancipations of the twentieth century probably meant little to this woman whose first thirty years of life were spent withstanding such blows of fate, while keeping, against the odds, her own 'sanity and self-control'. Understandably, Charlotte cultivated a manner of capriciously gauche, defiant detachment as protection against any further hurt. ' "I am credited with a more or less indifferent front to these things" ', she once wrote of her childhood pleasures, adding ' "the fact is they cut me to the heart" ' (in Fitzgerald, 1984: 37). The literary motif of burial gains from the real life of this poet a revived, if desolate conviction. After all, to be buried is at least to be out of reach of things that ' "cut . . . to the heart" '.

For the moment, however, Henry's death seems to have released Charlotte and Anne from their routine of domestic responsibility. They found a nurse for their mother and, in the summer of that year, went with four other women to stay at the convent of St Gildas de Rhuys in Brittany. It was their first holiday since the trips to the Isle of Wight in 'magical childhood' (*CPP*: 72), and it was to be the first of several. Charlotte seems to have been in high spirits, keeping the company amused on the passage with her stories and dancing a can-can for them in her silk knickers. When her sense of secrecy lifted, she could evidently be outrageously entertaining. On returning to Britain, she gave a lively account of the whole holiday in an essay, 'Notes in a Brittany Convent' (1901), where, in particular, she remembers the 'little portress' (*CPP*: 353), whose duties of mediation between the world and the convent, between life and self-denial, gave her a recurring figure for the double loyalties of her own imagination.

Charlotte returned to France many times, either with Anne or alone, and revelled, in her usual gamesome, self-possessed way, in its foreignness. In her letters, she describes impromptu trips into the countryside on the roofs of buses crammed with peasants (Davidow: 290), friendships struck up with the local working people (296) and even the occasional spin at the Casinos: ' "but I shall keep away from them as the attractions of gambling are irresistible, and I have no money to lose" ' (297), she vowed. Many of her poems and stories are set in France and have French protagonists: prostitutes, a curé, a schoolboy, two sisters, a fisherman. It is as if French life spoke more closely to her imagination than English, or else because, like Webster, to speak in the voice of another, in dramatic monologue, freed her from the eccentric, self-imposed proprieties of a 'strict moral code' – a code which caused her, as one friend noted, to 'absolutely cut out from her friendship anyone on whom a breath of scandal blew' (A. Monro, 1953: xii). Such double standards of life and of the imagination were yet another essentially Victorian inheritance.

Back in London in the early 1890s, Charlotte fell in with the spirit of the times. She took to wearing a black mannish jacket and to smoking cigars. In 1894 she submitted her story, 'Passed', to the editor of *The Yellow Book*, Henry Harland. He accepted it with enthusiasm, and it appeared in the second volume alongside works by Henry James, Ella D'Arcy and Beardsley, in the very issue which provoked scandalised indignation in Michael Field and caused them to retract the poem they themselves had submitted. For a short time, Mew's literary future and her place within a literary movement seemed assured. Then, in 1895, the arrest of Oscar Wilde, reportedly with a yellow book in his hand, caused the downfall of the magazine, at least in its original form. The public scandal associated with Wilde, and the attack on John Lane's offices as a result of his arrest, frightened many writers away. None the less, unlike Michael Field, Mew did not entirely withdraw her support, although she did disguise her connection with the magazine. In 1896, two of her poems appeared in a cleaned-up issue under the rather obvious pseudonym of Charles Catty (Davidow: 66). Publicly, however, Mew found it easier to withdraw into herself than to fight on against the backlash of opinion. The permissive 1890s had come to an abrupt end, and most of those who had been associated with John Lane either insisted he change his style (the Meynells were vociferous in their demand for Beardsley's dismissal) or simply lost their literary nerve. Charlotte, who had only just tasted some success, belonged among the latter. She seems to have returned to her largely reclusive domestic life with Anne, to have written increasingly less and to have become markedly unpredictable in company, either shy and silent or rather testy and rude: 'Smirking and speaking rather loud' (*FB*: 11), as she puts it. Perhaps the front of prim severity was now even more necessary. The atmosphere of the 1890s, which was much more congenial to her 'foreign' and sensually exotic imagination than that of the English Georgians with whom she is more often classed, might have provided a natural context for her gifts. But as her brief success with 'Passed' turned to scandal, she missed her moment and never found it again. She also perhaps missed the opportunity for a personal emancipation which, paradoxically, the advent of the twentieth century diminished rather than increased.

Unfortunately, the stories of the two great passions of Charlotte's life remain shrouded in hearsay. In 1902, she went to Paris for two months to visit Ella D'Arcy, and behaved with her customary timidity and oddness, failing to turn up for pre-arranged meetings, and seeming most offhand when perhaps she was most vulnerable. It seems that her love for Ella, however expressed, was politely if forcefully rejected (see Fitzgerald, 1984: 86). Years later, in 1913, a similar rejection took place. Charlotte evidently fell in love with May Sinclair, though it is a pity that only May's side of the story remains, in the barest details and at several removes. A certain G. B. Stern recalled how May had told him that ' "a lesbian poetess, Charlotte M., had chased her upstairs into the bedroom" ' and that she had had ' "to leap the bed five times!" ' (in Fitzgerald, 1984: 133). The element of histrionic absurdity, here, suggests an event elaborated for entertainment. For her part, Charlotte remained absolutely silent on this as on most other aspects of her private life. Like Rossetti, she was assiduous in destroying evidence which might expose that life to the public, and the two large trunks, which may once have been full of manuscripts and letters, and which she forbade even Anne to look into (A. Monro, 1953: xx), were found empty after her death.

The rest of Charlotte's life was one of quiet confinement with Anne, their invalid mother and their ferocious parrot, Wek, who was noted in particular for his noisy objections to male visitors. Then, eventually, in 1916, when Charlotte was 47, Harold and Alida Monro of the Poetry Bookshop published her first volume of poems, *The Farmer's Bride*. The title poem had first been published in *The Nation* in 1912, and had roused considerable interest. Spoken by a rough farmer whose young bride has turned from him in sexual terror, it uses the sexually and idiomatically 'other' voice of the monologue to express a maddening, tender, violent lust, which might otherwise have been inexpressible to, though perhaps not unfelt by, the prickly, defiant spinster Charlotte seemed to have become:

> She sleeps up in the attic there
> Alone, poor maid. 'Tis but a stair
> Betwixt us. Oh! my God! the down,
> The soft young down of her, the brown,
> The brown of her – her eyes, her hair, her hair!
>
> (*FB*: 10)

She herself took to helping out at the Bookshop, and attended some readings of her own poetry there. In spite of her public awkwardness, she struck up a kind of friendship with Alida Monro, whom she even invited to Gordon Street. There, Alida remembered, Charlotte would often smoke a cigarette and casually make spills out of the papers from the mysterious trunks, which she either burned or gave to Wek to chew up. On being questioned, she replied: ' "I'm burning up my work. I don't know what else to do with it" ' (A. Monro: xx). Certainly Alida remembered poems which Charlotte would recite to her but of which no trace remains. In a typically macabre and rather heartless gesture, Charlotte left one of the trunks to Alida in her will, but emptied of its contents.

When the time came, it was Alida who was called in to put an end to Wek. She describes how, after the due wait for the chloroform to take effect, she left Charlotte and Anne sitting miserably in another room, and went upstairs alone. As she tentatively put her hand into the covered cage, the old parrot took his last revenge and gave her 'a smart nip on the finger' (A. Monro: x–xi). Feeling that the sisters could take no more, she quickly wrung his neck. Yet even Alida, who was trusted more than most, was never told of the existence of Henry and Freda, or of the deaths of three brothers in childhood. Certain facts in Charlotte's life were not for public communication, even between friends, but only for poetry.

A few late-flowering friendships alleviated the poet's increasingly lonely last years. In 1918 she was invited to Max Gate. Hardy had read *The Farmer's Bride*, and had expressed his belief that Mew was ' "far and away the best living woman poet" ' (in Fitzgerald, 1984: 174), although it was with Florence Hardy that Charlotte struck up a more durable relationship. One of the last friends of her life was Sydney Cockerell, the director of the Fitzwilliam Museum in Cambridge. Charlotte visited him in Cambridge a number of times, and he showed her, for instance, a lock of Lizzie Siddal's hair – a sight which may indeed have dazzled this poet who was herself so sensitive to 'bright hair!' ('Fame', *FB*: 11), as well as so obsessed with the Rossettian mystique of burial. She seems to be recalling the still legendary story of the exhumation in her own poem, 'The Forest Road' (1916), when she writes: 'But death would spare the glory of your head / In the long sweetness of the hair that does not die' (*FB*: 37). Cockerell also allowed her to hold in her hand another literary relic which would have pleased her: a letter by one of the Brontës. At this time, he noted with surprise, she was in the habit of going out to morning mass, though, unlike many of her contemporaries, she never became a Catholic.

Then, in 1923, old Mrs Mew died. Without her family annuity, Charlotte and Anne were left even more impoverished, though Cockerell and other friends succeeded in securing Charlotte a small Civil List pension. However, the blow from which she never recovered came four years later. In 1927, Anne was diagnosed as having cancer of the liver and was given just three months to live. Alida, who visited her near the end, wrote anxiously about Charlotte: ' "Her rough little harsh voice and wilful ways hiding enormous depth of feeling – now she will be entirely alone and her relation with Anne has been one of complete love" ' (in Fitzgerald, 1984: 205). Anne died in June, and Charlotte fell into a deep depression from which she never recovered.

Anne's death also seems to have released in her sister certain terrors and manias which had lain under layers of control for years. In her own will she left instructions that her main artery should be cut before burial – a form of 'posthumous' literal-mindedness very like Christina Rossetti's, who had left instructions that she desired a '*perishable* coffin'. Now Charlotte began to be tormented by the idea that Anne had been buried alive. Such a notion, as a number of her short stories tell, was not new. But it became increasingly obsessive, drawing, no doubt, on a mixture of lifelong phobias long held in check, and literary images familiar since her schooldays. At one point, her doctor tried to persuade her to enter an asylum of her own accord. She refused, but then, in semi-capitulation, entered a dreary little nursing home where her room looked out onto a blank wall. She was there for just over a month. A last letter explains: ' "I just tried my best to keep going and broke down – it was so lonely – I try still but it is lonelier here" ' (in Fitzgerald, 1984: 213). On 24 March 1928, she went out and bought a bottle of Lysol, a form of domestic disinfectant, returned to her room, and drank it. After a painful struggle, during which she begged a doctor not to bring her back to life, she died. She was 59.

Mew had published in her lifetime only two volumes of poetry, her reputation resting on a mere twenty-eight poems, most of them written before 1916. In addition, she had published nine stories and twelve essays. Marsh never included her in his anthologies of *Georgian Poetry*, mainly because he objected to her irregular metres – that old source of provocation in women's poetry – while Ezra Pound, though he accepted

'The Fête' for *The Egoist* in 1914, was no more inclined to help a poet who did not fit the new movements of Imagism and modernism than Marsh was to help a poet, particularly a woman, who broke the rules of metricality. In 1920 Virginia Woolf, having just read *The Farmer's Bride* (1916), commented in a letter: 'I think her very good and interesting and unlike anyone else' (1975–80: II, 419). It was Mew's fate as a poet, but also her greatness, at a time when new movements and new canons were replacing the old, to remain unplaced and, indeed, in many ways 'unlike anyone else'. Her quirky originality is won, not from the experimentalist freedoms of modernism, like Anna Wickham's or Stevie Smith's, but from a complex echoing of the voices of her predecessors, as her imagination returns 'home' in a ghostly, posthumous foraging of her literary past.

PAYING SO HEAVILY

In sensibility and imagery, Mew looks back to the women poets who preceded her. Her poetry is rich in echoes, not only of Meynell, Rossetti and the Brontës, but also of Webster and Michael Field. In particular, her imagination, like theirs, is troubled by the problem of experience, that quantity of emotional or sexual reality which was likely to be, for the nineteenth-century woman, either too little or too much, the lot either of the nun or of the prostitute. Hers is still the scarlet and white imagery of a moral sexual code loaded with myth, and ordered round an opposition of innocence and experience which carries heavy penalties either way. The disappearance of the nun and the prostitute from women's writing of the twentieth century is itself a sign of a new attitude towards sexual experience. As Freudian theories of repression became increasingly well known from 1910 onwards (when the word first appeared in English translation), and thus offered a means of naming and decoding certain Victorian symbols, those symbols lost their artistic resourcefulness. Although in many ways modernism exaggerated the repressions of Victorianism for its own purposes of rebellion, and simultaneously made repression an inhibitingly named fact, it also provided a release, for many writers, from the carefully chiselled tombstones of their forbears. Both Sinclair and Woolf acted out their imaginative liberation through exorcising the Oedipal power of their real if somewhat over-monumentalised Victorian parents.

Mew, however, never does so. Whether because she lived longer in the Victorian age herself, because her parents were not dominant intellectual forces to be rejected or because her fear of what looked like hereditary insanity re-affirmed a Victorian morality of self-denial in women, her writing remains very much within the old structures. Her strategies of control and displacement, desire and debt, are familiar ones, and her highly charged gestures of sexual invitation and rejection are loaded with connotations of the cloister, the street or the grave. The idea that experience must be paid for, and paid for in the currency of the immortal soul itself, gives to Victorian women's poetry some of its distinctive intensities and inner scepticisms, and Charlotte Mew's writing belongs to the last, almost spent stages of this tradition.

One of the poets most openly admired by Mew was Emily Brontë, in particular, the Emily of 'No Coward Soul is Mine' – a poem which celebrates a Shelleyan spirit of intellectual beauty in language which rings with the soldiering confidence of a Nonconformist hymn:

> No coward soul is mine
> No trembler in the world's storm-troubled sphere
> I see Heaven's glories shine
> And Faith shines equal arming me from Fear
>
> O God within my breast
> Almighty ever-present Deity
> Life, that in me hast rest
> As I, Undying Life, have power in Thee
>
> Vain are the thousand creeds
> That move men's hearts, unutterably vain,
> Worthless as withered weeds
> Or idlest froth amid the boundless main
>
> (1941: 243)

Mew declared of her idol: 'It was with the face of a pagan warrior that she confronted life and met death. A pagan above all she was: the centuries of revelation behind her seem not to have won a glance of question or of recognition' (*CPP*: 361). Brontë's apparently effortless rejection of 'the thousand creeds' is an object of envy and admiration to her more faith-entrammelled follower. To be a pagan remains, for Mew, as late as 1904, an imaginative goal still seemingly incompatible with the ideals of womanliness. Like Dora Greenwell years before, she recognises the pagan element in women's poetry as a force of rebellious honesty, a 'warrior' attitude to 'life' and 'death' which refuses to be cowed into submission.

In fact, however, the poet who most powerfully dominates her consciousness is not the 'pagan warrior', but the inwardly repressed and tormented believer. Between Rossetti and Mew there is a relation which carries over from literary imitation into life, as the myth of the woman poet so elaborately woven by the one is inherited by the other. Just as Rossetti adopts the melancholy poses of L.E.L., so Mew enters the displacements and secrets of Rossetti's imagination: its ghostly mis-encounters, its sense of the penalties of sexuality and its obsession with burial. Her writing finds its own originality through an extraordinarily close re-writing of the characteristic motifs of her predecessor, in a lineage which comes, in Mew, historically and symbolically, to the end of its road.

Thus, for instance, Rossetti's 'Remember me when I am gone away' (*CP*: I, 37) is recalled in Mew's 'Remember me and smile, as smiling too' ('A Farewell'). The older poet's many homeless ghosts who try to return, like the speaker of 'At Home': 'When I was dead, my spirit turned / To seek the much frequented house' (*CP*: I, 28), give Mew her own figure for the revisited home in 'Passed', as well as for that in 'Péri en Mer', where the dead sailor remembers that: 'I, no longer I, / Climbed home, the homeless ghost I was to be' (*CPP*: 61). Home, for both these poets who never left it in real life, is an ideal full of inner alienations and absences. Neither of them feels 'at home' in their imaginations, and both exploit ghostliness with an exquisite, shrugging irony which, as in Mew's 'A Quoi Bon Dire', turns loss into the condition of love:

> Seventeen years ago you said
> Something that sounded like Good-bye;
> And everybody thinks that you are dead,
>   But I.
>
> So I, as I grow stiff and cold
> To this and that say Good-bye too;
> And everybody sees that I am old
>   But you.
>
> And one fine morning in a sunny lane
> Some boy and girl will meet and kiss and swear
> That nobody can love their way again
>   While over there
> You will have smiled, I shall have tossed your hair.
>   (*FB*: 30)

The imperceptible dislocations of time and place, here – the way that 'Seventeen years' is also a time stood still for 'I' and 'you', while 'over there' is somewhere both in and not in the 'sunny lane' – are ghost-effects which leave the speaker and her object timeless and placeless by the end, either still young or long dead. Like Rossetti, Mew sets love at odds with reality, smiling and careless, in another place.

Like Rossetti, too, is Mew's early poem, 'At the Convent Gate', which repeats the situation of 'The Convent Threshold':

'Ah! sweet, it is too late:
You cannot cast these kisses from your hair.
Will God's cold breath blow kindly anywhere
Upon such burning gold?'

(*RS*: 39)

Both Lizzie Siddal's 'burning gold' hair and Rossetti's threshold of choice come together, here, in a scene which belongs to a literary tradition almost over-ripe with use. To be always, not here, but 'over there', whether in some ghostly afterlife of strange meetings, or inaccessibly over the threshold of the closed convent, is characteristic of both poets whose imaginations enter into a toying game of desire and denial with life itself. Such perverse distances lie at the heart of their work, as well as being, indeed, perverse distances of the heart.

One poem of Rossetti's which seems to have lurked deep in Mew's subconscious is her sonnet 'On the Wing'. This, which was no doubt one of Christina's inventively untrue dreams, plays out an allegory of pleasure and violence which then turns into one of her dramas of missed love:

Once in a dream (for once I dreamed of you)
    We stood together in an open field;
    Above our heads two swift-winged pigeons wheeled,
Sporting at ease and courting full in view.
When loftier still a broadening darkness flew,
    Down-swooping, and a ravenous hawk revealed;
    Too weak to fight, to [*sic*] fond to fly, they yield;
So farewell life and love and pleasures new.
Then as their plumes fell fluttering to the ground,
    Their snow-white plumage flecked with crimson drops,
    I wept, and thought I turned towards you to weep:
But you were gone; while rustling hedgerow tops
Bent in a wind which bore to me a sound
    Of far-off piteous bleat of lambs and sheep.

(*CP*: I, 138–9, ll. 1–14)

The dream allegory of pigeons and hawk in the first part obliquely premonitions the 'waking' reality of the second part, as some unknown force drives away the presence who was standing by the speaker, and interrupts the implicit scene of courtship between them. However, the connection remains, as Cora Kaplan notes, 'unspecified, incomplete' (1986: 112). Certainly, the poem enacts one of those shocks of sudden emptiness which so often spoil Rossetti's dreams of love. 'But you were gone' is almost offhand in its surprise. Instead of 'life and love and pleasures new', represented by the pigeons, there is only the unexpected chilliness of a 'rustling' wind and the 'far-off piteous bleat of lambs and sheep'. This echo of the end of Keats's ode 'To Autumn', where 'full-grown lambs loud bleat from hilly bourn' (1970: 219), also signals its difference from the winter meaning of the earlier poem. Certainly, on one level, this is the old tale of lost or betrayed love, in which the inexplicable disappearance of the lover leaves universal cold and loneliness at the end. But on another level, this is a tale of flaunted sexuality, 'courting full in view', which ends in the displaced, but strangely harmonious, maternal and spring-like scene of 'lambs and sheep'. The pattern is like that of *Goblin Market*, where the pleasure and violence of the encounter with 'merchant-men' is imaginatively, though not narratively, related to the separate female place of mothers and daughters at the end. Although the hawk and the lover have each destroyed love, there is a kind of 'far-off' consequence, at once bleak and yet conclusive, in the idea of 'lambs and sheep' at the end. Sexual desertion yields its quietly visionary compensation, however cold and 'piteous', in this underlying, reproductive cycle of the imagery. The ghostly lover who casually disappears leaves the speaker not altogether comfortless and alone, but listening to other sounds in the distance. As so often in Rossetti's poems, the speaker is distracted from emotional loss by something else, a riddling other meaning, which does not quite fit the pattern of love and desertion, but comes from some other place, 'far-off'.

'On the Wing' evidently haunted Mew. Her own unpublished poem, 'Ne Me Tangito', is full of echoes from it, as well as reproducing the idea of sexual compensation which Rossetti keeps buried in her imagery. The title is a variant, correct, but in an older form (Lewis and Short, 1962: 1840), of 'Noli Me Tangere', which was the command given by Christ to Mary Magdalene in the Easter Garden: 'do not touch me'. Mew's poem is spoken by Mary herself, who suddenly breaks off her puzzled meditation on Christ's fear of touch to tell a dream:

> So I will tell you this. Last night, in sleep,
> Walking through April fields I heard the far-off bleat of sheep
> And from the trees about the farm, not very high,
> A flight of pigeons fluttered up into an early evening mackerel sky.
>> Someone stood by and it was you:
>> About us both a great wind blew.
>> My breast was bared
>> But sheltered by my hair
>> I found you, suddenly, lying there,
> Tugging with tiny fingers at my heart, no more afraid:
>> The weakest thing, the most divine
>> That ever yet was mine,
>> Something that I had strangely made,
>> So then it seemed –

The child for which I had not looked or ever cared,
Of whom, before, I had never dreamed.

(*RS*: 24)

Here Mary dreams, in an intriguing reversal both of the resurrection story and of Rossetti's poem, that, instead of leaving her, Christ 'stood by' and then became, in an even more recognisable birth event than Rossetti's 'lambs and sheep', a child in her arms: 'Something that I had strangely made.' The landscape of open 'fields', bleating 'sheep', fluttering 'pigeons' and a sudden 'wind' comes direct from 'On the Wing', and so, too, does the whole casually told dream frame of the event: 'So I will tell you this.' But instead of being displaced 'far-off', motherhood, here, is erotically and intimately realised in a reversal of roles which returns the power of creation and new life to Mary. The sexual fear of the man is thus turned into the fearless, physical dependency of the child, 'Tugging with tiny fingers at my heart'; the resurrection story is turned into a dream of maternity by the woman whom Christ finally would not touch. For once – and this is almost the only occasion in all Mew's writings – the dream vision actually fills her arms.

This odd poem suggests how close is the relationship between herself and her predecessor. The fantasy of motherhood, which serves as a kind of quiet epiphany in Rossetti's sonnet – at once a figure for something and nothing, vision and emptiness at the end – provides the later poet with her own distinctive and recurrent image for creativity. The mischances of life, whether chosen or simply suffered, find their compensations, in her verse, in the child dream which is, ambiguously, both a child and a dream. The pattern recurs throughout Mew's writings, though the dream of motherhood or the mothering of a dream becomes ever more empty-handed. It finds its most desolating, powerful expression in a poem which seems to recall, once again 'far-off', the 'lambs' of Rossetti's achieved inspiration: 'Fame'. Meanwhile, 'Ne Me Tangito' shows the extent to which Mew's own voice comes out of the house of literary echoes, where the 'dearest names' of the old poets are like 'an unlearned language', to be re-learned and re-dreamed by their successor.

Throughout her life, Mew was obsessed with the figure of the Magdalen. Her self-imposed chastity perhaps threw into fascinating relief the idea of the other woman of the streets, who had haunted her since Miss Bolt's stories in childhood. Such a figure, however, also belongs to the poetry of the past. In her, the language of sexuality remains crossed with the language of religion, and womanhood remains poised on a 'convent' threshold of innocence and experience, heaven and hell, which are the heavy balances of Victorian morality. Mew thus returns to a topic which Michael Field and Alice Meynell both, for different reasons, ignore: the exchange mechanisms of love, money and salvation which account for the nature of female desire. The fallen woman is specifically one who has been paid, but who also, in another scale of values, pays. She exists in a place between the socio-economic and spiritual systems, where the coin of the one is easily changed for the coin of the other. However, by the 1890s, such sexual marketing has lost much of its seriousness, and Mew's many poems about prostitution have a lurid colourfulness which betrays their lack of moral conviction. 'Le Sacré-Coeur', for instance, presents Paris as a scarlet woman, giddy with secular pleasures, while the God on the hill dies 'of his immortal smart' (*FB*: 50). In 'Pécheresse', the woman paces the Paris quay, knowing that, although she waits for one particular man among the many she has known, the system of exchange in love is the same: 'A gold piece for a scarlet shame' (*FB*: 23). Such colours are out of date by 1916, and certainly Mew's more jewelled, *fin-de-siècle* vocabulary of guilt clinks somewhat. Unlike *Goblin Market*, too little is at stake in her poems of sexual temptation. The soul itself has gone out of them.

It is only when she turns this absence of moral purpose to narrative account that she finds her own voice. The short story 'Passed', for instance, recounts the meeting in a church of the middle-class speaker and a poor girl which is rich in literary precedents: the meetings between Aurora and Marian Erle, Lizzie and Laura, Margaret and Lilian Gray. However, there is a difference here. At first, the two women's encounter is charged with recognition: 'we met, and her hand, grasping mine, imperatively dragged me into the cold and noisy street' (*CPP*: 68). This sistering gesture, like that of Aurora who, having found Marian, 'held her two slight wrists with both [her] hands' (*AL*: VI, 443), appears to herald another love story between women. But in Mew that story is abruptly avoided instead of developed. At the poor girl's house, the speaker realises that: 'The magnetism of our meeting was already passing; and, reason asserting itself, I reviewed the incident dispassionately, as she lay like a broken piece of mechanism in my arms' (*CPP*: 69). Brutally, she abandons the weeping girl she has embraced and returns to her safe home. The encounter turns out to be neither scandalous nor redeeming; it is simply morally and socially meaningless.

It may be that the love between women which was still 'free' to be imagined by Barrett Browning and Rossetti has become named and blocked in the later poet, who herself knew the cost and stigma of such love, or it may be that Mew is realising the redundancy of the myth itself. In either case, the other woman is, indeed, 'a broken piece of mechanism', a creature of the imagination who has lost her 'magnetism', her allure of the forbidden and the transgressive. Such an object can only be rejected. When, months later, the speaker encounters the girl, rather obviously dressed in 'brilliant crimson' (77) and hanging on the arm of the same man who betrayed her dead sister, she realises that, in fact, it is she who is redundant, she who is the unseen, unrecognised object of the story, an emptiness at its heart: 'The man and woman met my gaze with a void incorporate stare' (77). The sistering impulse of the earlier poems has been blanked out, and 'the human mart' (76), as Mew still calls it, is left untricked at the end. Behind all the flaunted pseudo-sinfulness of its Nineties' style, the story is really not about the fallen woman at all, but about the self's ghostly absence from experience. Where there should have been passion, love or even just kindness, there was a mechanical and futile embrace. The description of the girl as 'a broken piece of mechanism in my arms' is like a negative of the child dream in 'Ne Me Tangito'. Not only is this speaker heartless, she is also irrelevant, herself a ghost from the past whom no one sees or recognises. The subject of the story, as she resonantly puts it, is: ' "Not the desolation of something lost, but of something that had never been" ' (72). Such a conclusion presents the whole narrative as the elaboration of a missing purpose, a missing life. This absent motive becomes Mew's characteristic self-signature.

In one poem about the Magdalen, the old structures of sin and payment momentarily come back to life. 'Madeleine in Church' is written in a colloquially wandering metre, ranging from two feet to twelve, which shows Mew at her most inventive and modern. Yet, paradoxically, like much of her work, the poem also echoes uncannily with voices from the past. For instance, in one place the tones of Augusta Webster's Castaway clearly speak through Mew's own. Madeleine's exclamation:

> Oh! I know Virtue, and the peace it brings!
> The temperate, well-worn smile
> The one man gives you, when you are evermore his own . . .
> *(FB:* 40)

echoes the 'shrill carping virtues' of Webster's wives, who 'wear / No kisses but a husband's upon lips / There is no other man desires to kiss' *(Portraits:* 40), while Madeleine's mockery of 'the parsons' tags – / Back to the fold, across the evening fields, like any flock of baa-ing sheep' (41) repeats the Castaway's mockery of preachers who would 'teach all us wandering sheep . . . to stand in rows / And baa them hymns and moral songs' (47). The outward evidence of Mew's poetry is that it is steeped in the voices of her predecessors. She rings the last changes on their patterns of desire and guilt, and gives to their images of flowers, coins and laughter perhaps no more than a belated, hallucinatory intensity.

Yet, out of this peal of images from the past comes a voice which is, syntactically and metrically, profoundly original:

> We are what we are: when I was half a child I could not sit
> Watching black shadows on green lawns and red carnations burning in the sun,
> Without paying so heavily for it
> That joy and pain, like any mother and her unborn child were almost one.
> I could hardly bear
> The dreams upon the eyes of white geraniums in the dusk,
> The thick, close voice of musk,
> The jessamine music on the thin night air,
> Or, sometimes, my own hands about me anywhere –
> The sight of my own face (for it was lovely then) even the scent of my own hair,
> Oh! there was nothing, nothing that did not sweep to the high seat
> Of laughing gods, and then blow down and beat
> My soul into the highway dust, as hoofs do the dropped roses of the street.
>
>   (39)

This is probably one of the last 'fallen woman' poems in English. At least, it is one of the last in which the fall is internalised as a penalty for passion, and the Magdalen recognised as the figure for what has been forbidden, denied or divided in the self. All the imagery of the fall: the idea of 'paying so heavily for it' and of being trampled underfoot by the 'hoofs' of horses, have been displaced, here, into an account, not of rape or seduction, but of the girl's own generalised sensuousness. The idea of the fall is not a specific event in the sexual market of the world, but a system of exacted retribution which lies deep within the very aesthetic responses of the self. The pleasures of the senses are still being described as pagan forces, belonging to the 'laughing gods' of Olympus and not to the suffering God of the crucifix which Madeleine observes before her. The old Pans and goblins of the imagination re-surface in this late poem to play their games of pleasure and art against the sighing responsibility of the true God on the cross: 'too gravely looking at me' (43). Perhaps the Methodist compositor who refused to set the poem because he thought it blasphemous (A. Monro, 1953: xvi) was not entirely imperceptive. The very line lengths, which straggle beyond any proper accounting of the metre, seem like a culmination of earlier poets' provocative resistance to form. These unruly rhythms and unpredictable, unsatisfied rhymes express Madeleine's desires more powerfully than the gaudy jewel box of imagery which Mew plunders from the past.

'Madeleine in Church' is a technical *tour de force*, which none the less reiterates certain dated conventions of desire. Its language is a little too plush, its reds and whites too obviously painted and its musky sensuousness a little too comfortably sinful. Mew's aestheticism in these Magdalen poems evokes a belated decadence, in which the beautiful, unpremeditated ease of the speaking voice insinuates itself round the studded symbols of a forbidden, literary sexuality. In them, she is writing poems within poems, dreams within dreams. The contradiction between the demands of art and the demands of morality, between music and truth, pleasure and payment, which, after her, will largely cease to trouble the woman poet, is given a last, somewhat exotic revival by her, as her Madeleine repeats the old catch in women's pleasure: that it cannot be had without 'paying so heavily for it'. Although the currency has become debased, the market morality is the same.

However, Mew's best works break free of this derivative emotional colourfulness, and assert, in its place, a wintriness of the spirit which is her true landscape and true colour. To be free of the allure of the sexual market is to enter a world of bleakly self-denying dream, in which the heart is not penalised by guilt and appetite, but simply frozen to death or lost. Mew's best stories and poems push towards this ultimate territory of the sentimentalist tradition of women's poetry.

INTO WHITE WORLDS

In the summer of 1913, Charlotte was in Dieppe by herself on holiday. A year later, she remembered the thrill of that solitude and of the creativity which went with it: ' "One realizes the place much more alone, I think. It's all there is – and you don't feel it through another mind which mixes up things. I wonder if Art, as they say, is a rather inhuman thing?" ' (in Davidow, 1960: 75). The idea of that ' "inhuman thing" ' gives to her poetry a colour which negates its sensuousness. While red represents experience, deep-dyed in a Victorian mythology of woman's sexual guilt, its opposite white is the colour, not of innocence, but of vision and desolation, of that ' "inhuman thing" ' which turns experience into art. Mew's fascination with whiteness as ' "something that had never been" ' (*CPP*: 72), like the white of Rossetti's denied passion in 'Winter: My Secret', sets up a hollowness of reference, a revoked or negative significance, which itself becomes the object of her best writings. Where there should have been something loved, met or at least longed for, there is nothing. This gesture of ultimate refusal, however much regretted in her life, becomes the secret of her originality as a poet.

It is in some of her short stories that this imaginative road to nowhere is plotted. 'White World', for instance, which remained unpublished in Charlotte's lifetime, is a quest story which recalls Rossetti's *Prince's Progress*, though its obsessive, over-written length suggests a private trauma not quite worked into art. Two sisters live at home with their father. One is pining for her lover and slowly dying as a result; the other seems to take her father's part in keeping her younger sister imprisoned, though, in a moment of sudden fellow-feeling, they recognise 'their mutual doom' and 'found each other's hands and clung together' (267). But this politically loaded gesture is once again meaningless. So far, the story falls into the old patterns of the ballad: one sister against another, life against death, love against frigidity. However, that same night, the lover reappears, and the younger sister greets him with: ' "So you have come for me" '. His reply, though apparently affirmative, hints at an obliqueness of motive which the rest of the story plays out:

> 'I came . . . because the world was white, white like the waste through which tonight I travelled . . . There was but one thing audible and recognizable in the wide earth, one thing alone life-painted, speech-endowed. Dazzled, possessed and deaf, what wonder if I fled towards it – though to you.' (270)

The dazzling, possessing, deafening object he seeks is evidently not her, 'though' he flees in her direction. This unknown, compulsive object then flits across the long, monotonous path of the story. The two lovers set out through the snow in search of some vague goal which, like the Prince's, eludes them. Just as they reach the man's ancestral home, 'the bridegroom bringing home his bride' (280) as Mew puts it, she collapses and dies. Just when she should be won, the woman characteristically takes flight.

The point of the story is itself elusive, as the journey through the white world is described with an intensity which seems disproportionate to the facts. Evidently not love and marriage, but the white cold road to nowhere is the self-reflexively aimless object of this story. Both Rossetti and Mew, whatever the personal, emotional reasons, delay reaching home. Both poets, instead, seem fascinated by the intervening road, the dream; with the fiction which interferes with foregone conclusions and satisfied desires. Mew's winter secret, like Rossetti's, is an idea of inspiration so self-contained and 'inhuman', that it has no reference beyond itself. Such an idea, like the snow which covers the path, makes the direction of the quest uncertain: ' "what wonder if I fled towards it – though to you" '. This is the heart's familiar dodge: 'As he reached me my heart took flight.' Such an internalization of quest-romance by women writers results in a narrative which cannot altogether exclude the goals of home and love from the inner map of Romantic 'subjectivity' (Bloom, 1971: 18), but which, at the last minute, swerves away from both home *and* from subjectivity, by dying. The white world is a figure for that emptiness within and without. As the child who was seduced from her warm home by inhuman fairies already foresaw: 'I shall always, always be very cold'. White is the colour of that coldness which is ambiguously both the fairies' punishment and also, for those who must live outside, their protective gift.

In her poem 'The Call' (1929), Mew seems to repeat the situation of 'White World', as well as to echo another poem by Rossetti. In 'Love from the North', Rossetti tells of a man, cold and 'Light-locked' (*CP*: I, 29–30, ll. 22), who kidnaps a bride at her wedding and takes her to live with him in the bleak north, where 'He made me fast with book and bell' (29). The muse of writing and music is a ruthless, cold-hearted creature, who destroys human love and choice. In 'The Call' the intruder from the cold is even more deathly and irresistible:

> Something swift and tall
> Swept in and out and that was all.
> Was it a bright or a dark angel? Who can know?
> It left no mark upon the snow,
>   But suddenly it snapped the chain
>   Unbarred, flung wide the door
>   Which will not shut again;
> And so we cannot sit here any more.
>   We must arise and go:
>   The world is cold without
>   And dark and hedged about
> With mystery and enmity and doubt,
>   But we must go
>   Though yet we do not know
> Who called, or what marks we shall leave upon the snow.
>   (*RS*: 32)

The purposeful exhilaration of going out into the 'mystery and enmity and doubt' keeps its connotation of ambition and progress which may, or may not, leave 'marks' upon the snow. The 'blank page' of Mew's writing is a place of risk, winter and 'doubt'. Its whiteness may be death and desolation, but it may also be vision and writing, in a doubleness which has a long literary tradition in women's poetry. Very often in Mew they seem almost identical, the one missing the other by a hair's breadth, a high gamble of the imagination which cannot ever know, in advance, 'Who called, or what marks we shall leave upon the snow.' None the less, once this real or unreal, 'bright' or 'dark angel' has appeared, the door of home 'will not shut again', and the speaker has no choice but to take to the winter road.

However, such whiteness is not achieved without effort, as the extraordinary short story, 'A White Night' (1903), suggests. It tells how a group of travellers, two men and a woman, are accidentally locked overnight in the church of a Spanish monastery. There, they become the reluctant witnesses of a macabre ritual. The events are set in the past and dated 1876 – the unforgotten year, for Charlotte, of her two younger brothers' deaths. A line of monks enters the church chanting a mass for the dead, followed by a single woman in white, whose voice rises above the men's: 'a piercing intermittent note, an awful discord, shrilling out and dying down and shrilling out again – a cry – a scream' (*CPP*: 151). This note of female passion is one which both the monks' religious ritual and the male narrator's impassive voice control, but only just. Against that male order, the various gradations of the woman's voice, expressing terror, acquiescence, vision and protest, clashes powerfully. Then, as the three observers look on in disbelief, the woman is buried alive under a stone in the aisle. For all its Gothic accoutrements, the motif of burial which Mew revives so extravagantly keeps a coolness of purpose which is even more disturbing than the actual details of the scene.

This coolness is insisted on by the male narrator. It is he who, with Jamesian fastidiousness, declares that the woman 'wasn't altogether real, she didn't altogether live, and yet her presence there was the supreme reality of the unreal scene' (152). He finds in the whole macabre ritual a symbol of some perfectly disembodied art, which his own style impeccably reproduces: 'I, too, was quite incredibly outside it all' (154), he assures us. The live burial is, for him, a formal tragedy, an art of death performed to the life. As he explains: 'the row of faces seemed to merge into one face – the face of nothing human – of a system, of a rule' (153). '"I wonder if Art . . .", Charlotte herself asked, 'is a rather inhuman thing?"' The white woman seems, in part, to be a willing accomplice in the '"inhuman"' system which transcends and rules her emotion, while the artistic message is given at the end by the male speaker: 'What counted chiefly with her, I suspect, was something infinitely greater to her vision than the terror of men's dreams' (159).

However, this tone of suave control is challenged by something else. The 'system' which seems 'infinitely greater' than the 'terror' which it inspires is conspicuously male; the 'row of faces' may seem to 'merge' into an abstract form, but they remain the faces of monks. Against this impassive order, the voice of the woman makes 'an awful discord', while her acquiescence is touched with ambiguous resistance. For, as the narrator tells, 'she yielded to an impulse of her lips, permitted them the shadow of a smile. But for this slip she looked the thing of death they reckoned to have made of her' (154). This lets 'slip' that 'the thing of death' is very much a construction of what 'they', the monks, have invented. The woman is their effigy, the embodiment of their systematic fantasy. The brief smile on her lips, however, although it cannot make any difference, suggests an inner mockery of the mould in which they have cast her. Although she performs 'the thing of death' for them, the smile lets 'slip' that it is, indeed, for her, only a performance. As with Rossetti's dead or dying women, there is a hidden smile in this over-rehearsed morbidity which is sceptical and resisting. The 'thing of death' is the part women have played, in life and art, for at least a century, but their reasons may not be entirely submissive or credulous. They may, deep down, be laughing.

The story also contains another 'discordant' female voice: that of Ella, the narrator's sister. Unlike him, she is disturbed and upset by the scene she has witnessed, and attacks her brother for his *sang froid*: ' "Oh, for you," she says, and with a touch of bitterness, "it was a spectacle. The woman didn't really count" ' (159). By contrast to his aestheticism, hers is the literal-minded, human response. For her, what counts is not the male 'system', whether of monks or of artists, paring their finger nails, but the real life of the woman. Against her brother's detached curiosity, she asserts the truth of objective fact and suffering. Ella's is the voice, at the end, which keeps a human perspective on this self-consciously literary and yet profoundly disturbing story. It is she who remembers the real woman who must die, and who counts 'the cost and pain'.

'A White Night' is evidently drawing on a mixture of unsorted private phobias and a well-worn Gothic inheritance. Charlotte's own terror of being buried alive lies deeply 'buried' in it, but the pathology of that terror is held in extreme check by the dispassionate, arm's length of the style. It is as if the story were itself modelling the opposition between subconscious trauma and literary form, between real suffering and its artistic control, which is, in a sense, also its very subject matter. The tension between the two comes near to breaking at times, as the story veers from a nearly pathological, literal-minded horror of live burial to an extreme, aestheticist appreciation of death as an artistic metaphor. A schizophrenia deep, perhaps, as Charlotte's own, between madness and control, suffering and form, pain and play, pervades this story and almost wrecks it.

But in the end, the point is not to offer a choice of opposites, but to force them together. The tension between the subjective gratifications of the narrator and the objective protest of Ella, between the abstract idea and the literal event, runs through this story as an ambiguity which is the very raw stuff of fiction. The 'white' woman at the centre holds the two together, as, on the one hand, she plays to the rules of the male order, real or symbolic, and, on the other hand, smiles, dissentingly, within it. As the woman artist, she plays 'the thing of death' prescribed for her, but plays it in her own way, and with a different meaning. That 'shadow of a smile' provides a tiny commentary on the monoliths of religion and art within which the woman takes her place, but only by becoming her own player, her own artist. In 'A White Night', Mew is perhaps offering a strange and haunting tribute to the great poet of white visions before her, who submitted to the 'mortification' of her faith, but who also, from within her self-burial, found secrets to laugh at. The white woman of Mew's imagination, who is both muse and poetic mother, is, all the evidence suggests, Christina Rossetti.

> 'What', said they, 'if her brow be white as the mountain-tops, it is as cold as snow!'
> 'But her glance', says he at the window dreamily, 'sends brighter gleams than the sun over hills and hamlets, in the break of a dark day.' (*CPP*: 196)

Mew published 'The Smile' in 1914. This fairy-tale, which tells of an 'old woman' who lives 'at the top of a wonderful Tower' (195), an object of dispute and disbelief, is her 'Lady of Shalott'. For the chosen few, the idea of her smile, though ' "it is as cold as snow" ', is worth losing everything to find. One day, the old woman is 'seized with sudden love' for a baby girl. As the baby grows up, she is 'filled with delight at the beautiful Face' (198), but is not ambitious to climb the mountain and meet its smile. It is only when, in despair, the old woman turns her face away, that the girl, abandoning her mother and rejecting her lover, 'with a liberated cry' (199), sets off on her progress up the mountain. But she reaches the top too late. The beautiful Face is 'looking another way' (200), and the girl drops dead from weariness and despair. The story seems to be about Mew's sense of failure as an artist; about her inability to reach the Face of her white woman muse. It is perhaps also about the real misunderstandings and misencounters of her own life – encounters between women which were doomed to fail. 'The old woman heard, and turned to her beloved' (200), but it is, as always, too late for love. The old swerve of loss and denial is enacted once again, as the girl looks for the Smile of success, requital, inspiration, whatever it is, and finds it missing.

The story then ends with a familiar scene: 'Some have seen the Tower, and a strange white figure at the summit, clothed in tossed hair. It stands, they say, for ever speechless, desolate, striving to waken a burden in its arms' (200). This unchilded, white woman with the 'tossed hair', so much like Charlotte's own, is a figure both for the inspiration which is easily missed and for the object of the dream which dies as it is clasped. It is a losing either way. The idea of the lost child, whether deriving from the memory of those early lost brothers, from Charlotte's feelings of thwarted motherhood or perhaps from her equally thwarted love for other women, is turned into a figure for the emptiness at the heart of all vision. The object of the quest is elusive and hard to reach. If it is reached, it leaves the quester either dead or empty-handed. The white smile is indeed ' "as cold as snow" ' in its brilliant but 'inhuman' demands. The scene contains in miniature all the pathos, desire, renunciation and detachment of Mew's own vision. Over and over again, the 'burden' of her writing is something white with cold, found, too late, at the moment of rejection, repression or self-burial. Yet even this 'desolation of something lost' (*CPP*: 66) offers its wintry compensations.

These stories seem to be driving at an idea of empty-handedness which is fundamental to Mew's poetic vision. 'Saturday Market', although not one of her best poems, seems to hold the key to it. At first this seems to be another poem about the Victorian mart. Eggs and ducks can be bought there as well as women and men, for 'Silver pieces' (*CPP*: 33). This is the familiar coinage of moral double-dealing. But the poem then addresses a woman who brings back from the market something closer to heart:

> See, you, the shawl is wet, take out from under
> The red dead thing – . In the white of the moon
> On the flags does it stir again? Well, and no wonder!
> Best make an end of it; bury it soon.

This lurid imagery suggests the old burden: the dead child, the abortion, the failed life. Somehow, either the life or the death of this 'red dead thing' has been bought and shown at the market of the world. But the child dream, like many of Mew's, then shifts into another key. Having murdered the thing, the woman is advised by the speaker:

> Then lie you straight on your bed for a short, short weeping
> And still, for a long, long rest,
> There's never a one in the town so sure of sleeping
> As you, in the house on the down with a hole in your breast.

This may be a metaphorical statement, suggesting that the woman will be dead of grief, in some way pierced through the 'breast'. However, this image subtly revitalises the dead metaphors of the first stanza:

> Bury your heart in some deep green hollow
> Or hide it up in a kind old tree
> Better still, give it the swallow
> When she goes over the sea.

This gives the hole in the breast a new meaning. The woman has

293

murdered, not a child but her own heart. She has thus taken that traditionally shifty signifier, which was always easily misread for something else: faithfulness, feeling, womanliness, true religion, and draws it out of her literal 'breast'. Instead of burying or hiding her heart, as she should have, this woman first exposed it to the laughter of the market and then in humiliation murdered it. The poem offers a starkly literal allegory, rather like Doris Lessing's short story 'How I Finally Lost My Heart' (1965: 76–87), in which the much metaphorised organ of woman's sensibility is determinedly plucked out. Like the story, Mew's poem argues for a creativity which is altogether heart-free. However 'inhuman' and death-dealing the action, to pluck out the heart, to turn the red of passion into the cold 'white of the moon', is to be dead and buried, but for a reason. The 'white world' of the imagination is not exactly heartless, but it can be gained only after the poet has lost her heart.

'The Forest Road', a beautiful, tender, anti-love poem, begs precisely for this loss. The speaker, distanced but not dramatised as 'other', addresses a sleeping lover, friend, sister or even child, whose vulnerability at first holds her back from the road out:

> The forest road,
> The infinite straight road stretching away
> World without end: the breathless road between the walls
> Of the black listening trees: the hushed, grey road
> Beyond the window that you shut to-night
> Crying that you would look at it by day –
> There is a shadow there that sings and calls
> But not for you. Oh! hidden eyes that plead in sleep
> Against the lonely dark, if I could touch the fear
> And leave it kissed away on quiet lids –
> If I could hush these hands that are half-awake,
> Groping for me in sleep I could go free.
> I wish that God would take them out of mine
> And fold them like the wings of frightened birds
> Shot cruelly down, but fluttering into quietness so soon,
> Broken, forgotten things . . .
>
> (*FB*: 36)

The apparent tenderness of this is deceptive, hiding, as it does, a desire to destroy and leave the loved object. Instead of accepting the 'burden' in her arms, the speaker wishes that the clinging hands might be 'Shot cruelly down' like birds, and thus be, not only quiet, but also 'Broken, forgotten'. This, which echoes so many broken things in Mew's work, suggests, not loss, but deliberate, elated repudiation. The speaker wants to forget entirely the hands she has deserted. If she 'could go free', even of the memory of them, she might find the other object, once again cross-purposed with love, and once again outside the home, on the white road out: 'a shadow there that sings and calls'. This, then, is the other side to Mew's sense of empty-handedness, as it is the other side to Rossetti's broken-heartedness. Both are states which are intrinsically desired, because they untie the imagination from duty, care, love and pain, and leave it free, if also desolate, to sing.

'The Forest Road' ends with a repetition of the action of 'Saturday Market'. The speaker first rids herself of her heart, and then makes for the shadow in the trees:

> and I will strike and tear
> Mine out, and scatter it to yours. Oh! throbbing dust,
> You that were life, our little wind-blown hearts!
> The road! the road!
> There is a shadow there: I see my soul,
> I hear my soul, singing among the trees!
>
> (37)

There is no evidence that Charlotte knew Katherine Bradley and Edith Cooper personally, but it seems highly likely that she had read their poetry. This picture of the 'soul, singing among the trees' strongly recalls the mummy's soul perched 'on the summer trees' (*WH*: 88) in Michael Field's 'The Mummy Invokes his Soul'. The idea of trees harbouring some forbidden, ancient law of pleasure, heartless and laughing, seems to have been as dear to Mew as it was to her younger contemporaries. In 'Afternoon Tea', for instance, she declares 'my heart's in the wood', and then, in two lines which strongly echo Michael Field's 'Nests in Elms', in which the speaker asked to lie down and die where 'rooks are cawing up and down the trees' (*WH*: 62), asserts: 'I'd rather lie under the tall elm-trees, / With old rooks talking loud overhead' (*CPP*: 54). This Neoplatonic retreat of the soul in trees is a figure specifically of escape from the ties of the heart and all its emotional expense. Mew, like Michael Field, looks to trees as to a place of free, careless 'singing', on a road out from duty and devotion which, for the woman poet, can often only be reached through some symbolic act of death. 'The road, the road, beyond men's bolted doors' (*FB*: 22), as Mew calls it in 'The Pedlar'. The road that Charlotte herself loved to travel alone on her trips to Brittany is one which leads, not to love, fulfilment, or any human goal, but to art, the '"inhuman thing"'.

However, this 'hard & cold thing' in Mew's poetry is gained, not through a celebrated paganism and rebellion, as in Michael Field, but in a struggle through love, belief and guilt which must all be broken from within. The 'broken, forgotten things' which 'burden' her imagination, like all its dead children, deserted sisters and unmet lovers, are also things which she cruelly desires to leave and forget. The first and foremost of these, which is the symbol of all the others, is her own woman's heart: that brittle, powerful, allegorical emblem of feminine sensibility, which has troubled poets throughout the nineteenth century. Its absence gives her, on the one hand, a waste of reference and imaginative empty-handedness which is desolating and terrible, but also, on the other, a freedom of the spirit to leave and sing, which is exhilarating and strong: 'I hear my soul, singing among the trees!' Her white worlds express not only the absence of something which was never known, but also, ultimately, the freedom not to need it.

The paradox of this 'white' aesthetic is confronted, finally, in one of Mew's best poems, which was also her own favourite, 'Fame':

> Sometimes in the over-heated house, but not for long,
>> Smirking and speaking rather loud,
>> I see myself among the crowd,
> Where no one fits the singer to his song,
> Or sifts the unpainted from the painted faces
> Of the people who are always on my stair;
> They were not with me when I walked in heavenly places;
>> But could I spare
> In the blind Earth's great silences and spaces,
>> The din, the scuffle, the long stare
>> If I went back and it was not there?
> Back to the old known things that are the new,
> The folded glory of the gorse, the sweet-briar air,
> To the larks that cannot praise us, knowing nothing of what we do
>> And the divine, wise trees that do not care
> Yet, to leave Fame, still with such eyes and that bright hair!
> God! If I might! And before I go hence
>> Take in her stead
>> To our tossed bed,
> One little dream, no matter how small, how wild.
> Just now, I think I found it in a field, under a fence –
> A frail, dead, new-born lamb, ghostly and pitiful and white,
>> A blot upon the night,
>> The moon's dropped child!

$(FB: 11)$

With its breath-catching sprung rhythms of speech, this seems, at first, to offer a conventional opposition between 'the over-heated house' of Fame and the poet's cool spaces of vision, anonymous and open. So far, the message is clear. The speaker despises the house of Fame, and remains superciliously aloof from it, though appearing awkward and false in its 'over-heated' atmosphere. However, the note of qualm in 'But could I spare . . .' suddenly undercuts her confidence in the other world outside. If the 'heavenly places' were to prove simply empty, the larks simply indifferent and the trees always careless, could she afford to relinquish the human comforts? It is at this point that the idea of Fame starts to merge into another figure: 'Yet, to leave Fame, still with such eyes and that bright hair!' As in 'The Forest Road', this is the imagery of human passion, of a commitment to the 'tossed bed' of love, which everywhere in Mew stands in opposition to the dream. Here, the poet seems less tempted by the road out than by an emotional faithfulness which might at least have its compensations when the trees are too careless and the dream 'not there'. On balance, she wonders if the other were worth the risk.

However, at this point the poem offers its triumphantly bleak dénouement. The dream is found, dead. In this, the most powerful of all Mew's images of miscarried birth, denied motherhood, of 'white' desire, the paradox of her imagination is affirmed. The 'frail, dead, new born lamb' is a spoiled creation and it spoils the night. Yet, against the logic of these sad adjectives, 'ghostly and pitiful and white', the poem has had its vision and has made its discovery. Mew has 'found it', the inspiration, the dream, implicitly the poem itself, 'just now', in a figure which characteristically leaves her arms empty, but haunts her imagination with its strange, 'inhuman' whiteness. The 'moon' and her 'child' are doomed never to meet, never to embrace. Their separation, however, is the negatively achieved thing of the 'dream'. That dream, when the speaker finds it, is both 'new-born' and 'dead', both found and lost, in a grimly exhilarating riddle of something and nothing which constitutes the ambiguous object of many of Mew's best works.

Thus, like all the other 'broken things', this one too hints at an aesthetic of poetry which must be won from the absences of real life. The idea of 'the child who went or never came' ('Madeleine in Church': 41), however much drawn from the depths of Charlotte's own bereaved psyche, also figures as the heart-free, white-cold dream of the imagination, 'no matter how small, how wild'. After all the painted colours of her more derivative, decadent poems, this sense of the imagination as a 'white world', in which the dream is found like a negative epiphany, at cross-purposes to all the driving, human desires of the heart, is a sign of a truth eventually won from the old house of echoes from the past. In 'Fame' the dream is 'found', in all its bleak and yet exhilarating contradiction, at the end of a long road which is both Mew's own and that of the tradition of women's poetry which she inherits, and concludes.

★   ★   ★

Thus Victorian women's poetry, while not falling into any simply homogeneous or neatly progressivist tradition, does none the less reflect a general movement away from the cult of sensibility at the beginning of the century, towards, on the one hand, a socio-political reassessment of that sensibility from the outside or, on the other, an existential emptying of it from within. Like Rossetti, Mew exemplifies the latter. She is, like her predecessor, essentially a love poet, but a love poet who, at some level, has ceased to believe in love. This very failure of belief, which goes against all the inherited assumptions about woman's nature, is the source of her imaginative power. Where Hemans and L.E.L. generally sing too readily from the heart, and thus miss the other truths, the poets who follow them learn, in their different ways, to 'draw out the heart' and thus to sing of what it has excluded. It is that residue from feeling, whether it takes the form of Barrett Browning's, Webster's and Meynell's social vision or Rossetti's, Michael Field's and Mew's secretive, cryptic games of desire, which constitutes the strength of their best works. Ultimately the buried women and the white, empty burdens of Charlotte Mew's writing affirm her place in a tradition of poetry which is essentially Victorian, not because it is morbidly sentimental or self-pityingly exposed, as has too often been assumed, but because it has a sense of the constant fret of life against art, truth against beauty, conscience against dream, and thus of the special toll exacted from women for the amoral, objectless pleasures of their imaginations. After Mew, women poets – Anna Wickham, Stevie Smith, Amy Lowell, H.D., Laura Riding and Mina Loy, for instance – whatever other problems their sexual emancipation and formalist freedoms present, will at least be free from the paying, evading and burying motifs of having to write like these, their Victorian predecessors, against the heart.

Notes

CHAPTER 1 FELICIA HEMANS

1. There is some dispute about the date of Hemans' birth. Harriett Hughes, in her 'Memoir', gives 1793, but her brothers, 1794. Norma Clarke has argued for the second, on the basis of Felicia's age at the publication of her first volume of poems in 1808 (Clarke, 1989: 6). However, this seems to me not entirely conclusive, and as the age on Hemans' tombstone agrees with the 1793 date of birth, and as I am inclined to think Harriett more reliable than Felicia's more distant brothers, I have decided to stick with 1793. The date of 1795, given by B. E. Schneller in the entry on Hemans for Janet Todd's *Dictionary of British Women Writers* seems to have no basis in fact.

2. For some of the most interesting accounts of women writers' relationship with Romanticism, see especially Mary Poovey, *The Proper Lady and the Woman Writer* (Chicago and London: University of Chicago Press, 1984); Anne K. Mellor, *Mary Shelley: Her life, her fiction, her monsters* (New York and London: Routledge, 1988); Anne K. Mellor (ed.), *Romanticism and Feminism* (Bloomington and Indianapolis: Indiana University Press, 1988); Marlon Ross, *Contours of Masculine Desire: Romanticism and the rise of the woman writer* (New York and Oxford: Oxford University Press, 1989).

3. My interpretation of this poem differs somewhat from Ross's, who argues that the men are able to continue their journey because they 'incorporate the feminine affection' (1989: 293) of the dead wife. This more 'appropriative' reading seems to me to soften the dramatic and gender tensions of the poem.

4. Dorothy Mermin, in *Elizabeth Barrett Browning* (Chicago and London: University of Chicago Press, 1989) gives a slightly different interpretation of this revisionary poem, claiming that Barrett Browning is in agreement with Hemans 'that suffering and writing poetry are intimately connected' (75). This, it seems to me, is rather the main source of their differences.

CHAPTER 3 ELIZABETH BARRETT BROWNING

1. Helen Cooper, in *Elizabeth Barrett Browning: Woman & artist* (Chapel Hill and London: The University of North Carolina Press, 1988), gives an account of the sexual politics of this poem which is in some ways similar to my own.
2. In particular, Cora Kaplan, in her Introduction to *Aurora Leigh* (London: The Women's Press, 1978), takes Barrett Browning to task for her 'reactionary' rejection of Romney's socialism and for her middle-class lack of sympathy for the poor in the church scene (32). Deirdre David, in *Intellectual Women and Victorian Patriarchy* (London: Macmillan, 1987), is even more politically inquisitional, though her terms are somewhat baffling. She writes that 'As a political conservative favouring the values of the landowning classes in England, as a conservative poet lamenting the "defilement" of a once heroic culture, Barrett Browning speaks as a Gramscian traditional intellectual and abhors the liberalism and mercantilism of the swelling middle classes' (136). The problem with such anachronistic judgments is that they ignore the political realities and terminologies of Barrett Browning's own times.

CHAPTER 4 CHRISTINA ROSSETTI

1. For other discussions of the idea of the female Christ, see Marian Shalkhauser, 'The feminine Christ', *Victorian Newsletter*, 10(1957), 19–20, and Janet Galligani Casey, 'The potential of sisterhood: Christina Rossetti's *Goblin Market*', *Victorian Poetry*, 29(1991), 63–78. The best, however, which is also the best article on Rossetti in general, is Dorothy Mermin's 'Heroic sisterhood in *Goblin Market*', *Victorian Poetry*, 21(1983), 107–18.
2. Ellen Moers, in *Literary Women* (London: The Women's Press, 1978), first pointed out that the energy of *Goblin Market* recalls the 'rough-and-tumble sexuality of the nursery' (105). Many critics have discussed the 'market' imagery of the poem, most notably Terence Holt in '"Men sell not such in any town": exchange in *Goblin Market*', *Victorian Poetry*, 28(1990), 51–67.
3. In this, I take issue with Terrence Holt's Freudian reading of the poem, in which he claims that the 'penny' is 'yet another sign of an inescapable taint, an original guilt as well as an originary lack' (1990: 58) in woman.
4. Bodleian Library MS. Facs. 285, fols 17–20. (Originals in the University of British Columbia.)
5. Kathleen Blake is rare among Rossetti's critics in taking *The Prince's Progress* seriously (see *Love and the Woman Question in Victorian Literature*, Hemel Hempstead: Harvester Wheatsheaf, 1983, pp. 5–8).

CHAPTER 5 AUGUSTA WEBSTER

1. My thanks to Marysa Demoor for this information.
2. On Robert's tendency to put the responsibility for sincerity onto Elizabeth, see Daniel Karlin, *The Courtship of Robert Browning and Elizabeth Barrett* (Oxford: Oxford University Press, 1987), 181–90. Also, Angela Leighton, '"Stirring a dust of figures": Elizabeth Barrett Browning and love', in *Browning Society Notes*, 17(1987–8), 11–24.

CHAPTER 6 MICHAEL FIELD

1. *Diary of K. Bradley 1867–8*. Bodleian Library MS. Eng. misc. e. 33b, fol. 3.
2. *ibid.*, fol. 17.
3. *ibid.*, fol. 37.
4. *ibid.*, fol. 49.
5. *ibid.*, fol. 39.
6. *ibid.*, fol. 32.
7. British Library Add. MS. 46782, fol. 38a.
8. *ibid.*, 46779, fol. 29a.
9. *ibid.*, 46782, fols 37b, 38a.
10. *ibid.*, 46778, fol. 119b.
11. *ibid.*, 46797, fol. 52b.
12. *ibid.*, 46797, fol. 77a.
13. *ibid.*, 46781, fol. 6b.
14. Christine White suggests that this is 'no sexless romance between friends, but rather a dangerous eroticism' (' "Poets and lovers evermore": interpreting female love in the poetry and journals of Michael Field', *Textual Practice*, 4(1990), 199). In my view, there is more playfulness than danger in the poem.
15. I disagree, here, with Joyce Zonana's claim that Swinburne's identification of Sappho as a Muse helps to recuperate 'female creativity and female sexuality' ('Swinburne's Sappho: the muse as sister-goddess', in *Victorian Poetry*, 28(1990), 48). By comparison with Michael Field, Swinburne violently and sadistically appropriates the voice of Sappho for his own fantasies.
16. Bodleian Library MS. Eng. misc. e. 33b, fol. 24.
17. As those of old drank mummia
        To fire their limbs of lead,
   Making dead kings from Africa
        Stand pandar to their bed;

   Drunk on the dead, and medicined
        With spiced imperial dust,
   In a short night they reeled to find
        Ten centuries of lust.
                                (Brooke, 1918: 70)
18. In his *Selection from the Poems of Michael Field* (London: The Poetry Bookshop, 1923), T. Sturge Moore has almost certainly correctly subtitled this sonnet 'Syrinx to Pan' (59).
19. British Library Add. MS. 46783, fol. 151b.

CHAPTER 7 ALICE MEYNELL

1. On the subject of silence in Meynell's poetry, see Beverly A. Schlack, 'The poetess of poets: Alice Meynell rediscovered', *Women's Studies*, 7(1980), 113–14.
2. MS. letter to Katharine Tynan, in the John Rylands University Library of Manchester, fol. 115.
3. *ibid.*, fol. 94.
4. *ibid.*, fols 141–2.
5. *ibid.*, fol. 77.

Bibliography

(Primary texts are listed under name of author rather than of editor.)

Abel, Elizabeth (ed.) (1982) *Writing and Sexual Difference*, Hemel Hempstead: Harvester Wheatsheaf.

Adburgham, Alison (1972) *Women in Print: Writing women and women's magazines from the restoration to the accession of Victoria*, London: Allen and Unwin.

Armstrong, Isobel (1987) 'Christina Rossetti: diary of a feminist reading', in *Women Reading Women's Writing*, ed. Sue Roe, Hemel Hempstead: Harvester Wheatsheaf.

Ashton, Helen (1951) *Letty Landon*, London: Collins.

Badeni, June (1981) *The Slender Tree: A life of Alice Meynell*, Padstow, Cornwall: Tabb House.

Baillie, Joanna (1851) *The Dramatic and Poetical Works of Joanna Baillie*, London.

Bald, Marjorie A. (1922; 1923) *Women-Writers of the Nineteenth Century* Cambridge: Cambridge University Press.

Barbauld, Anna Laetitia (1825) *The Works of Anna Laetitia Barbauld with a Memoir by Lucy Aiken*, 2 vols., London.

Barrett Browning, Elizabeth (1897) *The Letters of Elizabeth Barrett Browning*, 2 vols., ed. Frederic G. Kenyon, London.

Barrett Browning, Elizabeth (1900) *The Complete Works of Elizabeth Barrett Browning*, 6 vols., ed. Charlotte Porter and Helen A. Clarke, New York: Crowell.

Barrett Browning, Elizabeth (1914) *New Poems by Robert Browning and Elizabeth Barrett Browning*, ed. Frederic G. Kenyon, London.

Barrett Browning, Elizabeth (1929) *Elizabeth Barrett Browning: Letters to her sister, 1846–1859*, ed. Leonard Huxley, London: John Murray.

Barrett Browning, Elizabeth (1955) *Elizabeth Barrett to Mr. Boyd: Unpublished letters of Elizabeth Barrett to Hugh Stuart Boyd*, ed. Barbara P. McCarthy, London: John Murray.

Barrett Browning, Elizabeth (1958) *Letters of The Brownings to George Barrett*, ed.

302

Paul Landis, with the assistance of Ronald E. Freeman, Urbana: University of Illinois Press.

Barrett Browning, Elizabeth (1969a) *Diary by E.B.B.: The unpublished diary of Elizabeth Barrett Barrett, 1831–1832*, ed. Philip Kelley and Ronald Hudson, Athens, Ohio: Ohio University Press.

Barrett Browning, Elizabeth (1969b) *The Letters of Robert Browning and Elizabeth Barrett 1845–1846*, 2 vols., ed. Elvan Kintner, Cambridge, Mass.: Harvard University Press.

Barrett Browning, Elizabeth (1974) *Elizabeth Barrett Browning's Letters to Mrs. David Ogilvy: 1849–1861*, ed. Peter N. Heydon and Philip Kelley, London: John Murray.

Barrett Browning, Elizabeth (1978) *Aurora Leigh and Other Poems*, intro. Cora Kaplan, London: The Women's Press.

Barrett Browning, Elizabeth (1983) *The Letters of Elizabeth Barrett Browning to Mary Russell Mitford: 1836–1854*, 3 vols., ed. Meredith B. Raymond and Mary Rose Sullivan, Winfield, Kans.: Wedgestone Press.

Barrett Browning, Elizabeth (1984–) *The Brownings' Correspondence*, 4 vols. to date, ed. Philip Kelley and Ronald Hudson, Winfield, Kans.: Wedgestone Press.

Barthes, Roland (1967) *Writing Degree Zero*, London: Jonathan Cape.

Barthes, Roland (1977) *Image/Music/Text*, essays sel. and ed. Stephen Heath, Glasgow: Fontana/Collins.

Basche, Françoise (1974) *Relative Creatures: Victorian women in society and the novel 1837–67*, trans. Anthony Rudolf, London: Allen Lane.

Battiscombe, Georgina (1981) *Christina Rossetti*, London: Constable.

Baudelaire, Charles (1982; 1987) *Les Fleurs du Mal*, trans. Richard Howard, London: Picador.

Bayne, Peter (1880) *Two Great Englishwomen: Mrs. Browning & Charlotte Brontë*, London.

Beckson, Karl (1987) *Arthur Symons: A life*, Oxford: Clarendon Press.

Bell, Mackenzie (1898) *Christina Rossetti: A biographical and critical study*, London.

Besant, Walter (1892) 'On literary collaboration', *The New Review*, 6(1892), 200–9.

Bethune, Geo W. (ed.) (1848) *The British Female Poets: with biographical and critical notices*, Philadelphia.

Birkhead, Edith (1930) *Christina Rossetti & Her Poetry*, London: George Harrap.

Bishop, Elizabeth (1970) *Elizabeth Bishop: The complete poems*, London: Chatto and Windus.

Blake, Kathleen (1983) *Love and the Woman Question in Victorian Literature: The art of self-postponement*, Hemel Hempstead: Harvester Wheatsheaf.

Blanchard, Laman (1841) *Life and Literary Remains of L.E.L.*, 2 vols., London.

Bloom, Harold (1971) *The Ringers in the Tower: Studies in romantic tradition*, Chicago and London: The University of Chicago Press.

Boll, Theophilus E. M. (1973) *Miss May Sinclair: Novelist, a biographical and critical introduction*, Rutherford: Fairleigh Dickinson University Press.

Bottome, Phyllis (1952) *The Challenge*, London: Faber.

Brennan, Teresa (ed.) (1989) *Between Feminism and Psychoanalysis*, London and New York: Routledge.

Bristow, Joseph (1991) *Robert Browning*, New York, London, Hemel Hempstead: Harvester Wheatsheaf.

Brittain, Vera (1953) *Lady into Woman: A history of women from Victoria to Elizabeth II*, London: Andrew Dakers.

Brontë, Charlotte (1932) *The Brontës: Their lives, friendships and correspondence*, 4 vols., ed. Thomas James Wise and John Alexander Symington, Oxford: Basil Blackwell.

Brontë, Charlotte (1984) *The Poems of Charlotte Brontë*, ed. Tom Winnifrith, Oxford: Basil Blackwell.

Brontë, Emily (1941) *The Complete Poems of Emily Jane Brontë*, ed. C. W. Hatfield, New York: Columbia University Press.

Brooke, Rupert (1918) *The Collected Poems of Rupert Brooke*, London: Sidgwick & Jackson.

Browning, Robert (1970; 1980) *Browning: Poetical works*, ed. Ian Jack, Oxford: Oxford University Press.

Browning, Robert (1985) *More Than Friend: The letters of Robert Browning to Katharine de Kay Bronson*, ed. Michael Meredith, Winfield, Kans.: Wedgestone Press.

Buckley, Jerome Hamilton (1951) *The Victorian Temper: A study in literary culture*, New York: Alfred A. Knopf.

Burch, Joanna (1991) *The Literary Life of L.E.L.* Unpublished Ph.D. Thesis, Faculty of English, University of Cambridge.

Burdett, Osbert (1928) *The Brownings*, London: Constable.

Burton, Hester (1949) *Barbara Bodichon: 1827–1891*, London: John Murray.

Butler, Elizabeth (1922) *An Autobiography*, London: Constable.

Butler, Marilyn (1981) *Romantics, Rebels and Reactionaries: English literature and its background 1760–1830*, Oxford: Oxford University Press.

Byron, Lord (1945; 1970) *Byron: Poetical works*, ed. Frederick Page, corr. John Jump, London: Oxford University Press.

Byron, Lord (1973–82) *Byron's Letters and Journals*, 12 vols., ed. Leslie A. Marchand, London: John Murray.

Case, Alison (1991) 'Gender and narration in *Aurora Leigh*', *Victorian Poetry*, 29(1991), 17–32).

Chesterton, G. K. (1903) *Robert Browning*, London: Macmillan.

Chesterton, G. K. (1913) *The Victorian Age in Literature*, London: Williams & Norgate.

Chesterton, G. K. (1923) 'Alice Meynell', *Dublin Review*, 172(January–March 1923), 1.

Chorley, Henry F. (1836) *Memorials of Mrs. Hemans: With illustrations of her literary character from her private correspondence*, 2 vols., London.

Chorley, Henry F. (1873) *Autobiography, Memoir, and Letters*, 2 vols., compiled Henry G. Hewlett, London.

Cixous, Hélène (1980) 'The laugh of the medusa', in *New French Feminisms: An anthology*, ed. Elaine Marks and Isabelle de Courtivron, Amherst, Mass.: The University of Massachusetts Press, 245–64.

Cixous, Hélène (1981) 'Castration or decapitation?', trans. Annette Kuhn, *Signs*, 7(1981), 41–5.

Clarke, Norma (1989) 'Burning decks: battle fires and home fires in the poetic life of Felicia Hemans 1794–1835'. Unpublished paper given at the International Conference on Romanticism and Revolution, Lancaster University, July 1989.

Clarke, Norma (1990) *Ambitious Heights: Writing, friendship, love – the Jewsbury sisters, Felicia Hemans, and Jane Welsh Carlyle*, London and New York: Routledge.

Clément, Catherine (1980) 'Enclave esclave', in *New French Feminisms*, ed. Elaine Marks and Isabelle de Courtivron, Amherst, Mass.: The University of Massachusetts Press, 1980, 130–6.

Cobbe, Frances Power (1863) *Essays on the Pursuits of Women*, London.

Cobbe, Frances Power (1883) *Light in Dark Places: Comments on vivisection*, London.

Cobbe, Frances Power (1889) *The Friend of Man; and his friends the poets*, London.

Cobbe, Frances Power (1894; 1904) *Life of Frances Power Cobbe: As told by herself*, London.

Coleridge, Mary E. (1910) *Gathered Leaves: From the prose of Mary E. Coleridge*, with a Memoir by Edith Sichel, London: Constable.

Coleridge, Mary E. (1954) *The Collected Poems of Mary Coleridge*, ed. Theresa Whistler, London: Hart-Davis.

Coleridge, Samuel Taylor (1906; 1971) *Biographia Literaria: Or biographical sketches of my literary life and opinions*, ed. George Watson, London: Dent.

Coleridge, Samuel Taylor (1956–71) *Collected Letters of Samuel Taylor Coleridge*, 6 vols., ed. Earl Leslie Griggs, Oxford: Clarendon Press.

Conor, Steven (1984) '"Speaking likenesses": language and repetition in Christina Rossetti's *Goblin Market*', *Victorian Poetry*, 22(1984), 439–48.

Cook, Eliza (1870) *The Poetical Works of Eliza Cook*, London.

Cooper, Helen (1988) *Elizabeth Barrett Browning, Woman & Artist*, Chapel Hill and London: The University of North Carolina Press.

Courtney, Janet E. (1933) *The Adventurous Thirties: A chapter in the women's movement*, London: Oxford University Press.

Crosland, Mrs Newton (Camilla Toulmin) (1893) *Landmarks of a Literary Life: 1820–1892*, London.

Cruse, Amy (1935) *The Victorians and Their Books*, London: Allen and Unwin.

Curran, Stuart (1971) 'The lyric voice of Christina Rossetti', *Victorian Poetry*, 9(1971), 287–99.

Curran, Stuart (1988) 'Romantic poetry: the I altered', in *Romanticism and Feminism*, ed. Anne K. Mellor, Bloomington and Indianapolis: Indiana University Press, 185–207.

Dale, Peter Allen (1977) *The Victorian Critic and the Idea of History: Carlyle, Arnold, Pater*, Cambridge, Mass.: Harvard University Press.

Darwin, Charles (1859; 1968) *The Origin of Species By Means of Natural Selection*, ed. J. W. Burrow, Harmondsworth: Penguin.

David, Deirdre (1987) *Intellectual Women and Victorian Patriarchy: Harriet Martineau, Elizabeth Barrett Browning, George Eliot*, London: Macmillan.

Davidow, Mary Celine (1960) *Charlotte Mew: Biography and criticism*, Unpublished Ph.D. Thesis, Brown University.

Davies, Margaret Llewelyn (ed.) (1931; 1977) *Life As We Have Known It: By co-operative working women*, intro. Virginia Woolf, new intro. Anna Davin, London: Virago.

de Beauvoir, Simone (1949; 1972) *The Second Sex*, trans. H. M. Parshley, Harmondsworth: Penguin.

DeJean, Joan (1989) *Fictions of Sappho: 1546–1937*, Chicago and London: University of Chicago Press.

de Man, Paul (1971; 1983) *Blindness and Insight: Essays in the rhetoric of contemporary criticism*, London: Methuen.

de Man, Paul (1979) *Allegories of Reading: Figural language in Rousseau Nietzsche, Rilke, and Proust*, New Haven and London: Yale University Press.

de Staël, Mme. (1833) *Corinne: or Italy*, trans. Isabel Hill, with metrical versions of the odes by L. E. Landon, London.

de Staël, Mme. (1836) *Sapho*, in *Oeuvres de Madame de Staël*, 3 vols., Paris, III, 693–711.

Devey, Louisa (1887) *Life of Rosina, Lady Lytton*, London.

Dickens, Charles (1965–88) *The Letters of Charles Dickens*, 6 vols., ed. Madeline House, Graham Storey, Kathleen Tillotson, Oxford: Clarendon Press.

Diehl, Joanne Feit (1978) ' "Come Slowly – Eden": an exploration of women poets and their muse', *Signs*, 3(1978), 572–87.

Dijkstra, Bram (1986) *Idols of Perversity: Fantasies of feminine evil in fin-de-siècle culture*, New York: Oxford University Press.

Dorling, William (1885) *Memoirs of Dora Greenwell*, London.

Doughty, Oswald (1949) *A Victorian Romantic: Dante Gabriel Rossetti*, London: Frederick Muller.

Dowden, Edward (1886) *The Life of Percy Bysshe Shelley*, 2 vols., London.

Eliot, George (Mary Ann Evans) (1954–78) *The George Eliot Letters*, 9 vols., ed. Gordon S. Haight, London: Oxford University Press.

Eliot, George (1989) *George Eliot: Collected poems*, ed. Lucien Jenkins, London: Skoob Books.

Ellis, Henry Havelock (1897; 1911) *Studies in the Psychology of Sex*, 6 vols., London: Random House.

Ellmann, Richard (1987; 1988) *Oscar Wilde*, London: Penguin.

Elton, Oliver (1920; 1927) *A Survey of English Literature: 1830–1880*, 2 vols., London: Edward Arnold.

Elton, Oliver (1924) *The Brownings*, London: Edward Arnold.

Elwood, Mrs Anne K. (1843) *Memoirs of the Literary Ladies of England*, 2 vols., London.

Enfield, D. E. (1928) *L.E.L.: A mystery of the thirties*, London: Hogarth Press.

Engels, Frederick (1972) *The Origin of the Family, Private Property and the State*, intro. Eleanor Burke Leacock, London: Lawrence & Wishart.

Evans, Ifor B. (1933) 'The sources of Christina Rossetti's "Goblin Market" ', *Modern Language Review*, 28(1933), 156–65.

Evans, Ifor B. (1933; 1966) *English Poetry in the Later Nineteenth Century*, London: Methuen.

Evans, Joan (1954) *John Ruskin*, New York: Oxford University Press.

Faas, Ekbert (1988) *Retreat into the Mind: Victorian poetry and the rise of psychiatry*, Princeton, N.J.: Princeton University Press.

Faderman, Lillian (1981; 1985) *Surpassing the Love of Men*, London: The Women's Press.

Fass, Barbara (1976) 'Christina Rossetti and St. Agnes' Eve', *Victorian Poetry*, 14(1976), 33–46.

Field, Michael (1889) *Long Ago*, London.

Field, Michael (1892) *Sight and Song Written by Michael Field*, London.

Field, Michael (1893) *Underneath the Bough: A book of verses by Michael Field*, London.

Field, Michael (1908) *Wild Honey From Various Thyme*, London: T. Fisher Unwin.

Field, Michael (1912) *Poems of Adoration*, London and Edinburgh: Sands.

Field, Michael (1913) *Mystic Trees*, London: Eveleigh Nash.

Field, Michael (1914a) *Whym Chow: Flame of love*, London: privately printed at the Eragny Press.

Field, Michael (1914b) *Dedicated: An early work of Michael Field*, London: G. Bell.

Field, Michael (1923) *A Selection from the Poems of Michael Field*, London: The Poetry Bookshop.

Field, Michael (1933) *Works and Days: From the journal of Michael Field*, ed. T. and D. C. Sturge Moore, London: John Murray.

Fitzgerald, Penelope (1984) *Charlotte Mew and Her Friends*, London: Collins.

Forman, H. Buxton (1871) *Our Living Poets: An essay in criticism*, London.

Forster, Margaret (1988) *Elizabeth Barrett Browning*, London: Chatto & Windus.

Foster, Jeannette H. (1958) *Sex Variant Women in Literature*, London: Frederick Muller.

Foucault, Michel (1976; 1979) *The History of Sexuality*, vol. I, trans. Robert Hurley, Harmondsworth: Penguin.

Garlitz, Barbara (1955) 'Christina Rossetti's *Sing-Song* and nineteenth-century children's poetry', *PMLA*, 70(1955), 539–43.

Gaskell, Elizabeth (1857; 1975) *The Life of Charlotte Brontë*, ed. Alan Shelston, Harmondsworth: Penguin.

Gaskell, Elizabeth (1864–6; 1986) *Wives and Daughters*, ed. Frank Glover Smith, intro. Laurence Lerner, Harmondsworth: Penguin.

Gelpi, Barbara Charlesworth (1981) '*Aurora Leigh*: the vocation of the woman poet', *Victorian Poetry*, 19(1981), 35–48.

Gilbert, Sandra M. and Gubar, Susan (1979) *The Madwoman in the Attic: The woman writer and the nineteenth-century literary imagination*, New Haven and London: Yale University Press.

Gilbert, Sandra M. (1984) 'From *Patria* to *Matria*: Elizabeth Barrett Browning's Risorgimento', *PMLA*, 99(1984), 194–209.

Gilfillan, George (1847) 'Mrs. Hemans', *Tait's Edinburgh Magazine*, 14(1847), 359–63.

Gosse, Edmund (1893) 'Christina Rossetti', *The Century Magazine*, NS 24(1893), 211–17.

Green-Armytage, A. J. (1906) *Maids of Honour: Twelve descriptive sketches of single women who have distinguished themselves*, Edinburgh and London: Blackwood.

Greene, Gayle and Kahn, Coppélia (eds) (1985) *Making a Difference: Feminist literary criticism*, London and New York: Methuen.

Greenwell, Dora (1861) *Poems*, Edinburgh.

Greenwell, Dora (1862) 'Our Single Women', *The North British Review*, 36(1862), 62–87.

Greenwell, Dora (1906) *Selected Poems*, intro. Constance L. Maynard, London: H. R. Allenson.

Greer, Germaine (1979; 1981) *The Obstacle Race: The fortunes of women painters and their work*, London: Picador.

Greer, Germaine (ed.) (1988) *Kissing the Rod: An anthology of seventeenth-century women's verse*, London: Virago.

Greg, W. R. (1850) 'Prostitution', *Westminster Review*, 53(1850), 448–506.

Gubar, Susan (1984) 'Sapphistries', *Signs*, 10(1984), 43–62.

Gutwirth, Madelyn (1978) *Madame de Staël, Novelist: The emergence of the artist as woman*, Urbana, Chicago and London: University of Illinois Press.

Hake, T. E. and Compton-Rickett, A. (1916) *The Life and Letters of Theodore Watts-Dunton*, 2 vols., London: T. C. Jack.

Hall, S. C. (1871) *A Book of Memories of Great Men and Women of the Age, from Personal Acquaintance*, London.

Hallett, Judith P. (1979) 'Sappho and her social context: sense and sensuality', *Signs*, 4(1979), 447–64.

Harris, Daniel A. (1984) 'D. G. Rossetti's "Jenny": sex, money, and the interior monologue', *Victorian Poetry*, 22(1984), 197–215.

Harrison, Antony (1988) *Christina Rossetti in Context*, Hemel Hempstead: Harvester Wheatsheaf.

Hawthorne, Nathaniel (1850; 1970) *The Scarlet Letter*, Harmondsworth: Penguin.

Hawthorne, Nathaniel (1852; 1983) *The Blithedale Romance*, Harmondsworth: Penguin.

Hayter, Alethea (1962) *Mrs Browning: A poet's work and its setting*, London: Faber.

Hemans, Felicia (1839) *The Works of Mrs Hemans: With a memoir of her life by her sister*, 7 vols., Edinburgh.

Hemans, Felicia (1873) *The Poetical Works of Mrs. Felicia Hemans*, ed. William Michael Rossetti, London.

Hewlett, Dorothy (1952; 1972) *Elizabeth Barrett Browning: A life*, New York: Octagon Books.

Hickok, Kathleen (1984) *Representations of Women: Nineteenth-century British women's poetry*, Westport, Conn.: Greenwood Press.

Hirsch, Marianne and Keller, Evelyn Fox (eds) (1990) *Conflicts in Feminism*, New York and London: Routledge.

Holt, Terrence (1990) ' "Men sell not such in any town": exchange in *Goblin Market*', *Victorian Poetry*, 28(1990), 51–67.

Homans, Margaret (1980) *Women Writers and Poetic Identity: Dorothy Wordsworth, Emily Brontë, and Emily Dickinson*, Princeton, N.J.: Princeton University Press.

Howitt, Mary (1889) *An Autobiography*, 2 vols., ed. Margaret Howitt, London.

Hunt, Violet (1932) *The Wife of Rossetti: Her life and death*, London: John Lane.

Huysmans, J. K. (1884; 1959) *Against Nature*, trans. Robert Baldick, Harmondsworth: Penguin.

Irigaray, Luce (1980) 'When our lips speak together', trans. Carolyn Burke, *Signs*, 6(1980), 69–79.

Jacobus, Mary (ed.) (1979) *Women Writing and Writing about Women*, London: Croom Helm.

Jameson, Mrs Anna (1826; 1836) *Diary of an Ennuyée*, London.

Jameson, Mrs Anna (1855) *Sisters of Charity: Catholic and Protestant, abroad and at home*, London.

Jardine, Alice and Smith, Paul (eds) (1987) *Men in Feminism*, New York and London: Methuen.

Jewsbury, Maria Jane (1830) *The Three Histories*, London.

Jones, Kathleen (1991) *Learning Not To Be First: The life of Christina Rossetti*, Moreton-in-Marsh, Gloucestershire: The Windrush Press.

Kaplan, Cora (1975) *Salt and Bitter and Good: Three centuries of English and American women poets*, New York and London: Paddington Press.

Kaplan, Cora (1978) Introduction to *Aurora Leigh and Other Poems*, London: The Women's Press.

Kaplan, Cora (1986) 'The indefinite disclosed: Christina Rossetti and Emily Dickinson', in *Sea Changes: Essays on culture and feminism*, London: Verso.

Karlin, Daniel (1987) *The Courtship of Robert Browning and Elizabeth Barrett*, Oxford: Oxford University Press.

Keats, John (1956; 1970) *Keats: Poetical works*, ed. H. W. Garrod, London: Oxford University Press.

Kemble, Frances Ann (1878) *Record of a Girlhood*, 3 vols., London.

Kent, David A. (ed.) (1987) *The Achievement of Christina Rossetti*, Ithaca and London: Cornell University Press.

Keohane, Nannerl O., Rosaldo, Michelle Z. and Gelpi, Barbara C. (eds), (1981; 1982), *Feminist Theory: A critique of ideology*, Hemel Hempstead: Harvester Wheatsheaf.

Kinglake, A. W. (1844) 'The rights of women', *Quarterly Review*, 75(1844), 94–125.

Landon, Letitia Elizabeth (L.E.L.) (1831) 'Living literary characters, no. V. Edward Lytton Bulwer' *New Monthly Magazine*, 31(1831), 437–50.

Landon, Letitia Elizabeth (L.E.L.) (1835) 'On the characteristics of Mrs. Hemans's writing', *New Monthly Magazine*, 44(1835), 425–33.

Landon, Letitia Elizabeth (L.E.L.) (1836) *Traits and Trials of Early Life*, London.

Landon, Letitia Elizabeth (L.E.L.) (1837) *Ethel Churchill: Or, the two brides*, 3 vols., London.

Landon, Letitia Elizabeth (L.E.L.) (1873) *The Poetical Works of Letitia Elizabeth Landon*, ed. William B. Scott, London.

Langbaum, Robert (1957; 1974) *The Poetry of Experience: The dramatic monologue in modern literary tradition*, Harmondsworth: Penguin.

Lecky, William (1869; 1955) *History of European Morals from Augustus to Charlemagne*, 2 vols. in one, New York: George Braziller.

Le Gallienne, Richard (1925; 1926) *The Romantic '90s*, London: Putnam.

'Leigh, Arran' (Katherine Bradley) (1875) *The New Minnesinger and other poems*, London.

'Leigh, Arran and Isla' (Katherine Bradley and Edith Cooper) (1881) *Bellerophôn*, London.

Leighton, Angela (1986) *Elizabeth Barrett Browning*, Hemel Hempstead: Harvester Wheatsheaf.

Leighton, Angela (1987–8) '"Stirring a dust of figures": Elizabeth Barrett Browning and love', *Browning Society Notes*, 17(1987–8), 11–24.

Leighton, Angela (1989) '"Because men made the laws": the fallen woman and the woman poet', *Victorian Poetry*, 27(1989), 109–27.

Leighton, Angela (1990) '"When I am dead, my dearest": the secret of Christina Rossetti', *Modern Philology*, 87(1990), 373–88.

Lessing, Doris (1958; 1965) *A Man and Two Women*, St Albans: Panther.

L'Estrange, A. G. (ed.) (1882) *The Friendships of Mary Russell Mitford*, 2 vols., London.

Levy, Amy (1884) *A Minor Poet And other Verse*, London.

Levy, Amy (1888) 'The poetry of Christina Rossetti', *The Woman's World*, 1(February 1888), 178–80.

Levy, Amy (1889) *A London Plane-Tree, and other Verse*, London.

Lewis, Charlton T. and Short, Charles (1879; 1962) *A Latin Dictionary*, Oxford: Clarendon Press.

Lipking, Lawrence (1983) 'Aristotle's sister: a poetics of abandonment', *Critical Inquiry*, 10(1983), 61–81.

Lockhart, John G. (1840) 'Modern English poetesses', *Quarterly Review*, 66(September 1840), 374–418.

Lonsdale, Roger (ed.) (1989) *Eighteenth Century Women Poets: An Oxford anthology*, Oxford and New York: Oxford University Press.

Louÿs, Pierre (1894; 1949) *Les Chansons de Bilitis*, Paris.

Lucas, F. L. (1930; 1966) *Ten Victorian Poets*, New York: Archon Books.

Lytton, Bulwer (1831) 'Romance and reality. By L.E.L.', *New Monthly Magazine*, 32(1831), 545–51.

Marks, Elaine, and de Courtivron, Isabelle (1980) *New French Feminisms: An Anthology*, Amherst, Mass.: The University of Massachusetts Press.

Marsh, Jan (1991) *Elizabeth Siddal 1829–1862: Pre-Raphaelite artist*, Sheffield: Ruskin Gallery.

Martineau, Harriet and Atkinson, Henry (1851) *Letters on the Laws of Man's Nature and Development*, London.

McGann, Jerome J. (1980) 'Christina Rossetti's poems: a new edition and a revaluation', *Victorian Studies*, 23(1980), 237–54.

McGann, Jerome J. (1985) *The Beauty of Inflections: Literary investigations in historical method and theory*, Oxford: Clarendon Press.

Mellor, Anne K. (1988a) *Mary Shelley: Her life, her fiction, her monsters*, New York and London: Routledge.

Mellor, Anne K. (ed.) (1988b) *Romanticism and Feminism*, Bloomington and Indianapolis: Indiana University Press.

Meredith, George (1970) *The Letters of George Meredith*, 3 vols., ed. C. L. Cline, Oxford: Clarendon Press.

Merivale, Patricia (1969) *Pan the Goat-God: His myth in modern times*, Cambridge, Mass.: Harvard University Press.

Mermin, Dorothy (1983) 'Heroic sisterhood in *Goblin Market*', *Victorian Poetry*, 21(1983), 107–18.

Mermin, Dorothy (1986) 'The damsel, the knight, and the Victorian woman poet', *Critical Inquiry*, 13(1986), 64–80.

Mermin, Dorothy (1989) *Elizabeth Barrett Browning: The origins of a new poetry*, Chicago and London: The University of Chicago Press.

Mew, Charlotte (1916; 1929) *The Farmer's Bride*, London: The Poetry Bookshop.

Mew, Charlotte (1929) *The Rambling Sailor*, London: The Poetry Bookshop.

Mew, Charlotte (1953) *Collected Poems of Charlotte Mew*, with 'A memoir' by Alida Monro, London: Gerald Duckworth.

Mew, Charlotte (1981) *Charlotte Mew: Collected poems and prose*, ed. Val Warner, Manchester: Carcanet Press with Virago Press.

Meynell, Alice (ed.) (n.d.) *Elizabeth Barrett Browning*, London.

Meynell, Alice (1889) *The Poor Sisters of Nazareth: An illustrated record of life at Nazareth House*, London.

Meynell, Alice (1895) 'Christina Rossetti', *The New Review*, NS 12(1895), 201–6.

Meynell, Alice (1896) 'My faith and my work', *Woman* (12 August 1896), 7–8.

Meynell, Alice (ed.) (1903) *Poems by Elizabeth Barrett Browning*, London: Red Letter Library.

Meynell, Alice (ed.) (1906) *Poems by Christina Rossetti*, London: Blackie and Son.

Meynell, Alice (1912) *Mary, the Mother of Jesus: An essay*, London: Lee Warner.

Meynell, Alice (1914) *Essays by Alice Meynell*, London: Burnes & Oates.

Meynell, Alice (1940) *The Poems of Alice Meynell*, London: Oxford University Press.

Meynell, Alice (1947) *Alice Meynell: Prose and poetry*, intro. V. Sackville-West, London: Jonathan Cape.

Meynell, Viola (1929) *Alice Meynell: A memoir*, London: Jonathan Cape.

Meynell, Viola (ed.) (1940) *Friends of a Lifetime: Letters to Sydney Carlyle Cockerell*, London: Jonathan Cape.

Miles, Alfred H. (ed.) (1891–7) *The Poets and the Poetry of the Century*, 10 vols., London.

Mill, John Stuart (1859; 1974) *On Liberty*, ed. Gertrude Himmelfarb, Harmondsworth: Penguin.

Mill, John Stuart and Mill, Harriet Taylor (1970) *Essays on Sex Equality*, ed. Alice S. Rossi, Chicago and London: The University of Chicago Press.

Mill, John Stuart (1981) *Autobiography and Literary Essays*, in *Collected Works of John Stuart Mill*, vol. I., ed. John M. Robson and Jack Stillinger, London: Routledge.

Millett, Kate (1969; 1977) *Sexual Politics*, London: Virago.

Minogue, Sally (ed.) (1990) *Problems for Feminist Criticism*, London and New York: Routledge.

Mitchell, Sally (1981) *The Fallen Angel: Chastity, class and women's reading, 1835–1880*, Bowling Green, Ohio: Bowling Green University Popular Press.

Mix, Katherine Lyon (1960) *A Study in Yellow: 'The Yellow Book' and its contributors*, London: Constable.

Moers, Ellen (1963; 1978) *Literary Women*, London: The Women's Press.

Monro, Alida (1953) 'Charlotte Mew – a memoir', in *Collected Poems of Charlotte Mew*, London: Gerald Duckworth.

Monro, Harold (1920) *Some Contemporary Poets: (1920)*, London: Leonard Parsons.

Moore, Virginia (1934; 1968) *Distinguished Women Writers*, Port Washington, N.Y.: Kennikat Press.

Moorman, Mary (1957–65) *William Wordsworth: A biography*, 2 vols., Oxford: Clarendon Press.

More, Hannah (1835) *The Complete Works of Mrs. Hannah More*, 2 vols., London.

Nicholson, Linda J. (ed.) (1990) *Feminism/Postmodernism*, New York and London: Routledge.

Nightingale, Florence (1859; 1978) 'Cassandra', in Ray Strachey, *The Cause*, pp. 395–418, London: Virago.

Noble, James Ashcroft (1895) 'The burden of Christina Rossetti', in *Impressions and Memories*, London, pp. 55–64.

Norton, Caroline (1863) ' "The Angel in the House", and "The Goblin Market" ', *Macmillan's Magazine*, 8(September 1863), 398–404.

Noyes, Alfred (1924) *Some Aspects of Modern Poetry*, London: Hodder & Stoughton.

Packer, Lona Mosk (1963) *Christina Rossetti*, Cambridge: Cambridge University Press.

Pater, Walter (1873; 1910) *The Works of Walter Pater*, 10 vols., London: Macmillan.

Patmore, Coventry (1921) *Poems by Coventry Patmore*, intro. Basil Champneys, London: Bell.

Patmore, Peter George (1854) *My Friends and Acquaintance*, 3 vols., London.

Poovey, Mary (1984) *The Proper Lady and the Woman Writer: Ideology as style in the works of Mary Wollstonecraft, Mary Shelley, and Jane Austen*, Chicago and London: The University of Chicago Press.
Pope, Alexander (1963; 1968) *The Poems of Alexander Pope*, ed. John Butt, London: Methuen.
Proctor, Ellen A. (1895) *A Brief Memoir of Christina G. Rossetti*, London.
Proust, Marcel (1971; 1988) *Against Sainte-Beuve and Other Essays*, trans. John Sturrock, Harmondsworth: Penguin.
Radford, Dollie (1895) *Songs and Other Verses*, London.
Rich, Adrienne (1977) *Of Woman Born: Motherhood as experience and institution*, London: Virago.
Rich, Adrienne (1980) *On Lies, Secrets, and Silence: Selected prose 1966–1978*, London: Virago.
Roe, Sue (ed.) (1987) *Women Reading Women's Writing*, Hemel Hempstead: Harvester Wheatsheaf.
Robertson, Eric S. (1883) *English Poetesses: A series of critical biographies, with illustrative extracts*, London.
Robinson, David M. (1924) *Sappho and her Influence*, London: Harrap.
Robinson, Mary (1800; 1989) *Lyrical Tales 1800*, Oxford; Woodstock Books.
Rosenblum, Dolores (1983) 'Face to face: Elizabeth Barrett Browning's *Aurora Leigh* and nineteenth-century poetry', *Victorian Studies*, 26(1983), 321–38.
Rosenblum, Dolores (1986) *Christina Rossetti: The poetry of endurance*, Carbondale and Edwardsville: Southern Illinois University Press.
Ross, Marlon B. (1989) *The Contours of Masculine Desire: Romanticism and the rise of women's poetry*, New York and Oxford: Oxford University Press.
Rossetti, Christina G. (1870) *Commonplace, and Other Short Stories*, London.
Rossetti, Christina G. (1874) *Speaking Likenesses*, London: Macmillan.
Rossetti, Christina G. (1881) *Called to be Saints: The minor festivals devotionally studied*, London.
Rossetti, Christina G. (1884) 'Dante: the poet illustrated out of the poem', *The Century* (February 1884), 566–73.
Rossetti, Christina G. (1885) *Time Flies: A reading diary*, London.
Rossetti, Christina G. (1892) *The Face of the Deep: A devotional commentary on the Apocalypse*, London.
Rossetti, Christina (1904) *The Poetical Works of Christina Georgina Rossetti*, with memoir and notes by William Michael Rossetti, London: Macmillan.
Rossetti, Christina (1908) *The Family Letters of Christina Georgina Rossetti*, ed. William Michael Rossetti, London: Brown, Langham.
Rossetti, Christina G. (1976) *Maude: Prose and verse*, ed. R. W. Crump, Hamden, Conn.: Archon Books.
Rossetti, Christina (1979–90) *The Complete Poems of Christina Rossetti: A variorum edition*, 3 vols., ed. R. W. Crump, Baton Rouge and London: Louisiana State University Press.
Rossetti, Dante Gabriel (1913) *Rossetti: Poems and translations 1850–1870*, London: Oxford University Press.
Rossetti, Dante Gabriel (1965–7) *Letters of Dante Gabriel Rossetti*, 4 vols., ed. Oswald Doughty and John Robert Wahl, Oxford: Clarendon Press.
Rossetti, William Michael (1873) Introduction to *The Poetical Works of Mrs. Felicia Hemans*, London.
Rossetti, William Michael (1899) *Ruskin: Rossetti: Preraphaelitism: Papers 1854 to 1862*, London.

Rossetti, William Michael (1903) *Rossetti Papers: 1862 to 1870*, London: Sands & Co.

Rossetti, William Michael (1904) 'Memoir' in *The Poetical Works of Christina Georgina Rossetti*, London: Brown, Langham.

Rossetti, William Michael (1906) *Some Reminiscences of William Michael Rossetti*, 2 vols., London: Brown Langham.

Rossetti, William Michael (1977) *The Diary of W. M. Rossetti 1870–1873*, ed. Odette Bornand, Oxford: Clarendon Press.

Rowton, Frederic (ed.) (1848; 1853) *The Female Poets of Great Britain*, facsimile edition, intro. Marilyn L. Williamson, Detroit: Wayne State University Press.

Ruskin, John (1903–12) *The Works of John Ruskin*, 39 vols., ed. E. T. Cook and Alexander Widderburn, London: George Allen.

Sackville-West, Vita (1929) 'The women poets of the 'seventies', in *The Eighteen-Seventies*, Cambridge: Cambridge University Press, pp. 111–32.

Sadleir, Michael (1931) *Bulwer: A panorama. Edward and Rosina: 1803–1836*, London: Constable.

Sadleir, Michael (1933) *Blessington-D'Orsay: A masquerade*, London: Constable.

Saintsbury, George (1896; 1912) *A History of Nineteenth Century Literature (1780–1900)*, London, Macmillan.

Sappho (1885; 1895) *Sappho: Memoir, text, selected renderings, and a literal translation*, by Henry Thornton Wharton, London: John Lane.

Sappho (1922) *Lyra Graeca*, vol.1, ed. J. M. Edmonds, Loeb Classical Library, London: Heinemann.

Sawtell, Margaret (1955) *Christina Rossetti: Her life and religion*, London: A. R. Mowbray.

Schlack, Beverly Ann 'The poetess of poets: Alice Meynell rediscovered', *Women's Studies*, 7(1980), 111–26.

Shalkhauser, Marian (1957) 'The feminine Christ', *Victorian Newsletter*, 10(1957), 19–20.

Shaw, Marion (1988) *Alfred Lord Tennyson*, Hemel Hempstead: Harvester Wheatsheaf.

Shelley, Mary (1826; 1985) *The Last Man*, intro. Brian Aldiss, London: Hogarth Press.

Shelley, Percy Bysshe (1970) *Shelley: Poetical works*, ed. Thomas Hutchinson, corr. G. M. Matthews, London: Oxford University Press.

Sheppard, Sarah (1841) *Characteristics of the Genius and Writings of L.E.L.*, London.

Showalter, Elaine (1977; 1978) *A Literature of Their Own: British women novelists from Brontë to Lessing*, London: Virago.

Smith, Logan Pearsall (1936) *Reperusals and Re-Collections*, London: Constable.

Stedman, Edmund Clarence (1873; 1887) *Victorian Poets*, London.

Stevenson, Lionel (1947) 'Miss Landon: "The Milk-and-Watery Moon of our Darkness", 1824–30', *Modern Language Quarterly*, 8(1947), 355–63.

Stevenson, Lionel (1972) *The Pre-Raphaelite Poets*, Chapel Hill: The University of North Carolina Press.

Stone, Marjorie (1987) 'Genre subversion and gender inversion: *The Princess* and *Aurora Leigh*', *Victorian Poetry*, 25(1987), 101–27.

Strachey, Ray (1928; 1978) *The Cause: A short history of the women's movement in Great Britain*, London: Virago.

Sturgeon, Mary (1921) *Michael Field*, London: George G. Harrap.

Swinburne, Algernon Charles (1904) *The Poems of Algernon Charles Swinburne*, 6 vols., London: Chatto & Windus.

Symonds, John Addington (1873; 1920) *Studies of the Greek Poets*, London: A. and C. Black.

Symonds, John Addington (1883; 1908) *A Problem in Greek Ethics*, London: privately printed.

Symonds, John Addington (1967–9) *The Letters of John Addington Symonds*, 3 vols., ed. Herbert M. Schueller and Robert L. Peters, Detroit: Wayne State University Press.

Symons, Arthur (1897) 'Christina Rossetti', in *Studies in Two Literatures*, London, pp. 135–49.

Symons, A. J. A. (1928) *An Anthology of 'Nineties' Verse*, London: Elkin Matthews.

Taplin, Gardner B. (1957) *The Life of Elizabeth Barrett Browning*, London: John Murray.

Tennyson, Alfred Lord (1969) *The Poems of Tennyson*, ed. Christopher Ricks, London: Longmans.

Tennyson, Charles (1968) *Alfred Tennyson*, London: Macmillan.

Thackeray, William Makepeace (1837) 'A word on the annuals', *Fraser's Magazine*, 16(1837), 757–63.

Thomas, Eleanor Walter (1931) *Christina Georgina Rossetti*, New York: Columbia University Press.

Thompson, Francis (1913; 1925) *The Works of Francis Thompson*, 3 vols., London: Burnes Oates & Washbourne.

Thomson, Patricia (1977) *George Sand and the Victorians: Her influence and reputation in nineteenth-century England*, London: Macmillan.

Todd, Janet (1986) *Sensibility: An introduction*, London: Methuen.

Todd, Janet (ed.) (1989) *Dictionary of British Women Writers*, London: Routledge.

Tompkins, J. M. S. (1961–2) *Aurora Leigh*, The Fawcett Lecture, London.

Tristan, Flora (1842; 1982) *The London Journal of Flora Tristan: 1842*, trans. Jean Hawkes, London: Virago.

Troxell, Janet Camp (ed.) (1937) *Three Rossettis: Unpublished letters to and from Dante Gabriel, Christina, William*, Cambridge, Mass.: Harvard University Press.

Tuell, Anne Kimball (1925) *Mrs. Meynell and Her Literary Generation*, New York: Dutton.

Tynan, Katharine (1885) *Louise de la Vallière and Other Poems*, London.

Tynan, Katharine (1913) *Twenty-five Years: Reminiscences*, London: Smith Elder.

Walker, Hugh (1910; 1921) *The Literature of the Victorian Era*, Cambridge: Cambridge University Press.

Watts, Theodore (1894) 'Mrs. Augusta Webster', *Athenaeum* (15 September 1894), 355.

Watts-Dunton, Theodore (1916) *Old Familiar Faces*, London: Herbert Jenkins.

Waugh, Arthur (1915) *Reticence in Literature: And other papers*, London: Wilson.

Weathers, Winston (1965) 'Christina Rossetti: the sisterhood of self', *Victorian Poetry*, 3(1965), 81–9.

Webster, Augusta (Cecil Home) (1860) *Blanche Lisle and other Poems*, Cambridge.

Webster, Augusta (Cecil Home) (1864) *Lilian Gray*, Cambridge.

Webster, Augusta (1866) *Dramatic Studies*, London and Cambridge.

Webster, Augusta (1867) *A Woman Sold, and Other Poems*, London.

Webster, Augusta (1870; 1893) *Portraits*, London.
Webster, Augusta (1878) *Parliamentary Franchise for Women Ratepayers*, London.
Webster, Augusta (1879) *A Housewife's Opinions*, London.
Webster, Augusta (1881) *A Book of Rhyme*, London.
Webster, Augusta (1887) *The Sentence: A drama*, London.
Webster, Augusta (1893) *Selections from The Verse of Augusta Webster*, London.
Webster, Augusta (1895) *Mother & Daughter: An uncompleted sonnet-sequence*, intro. William Michael Rossetti, London.
Wellesley, Dorothy (ed.) (1930) *The Annual*, London: Cobden-Sanderson.
Wharton, Grace and Philip (1860; 1861) *The Queens of Society*, London.
Wharton, Henry Thornton (ed.) (1885; 1895) *Sappho: Memoir, text, selected renderings, and a literal translation*, London: John Lane.
White, Christine (1990) ' "Poets and lovers evermore": interpreting female love in the poetry and journals of Michael Field', *Textual Practice*, 4(1990), 197–212.
Wilcox, Ella Wheeler (1909a) *Poems of Pleasure*, London: Gay and Hancock.
Wilcox, Ella Wheeler (1909b) *Poems of Sentiment*, London: Gay and Hancock.
Wilde, Oscar (1990) *The Complete Stories, Plays and Poems of Oscar Wilde*, London: Michael O'Mara Books.
Williams, Jane (1861) *The Literary Women of England*, London.
Winwar, Frances (1934) *The Rossettis and Their Circle*, London: Hurst & Blackett.
Wollstonecraft, Mary (1976) *Mary and The Wrongs of Woman*, ed. Gary Kelly, Oxford: Oxford University Press.
Woolf, Virginia (1932; 1986) *The Common Reader*, Second Series, ed. Andrew McNeillie, London: Hogarth Press.
Woolf, Virginia (1975–80) *The Letters of Virginia Woolf*, 6 vols., ed. Nigel Nicolson, London: Hogarth Press.
Woolf, Virginia (1976) *Moments of Being: Unpublished autobiographical writings*, ed. Jeanne Schulkind, London: Chatto & Windus.
Woolf, Virginia (1977–84) *The Diary of Virginia Woolf*, 5 vols., ed. Anne Olivier Bell, London: Hogarth Press.
Wordsworth, William (1940–9) *The Poetical Works of William Wordsworth*, 5 vols., ed. E. de Selincourt and Helen Darbishire, Oxford: Clarendon Press.
Wordsworth, William (1967–88) *The Letters of William and Dorothy Wordsworth*, 7 vols., ed. Ernest de Selincourt, rev. Alan G. Hill *et al.*, Oxford: Clarendon Press.
Yeats, W. B. (1936) *The Oxford Book of Modern Verse: 1892–1935*, ed. W. B. Yeats, Oxford: Clarendon Press.
Yeats, W. B. (1954) *The Letters of W. B. Yeats*, ed. Allan Wade, London: Rupert Hart-Davis.
Yeats, W. B. (1986) *The Collected Letters of W. B. Yeats*, vol. 1 to date, ed. John Kelly, Oxford: Clarendon Press.
Zaturenska, Marya (1949) *Christina Rossetti: A portrait with background*, New York: Macmillan.
Zonana, Joyce (1990) 'Swinburne's Sappho: the muse as sister-goddess', *Victorian Poetry*, 28(1990), 39–50.

Index

INDEX